Frequency of the Fourth Industrial Revolution

WONCHAN LEE

Author's Note

Before writing this book, I took a lot of things into consideration. I have been working in the ICT industry for over 20 years, but when I used ICTs to live my life and conduct business myself, I often overlooked the social value of information and the value of books as a medium of information transmission. However, now, books change their forms, such as e-books and Internet books, and share their fate with human history as a medium of information transmission, and their meaning will remain unchanged no matter what multimedia information transmission media comes out in the future. It seems that books have the power to acquire certain information and create something out of it. In that sense, I would like to define all multimedia these days as a kind of book.

I have written this book from the perspective that I can provide a wider range of knowledge and ideas to people living in the era of the Fourth Industrial Revolution through the various experiences and knowledge I have acquired while working in the ICT industry for more than 20 years, starting as a developer and serving as the CEO of the company. The Third Industrial Revolution occurred in the 20th century, but people did not expect that this technology would change the world. They just thought that everything would be convenient. But now, technology is changing the world, and it is changing into a world where technology leads people, not people lead technology. Its beginning is the Fourth Industrial Revolution. Therefore, this book was written to help people understand and adapt properly to the Fourth Industrial Revolution.

WONCHAN LEE from Republic of KOREA

CONTENTS

Drawing of Contents

Figure of Contents

Part 1 Fourth Industrial Revolution 1

1.1 Why the Fourth Industrial Revolution 1

1.2 Beginning of the First Industrial Revolution 39

1.3 What is the Second and Third Industrial Revolution?.. 45

1.4 History of the Industrial Revolution 49

1.5 The Birth of the Fourth Industrial Revolution 55

Part 2 Blockchain and Virtual Currency 61

2.1 Creation of Blockchain Technology 61

2.2 Virtualization Technology and Virtual Solution 79

2.3 Virtual Currency and Financial Security System 127

Part 3 Big Data Business 157

3.1 Mobile Communication Technology and IoT 157

3.2 Internet of Things Business 183

3.3 Big Data Production and Technology 203

3.4 Big Data Business 211

3.5 The Future of Big Data 219

Part 4 Artificial Intelligence and Robots 223

4.1 Artificial Intelligence on The Internet of Things 223

4.2 Artificial Intelligence with Big Data 235

4.2.1 Pattern Recognition and Artificial Intelligence 235

4.2.2 Distributed Processing System and AI 265

4.2.3 AI in 5G Communication Network 279

4.3 Artificial Intelligence and Robot Technology ·············· 287

   4.3.1 Atom, Mazinger Jet and Terminator ···························· 287

   4.3.2 From Robot Vacuums to Spaceships ··························· 297

Part 5 Future of the Fourth Industrial Revolution ····· 321

   5.1 50 Knowledges for The Fourth Industrial Revolution 321

   5.2 Nano Technology and The Time Machine ····················· 379

   5.3 Prediction of the Fourth Industrial Revolution ············· 393

Bibliography ··· 403

Closing Remarks ·· 407

Drawing of Contents

Drawing 1 (Patent 1) ·· 114

Drawing 2 (Patent 1) ·· 114

Drawing 3 (Patent 1) ·· 115

Drawing 4 (Patent 1) ·· 115

Drawing 5 (Patent 1) ·· 116

Drawing 6 (Patent 1) ·· 116

Drawing 7 (Patent 1) ·· 117

Drawing 8 (Patent 1) ·· 117

Drawing 9 (Patent 1) ·· 118

Drawing Abstract (Patent 1) ·· 118

Drawing 1 (Patent 2) ·· 146

Drawing 2 (Patent 2) ·· 146

Drawing 3 (Patent 2) ·· 147

Drawing 4 (Patent 2) ·· 147

Drawing 5 (Patent 2) ·· 148

Drawing Abstract (Patent 2) ·· 148

Drawing 1 (Patent 3) ·· 194

Drawing 2 (Patent 3) ·· 194

Drawing 3 (Patent 3) ·· 195

Drawing 4 (Patent 3) ·· 195

Drawing 5 (Patent 3) ·· 196

Drawing 6 (Patent 3) ·· 196

Figures of Contents

Figure 1-1 Fourth Industrial Revolution in life ·· 4

Figure 1-2 Production of big data in daily life ·· 7

Figure 1-3 Living Location Big Data (Google Maps) ·· 7

Figure 1-4 Information guide robot at International Airport ······················ 9

Figure 1-5 Robots used in factories ··· 10

Figure 1-6 Qualcomm's dedicated IoT chip ··· 11

Figure 1-7 Introduction of Qualcomm's IoT solution ··································· 13

Figure 1-8 Qualcomm's IoT KIT ··· 13

Figure 1-9 Chinese IoT products ·· 14

Figure 1-10 Self-driving car manufacturing site ·· 17

Figure 1-11 Drones used in IoT services ·· 19

Figure 1-12 Unmanned aerial vehicle exhibited at CES ······························ 20

Figure 1-13 US military unmanned aerial vehicle ·· 22

Figure 1-14 Unmanned aerial vehicles used for military purposes ·········· 32

Figure 1-15 3D printer that creates a model of human hand ···················· 35

Figure 1-16 Molecular-level quantum mechanics ·· 36

Figure 1-17 The birth of the Fourth Industrial Revolution 37

Figure 1-18 The steam locomotive 40

Figure 1-19 James Watt's steam engine 41

Figure 1-20 Workers in modern society 42

Figure 1-21 Light bulb invented in the Second Industrial Revolution 46

Figure 1-22 Machines invented in the Third Industrial Revolution 47

Figure 1-23 Satellites at the American Space Center 50

Figure 1-24 Transition to the Fourth Industrial Revolution 52

Figure 1-25 Issues of the Industrial Revolution 56

Figure 1-26 Shenzhen-City of the Fourth Industrial Revolution 57

Figure 1-27 CES Expo-Leader of the Fourth Industrial Revolution 58

Figure 2-1 Cryptocurrency and GACOIN using blockchain technology .. 63

Figure 2-2 ICO history of cryptocurrency 66

Figure 2-3 Cryptocurrency Types and Mining Methods 68

Figure 2-4 Cryptocurrency ICO method 70

Figure 2-5 Gartner Hype Cycle 2015 on Blockchain Technology 72

Figure 2-6 Blockchain Network 73

Figure 2-7 Time of application of hash ·· 74

Figure 2-8 Reasons for applying Hash ··· 75

Figure 2-9 How to apply Hash ·· 76

Figure 2-10 Block branch of blockchain ··· 76

Figure 2-11 Asymmetric key of blockchain technology ························· 78

Figure 2-12 The concept of Virtualization ·· 80

Figure 2-13 The evolution of Virtualization ··· 81

Figure 2-14 The definition of Virtualization ··· 82

Figure 2-15 Expected Effects of Virtualization ····································· 83

Figure 2-16 Features of Virtualization technology ······························· 85

Figure 2-17 Virtualization Migration ··· 85

Figure 2-18 Detailed policies for virtualization Migration ···················· 86

Figure 2-19 Disk Utilization for Virtualization ····································· 87

Figure 2-20 Dynamic storage management in Virtualization················ 87

Figure 2-21 Failover function of Virtualization solution······················· 88

Figure 2-22 Disaster recovery logic of Virtualization solution·············· 88

Figure 2-23 The first core attribute of Virtualization solution ············· 120

Figure 2-24 The second key attribute of Virtualization solution ············ 120

Figure 2-25 Central management solution of Virtualization system······· 120

Figure 2-26 Gartner Comparison Table by Virtualization solution ········ 122

Figure 2-27 Performance comparison graph of Virtualization ············· 122

Figure 2-28 Organize supported OS by Virtualization solution ············ 123

Figure 2-29 Business efficiency increase graph of Virtualization ·········· 123

Figure 2-30 Wallet to store cryptocurrencies ···································· 127

Figure 2-31 Arbitrage for cryptocurrency trading ······························ 128

Figure 2-32 Auto Trading cryptocurrency ······································· 129

Figure 2-33 Investment amount in the cryptocurrency market ············· 130

Figure 2-34 Financial Security Control Center Operation System ········ 150

Figure 2-35 Fintech service development progress ··························· 152

Figure 2-36 Fintech field belonging to financial security system ·········· 155

Figure 3-1 The world's first mobile phone ······································· 158

Figure 3-2 Mobile communication technology by generation ·············· 159

Figure 3-3 Characteristics of mobile communication by generation······· 160

Figure 3-4 Frequency usage by generation in mobile communication ··· 161

Figure 3-5 The 3rd generation mobile communication technology 161

Figure 3-6 Mobile terminal connection status 162

Figure 3-7 Location tracking technology 163

Figure 3-8 Comparison of the 4th and the 5th generation mobile 167

Figure 3-9 Trend of global 5G market size 168

Figure 3-10 Global service change trend through 5G 169

Figure 3-11 Service usage by frequency band 170

Figure 3-12 Usage by band of electromagnetic waves 171

Figure 3-13 Changes in frequency usage from 3G to 5G 172

Figure 3-14 5G's main technical features 173

Figure 3-15 5G technology evolution direction 174

Figure 3-16 5G high-capacity multi-antenna technology 176

Figure 3-17 Required technology for 5G performance 177

Figure 3-18 Next-generation network configuration centered on 5G 178

Figure 3-19 SD-IOT for Next-generation network hyper connection 179

Figure 3-20 Internet of Things service application main screen 180

Figure 3-21 The concept of IoT service 182

Figure 3-22 The barometer beacon of the Internet of Things ············ 184

Figure 3-23 Changing the size of the IoT business ····························· 197

Figure 3-24 The concept of Internet of Things business ······················ 198

Figure 3-25 IBM Watson Internet of Things Platform ························· 199

Figure 3-26 IoT Platform and 5G ·· 200

Figure 3-27 The principle of AlphaGo using big data ························· 204

Figure 3-28 VR Glass to improve user experience ······························ 205

Figure 3-29 Artificial intelligence implementation process ················· 206

Figure 3-30 Qualcomm's Internet of Things Big Data Platform ·········· 207

Figure 3-31 Big data production by Vote Builder ······························· 208

Figure 3-32 Big data market analysis (service, software, and hardware)· 212

Figure 3-33 Predictive delivery system using Amazon's big data ········ 212

Figure 3-34 Business use cases of big data ··· 213

Figure 3-35 The Money Ball of Soccer Evolved with Big Data ············· 214

Figure 3-36 Money Ball Theory ··· 215

Figure 3-37 Application of Money Ball Theory - Defense Budget ········ 216

Figure 3-38 Aircraft flight information stored as big data ·················· 217

Figure 3-39 Gartner's Analysis of Big Data Usage Purposes 219

Figure 3-40 America's leading low-cost airline 220

Figure 3-41 US President Trump's Twitter Politics 221

Figure 4-1 Examples of Intelligent Internet of Things 223

Figure 4-2 Intelligent IoT Platforms 224

Figure 4-3 The advent of artificial intelligence 225

Figure 4-4 The human brain, the motif of artificial intelligence 227

Figure 4-5 Comparison of human brain and artificial intelligence ... 227

Figure 4-6 History of artificial intelligence 229

Figure 4-7 The singularity of artificial intelligence and intelligence 229

Figure 4-8 Analysis of current issues 231

Figure 4-9 Home appliances with Intelligent IoT 232

Figure 4-10 Intelligent IoT device 232

Figure 4-11 Cognitive transmission process in the human brain 236

Figure 4-12 Pattern classification for objects to be recognized 237

Figure 4-13 Pattern classification based on the human brain 237

Figure 4-14 A network that mimics the human brain (Perceptron) 238

Figure 4-15 The principle of artificial intelligence ············· 239

Figure 4-16 Perceptron Hidden Layer ················ 240

Figure 4-17 Perceptron Hidden Layer position ················ 241

Figure 4-18 LNS as an AI Network (Perceptron) Exception ············ 242

Figure 4-19 Clustering of radio frequency training data ············· 246

Figure 4-20 Recognition, classification, and clustering ············· 247

Figure 4-21 Optimization for data recognition ················ 248

Figure 4-22 Setting patterns in real-world data ················ 249

Figure 4-23 Artificial intelligence, machine learning, and deep learning 251

Figure 4-24 4 stages of machine learning ················ 252

Figure 4-25 Data storage among the 4 stages ············· 253

Figure 4-26 Abstraction among the 4 stages ················ 253

Figure 4-27 Generalization of the 4 stages ················ 255

Figure 4-28 Evaluation of the 4 stages ················ 255

Figure 4-29 Deep Learning Algorithm Flowchart ················ 256

Figure 4-30 Data Architecture in Machine Learning ············· 257

Figure 4-31 Errors in generalization of objects to be recognized ············ 258

Figure 4-32 Classification of objects to be recognized ·········· 259

Figure 4-33 Euclidean equation ·········· 259

Figure 4-34 Evaluation of Machine Learning ·········· 261

Figure 4-35 Decision Tree in Machine Learning ·········· 261

Figure 4-36 Numeric Features Sample ·········· 263

Figure 4-37 Large-capacity deep learning ·········· 266

Figure 4-38 Data parallel processing ·········· 267

Figure 4-39 Distributed processing system configuration diagram ·········· 268

Figure 4-40 Deep Learning Model Distributed Learning System ·········· 270

Figure 4-41 Distributed processing system IBM WORKLOAD ·········· 272

Figure 4-42 PETUUM Distributed Processing Architecture ·········· 275

Figure 4-43 PETUUM Distributed processing logic ·········· 275

Figure 4-44 Reinforcement learning through four-step ·········· 276

Figure 4-45 CES First ·········· 280

Figure 4-46 CES Second ·········· 281

Figure 4-47 CES Third ·········· 282

Figure 4-48 CES Four ·········· 283

Figure 4-49 CES Five ········· 284

Figure 4-50 History of robots ········· 288

Figure 4-51 Spaceship's robot Arm ········· 289

Figure 4-52 Robot arm with tactile sensor developed by MIT ········· 291

Figure 4-53 The battle robot from the movie Terminator ········· 291

Figure 4-54 T800 in the movie Terminator ········· 292

Figure 4-55 Robot with autonomous intelligence ········· 293

Figure 4-56 Humanoid Robot ········· 293

Figure 4-57 Japanese Manga and Robot Industry - Mazinger Jet ········· 295

Figure 4-58 Japanese Manga and Robot Industry - Atom ········· 295

Figure 4-59 Cotton candy making robot exhibited at CES ········· 298

Figure 4-60 Robot with optical sensor ········· 300

Figure 4-61 Increasing trend by use of robot industry ········· 304

Figure 4-62 Increasing trend by user in the robot industry ········· 305

Figure 4-63 Robot industry market size and forecast by service ········· 306

Figure 4-64 3D printer principle ········· 310

Figure 4-65 Rocket engine test made with 3D printer ········· 313

Figure 4-66 Small 3D printer exhibited at CES ·········· 315

Figure 4-67 A car made with a 3D printer exhibited at CES ·········· 319

Figure 5-1 World of Nano Technology ·········· 384

Figure 5-2 Nanotechnology - Catenane ·········· 385

Figure 5-3 Nanotechnology - Rotaxane ·········· 386

Figure 5-4 Time and space exist in multiple dimensions ·········· 388

Figure 5-5 Gartner's Top 10 Strategic Technology Keywords ·········· 394

Figure 5-6 Global artificial intelligence market Trend ·········· 395

Figure 5-7 Global Human Enhancement Market Trend ·········· 396

Figure 5-8 Artificial intelligence patent applications ·········· 397

Figure 5-9 Artificial intelligence papers around the world ·········· 398

Part 1 Fourth Industrial Revolution

1.1 Why the Fourth Industrial Revolution

The purpose of this book is to convey the basic knowledge that college students and modern people living in the era of the Fourth Industrial Revolution should have. Even if you live independently of modern technology, you have to use a smartphone, use a computer, and ride a car in order to live in harmony with people in today's society. (Even if you live independently of modern technology, you can live in harmony with people in modern society by using smartphones, computers, and automobiles) In other words, imagine that when we live in the world with people, we go to a golf course and play golf for a social life. Not everyone needs to have Tiger Woods skills to go out and play golf. In other words, you don't have to be the best player in the world like Tiger Woods to live with people. However, to go to the golf course and play golf, you need to know how to hold a golf club and swing, and if you know the basic rules of golf, you can get along with other people and enjoy socializing or the sport of golf, which is the original purpose of going to the golf course. Likewise, it is not necessary for everyone to know the technologies of the Fourth Industrial Revolution, which are called modern cutting-edge technologies, at the academic level. However, the modern society is a technology-oriented society that is more developed and rapidly changing than any other period in history. Technology is leading the lives of each individual and the group of society. Also, information becomes the basic knowledge to live in the modern age. In particular, the present living in 2020 is already in a period of rapid technological transformation that is called the Fourth Industrial Revolution. Children born these days are born and grow up in the arms of technology. These days, people are not born at home but mainly in hospitals, and the hospital itself is the crystallization of modern science and technology. And before going to kindergarten, they watch TV, use a smartphone, get in a car before they even start to walk, move to a certain place, and live in a house with home automation installed.

As an example, in modern times, all human life and death are related to technology. From birth, they are intensively observed in hospital incubators, prevent aging through various medical technologies, discover diseases with advanced computer diagnostics such as MRI, and medical equipment such as laser surgery equipment or robots treat diseases. When they die, they are automatically buried in a computerized system from the crematorium serviced by the state-of-the-art funeral system, and the burial map is distributed through the computerized system. Therefore, this book is designed to provide easy-to-understand information on the environment of the Fourth Industrial Revolution technology necessary for basic living to university students and ordinary people living in the modern age from the perspective of a technology-oriented human society that modern people face in life, especially at birth, and to help them adapt well to the technological society and utilize those technologies well.

The Fourth Industrial Revolution is a word that has never been said before. Maybe that's a given. It was not long before the advancement of technology that existed on Earth was named the industrial revolution, and it was because the term industrial revolution began to be given through the social changes that appeared after the advent of technology.

We are realizing the impact of technology on human life through experiences in modern times. If there were no smartphones, no cars, and no airplanes, what would our life be like? There will be a very different form of life than today.

It is not so long ago that the development of such technology began to have a very large impact on human life. Just as an agricultural society hundreds of years ago, technology was only a simple tool, as it could have sold land with a hoe without a plow.,

However, not many people would disagree that modern technology has become a lifestyle rather than a simple tool, and that the development of technology that regulates such life changes has become a major change factor that brings the revolution to human life.

For example, consider artificial intelligence, which is heralding the era of the Fourth Industrial Revolution in its midst.

Many people must have watched the Go game between humans and Alpha Go with artificial intelligence. It now means that electronic calculators have already surpassed the human brain. Except for the emotional part, arithmetic ability has long since surpassed human ability. Machine learning is a word that describes this incredibly advanced artificial intelligence. This means that machines can study.

The Fourth Industrial Revolution is described in the encyclopedia as follows. It is the next industrial revolution created by the convergence of information and communication technology. It is the fourth most important industrial age since the Industrial Revolution in the early 18th century. At the heart of this revolution are new technological innovations in six major fields: Big Data and Artificial Intelligence, Robotics, Internet of Things, Unmanned Vehicles (Unmanned Aerial Vehicles, Unmanned Vehicles), 3D Printing, and Nanotechnology.

The term was coined at the 2016 World Economic Forum (WEF) chaired by Klaus Schwab. Jeremy Rifikin, author of The Third Industrial Revolution, says the Third Industrial Revolution is still underway.

The Fourth Industrial Revolution can be explained by various new technologies that integrate the physical, biological, and digital worlds based on big data and affect all fields, including economy and industry. The integration of the physical and digital world is performed through O2O (online to offline), and in the biological world, mobile health care can be implemented using smart watches or smart bands, which are technologies that grafting human information into the digital world. Virtual reality (VR) and augmented reality (AR) may also be the fusion of the physical world and the digital world. In other words, it can be said that the current new technology and all future ICT fall into the category of the Fourth Industrial Revolution.

Figure 1-1 Fourth Industrial Revolution in life

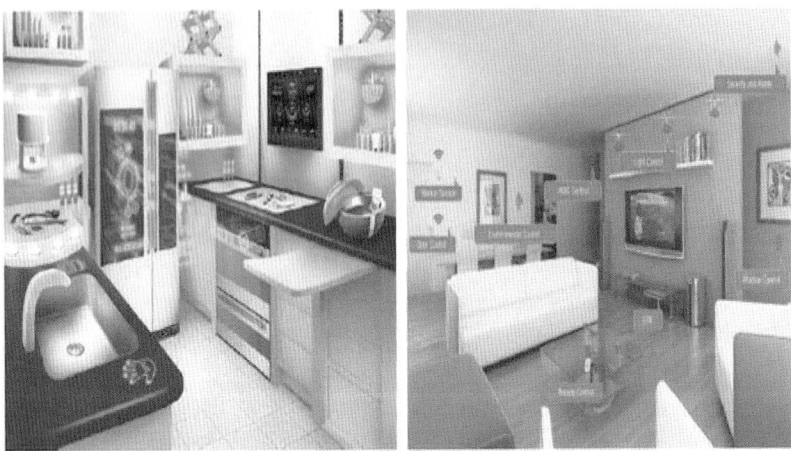

As mentioned earlier, the Fourth Industrial Revolution refers to six major technological innovation fields such as big data, artificial intelligence, robots, the Internet of Things, autonomous vehicles or aircraft, 3D printers, and nanotechnology.

First, big data refers to large-scale data that is generated in a digital environment, has a short generation cycle and includes not only numerical data but also text and image data. In the big data environment, the amount of data has increased dramatically compared to the past, and the types of data have also been diversified. It has the characteristic of regenerating various technologies using such a large amount of data.

Video contents, including personal broadcasts created by users, and text messages generated from smartphones and SNS (Social Network Service) such as Facebook, Twitter, and KakaoTalk are different from the existing ones in terms of form and quality as well as the rate of increase in data volume. In particular, textual information used in blogs and social networking can analyze not only the tendency of the person who wrote the article through the content but also the connection relationship of the other party with whom they communicate. In addition, the use of photos and video contents on PCs has been common since long ago, and broadcasting programs are mainly viewed on PCs or smartphones rather than through TV sets.

For example, Twitter alone, which President Trump primarily uses to express his political views, generates an average of 155 million videos per day, and YouTube averages more than 4 billion video views per day. The global data volume has already increased to 2.7 zetta bytes in 2012 and 7.9 zetta bytes in 2015. It is said that 1 zetta byte is 1000 exa bytes, and 1 exa byte is the amount of information equivalent to 100,000 times the printed materials of the US Library of Congress. In other words, the amount of data currently circulating in the human world is vast beyond comparison with the Third Industrial Revolution era, and large amounts of data are produced every day.

The amount of data from cameras installed on roads and buildings, as well as even in apartment elevators, and from various beacon sensors and environmental sensors installed in each facility these days is beyond imagination. In fact, every single action of a person's daily life is stored as data.

In the Fourth Industrial Revolution, big data is transformed into artificial intelligence technology. Now, it is not just a stage that exists as data, but a technological unit.

Artificial intelligence technology is producing a lot of issues, especially in recent years.

Not only the case in Korea but also around the world, a variety of new artificial intelligence services using Alpha Advanced Machine Learning are emerging.

The Fourth Industrial Revolution can be realized through technological advancements in six major fields: big data, artificial intelligence, robots, Internet of Things, autonomous vehicles or aircraft, 3D printers, and nanotechnology. The innovation in such technologies changes the structure of the economy. Now, let's take a look at robotics.

Robotics has its origins in mechanical engineering, which has been steadily developing since the 19th century. As mechanical engineering developed through the steam engine, robotics developed into a new form from the 20th century.

In the Fourth Industrial Revolution, a robot means that the human-like mechanical robot we saw in cartoons as a child is now a reality. In the past, robots have developed by using the principles of mechanical engineering for tasks that require the same level of power as production machines or construction equipment in factories that perform simple tasks. But now the level of use is changing. In particular, a robot that combines big data and artificial intelligence means that we can make robots that we previously saw in cartoons in real life.

Figure 1-2 Production of big data in daily life

Figure 1-3 Living Location Big Data (Google Maps)

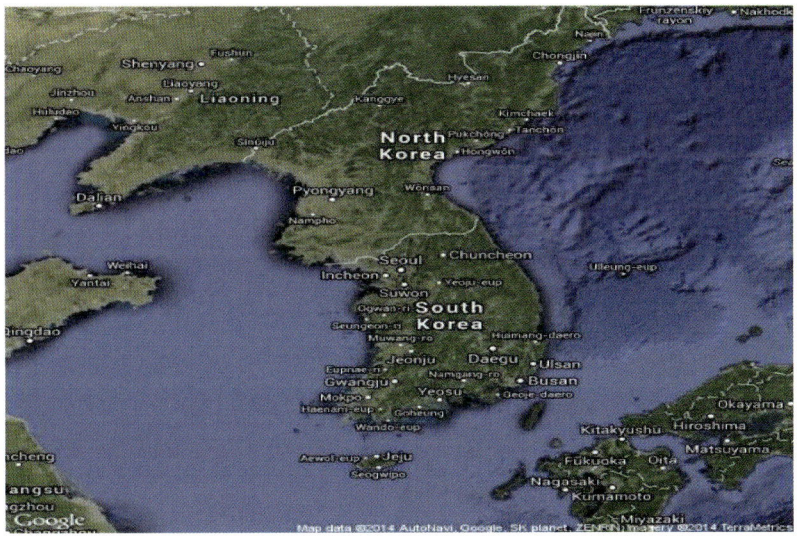

The robot appears in the encyclopedia as follows: A robot is a machine with a human-like appearance and function, or a machine or form that has the ability to work on its own, is a machine with the ability to think for itself. In other words, a robot is a kind of mechanical human based on engineering.

In general, an automated robot that performs assembly, welding, and handling in a manufacturing plant is called an industrial robot, and a robot that recognizes the environment and makes self-judgment is called an intelligent robot. Robots that resemble humans are sometimes called androids.

Intelligent Robots recognize the external environment, judge the situation on their own, and operate autonomously.

What set them apart from the existing robot is the addition of a situation judgment function and an autonomous operation function.

The situation judgment function is further divided into an environment recognition function and a location recognition function, and the autonomous operation function can be divided into an operation control function and an autonomous movement function. Therefore, the technology that enables these four functions is called the four core technologies of intelligent robots.

A negative image of the future of intelligent robots is fear of taking away human jobs and a world ruled by robots such as Terminator, and a positive image is that the advent of intelligent robots in various fields is expected to provide new jobs and convenience to many people.

Numerous physics, chemistry, and bioengineering are required to realize intelligent robots, and mechanical engineering, electronic engineering, and software engineering elements are also required.

In other words, intelligent robots can be described as the process of creating a new type of person. What a difficult yet creative process. Such robotics will be the barometer to realize the era of the Fourth Industrial Revolution.

In addition to such robotics, the field of the Internet of Things is most easily approaching our daily life in the era of the Fourth Industrial Revolution is

The Internet of Things (IoT) is being evaluated as the hottest innovative technology that is expanding to the Internet of Everything (IoE).

Internet of Things (IoT) is an abbreviation of Internet of Things in English.

Figure 1-4 Information guide robot at International Airport

The Internet of Things refers to a technology that connects various objects to the Internet by embedding sensors and communication functions in various objects, that is, a technology that connects various objects through wireless communication. It is an artificial intelligence technology that allows objects connected to the Internet to exchange data, analyze and provide learned

Figure 1-5 Robots used in factories

information to the user, or remotely control it. Here, things refer to various embedded systems such as home appliances, mobile devices, and wearable devices. Things connected to the Internet of Things need to be connected to the Internet with a unique ID that can identify themselves, and sensors can be embedded to acquire data from the external environment. Since any object can be a target for hacking, the development of the Internet of Things and the improvement of security systems have no choice but to go together.

According to Gartner, a global industrial economy research and advisory firm, the number of objects using Internet of Things technology was about 900 million until 2009, but this number is expected to reach 26 billion by 2020. When many things are connected in this way, vast amounts of data are collected through the Internet, and the collected data becomes so vast that it is difficult to analyze with existing technologies. This is often referred to as big data.

Figure 1-6 Qualcomm's dedicated IoT chip

Therefore, the need for technology to develop efficient algorithms to analyze big data is emerging with the advent of the Internet of Things. These days, it is expected that we will arrive in the era of the Internet of Everything, in which almost all entities in this world expanded from the Internet of Things are networked.

According to a study by Cisco, a network solutions company, the Internet of Things (IoT) is expected to have an economic value of $14.4 trillion over 10 years from 2013 to 2022, and its growth prospects are expected to increase exponentially along with other technologies of the Forth Industrial Revolution. It is expected to increase exponentially

In general, in IoT technology, each entity participating in the network requires authentication that allows other entities to identify themselves.

RFID technology authenticates objects located within a very short distance, but to verify the identity of an individual object on a wider network, an ID address must be assigned to an individual object. Accordingly, the demand for IP (Internet Address Protocol) addresses increased, and the existing 32-bit IPV4 system had a limitation in that it was difficult to allocate all the addresses of the increasing objects. For this reason, the need for the 128-bit IPV6 scheme has emerged. However, this is a condition on the premise that each end-of-things object directly connects to the Internet network, and the end-of-things located in the local network, such as homes and businesses, use private IP addresses to send and receive information to the Internet via a local server. In this case, it is possible to prevent a sharp increase in demand. On the other hand, it is not a wise choice from a cost and efficiency standpoint because

ISPs, which are Internet service providers, partially limit the public IP addresses provided to subscribers, and have to pay for additional allocation.

Figure 1-7 Introduction of Qualcomm's IoT solution

Figure 1-8 Qualcomm's IoT KIT

In general, information created by IoT technology must satisfy two requirements: economic utility and social publicity. This is because public infrastructure must change to do business on the Internet of Things (IoT) environment where data is rapidly increasing. Cloud computing, virtualization, efficient storage operation, and big data analysis have been suggested as factors to overcome these infrastructure limitations. Among these infrastructure environment elements, the existing Internet environment and cloud service have opposite positions in terms of economics. Therefore, as the demand for products increases, there may be economic problems in that the maintenance cost of cloud service and the cost of content production increase.

Figure 1-9 Chinese IoT products

Usually, various technologies are applied to connect various devices to the

Internet, which inevitably requires massive computing processes and storage infrastructure, so the demand for cloud computing will continue to increase in the future.

As the technology of the Fourth Industrial Revolution, another issue these days is autonomous vehicles and unmanned aerial vehicles, that is, drones.

A self-driving car is a car that can drive automatically without human driving. These autonomous vehicles are equipped with sensors such as radar, light detection and ranging (LIDAR), GPS, cameras, and beacons.

It recognizes the surrounding environment and drives autonomously by simply designating a destination. Autonomous vehicles that are already being put into practical use include unmanned vehicles that patrol preset routes operated by the Israeli military and unmanned driving systems such as trucks operated at mines and construction sites in the United States.

Looking at the core technologies of autonomous driving, one of the technological innovations of the Fourth Industrial Revolution, the first is the autonomous driving system and the actual system. It is a technology that not only simulates in the laboratory but also actually builds an autonomous vehicle system. It implements driving devices such as accelerators, reducers, and steering devices for unmanned operation and controls them using the computer, software, and hardware installed in autonomous vehicle.

The second is a technology that receives and processes visual information using sensors. As the basis of autonomous driving for unmanned driving, it is a technology that accepts image information and extracts necessary information from this image. It uses not only a charge-coupled device (CCD) camera but also an ultrasonic sensor and range field sensor to fuse information necessary for distance and driving and analyze and process it to avoid obstacles and cope with unexpected situations.

The third is the integrated control system, operation monitoring, and fault diagnosis system technology.

This technology establishes a driving monitoring system that monitors vehicle operation and gives appropriate commands according to frequently changing situations, analyzes various situations that occur from individual processors and sensors, diagnoses system failures, and provides appropriate information to the operator. It can perform the function of notifying an alarm.

The fourth is intelligent control and intelligent operation devices. This is an unmanned driving technique that generates control commands based on mathematical analysis using real vehicle models and is currently applied to autonomous vehicles. The applied technology is the Adaptive Cruise Control system. Intelligent Forward Control is a system that maintains the distance from the vehicle or obstacles ahead by adjusting the speed by itself without the driver operating the pedals based on radar guide technology. When the driver inputs the distance to the vehicle ahead, the long-range radar attached to the front of the vehicle detects the position of the vehicle ahead, maintains a constant speed, decelerates, or accelerates, and stops completely, if necessary, which is useful in weather where visibility is difficult.

The fifth is the Lane Departure Prevention System. These days, many cars black boxes are equipped with this function. This is a technology that an installed camera detects a lane and informs the driver of an unintentional departure situation. An autonomous vehicle distinguishes between the lane and the center line of the road so that the vehicle can safely drive along the lane.

And additionally, there is a parking assist system, which helps the car park in reverse by adjusting the steering system when the driver selects the Assist button, puts in reverse gear, and presses the brake pedal. By automatically guiding the vehicle to the parking space based on the surrounding environment through the sensor installed on the vehicle, it saves unnecessary time and energy when parking, thereby minimizing cost and environmental pollution.

Figure 1-10 Self-driving car manufacturing site

This is also linked to the automatic parking system. After the driver stops the car in front of the parking lot, turns off the engine, and presses the remote-control lock switch twice in succession, the camera installed in the car detects the reflector pre-installed on the opposite wall of the garage and determines the appropriate approach route. There is also a technology that calculates and parks itself. In addition, there is a blind spot information guidance system, which warns the driver by judging whether there is another vehicle in the blind spot that is not visible through the side mirrors by sensors mounted on both sides of the car. It is used to change lanes. Even if it's not a self-driving car, most of the new cars these days are equipped with it for the safety and convenience of drivers.

The biggest advantage of autonomous vehicles is that the driving control system is further stabilized by using the matching of driving speed and traffic information to avoid repeated braking, which helps fuel efficiency and that people who cannot drive, such as children and the disabled, can use it. In addition, it solves fatigue caused by long-term driving, can greatly reduce the risk of traffic accidents, and has the advantage of speeding up road traffic and reducing traffic congestion.

In general, car accidents are mainly caused by driver mistakes. When people drive, they can't focus on anything other than driving. . In addition, humans have physical limitations such as drowsiness, eyesight, and reaction time. On the other hand, self-driving cars have a 360-degree field of view and can better understand the surrounding situation at night through infrared sensors, radar, and other sensors, so they can go beyond the human senses and reduce the likelihood of an accident.

Self-driving cars also reduce traffic congestion and driving time. At the same time, self-driving cars could reduce the amount of time it takes to find a parking spot and park it.

As described above, while self-driving cars have many advantages, they also necessarily have disadvantages.

Among them, the most controversial part is that there is still no regulation that can be dealt with legally if an accident occurs on the same road between an autonomous vehicle and a general manned vehicle. Also, there are no countermeasures or technologies for the security problems of autonomous vehicles, that is, accidents caused by hackers arbitrarily manipulating autonomous vehicles. Currently, Drones, which are unmanned aerial vehicles, are causing various social problems.

Since Google introduced its first self-driving car in 2010, automakers around the world have been spurring the development of self-driving cars. In 2013, Mercedes-Benz succeeded in autonomous driving for 100 km with its self-driving car, and Audi also unveiled its autonomous driving technology in 2014. In 2014, Korea also unveiled a self-driving car technology that drives without a driver and finds empty parking spaces by itself. However, Korea's self-driving car technology is still far behind compared to the developed countries in the United States and Europe. Realistically, we spend a lot of time following and imitating foreign autonomous driving technologies.

The autonomous flight of drones along with driverless cars is also a very important issue in the Fourth Industrial Revolution.

An unmanned aerial vehicle (UAV) or drone is a flying object that can fly without an actual pilot on board. It refers to a remote-controlled vehicle on the ground or a device that is programmed in advance and flies automatically or semi-automatically according to the route.

In the case of unmanned aerial vehicles, there are cases where a human is controlled on the ground and cases where they fly autonomously and autonomously, both of which can be referred to as unmanned aerial vehicles. Furthermore, it is a generic term for the entire system, including air vehicles, ground control equipment, communication equipment, and support equipment, which are equipped with artificial intelligence and perform missions according to their environmental judgment. In other words, you may not need a controller to control the drone.

Figure 1-11 Drones used in IoT services

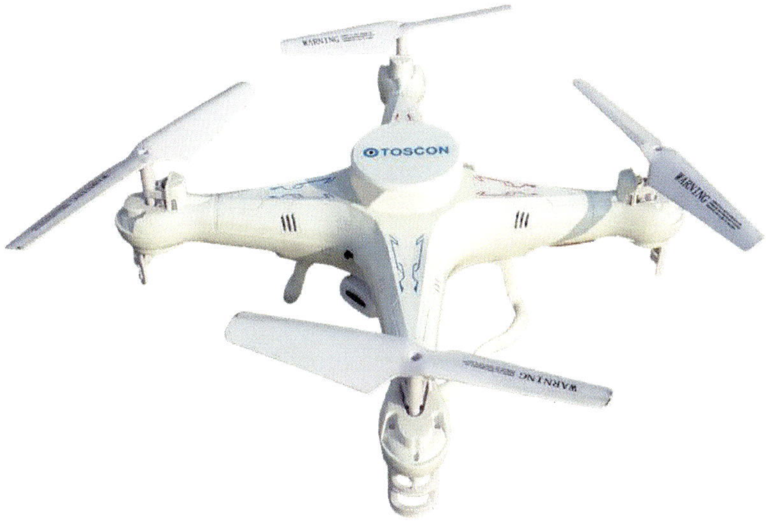

Technically, there is a tendency these days to include the technology field of unmanned aerial vehicles that can autonomously take off, fly, perform missions, and then land on their own following the flight path programmed by humans in the Fourth Industrial Revolution technology.

In general, unmanned aerial vehicles operate in conjunction with manned aircraft and other independent flight control systems. Depending on the field of application, various equipment (optical, infrared, radar, beacon sensor, etc.) are installed to perform missions such as surveillance, reconnaissance, the guidance of precision attack weapons, and communication (information relay). It has also been developed and put into practical use, drawing attention as a major military means in the future. Already in June 2017, Amazon applied for a patent for the flight control and operation system for the drone take-off and landing center and is now entering the business in earnest.

Figure 1-12 Unmanned aerial vehicle exhibited at CES

Let's take a look at the history of unmanned aerial vehicles here.

Before the first flight of manned aircraft in 1903, primitive unmanned aerial vehicles were used for combat and reconnaissance purposes. Think of it as the hot air balloon we saw in the movies. Its first form was Bombing by Balloon, invented in Austria in 1849. It was a method of dropping a bomb by attaching a bomb to a hot air balloon, and it is said that it was actually used in the battle against Venice. In the United States, there was a similar hot-air balloon, called Perley's Aerial Bomber, for which Charles Parley, a New York native, patented an unmanned bomber in 1863 after the Civil War. Perley's Aerial Bomber is a hot air balloon designed to drop bombs on a timer with a bomb basket loaded. Then, in 1883, Douglas Archibald developed Eddy's Surveillance Kite and succeeded in taking the first aerial photographs. It is said that the first unmanned aerial vehicle successfully flew in the United States during World War I. Because these unmanned aerial vehicles seemed to have great potential not only for reconnaissance but also for combat use, many countries, including the United States and Europe, recognized the need for unmanned aerial vehicles and began to study them. Starting from World War I, Britain developed the first reciprocating reusable unmanned aerial vehicle, the Queen Bee, and mass-produced more than 400. The Queen Bee can be said to be the progenitor of the unmanned target aircraft, commonly referred to as the Drone today. It was equipped with wheels for take-off at the airport and floats for use at sea. Meanwhile, the U.S. also started developing unmanned target aircraft, and Reginald Denny persuaded the U.S. Army about the usefulness of training in anti-aircraft gunfire using a radio-controlled model aircraft as a target in the 1930s. About 15,000 units were produced.

Then, during World War II, the Nazis put the V-1 combat unmanned aerial vehicle into combat, and in response, the United States began making unmanned aerial vehicles to destroy the V-1.

Figure 1-13 US military unmanned aerial vehicle

In Germany, an unmanned aerial vehicle called the Vergeltungswaffe was developed, and it is said that at the beginning of World War II, Hitler procured a cold flying bomb for the battlefield. The V-1 unmanned aerial vehicle is said to be equipped with a pulse jet engine that generates a signed bass signal. The V-1 could carry a warhead of 2000 pounds at a time and was pre-loaded to fly 150 Miles before dropping the bomb. The V-1 first entered the UK in 1944, killing over 900 civilians and injuring approximately 35,000 civilians in British cities. Here, Vergeltungswaffe, which means a retaliatory weapon, is a kind of flying bomb manufactured by Germany to counter the Allied Forces at the end of World War II, and it is the progenitor of modern missiles. In other words, it can be said that unmanned aerial vehicles were invented before missiles. As such, the R&D history of unmanned aerial vehicles is not short. It may be the cause of the preconceived notion that self-flying drones can be implemented more easily rather than self-driving cars.

The missile was inspired by the success of the 120 km-range Paris artillery that frightened Parisians during World War I. It was produced according to the

German Army's large rocket weapon development plan that began at the end of the year. It is divided into V-1 and V-2 according to the development order. V-1 is an unmanned aerial vehicle-type missile powered by the V-1 pulse jet, which corresponds to the current cruise missile, and became the beginning of an attack on the heart of the enemy by a long-range missile. In 1942, the Luftwaffe commissioned Fazela to develop the Fi103 modified FZG76, and after the first flight test in December of that year, it was mass-produced and used in practice in 1943. It has a total length of 7.9m, an overall width of 5.3m, a maximum diameter of 0.84m, a launch weight of 2.2t, a warhead weight of 850kg, a cruising distance of about 250km, and a cruising speed of 600km per hour, which was relatively low. It consisted of a warhead with a bomb on the fuselage, a fuel tank with a capacity of 640 liters, a high-pressure air tank for propulsion for flight, and a gyroscope for direction control. The accurate bombardment was impossible because the flight distance was calculated with the small propeller attached to the nose, but after the noise of the jet engine generated during flight stops, there is silence for a few seconds as it falls, which has sent Britain into a panic. In about 80 days from 13 June 1944, 8,070 were launched, of which 2,420 reached London, killing 5,864 people and destroying 24,481 buildings.

The V-2 is the first missile powered by a rocket engine and corresponds to the current intercontinental ballistic missile or submarine-launched ballistic missile. The V-2 means retaliatory weapon No. 2, and it was named by Hitler after completion, and the original name at the time of development was A-4.

The V-2 weighed 14 tons, 15 times that of the V-1, and flew at a speed of 8,000 km per hour, so it was faster than sound. The inertia induction method was mainly used, but in the end, about 20% of the beam writer method was also employed. It is a liquid rocket propelled by using a turbine pump to send liquid oxygen and alcohol into the combustion chamber. About 3,000 were built, of which 1,027 were used in the attack on London. This liquid engine structure and the induction control technology used were also used in the US Apollo spacecraft, Saturn 5, 20 years later. Meanwhile, the US developed the PB4Y-1 and BQ-7 unmanned aerial vehicles to counter the V-1. During World War II, the German V-1 influenced the U.S. Navy to develop unmanned aerial vehicles that could counter it. The US Navy Special Attack Unit-1 was converted into PB4Y-1 and BQ-7 to carry 25,000 pounds of explosives while flying remotely using a Television system. The unmanned aerial vehicle took off with two crew members setting the route for the German V-1 as it was mounted on a plane flying 2,000 feet. The crew disposed of the V-1 before it was retrieved from the landing. This, albeit dangerous, has been successful in effectively disposing of V-1.

After World War I and the Vietnam War, unmanned aerial vehicles began to be mainly used for the purpose of monitoring enemy positions.

In the 1960s, the United States developed a jet-powered drone called "Fire Bee" and operated it in Vietnam to monitor enemy positions. Firebee can be said to be the first surveillance drone. This is the predecessor of the unmanned aerial vehicle AQM-34 Rayn Fire Bee. In the 1960s, the U.S. Air Force started the first stealth aircraft program and said it would change to a combat unmanned aerial vehicle for reconnaissance missions. Engineers devised a way to avoid getting radar signals by placing a specially designed screen over the engine's air intakes, placing radar-absorbing pads on the sides of the aircraft, and covering the aircraft airframe with a newly developed radar paint. As a result, an unmanned aerial vehicle called the AQM-34 Rayn Fire Bee was developed.

During the Vietnam War, from October 1964 to April 1975, the United States conducted surveillance missions, flying over 34,000 flights of over 1,000 unmanned aerial vehicles over Southeast Asia. After that, the surveillance range was expanded to Japan, Korea, Vietnam, and Thailand. It carried out day and night surveillance and the mission of distributing leaflets. It also detected anti-aircraft missile radars across North Vietnam and China. In addition to the AQM-34, the U.S. Air Force has developed and deployed a hypersonic unmanned aerial vehicle called the "D-21" that can fly at an altitude of 90,000 ft at a speed of Mach 3. At that time, the Soviet Union and the Cold War era required high-quality reconnaissance images. In 1965, Lockheed's D-21 was released. The D-21 was the fastest aircraft of its time with a speed of Mach 4. The D-21 was released from the sky by the manned M-21 and was not detected by radar because of its stealth capabilities.

After the Fire Bee's great success in the Vietnam War, other countries also started developing unmanned aerial vehicles.

In the 1980s, the Israeli Air Force began developing a new unmanned aerial vehicle. Israel developed and used "Decoy" for the first time in the world. It has the meaning of a reconnaissance aircraft that deceives the enemy, and the Israeli Air Force developed it as a reconnaissance aircraft that deceives the enemy by using the Fire Bee introduced by the United States. In the 1980s, the Israeli Air Force pioneered the development of new unmanned aerial vehicles, and in the late 1980s, the United States and other countries were successful enough to introduce Israeli-made unmanned aerial vehicles. In 1978, Israel Aircraft Industries developed an unmanned aerial vehicle called the Scout, which was successfully put into service in 1982. The Scout had a piston engine and 13-foot wings made of fiberglass. It emitted a small radar signal and its small size made it nearly impossible to shoot down. And it was able to transmit real-time 360-degree monitoring data through the central TV camera. In fact, it was deployed to the Battle of Bekaa Valley between Israel, Lebanon, and Syria in 1982, destroying 15 of 17 Syrian missile bases, with great success. In the late 1980s, a cheap and lightweight unmanned aerial vehicle called the Pioneer was created. The Pioneer was equipped with a rocket booster engine, making it possible to take off from the deck of a ship on land or at sea. It performed its mission by performing 533 sorties in the Gulf War, has proven particularly effective for monitoring tasks and is still being used in Israel and the United States.

In the 1990s, unmanned aerial vehicles (UAVs) developed the Fire Bird2001, an unmanned aerial vehicle for reconnaissance in Israel. FireBird2001 uses GPS technology (Global Positioning System technology), GIS technology (Geographic Information Systems mapping), and forward surveillance cameras to accurately transmit the size, speed, surroundings, and movement of a forest fire in real-time. In the 1990s, the United States also actively participated in the development of unmanned aerial vehicles and developed five new models. First, the Pathfinder is a solar cell type ultra-light research aircraft developed for environmental research. A small sensor can be used to collect wind or weather data, and it can take and transmit high-resolution digital images. The Dark Star is also an unmanned aerial vehicle expected to have stealth capabilities while flying at 45,000 feet. It was created to perform unmanned reconnaissance missions under the leadership of the US Defense Advanced Research Projects Agency, but development was canceled due to financial problems. Next, the RQ-1 Predator was developed for pure reconnaissance, but some are equipped with anti-tank missiles and are successfully performing missions. The RQ-1 Predator has been valued in the Balkans and more recently in Afghanistan and the Middle East. Next, the RQ-4 Global Hawk is an unmanned aerial vehicle made by Teledyne Lion, a global unmanned aerial vehicle company.

The RQ-4 Global Hawk has a wingspan of 116 feet and is capable of monitoring and transmitting data at up to 65,000 feet.

The Helios is an unmanned aerial vehicle serving as a platform for atmospheric research work and communications, aiming to fly 100,000 feet above 50,000 feet for more than 14 hours in a 24-hour flight.

The Global Hawk, which the US military has been using since 2000, is the highest-performing unmanned reconnaissance aircraft in existence. It is a strategic weapon that can fly up to 20 km in height and can identify objects up to 30 cm above the ground. It can be operated for 35 hours, has an operational radius of 3000 km, and is known to be able to collect information day and night regardless of the weather with advanced synthetic image radar and electro-optical and infrared monitoring equipment. In addition, missions can be assigned in case of emergency according to the command of the pilot on the ground, and when the mission is set, take-off, mission flight, and landing are performed automatically. In the UK, the country's first unmanned aerial vehicle, the Taranis, was developed in 2013. Development began in 2005 and the first flight was completed in 2013. Its flight speed is supersonic and is said to have stealth capabilities. In the field of photography, an unmanned aerial vehicle called Helicam is used. Helicam is a compound word of Helicopter and Camera, and it is a small, unmanned helicopter for taking pictures of places that are difficult for humans to access. And unmanned aerial vehicles are also being used in the delivery field. Amazon's Prime Air is a small unmanned aerial vehicle that checks the location of the delivery destination and flies to deliver packages to your home. And in the telecom space, there is the Solara 50 from Titan Aerospace. The Solara 50 can fly at an altitude of 20,000m, which is twice as high as the normal drone flight route, and because it is powered by sunlight, it has the advantage of being able to use it for years without charging. As discussed above, there are no universal standards for classifying unmanned aerial vehicles and international weight standards, and the standards for unmanned aerial vehicles applied by country are also different. Some general methods for unmanned aerial vehicles are classification according to military use, classification according to flight radius, classification according to flight altitude, classification according to size, classification by flight mission method, and classification by takeoff and landing method.

If unmanned aerial vehicles are classified according to military use, they are called tactical unmanned aerial vehicles (UAVs) that are used for tactical purposes at cruising distance and below short-range and at altitude below medium altitude. An unmanned aerial vehicle that is used for strategic purposes and that requires long-term flight capability at high altitude is called a strategic unmanned aerial vehicle. There are also unmanned fighters, attack unmanned aerial vehicles, and jam unmanned aerial vehicles.

When classified according to flight radius, close-range UAVs that can operate within about 50 km are short-range UAVs that can operate within about 200 km and support units below corps. In addition, it is said that it is a medium-range unmanned aerial vehicle that can operate within about 650 km, that it can operate up to about 3,000 km, and that it mainly performs military strategic information support missions is called a long-range unmanned aerial vehicle.

When classified according to flight altitude, a Low Altitude UAV is an unmanned aerial vehicle of less than 6,200 m (20,000 ft) that flies at a low altitude and is equipped with an electro-optical camera and infrared detector. In addition, the Medium Altitude Endurance is an unmanned aerial vehicle of 13,950 m (45,000 ft) or less that flies in the troposphere and can be equipped with an electro-optical camera and a radar synthesis camera.

Lastly, it is a high-altitude unmanned aerial vehicle (High Altitude Endurance) that flies and hovers in the stratosphere of the Earth's atmosphere with an activity range of 13,950 m (45,000 ft) above the ground.

Unmanned aerial vehicles can also be classified by flight mission performance. As an early unmanned reconnaissance aircraft, after being launched, it flies along a pre-programmed flight path without artificial control and takes pictures with an attached camera. It is called a primitive reconnaissance aircraft that retrieves VCR tapes recorded after a flight and obtains information.

It is a type of unmanned attack aircraft that is often used to destroy enemy radar air defense networks. There is an attack aircraft that follows the radar signal and self-destructs when the enemy radar activates while flying in a certain sky. The unmanned aerial vehicle for this purpose is a reconnaissance aircraft. Nowadays, unmanned helicopters that have removed the restrictions on the location for take-off and landing are also being used a lot.

Unmanned aerial vehicles of this type (rotary wing aircraft or vertical take-off and landing aircraft) can take off and land with only a helipad without a runway and can take off and land in rough terrain or under poor natural terrain conditions. This can be said to be the drones based on vertical take-off and landing, which we are generally familiar with.

Looking at the development status of unmanned aerial vehicles by countries around the world, the United States paid attention to the military practicality of unmanned aerial vehicles from an early age. It is understood that more than 10,000 unmanned aerial vehicles (UAVs) of 120 types are currently in operation. Therefore, various policies have been established and implemented to subdivide and manage numerous unmanned aerial vehicles by each operational radius and payload weight.

The United States is strategically developing MQ model and RQ model among various types of unmanned aerial vehicles. They are mainly responsible for surveillance and reconnaissance, electronic warfare, maritime surveillance, and anti-submarine missions. Recently, the development of the Unmanned Combat Aerial Vehicle is the most focused. The development of the Unmanned Combat Aerial Vehicle was selected as a key research and development target after the completion of the development of the high-altitude unmanned aerial vehicle in the late 1990s.

At first, several companies such as Boeing and Lockheed participated mainly in the US Navy and US Air Force, but since 2007, they have been reorganized to focus on the US Navy, and Northrop and Lockheed are conducting business together. At that time, it is known that the contract amount was approximately KRW 700 billion, and the target price per unit of Unmanned Combat Aerial Vehicle is expected to be between KRW 27.5 billion and KRW 38.5 billion when mass-produced. If the program currently under development is successful, it is expected that by 2020, 4 to 12 unmanned fighters will be deployed per carrier to build an unmanned fighter squadron with a total size of 120 to 150 units.

The United States established a mid- to long-term development roadmap for unmanned systems and future development goal by analyzing the current situation and actual conditions by areas such as interoperability, autonomous flight, airspace management, communication technology, training technology, engine power technology, and unmanned integrated operation technology

Israel ranks second in the UAV sector.

Israel, which recognizes the defense industry as a national strategic nurturing industry due to the nature of the country located in the Middle East, is concentrating on developing an unmanned aerial vehicle with excellent cost-effectiveness.

Through the government-level export-led defense industry nurturing strategy, the worldwide unmanned aerial vehicle R&D project is being carried out, and the bestsellers in the unmanned aerial vehicle market are steadily being released. The United States, which perceives the world stage as a battlefield, can be seen as a rather special case, while small and medium-sized countries such as Israel focused on developing a system capable of tactical surveillance and small-scale attacks in a relatively limited area. Therefore, a small local target attack system and operation concept have been intensively developed. In other words, the technology related to operating system development is more prominent at the medium altitude and below than at the high-altitude long endurance level. The tactical monitoring capability was maximized by optimizing the intermediate level and below, and the mission requirement of the purchasing country was met at a lower price. It is being used in most countries, such as Russia and China, which are not enemies of Israel.

Since Israel starts system development with export in mind from the initial development stage, economic feasibility is a key issue in the concept of operation of Israeli unmanned aerial vehicles. By militarily commercializing inexpensive expendable UAVs and hand-launch UAVs that can also be used for strike purposes, the U.S. has a remarkable advantage in areas not focused on. UAVs such as Scout, Pioneer, Hunter, Searcher, Heron, Harpy, Hermes, Skylark, and Skylite whose practicality and economy have been proven worldwide are manufactured and operated based on Israeli technology. While maintaining the same performance, it is being recognized for its value in the global market by improving the system scale and cost. In addition, it is evaluated as having pioneered an area of the Israeli unmanned aerial vehicle market that is virtually independent by simultaneously promoting international joint R&D projects without borders. Pioneer (AAI in the US), Hunter (TRW in the US), and Ranger (RUGA Aerospace in Switzerland) are representative examples of unmanned aerial vehicles developed jointly with Israel.

Figure 1-14 Unmanned aerial vehicles used for military purposes

Europe is researching and developing different unmanned aerial vehicle systems for each country. In Sweden, SAAB produced SHARC and FILUR as shrink testers for technology research and succeeded in automatic control flight in August 2004. Although the tail wing and fuselage air intake design were different depending on the stealth performance, it is equipped with the same engine and aims to develop autonomous navigation and flight capabilities at the same level, so-called whole components are separately combined the modular strategy is applied. And it was intended to improve cost efficiency by using a common platform.

In other words, Sweden systematically integrates and manages various technologies such as engine, fuselage, ground control equipment, autonomous navigation, power management, collision avoidance, data link, stealth, and weapon loading by using the modular method and development platform in the unmanned aerial vehicle field.

In the case of France, in addition to national security purposes, unmanned aerial vehicle R&D projects are in progress taking into account political and economic specificities. France, Italy, Greece, Switzerland, Spain, and Sweden are promoting the NEURON R&D project in which six countries jointly participate. It is a project that costs about 500 billion won to develop a platform.

It is not a method in which several European countries or companies form a consortium and participate, but the French national government agency takes responsibility and leads the industry and program control.

Germany and Spain are jointly developing the Barracuda. It is being promoted jointly with companies belonging to each country, and it is characterized by a limited level of stealth performance and designed to make jamming, a method of hacking unmanned aerial vehicles impossible through radio wave disturbance.

The UK has manufactured the Raven as a scaled-down tester similar to the B-2 bomber and aims to commercialize unmanned aerial vehicles after 2020. Meanwhile, BAE systems' Taranis is the largest unmanned aerial vehicle known to date, can carry precision-guided bombs and is said to be capable of transcontinental flight.

Looking at China's unmanned aerial vehicle R&D, Yilong, known as the Chinese version of the Predator, was unveiled at the Paris Air Show in 2013. At that time, it was displayed along with the BA-7 air-to-air missile, the YZ-212 laser-guided bomb, the YZ-102 anti-personnel bomb, and a 50 kg small-sized guided bomb, demonstrating its performance as an unmanned attack aircraft. In addition, Xialong, the Chinese version of the Global Hawk, is known to reach an altitude of 57,000 feet and a range of about 7,500 km. It succeeded in a test flight in January 2013 and flew for a maximum of 10 hours at a speed of 750 km.

And the Lijien, a Chinese unmanned aerial vehicle, is the world's third self-made unmanned aerial vehicle with a stealth function after the United States and France.

Korea's unmanned aerial vehicles include the peregrine falcon for reconnaissance, which was developed by the Defense Science Research Center in the 1990s and has been operated by the military since 2004, a large medium-altitude unmanned aerial vehicle with a wingspan of 25 meters, and an unmanned aerial vehicle for close-up surveillance developed by Korean Air.

The Korean military peregrine falcon can operate within about 200 km and is a short range unmanned aerial vehicle (Short Range) that supports units below the corps. Its main task is reconnaissance. The development was completed in 2000. The characteristics of the Peregrine Falcon, whose main task is to collect information for artillery units, is that it can acquire long-distance real-time target image information day and night, and it is possible to take off the launch pad and automatically land the parafoil. It is also equipped with an automatic flight system as a pre-programmed program. And the smart unmanned aerial vehicle being developed by the Korea Aerospace Research Institute has been developed since 2002, and its main features are vertical take-off and landing and high-speed flight, and it is being developed to enable high-speed autonomous flight at a speed of 500 km/h.

The unmanned aerial vehicle being developed by Korean Air began development in 2004 and successfully flew publicly in 2007. Its main features are real-time surveillance and reconnaissance over a radius of 40 km or more for two and a half hours, and a zoom-in camera is installed to enable real-time observation and storage of mission area images from the ground control station.

As described above, countries around the world are competitively spurring the development of autonomous vehicles and unmanned aerial vehicles as major technologies in the era of the Fourth Industrial Revolution.

Next, the 3D printer is one of the six major technologies of the Fourth Industrial Revolution. 3D printing refers to the activity of three-dimensional electronic information for realizing a three-dimensional shape in an encyclopedia through an automated output device. To put it more simply, it refers to a machine that creates 3D objects based on 3D drawings. In the early days, plastic was mostly used as a material due to various reasons such as ease of processing, however, as the range of materials is gradually expanding from paper, rubber, concrete, and food to metal, it has become a promising field.

It is said that an idea product called a 3D pen that allows you to draw in 3D by yourself has come out. There has been a boom in 3D printers for a while, but there is an evaluation that the related industry has a bit of a stagnation due to the high price of 3D printers or prototype production using plastics. However, as the market price of 3D printers is formed at an appropriate level along with the boom of the Fourth Industrial Revolution, various types of 3D printers are being released from various companies, from low-cost assembly models to educational and industrial use. Also, Autodesk, which is famous for CAD, developed 123D Design, Tinker cad, etc.

Figure 1-15 3D printer that creates a model of human hand

with the intention of making modeling software that even elementary school students can use easily and distributed mainly as freeware. Other software, such as Blender, Free CAD, and Sketchup, can be used. It is true that the difficulty of modeling has decreased due to this, but there is still some academic difficulty in the production of drawings.

Finally, one of the technologies of the Fourth Industrial Revolution that should be noted is nanotechnology.

Nano(10^{-9}) means 10 to the minus (-)9th power, and nanotechnology refers to the field of precision technology centered on extremely fine sizes, such as those in Nano units.

Figure 1-16 Molecular-level quantum mechanics

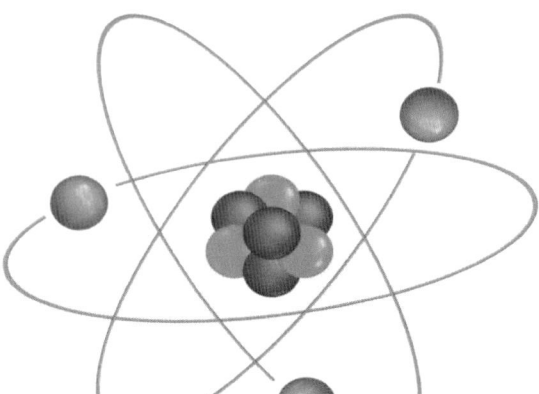

The fields covered are diverse, such as displays, semiconductors, and Nano-bio. The reason that nanotechnology is attracting attention these days is that it can be manipulated into a small size that was difficult to imagine before and new characteristics are being discovered due to such a small size. Therefore, it can be said that the potential is high due to the diverse fields to be dealt with, but it can also be said that the detailed definition of the discipline has not been fully established.

Figure 1-17 The birth of the Fourth Industrial Revolution

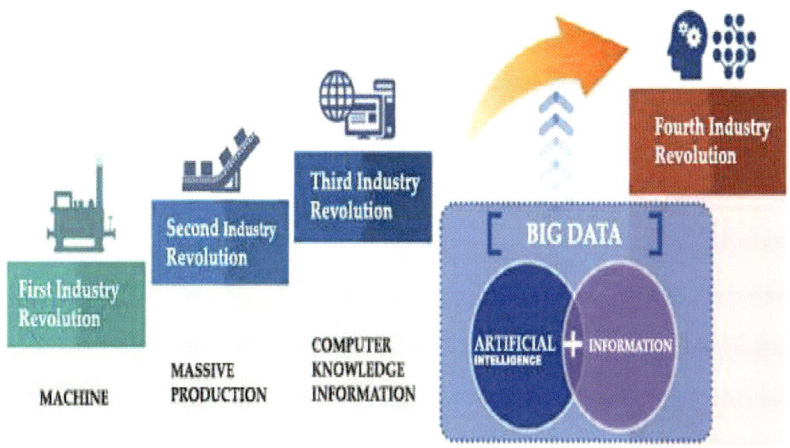

As seen above, the Fourth Industrial Revolution refers to six fields such as big data, artificial intelligence, robots, the Internet of Things, autonomous vehicles or aircraft, 3D printers, and nanotechnology. It has a powerful influence that can change even the structure and form of human society.

As a prime example, if self-driving cars become a stable reality, a world will come where no driver's license is required, and if big data and artificial intelligence take care of all the work that humans used to do, it could eliminate the need for people to go to work. Industrial Revolution means not only changes in industry or economy, but also changes in the way of life itself and society. Therefore, Fourth Industrial Revolution the contents of basic technological innovation in the era of the Fourth Industrial Revolution will become the common sense necessary for us to live in the present age.

1.2 Beginning of the First Industrial Revolution

In general, the Industrial Revolution is a social, economic, and cultural revolution that occurred in England between the mid-18th century and the early 19th century, that is, between 1760 and 1820, through technological innovation and new manufacturing processes.

Through this First Industrial Revolution, the textile industry, which used to produce simple clothes and fabrics, began to use modern production methods for the first time.

Afterward, the Industrial Revolution spread throughout the world and changed the world greatly. The term industrial revolution was first used by Friedrich Engels in 1844 in his book The Condition of the Working Class in England, and it was later embodied in the book "Lectures on the Industrial Revolution of the Eighteenth Century in England" by Toynbee in 1884.

In Europe, especially Britain, political maturity and stability were achieved due to the earlier revolution and feudalism than in other countries, resulting in the emergence of a freer peasant class. In addition, the woolen industry developed a lot in rural areas centering on this peasant class, and various mechanical industries began to develop based on this.

In England in the 18th century, when the demand for cotton fabrics surged, James Watt improved the steam engine and started mass production using these machines, which is generally regarded as the starting point of the Industrial Revolurion. After that, the textile industry using these machines led the Industrial Revolurion. During this First Industrial Revolurion, many machines related to the textile industry were invented. In the First Industrial Revolution, the production of textiles by hand was changed to production using a cotton spinning machine, Arclite's hand spinning machine,

Hargreaves' multi-axis spinning machine, and Cromton's mule spinning machine. The time was around 1769, and from that time on, the concept of a patent was first introduced in the industry. In other words, the beginning of the Industrial Revolurion has a very close relationship with the introduction of the concept of patents. Manufacturing by human hands was a kind of ability or knowledge known only to the person, but with the introduction of the concept of machine manufacturing, the knowledge and idea of the technology itself began to become an industrial property with a value.

Figure 1-18 The steam locomotive

The machine power transmission method using steam power, as we know it, is well known as an improved steam engine invented by James Watt. At first, it was mainly used to extract minerals from mines, and from the 1780s, it was developed as a motor to drive machinery. This steam engine technology enabled the rapid evolution of small, efficient semi-automated plants in an era when hydropower did not exist.

To use a steam engine, fuel was needed. In England, coal started to replace charcoal from the time of the industrial revolution, and a steam engine using coal was used for iron smelting instead of the charcoal used for iron smelting. The First Industrial Revolution not only brought revolutionary changes to the economic structure of the country but at the same time brought about significant changes in the political structure as well. The ruling system of royalty and nobility collapsed, and the electoral law was revised to allow the emerging bourgeoisie to participate in politics based on the wealth gained through mass production.

The notions of democracy and communism came into existence.

Figure 1-19 James Watt's steam engine

Figure 1-20 Workers in modern society

Through the Industrial Revolution, most of the rural population moved to the city, which resulted in an explosive growth of the urban population. However, in the end, during the Industrial Revolution, the city was transformed into an unsanitary, stinky, and filthy city crowded with smoke from burning coal. Human rights violations against workers also began to emerge during the Industrial Revolution. Factory owners forced their workers to work long hours, and consumption and rest were also partially restricted. In addition, an unusual incident of child labor took place.

At that time, capitalists seduced orphans from an orphanage, also called a poverty-stricken orphanage, and brought them to work. In addition, related laws such as banning night shifts were enacted, and in the United States, a labor movement demanded that workers work eight hours a day against wage cuts and long working hours despite government oppression and distorted reports from the media. The meal consisted mostly of bread and potatoes, and it was very poor compared to modern times when tea and butter were served. The miserable lives of workers caused a wave of socialist movements against capitalism, and the logic of Marx's scientific socialism establishment against socialism.

The emergence of a liberal economic system in most Western countries today or a distribution-oriented economic system under the jurisdiction of the state represented by communism is all related to the change in the social structure that began with the Industrial Revolution.

The First Industrial Revolution started in England at the end of the 18th century and became a catalyst for world modernization, and it made a turning point in human history that determined the structure of modern society represented by today's liberal democracy and communism.

1.3 What is the Second and Third Industrial Revolution?

The Second Industrial Revolution is a word used by historians to describe the second stage of the First Industrial Revolution. It is generally defined as the period from 1865 to the mid-1900s. It is widely used to distinguish it from the First Industrial Revolution, which was centered in England, as the productive capacity of factories in Germany and the United States grew innovatively during this period.

While the First Industrial Revolution had a mechanical industrial aspect mainly focused on "clothes" among textile machinery or food, clothing, and shelter, the Second Industrial Revolution carried out many technological innovations in chemical, electricity, oil, and steel fields. There were also structural advances in the mass production of consumer goods, and in the fields of processing, transportation, and even entertainment, films, radios and phonographs were developed, as well as machinery for manufacturing foodstuffs, beverages, and clothing. However, mass production by machines caused the Great Depression from 1873 to 1896, and so-called neo-imperialism, which plundered other powerless and poor countries.

The Second Industrial Revolution began to spread not only to England but also to all of Europe, and in particular, brought about the most changes in the United States. The reason that the United States has risen to the ranks of the world's most powerful power economically and militarily is also the driving force behind this Second Industrial Revolution. Edison, Tesla, Westinghouse, etc. of the United States invented and presented very useful inventions one after another using electricity. Some say that the Second Industrial Revolution was a time when new technologies that would surprise mankind after World

War I were spread around the world. During World War II, the world developed new technologies competitively with each other, and eventually achieved scientific and technological advances such as the atomic bomb that threatened even the survival of mankind.

Figure 1-21 Light bulb invented in Second Industrial Revolution

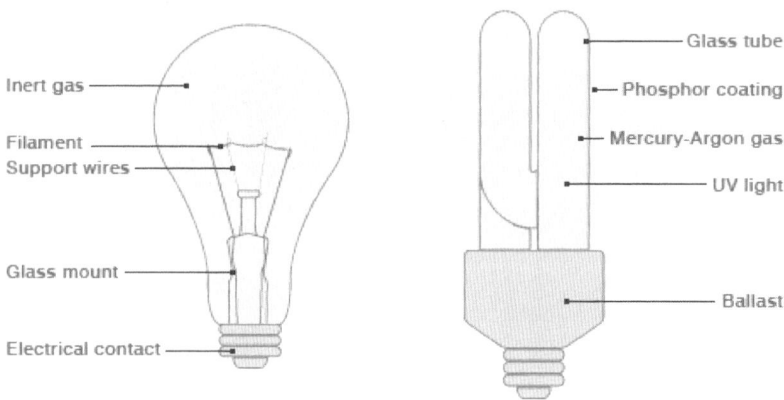

The Second Industrial Revolution was a time when innovative and useful inventions were developed one by one from electricity to phonographs, automobiles, airplanes, and even the atomic bomb.

The Third Industrial Revolution is the future predicted by American economist Jeremy Rifkin, etc., that is, the present appearance of us living in the present age. In particular, the market is growing centered on virtual goods, that is, contents, rather than actual factory products, and the market is reorganized centered on services. In other words, it means that the whole world is united into one factory or one market through a globally connected Internet network and a multitasking computer environment that can be used anywhere. It is the information age.

The emergence of telephone lines, radio, television, and the Internet created a wide range of communication, and a new form of Industrial Revolution was required. Scholars led by Jeremy Rifkin, under the title of the Third Industrial

Revolution, proposed the combination of Internet communication technology and renewable energy requested.

Figure 1-22 Machines invented in the Third Industrial Revolution

Therefore, it is the Third Industrial Revolution that mass customization occurs as the digitization of the manufacturing industry represented by factories and machines is promoted and the maker space of the factory in charge of actual manufacturing is expanded.

This means that the information age has arrived.

1.4 History of the Industrial Revolution

The history of the Industrial Revolution of mankind is the history of technology and the history of tools. From the prehistoric and Neolithic times, when humans first used stones, to the Stone Age, the Bronze Age, and the Iron Age, the use of tools, which is difficult to say as an industry compared to modern times, is human history. It wasn't long time ago. Until the First Industrial Revolution, life was based on animals and tools, and it was not at a level that could be called industry.

That is why the term Industrial Revolution is meaningful. This is because through the Industrial Revolution, the political structure of human society has changed, the lifestyles have changed, and the scale of thinking has changed. The impact of the Industrial Revolution on human history has taken on such a large proportion that it is not an exaggeration to say that it is human history itself. It wasn't long before technology began to influence human history in this way. Until now, human history has been dismissed as tens of thousands of years at the longest, or as short as thousands of years, which is the history of civilization, but the history of the Industrial Revolution has all happened within 200 years. The United States proves it. Although the United States was founded only 200 years ago, it has already been recognized as the most developed and strongest country in the world for 100 years. This was only possible because of the Industrial Revolution. And the cycle of change in the Industrial Revolution is getting faster.

The First Industrial Revolution occurred between about 1760 and 1820 in England, Europe, and the United States. There was a transition from mainly agricultural and rural societies to industrial and urban societies, and the steel industry play a key role in the Industrial Revolution with the development of steam engines.

The Second Industrial Revolution occurred between 1865 and the mid to late 1900s, before World War I. It was a period of growth of existing industries, and electric power was used for the expansion and mass production of new industries such as steel, oil, and electricity. It was a period when innovative and useful inventions were developed one by one.

Figure 1-23 Satellites at the American Space Center

The Third Industrial Revolution is, in other words, a virtual goods revolution or a digital revolution.

It refers to the fact that an analog signal derived from the Second Industrial Revolution has been replaced with a digital signal with content. It mainly refers to technological advances ranging from electronic and mechanical devices to digital technologies currently available. In general, there are many tendencies to think that it was after the rapid spread of computers in the 1960s and after the Internet began to spread. Personal computers, the Internet, and numerous information and communication technologies that are currently commercialized are included in the technology of the third Industrial Revolution. The Third Industrial Revolution is still evolving. Strictly speaking, this is a time when the technology of the Industrial Revolution and the technology of the Fourth Industrial Revolution coexist.

The title of this book is "Frequency of the Fourth Industrial Revolution". Perhaps the title of this book, frequency, is a word that specifies analog signals, expressing this current situation. Frequency is the most important technology keyword for information communication and analog-to-digital conversion, which are the main technologies of the Third Industrial Revolution. Just as the frequency leading to the analog signals is converted to digital to produce content, this book also intends to prepare for the Fourth Industrial Revolution from the perspective of the Third Industrial Revolution that is still in progress.

The Third Industrial Revolution is not over yet, and the Fourth Industrial Revolution has already begun. The Fourth Industrial Revolution is being built in the digital revolution that represents a new way in which technology is applied to society and even the human body is absorbed. As described above, the Internet of Things means that people or things become components of a network. It is not a concept of simply acquiring information and contents by accessing a network through a terminal like the existing Third Industrial Revolution.

Figure 1-24 Transition to the Fourth Industrial Revolution

The Fourth Industrial Revolution generally refers to six fields including big data, artificial intelligence, robotics, the Internet of Things, unmanned transportation (unmanned aerial vehicles, unmanned vehicles), 3D printers, and nanotechnology.

At the World Economic Forum, Klaus Schwab's book "The Fourth Industrial Revolution" mentions the fundamental differences from the previous First, Second, and Third Industrial Revolutions characterized by the development of technology. These technologies have great potential to keep billions of people connected to the Web, dramatically improving the efficiency of businesses and organizations, and regenerating the natural environment.

I completely agree with Klaus Schwab's opinion, and I expect it to bring about a much greater change. While the Fourth Industrial Revolution is the development of existing human society and technology that humans can imagine, artificial intelligence, robotics, and nanotechnology have the potential to make things that humans cannot imagine into reality.

As a single example, AI technology has already proven that it has superior learning and judgment abilities than humans through AlphaGo, a Go algorithm. In addition, robotics has already transcended the limits of the human body for a long time. And in the case of nanotechnology, it can bring about the birth of powerful creatures such as Hulk and Alien that we have seen in movies.

The Fourth Industrial Revolution is not a dream that becomes reality, but something beyond imagination can become a reality. Therefore, the Fourth Industrial Revolution has the potential to make things possible that humans cannot even imagine.

1.5 The Birth of The Fourth Industrial Revolution

How did the Fourth Industrial Revolution originate and for what purpose? Klaus Schwab describes the 10 leading technologies of the Fourth Industrial Revolution as unmanned transportation means, 3D printing, advanced robotics, new materials, IoTremote monitoring technology, blockchain Bitcoin, the sharing economy, genetic engineering, synthetic biology, and bioprinting were emphasized. Are all the above technologies essential for the Fourth Industrial Revolution? It can depend on the person, company, and institution that accepts it. And it must be different. Not everyone needs to know the sharing economy or bioprinting technology. Therefore, each scholar discusses the above-mentioned 10 technologies as technologies corresponding to the Fourth Industrial Revolution, minus and adding according to their respective standards. When the word Fourth Industrial Revolution was first coined, people thought that all the technologies mentioned would develop at once. However, it can change according to various variables such as social trends, people's interest and investment in technology. This is because not only the components of each technology are different, but also the issues of the new human society change every year.

As someone wrote in the column, the technology of the Fourth Industrial Revolution is a combination of the original technology area and the applied technology area, which looks like a new technology in some respects. There are those who say that it does not fit the technological revolution. Therefore, rather than vaguely mentioning new technologies, some argue that it is necessary to reflect on the purpose of introducing the technologies of the Fourth Industrial Revolution. I agree with a great deal on that.However, I do not think that the Fourth Industrial Revolution is a classification of technologies introduced by clarifying the standards based on existing standards and determining whether it is currently necessary or not. We have already learned many lessons from the Third Industrial Revolution, and we continue to learn lessons today. Before thinking about the conceptual technical classification, such as thinking about which one comes first, the egg or the chicken, I think it is right to introduce and study it first and consider the application as a second priority.

Figure 1-25 Issues of the Industrial Revolution

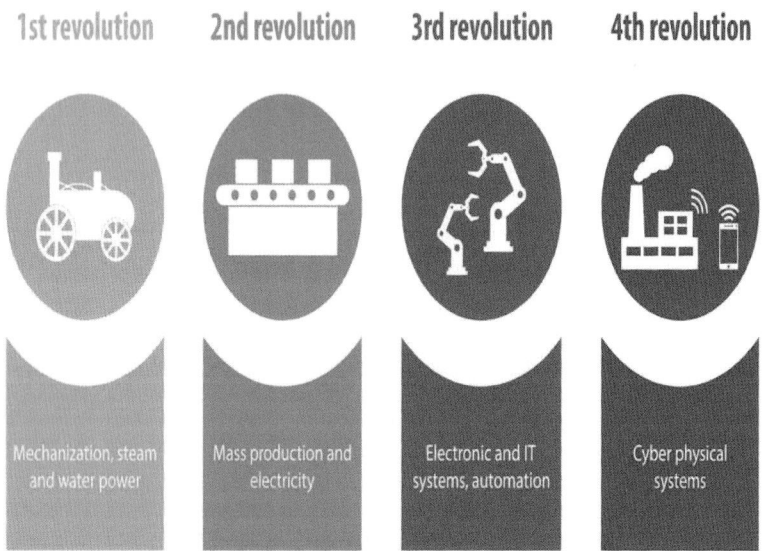

This is because, in the process of introducing the new technology, new innovations and ideas are continuously created.

This is because, as described earlier, the Fourth Industrial Revolution technology will be a technological revolution different from the Third Industrial Revolution we imagined and developed. While the Third Industrial

Revolution was the advancement of technology that could be imagined by the existing human society and human beings out of necessity, the Fourth Industrial Revolution has potential to make possible parts that humans could not even imagine in the case of artificial intelligence, robotics, and nanotechnology..

Figure 1-26 Shenzhen-City of the Fourth Industrial Revolution

Figure 1-27 CES Expo-Leader of the Fourth Industrial Revolution

I designated the six technologies referred to by the most scholars in this book as the core technologies of the Fourth Industrial Revolution.

It includes big data analysis, artificial intelligence, robotics, the Internet of Things, unmanned transportation (unmanned aerial vehicles, unmanned vehicles), 3D printers, and nanotechnology. All of these technologies are things that can become reality beyond imagination. Therefore, the Fourth Industrial Revolution will become the basic knowledge that we must accept, whether we understand it or not, and the basic knowledge we need to live in this era.

Part 2 Blockchain and Virtual Currency

2.1 Creation of Blockchain Technology

Blockchain technology began to attract attention in 2009 when a cryptocurrency called Bitcoin was born. Of course, Bitcoin is not the whole of blockchain technology. However, since Bitcoin was the one that introduced the blockchain technology to the world and widely publicized the usefulness of the technology, the concept will be explained using Bitcoin as an example. Bitcoin was created in 2009 with the purpose of creating an online currency that can improve the shortcomings of existing real money by an individual named Satoshi Nakamoto.

In the early days, no one expected it to become a technology that forms an axis of the Fourth Industrial Revolution. However, it is Bitcoin that has played a role in confirming the infinite potential of the technology called blockchain as many people form and develop systems based on its principle.

Under the legalized economic system, such as the real-name financial system, it became more widely known as it was used for the distribution of illegal funds, which is an issue these days, and the drug and arms trade based on unique anonymity.

The most important keyword of the blockchain is the integrity of information. That is, since it is almost impossible to change the information generated initially, the possibility of distortion or modulation is very low. Therefore, the reliability of the information increases.

A blockchain is a method of putting certain information in a certain section called a block, and when information is added/changed, another block is created and attached to the existing block to continue as a chain.

For example, in the case of Bitcoin, the information and hash value of the

Bitcoin holders are put into a block, and when there is a change in funds such as a transfer, a new block is created to bind a kind of chain to connect the information.

A block containing this information is called a Node, shared equally by users around the world, and the operation of adding a new block is proven by the participants in the block who want economic rewards, often called miners.

Mining is the task of finding a specific target value on a computer. If someone has to succeed in manipulating blocks for financial gain, that is, creating and propagating blocks that have been altered by hackers, the number of computers currently connected to the network is 550,000 times that of existing supercomputers. It is close to impossible to embed into the existing blockchain.

Therefore, it is practically impossible to instantaneously hack common information shared with nodes, and the integrity, or reliability, of information is secured here.

If a quantum computer appears, it is likely to exceed the number of computing on the network, but it seems that it will take a long time for quantum computers to become popular.

Bitcoin is like a note written on such a node how much the block is worth. No one in this world can edit the text of that note. Therefore, the face value of the block is a concept that can be used as money because its reliability can be assured by having the integrity of the information.

In general, Bitcoin, an acquisition method called mining, uses a proof-of-work method called POW (Proof of Work) that gives proof rights to those who own a lot of stakes, but in the case of other cryptocurrencies, a stake called POS (Proof of Stake) is used, and several other methods such as POI are used.

In general, it is not Bitcoin that professional cryptocurrency traders or engineers pay attention to, but the blockchain technology used in those cryptocurrencies.

Figure 2-1 Cryptocurrency and Gacoin using blockchain technology

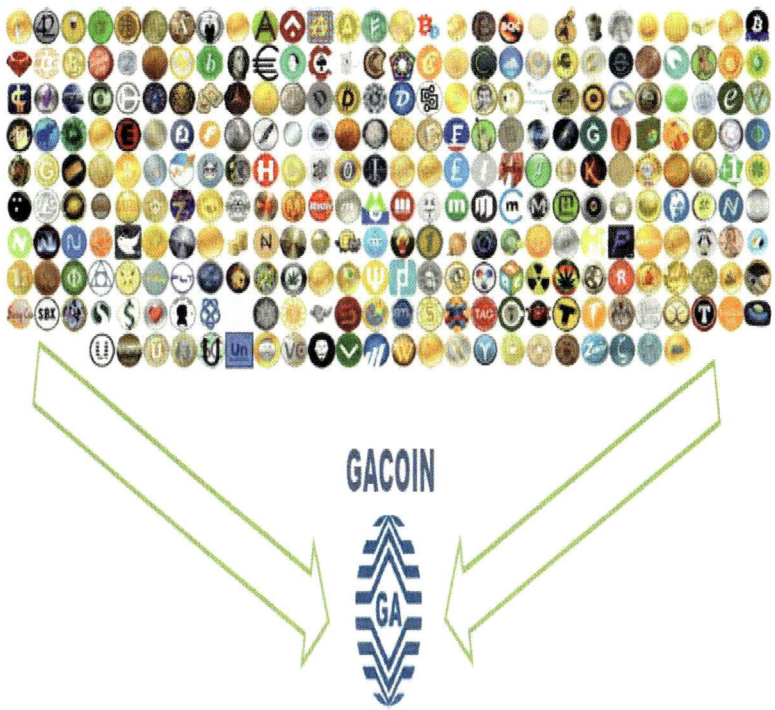

By using blockchain technology, it is possible to easily share and deliver a set of information without fear of hacking, and I believe that this work will bring about innovative changes in various fields.

The development of blockchain technology is the same as the development of security technology. This is because the most necessary part of the integrity of information is a security.

For example, an election verifies the integrity of information about whether you voted in person or if someone else deliberately manipulated your ballot. If you look around, there are countless areas where information distortion is likely to occur. As a security technology to protect the integrity of such information, a blockchain technology can be very useful.

Through the easy sharing of such flawless information, the development of technologies that have always been delayed in terms of information integrity can processed quickly in the wave of new technologies, such as the Internet of Things, financial innovation, multimedia, and artificial intelligence, commonly referred to as the Fourth Industrial Revolution.

For example, it has been found that currently about 60% of the world's population is unable to conduct active electronic financial transactions such as online finance, savings, or fund products.

In particular, African countries, which are difficult to own real assets due to government corruption or an underdeveloped financial system, have only primitive financial transactions such as labor and exchange of goods even in the 21st century. The theoretical advantage is that anyone with an internet connection can create a wallet and participate in transactions, and there is no need to worry about corruption in the national system. Therefore, if cryptocurrency using blockchain technology is activated globally, the number of economic participants will grow exponentially, and the global economy will enjoy a greater boom and develop theoretically. However, in my opinion, there has always been a gap between theory and the real market. Even if the cryptocurrency market using blockchain technology is activated, hacking technologies or vulnerabilities that coexist with blockchain technology will inevitably emerge, leading to a situation where only the underground economy is nurtured. Therefore, it would be a prerequisite to secure the stability of the technology by actively researching the complete system of blockchain technology and self-security than now.

To return, Bitcoin had no proper exchange like the existing stock market, gold market, or oil market at first, and was only traded as an exchange between individuals existing online.

Bitcoin was initially very low in exchange value for real money like a kind of discount coupon, with two pizzas exchanged for 10,000 pieces, but now the market price is changing dynamically from moment to moment, as it used to be more than $10,000 per bitcoin because many people are interested and participate in mining or trading. So far, its value remains the subject of interest rather than the function of a stabilized currency.

Bitcoin, which was previously programmed with a limited supply of 21 million pieces, will end when 21 million pieces are issued. In other words, it is not the concept of real money that can be printed infinitely but has the highest value at a certain point according to the rate of change in value, and then the value tends to decline again after a certain inflection point. It has a similar circulation flow of other types of speculative assets, such as stocks, gold, and money, which have similar monetary value to oil.

Initial miners were issued 50 Bitcoins each through mining, and after that, if the issuance amount exceeded a certain amount, 12.5 Bitcoins were given as a reward. However, if the actual mining program runs on a PC, the value may be less than the actual power consumption cost. Therefore, based on current value, mining may result in consumption rather than earning money.

However, creating and distributing cryptocurrencies using new blockchain technology raises issues such as whether as many people will actually use it and mine it compared to the cost of production. So these days, when investing in Korean companies abroad, there are cases where the company creates and sells cryptocurrency. This is often referred to as an ICO.

When explaining a block using a cryptocurrency called Bitcoin as an example, the data limit of the block is 1 MB, and the transfer and processing speed are quite slow, so it often takes half a day to use the exchange. It seems that there are various difficulties in being used as a substitute for real money. To solve this speed problem, several ideas that can apply the principles of blockchains well while making the algorithm simpler are emerging from various places.

Figure 2-2 ICO history of cryptocurrency

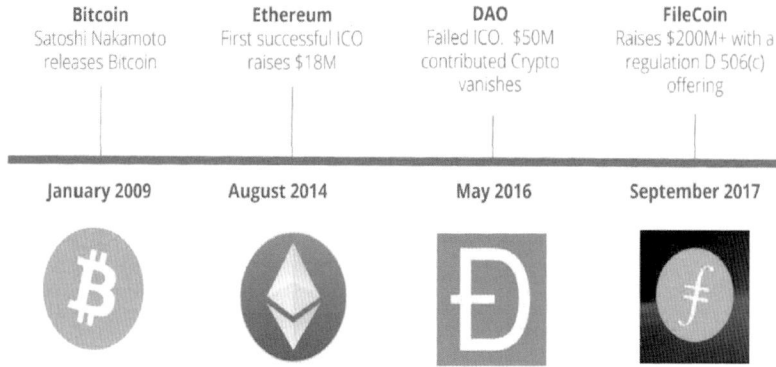

Currently, other coins other than Bitcoin can be bought and sold with Bitcoin on Poloniex, the world's No. 1 bitcoin exchange. Bitcoin is playing the role of a key currency that determines the value of various currencies, such as the dollar and yen.

If you look at other cryptocurrencies, there is LiteCoin, a currency that changed some variables in 2011 by applying this open source because the Bitcoin program code was open source.

Developed by Charlie Lee, a former Google employee, it is a cryptocurrency for smooth transactions by reducing block creation time and increasing the issuance volume compared to Bitcoin.

And Ethereum, as you may have heard, was created by Vitalik Buterin, who was inspired by Bitcoin.

With the development of Ethereum, Vitalik Buterin won the World Technology Information Technology Software Award, beating Mark Zuckerberg of Facebook.

This cryptocurrency, which started as an independent project in 2013, is not satisfied with the function of a simple currency but is equipped with a platform function that enables programming in a blockchain system. This is the function that makes Ethereum the most unique among other cryptocurrencies.

As a platform equipped with electronic contracts, it can be said that it is a cryptocurrency that has opened the era of blockchain 2.0 widely in name and reality.

As a platform that greatly increases the possibility of using block chain in reality, it is evaluated as a technology that will be importantly used and applied to the Internet of Things in the future. Applications using blockchain can be created within the Ethereum Platform, and the applications pay Eth (Ether) as a fee to the Ethereum Platform. In the platform, many developers are making various applications using blockchain, and applications that provide the current user's computing power to others for money or prediction market applications that receive bets and dividends according to certain results, etc., are being created and distributed within the Ethereum Platform.

As mentioned earlier, in modern society, the platform is the trend. Ethereum, which does not simply create and supply cryptocurrency, but also supplies a platform that can utilize it, is expected to have great development potential. It is also a platform that shows infinite possibilities, currently ranked second in terms of market capitalization of crypto currencies and is gaining huge popularity around the world. If cryptocurrency plays a big role in the Fourth Industrial Revolution, Ethereum will play a big role.

There is Ethereum Classic, which broke the block of the blockchain and started anew because the initial Ethereum was hacked. The newly created currency is Ethereum, which refers to using Ethereum's past blockchain, which includes even blocks hacked by some groups. In a word, it can be seen as an initial outdated version of Ethereum.

Figure 2-3 Cryptocurrency Types and Mining Methods

SORT	ALGORITHM	METHOD
BITCOIN(BTC)	SHA256	ASIC
BITCOIN CASH(BCH,BCC)	SHA256	ASIC
Ethereum(ETH)	Ethash	GPU
EthereumClassic(ETC)	Ethash	GPU
LITECOIN(LTC)	Scrypt	ASIC
DASH(DASH)	X11	ASIC
ZCASH(ZEC)	Equihash	GPU
GACOIN(GAC)	Ethash	GPU
DECRED(DCR)	Blake256	GPU

Ripple is a cryptocurrency that is faithful to the basics of blockchain technology. Although it does not have complex functions such as a platform like Ethereum, it is expected to be commercialized the fastest as a currency specialized in transmission speed and financial transactions.

While other currencies are aiming for decentralization, Ripple uses the method of having a central institution called Ripple Labs to exist. Since issuing the first 100 billion, Ripple Labs owns about 55 billion, and currently about 35 billion are traded in the market. Although the financial system is expected to be the first and most efficient application of blockchain technology, some say that Ripple intends to take an intermediate position in the fields of currency exchange and remittance. The transfer speed of Ripple is about 5 seconds, which is the same as the processing of Visa cards, and it is said that it can process about 50,000 transactions per second.

In addition, contracts are reported to have been signed with major banks such as SBI Financial Group of Japan, Bank of America of the US, and Abu Dhabi National Bank of the United Arab Emirates. The reason why banks use Ripple is that the cost of currency exchange and remittance can be reduced to 80% by using Ripple as an intermediary, and tests are being conducted in various places. Ripple ranks third in the overall cryptocurrency market. In other words, it is safe to say that Bitcoin, Ethereum, and Ripple are the three major cryptocurrencies. To date, the number of cryptocurrencies available around the world is roughly thousands. And this is expected to increase further in the future. As described in all of this chapter, cryptocurrency is more meaningful in that it was created using blockchain technology rather than its function as a currency. Cryptocurrency is used to verify the integrity of information in blockchain technology, not because of cryptocurrency. Therefore, for the Fourth Industrial Revolution, it is necessary to promote the development of blockchain technology through cryptocurrency and strategically research and prepare blockchain technology.

These days, many people have searched the cryptocurrency market while looking for a place to invest. Therefore, we describe how to trade cryptocurrencies in a simple common sense.

First, if you want to trade virtual currency, you can exchange won for coins through the Korean exchange. It is the same as buying securities with money on the stock exchange or buying gold on the gold exchange.

There are three main large exchanges in Korea, Bithumb, Coinone, and Korbit, and you can buy and sell coins freely like stock trading after registering as a member of the exchange. Just as we can buy stocks and gold at banks, there are also many people who use small and specific coin exchanges.

However, since it is not a real-name system like real money, if the security function of the registered website is lost, such as being hacked through careless information management, there is still no legal device to safely protect one's assets, such as the Depositor Protection Act, like a bank.

Figure 2-4 Cryptocurrency ICO method

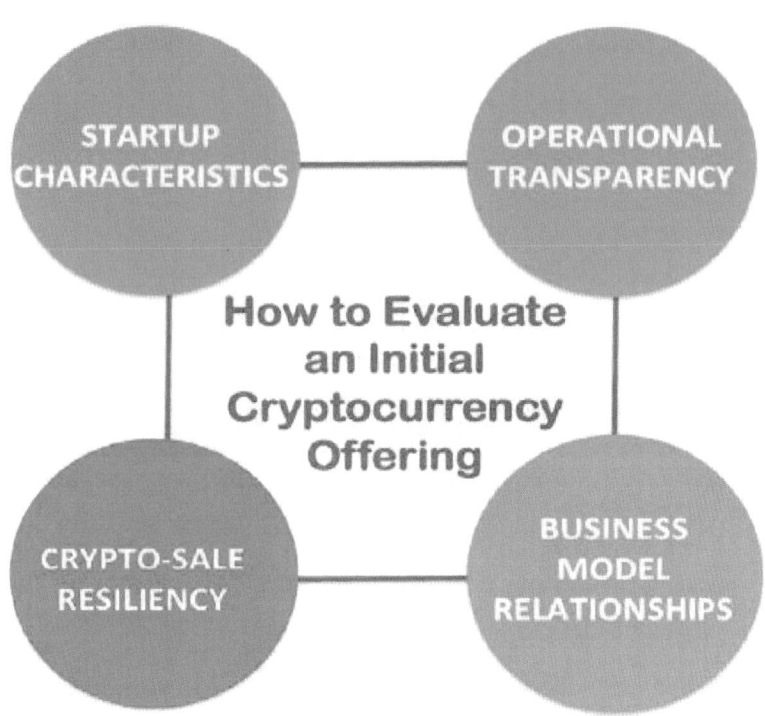

Currently, the coin trading market is not illegal, but the related management systems, enforcement rules, or related laws have not yet been established.

In fact, there is no definition of tax, and if you make a lot of money with coins, it may be a problem in the future to cash out.

There is also an ICO market where newly developed coins are issued like stocksare issued. The rate of return may be the best, but the risk is too high and it is currently overheated, so it is an investment method mainly used by Chinese investors.

Here, I would like to summarize the concepts of cryptocurrency, virtual currency, and digital currency that have been explained so far.

Cryptocurrency refers to electronic money that uses encryption technology.

And digital money can be thought of as a whole word that includes all kinds of money that is made up of digital information.

Cryptocurrency refers to money circulated online with mileage, game money, and points that we usually use.

In other words, cryptocurrency, digital currency, and virtual currency are strictly different words that have an intersection.

Bitcoin, for example, is a cryptocurrency, a digital currency, and a virtual currency. And it is a currency that uses blockchain technology. However, if you use the application and exchange Ethereum with the fee, this can be game money.

Let's find out why blockchain technology is used in cryptocurrency.

It is similar to the question of whether the chicken comes first or the egg comes first. This is a case in which blockchain technology was created to make cryptocurrency, but the importance of technology that guarantees the information integrity of blockchain technology has grown more than that of cryptocurrency. In other words, although cryptocurrency may be one of the major technological components of the Fourth Industrial Revolution, it is not a technology that forms a big axis like blockchain technology. Let's look at why this happens in the blockchain.

One thing to note here is that Bitcoin uses blockchain technology, and Bitcoin and blockchain are completely different.

Looking at the subprime mortgage crisisin the United States in 2007, financial institutions such as investment banks and fund companies were looking for high-yield investment destinations in the early 2000s. At that time, real estate prices soared day by day, and ordinary people were eager to buy houses, but financial institutions did not miss it. Financial institutions began to provide large-scale loans to prospective home buyers, and people took out loans believing that real estate prices would rise.

Figure 2-5 Gartner Hyper Cycle 2015 on Blockchain Technology

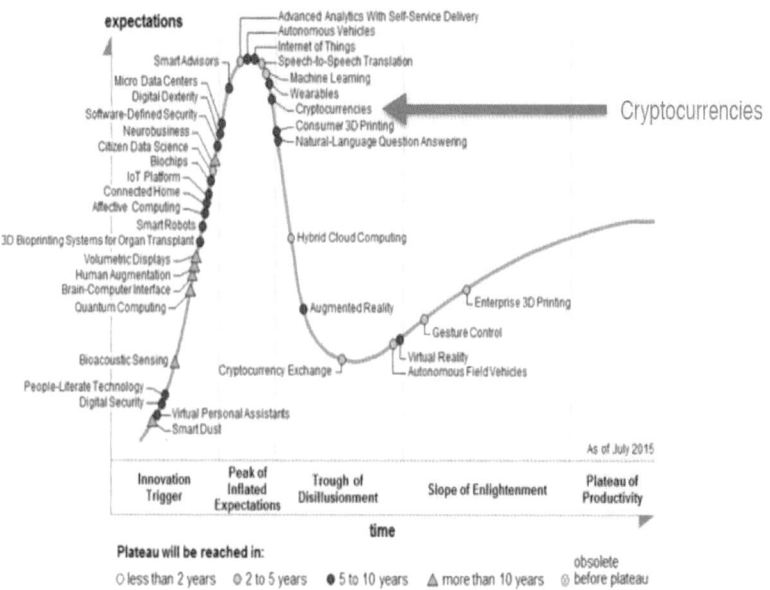

However, as the housing bubble burst, people were unable to pay off their loans, and as a result, financial institutions that could not pay off their loans went bankrupt. The most shocking of these was the bankruptcy of Lehman Brothers Holdings Inc, one of the four largest banks. When one of the four major banks went bankrupt, people did not trust financial institutions and became dissatisfied with such centralized financial institutions, and the idea of a virtual currency called Bitcoin was born.

In other words, in terms of server and client concepts, a distributed processing system, that is, a system in which each client divides and manages the server's resources, was conceived in a way that several clients access one computer to conduct financial transactions.

Figure 2-6 Blockchain Network

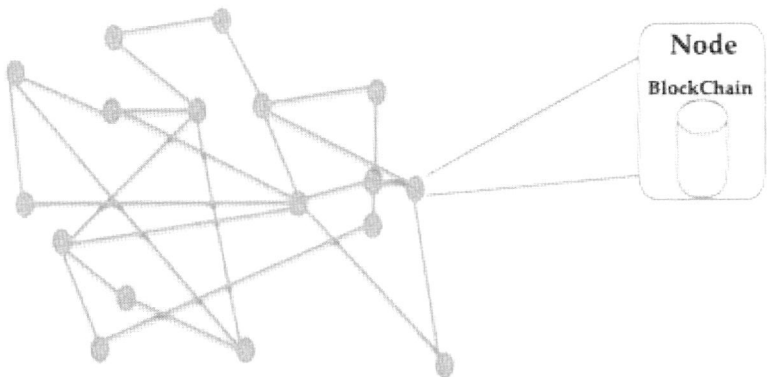

Each node has a blockchain

Cryptocurrency emerged from the financial transaction method that maximized this distributed processing system. Therefore, it is related to the security of the distributed processing system.

Blockchain technology is such a distributed processing system, in other words, having each block connected to the network, a book that is note and node, and entering the amount. This note is that several people have the same ledger, and it is not recognized if they are not the same compared to each other. What if 51 out of 100 notes are the same and 49 are not the same? This is called the 51% Rule in blockchain technology. That is, even a single block is recognized as the correct answer by a long chain. Simply put, a long chain, even one block, is recognized as a valid chain. Of course, there is the 51% Attack, a weakness that occurs in the 51% Rule. It is an act where a specific block group with more than 51% power manipulates the entire contents by attaching the manipulated blocks created by them.

An important concept in blockchain technology is hash. Hash is a method of converting a string into a hexadecimal number of a specified length. What's important here is the "determined length". Even if the input is jaggedly short or long, it always comes out with a fixed length.

Hash is made through a hash function, and if you use a hash function called SHA-256 to hash a string, whether you hash one word A or a relatively long string "Thank you" the same 64-digit result value is output. This is because it is a function designed to give a result value in that way.

Figure 2-7 Time of application of hash

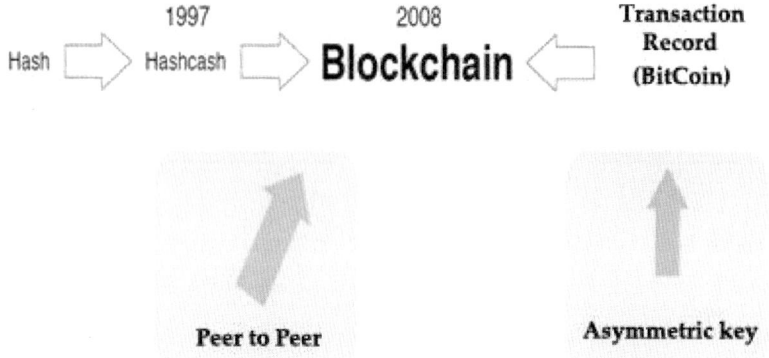

In other words, the number 256 in SHA-256 was given because 64 numbers consist of a total of 256 (64 x 4) combinations of 0 or 1. Then, the SHA-512 function is $512 \div 4 = 128$, that is, the SHA-256 always returns 64 numbers.

This hash function has the following four characteristics.

First, the use of hash functions can lead to redundant collisions.

Second, it is impossible to find the original input with only the hash result.

Third, a single digit change in the input will completely change the result.

Fourth, if both the input and the hashed result are known, verifying it consists of a very easy algorithm.

Hashes have different characteristics from general encryption techniques such as transposition (replacement of a character) and substitution (replacement of characters with other characters). In general encryption technology, the longer the characters to be encrypted, the longer the result. However, since the hash always outputs with the same length, the length of the original string cannot be known. Even if you are lucky enough to know the exact length, it is impossible to decipher.

Figure 2-8 Reasons for applying Hash

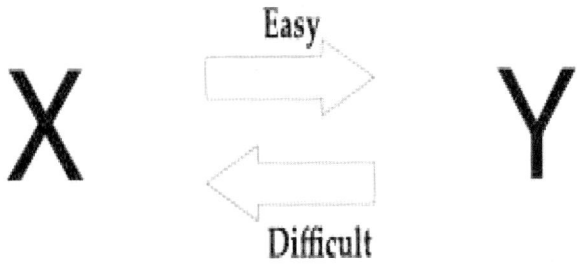

Example : The remainder function of a value divided by a specific decimal number (Modular)
When X = 19 Y=MOD7(19) = 5 [EASY]
INVERSE MOD7(5) = 5, 12, 19 .... [DIFFICULT]

General encryption technology has a certain pattern. For example, consider replacing the alphabet by pushing 3 spaces. When substituting with these rules (A=D, B=E, C=F), encrypting ABC, ACB, and CAB in the same manner as above results in certain patterns such as DEF, DFE, and FDE. Changing just one digit at the end gives a completely different result. Also, the verification of hash is fast when the answer is known, but when the answer is unknown, it takes a long time because it has to be solved only by pure assignment. In other words, since blockchain technology uses an encryption method called hash, the integrity of information is further protected.

Figure 2-9 How to apply Hash

How to find the original input value (X)
From the hash value (Y)

SHA-1 Calculation

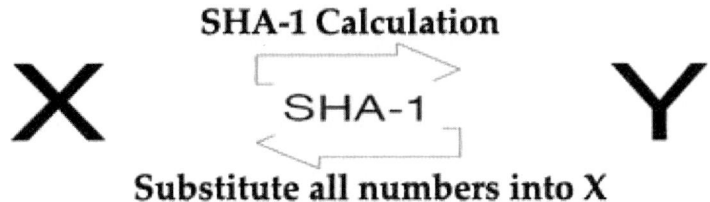

Substitute all numbers into X

To find the X where the exact Y comes FromSquared by the number of bits in Y of 2

Figure 2-10 Block branch of blockchain

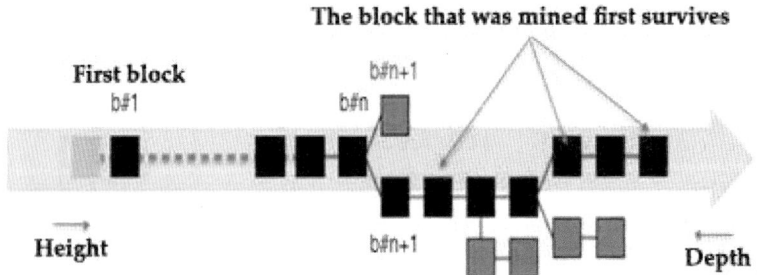

**Black is the main block,
Sometimes two chains are temporarily formed,
Chain is formed with the longest block**

The functions are largely divided into cryptographic hashes (SHA-256, SHA-512, Keccak, etc.) and non-cryptographic hashes (CRC32, FNV, etc.), both of which are actually used in the blockchain.

In the blockchain, each node of each block must be signed. It proves to other users on the network that it is my Note.

If you do not sign the note, various forgery and alterations may occur. Taking this as an example, there may be a problem of arbitrary creating a record that A made a remittance even though A did not actually make a remittance, or a problem of forging or altering records that A actually sent 100,000 won to B but claimed that he never sent it or sent 1 million won. Therefore, an authentication process is required. It is easy to understand if you take a look at the existing online authentication method. These days, people use accredited certificates countless times in banks, schools, or companies. From simple phone banking to online certificate issuance, it is widely used that it is difficult to find a place that does not use public certificates. This is the online key concept. You can think of it as the concept of having already made a lock and carrying the key. Of course, my online key is a public certificate password, and the lock is owned by a public certificate authority. The process of entering a password is exactly the process of turning it using a key that fits the lock. Originally, the key should be turned to the right, but turning to the left is the wrong password.

Similarly, electronic signatures are made for authentication. If it is a general-purpose public certificate that is authenticated by the government unit, it can be digitally signed in the same way as above, and if it is a cryptocurrency note that is not managed by the government like now, it is the opposite of the above. You can work to match the key with the lock you made in advance. At this time, the private key becomes a lock, and the public key can be thought of as a key to open the lock.

Of course, if you use a different key or a different public key, it won't open.

Figure 2-11 Asymmetric key of blockchain technology

Here, the private key is the secret key that only the sender has. In other words, the digital signature is a concept of a lock and a key, and its role can be both depending on the shape.

Through this type of digital signature, it is possible to authenticate the integrity of the notes included in the block and secure the reliability of information.

2.2 Virtualization Technology and Virtual Solution

Virtualization is a broad term for abstracting resources from computer. It is defined as a technology that hides the characteristics of a physical computer resource from the way in which other systems, applications, and end users interact with the resource. This creates a single physical resource, such as a server, operating system, application, or storage device, that appears to function as multiple logical resources. Alternatively, you can create multiple physical resources, such as storage devices or servers, that look like a single logical resource. In other words, in simple terms, it can be defined as a technology that makes the number and capacity of a single physical resource available to use multiple or more capacities.

In general, companies can run more than one operating system or switch at the same time on a single computer and network through server and network virtualization. Most servers use only 10-15% of their capacity, and virtualization can increase their efficiency to over 70%. A high level of utility serves to reduce the number of computers required to process the same amount of work.

Virtualization has been widely used since the 1960s and has been applied to many different aspects and areas of the computer, from the entire computer system to individual functions and components. A common theme of all virtualization technologies is to hide and publicize technical details. Virtualization creates an external interface that hides the underlying function additions, such as aggregating resources from different physical locations or simplifying control systems, such as multiple transmit/receive access.

Figure 2-12 Virtualization Concept

Such virtualization is mainly used as a concept opposite to the generalization of reality, such as abstraction and object-oriented terms. In particular, virtualization is used as an important concept even in environments where computers are not used.

Another concept opposite to virtualization is transparency, in which virtual artifacts can be seen and felt, but are not physically present. Transparent things are practically present, but invisible when used. Most forms of virtualization include design patterns that link computers and providers. Computers and providers interact using several interfaces. Virtualization puts an intermediary between consumers and providers acting on both sides of the interface, providing an interface for the real computer and consuming the interface of the real provider. This usually allows for both when multiple consumers to interact with one provider, or when one consumer interacts with multiple providers, or when there is an intermediary who is aware of the diversity.

Figure 2-13 The evolution of Virtualization

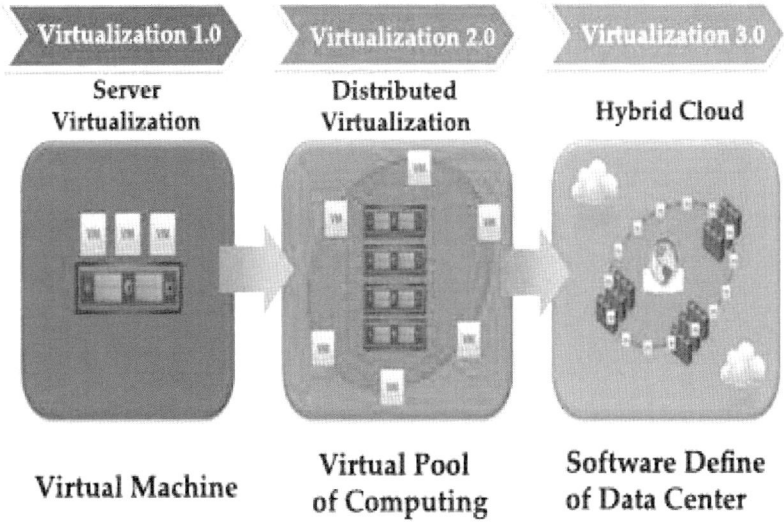

The original etymology of the term virtualization dates back to the 1960s when virtual machines that combine hardware and software were created. This is commonly referred to as platform virtualization. Virtual machines first appeared on the IBM M44/44X systems. Virtual machines are created and managed, and in the C-40 days and recently when the term server virtualization began to be used, it was called making a pseudo machine. The terms virtualization and virtual computers have acquired additional meanings over the years.

In the virtualization of the platform, the control program is executed through the host software on a given hardware platform. The host software creates a simulated computer environment called a virtual machine according to the Guest application under the host. Guest applications are called complete operating systems and run as if they were installed on an independent hardware platform. In general, most if these virtual machines are simulated on a single physical computer. However, their number is limited by the resource of the host hardware.

Figure 2-14 Virtualization Definition

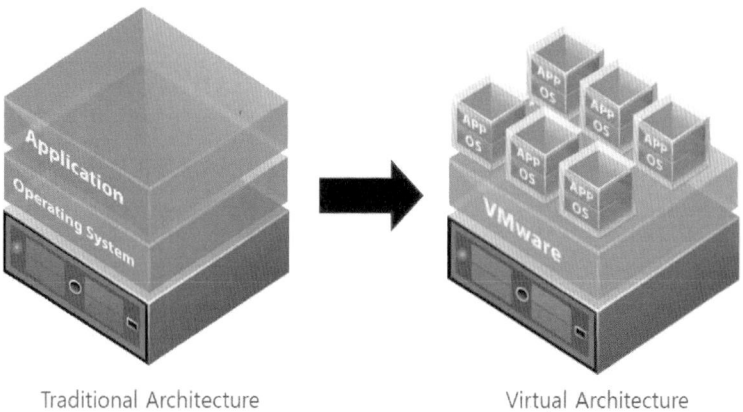

Traditional Architecture   Virtual Architecture

In general, the guest operating system does not need to be the same as the host operating system. Guest operating systems often require access to certain peripherals to function properly, so the simulation must support the guest's interfaces to those devices. In summary, virtualization is a technology that allows a single physical IT resource to be used as multiple logical IT resources at the same time. For example, in traditional computer, only a single operating system is performed on a single hardware, and the operating system monopolizes the hardware. Different types of operating systems may run independently. The virtualization software element that plays the most important role in the virtualization system is the hypervisor, or virtual machine monitor. The hypervisor is located between the virtual machine and hardware and provides a virtualization layer that allows multiple virtual machines to operate. To this end, the hypervisor provides a logically independent virtual machine environment so that each guest operating system (operating system of a virtual machine) can run and manages the execution of these guest operating system. Therefore, the main function of the hypervisor is to logically divide and allocate hardware resources including CPU and memory to each virtual machine and to take charge of their scheduling.

Figure 2-15 Expected Effects of Virtualization

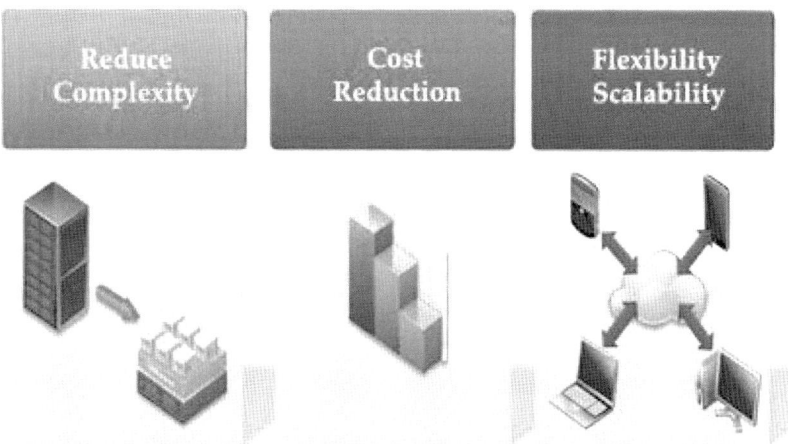

It also guarantees independence between virtual machines when sharing hardware resources.

One of the main differences between computing resources in a virtualized environment is the ease of installation and management of the virtualized resources. In the existing IT infrastructure environment, it takes weeks to months to introduce the necessary physical infrastructure resources (servers, network equipment, etc.). However, for virtual machines, installation and management processes such as creation, stopping, restarting, copying, shutting down, and removing can be done within a few minutes. A virtual machine in a virtualization environment is saved in the form of an image file and can be paused or terminated. When a paused or terminated virtual machine is restarted, the saved virtual machine image file is reloaded into the virtualization system and can be restarted immediately. In addition, when a problem such as malfunction or overload occurs in the physical host system in which the virtual machine is running, it is possible to move the running virtual machine to another physical host without stopping the execution. This function is called Live Migration. In the virtual network inside the virtualization environment, network packet switching is performed through a virtual switch. Through a virtual switch, network packets between virtual machines in the same virtualization system are directly switched. In addition, the network packet between the host outside the virtualization system and the internal virtual machine is switched to the outside of the virtualization system through the virtual switch. However, in this case, communication with the outside of the virtualization system is performed through a physical NIC (Network Interface Card).

The virtualization infrastructure in the cloud environment has the following major security vulnerabilities.

First, the internal area of the virtualization system cannot detect security vulnerabilities with existing security technologies such as firewall, IPS, and anti-virus.

As for the security issues in virtual systems, existing network security devices perform intrusion detection by analyzing network packets delivered through a physical network. However, communication between virtual machines in the area inside the virtualization system is delivered only through the virtual switch in the virtualization system. That is, it is not transmitted through the network line connected to the outside of the physical host where the virtualization system is built. This characteristic creates a security blind spot where the existing security equipment cannot detect network communication between virtual machines in the area inside the virtualization system. The virtualization layer inside the virtualization system is a layer that becomes a security blind spot because technologies such as existing security solutions do not understand the structure.

In general, the structural difference in the virtualization layer for each virtualization hypervisor aggravates this security issue. Therefore, an intrusion detection technology capable of monitoring by understanding the internal structure of the virtualization system and resolving the security blind

Figure 2-16 Features of Virtualization technology

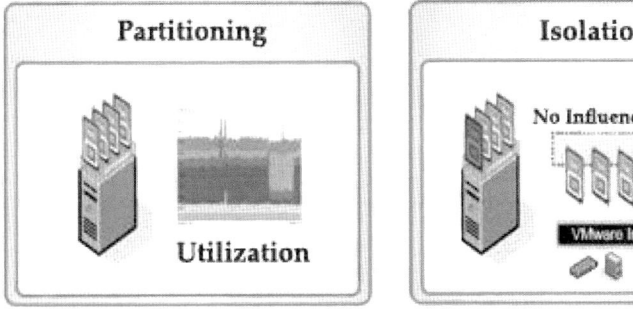
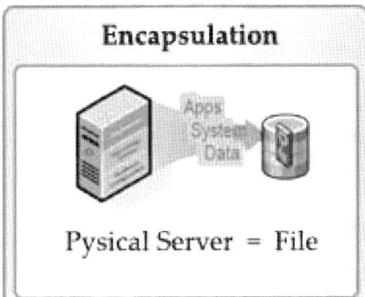
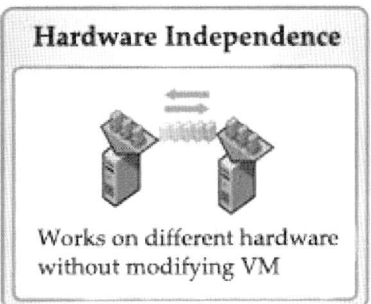

Figure 2-17 Virtualization Migration

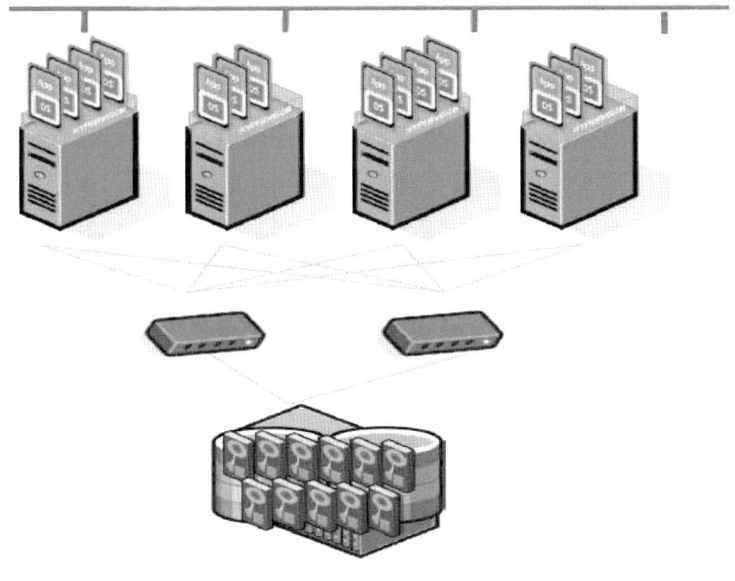

Figure 2-18 Virtualization Migration Detailed Policy

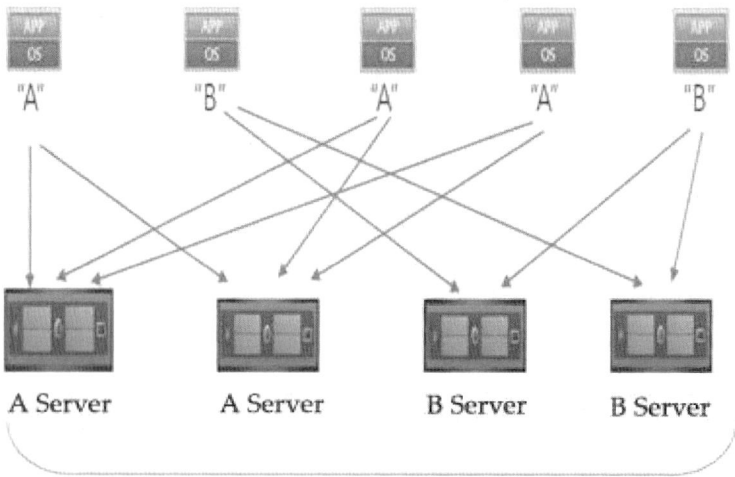

spots in the internal area of the virtualization system is required.

Second, in the internal area of the virtualization system, virtual machines from different user groups with the characteristics of multi-tenancy are interconnected, so there are many paths that can be attacked by various hacking and malicious code propagation. First, creation stop, restart, move, copy, deletion, etc. occur dynamically, and it is difficult to separate static virtual networks using VLANs on a virtual switch due to the characteristics of virtual machines that can be leased to different users and organizations like AWS. Due to this, it may be vulnerable to various attacks, such as sniffing attacks such as ARP Cache Poisoning and malicious code propagation that are possible on the same network. In addition, if the hypervisor is successfully hacked, control over all virtual machines in the virtualization system may be lost, and thus all systems on the entire public network may be destroyed. Therefore, dynamic access control change management is required on the virtual network, and it is necessary to respond to new types of attacks against virtualization layers, such as hypervisors, as well as various existing network-based attacks.

Figure 2-19 Disk Utilization for Virtualization

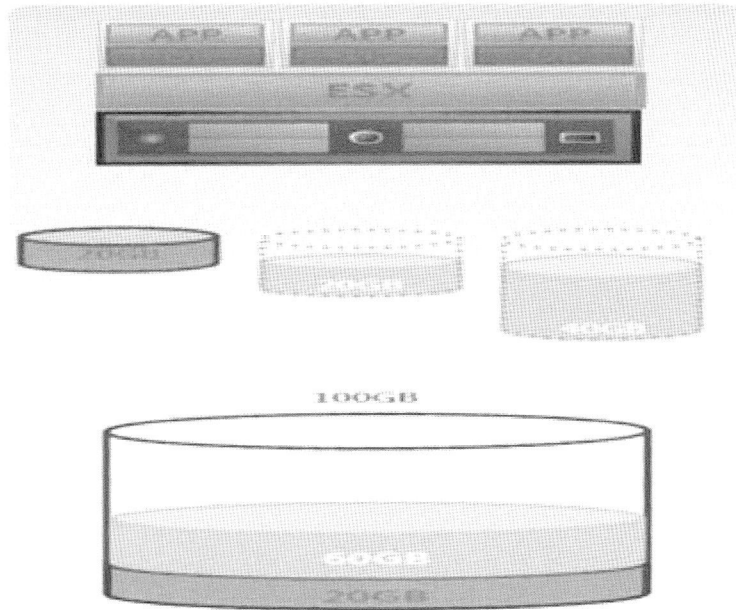

Figure 2-20 Dynamic storage management in Virtualization

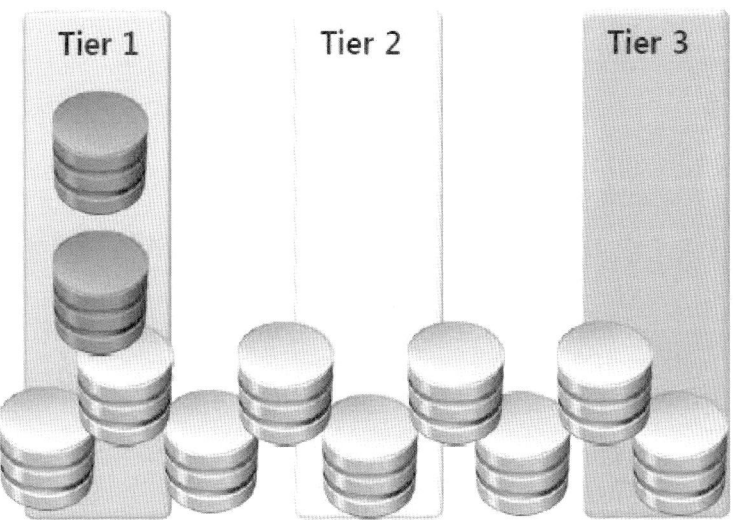

Figure 2-21 Failover function of Virtualization solution

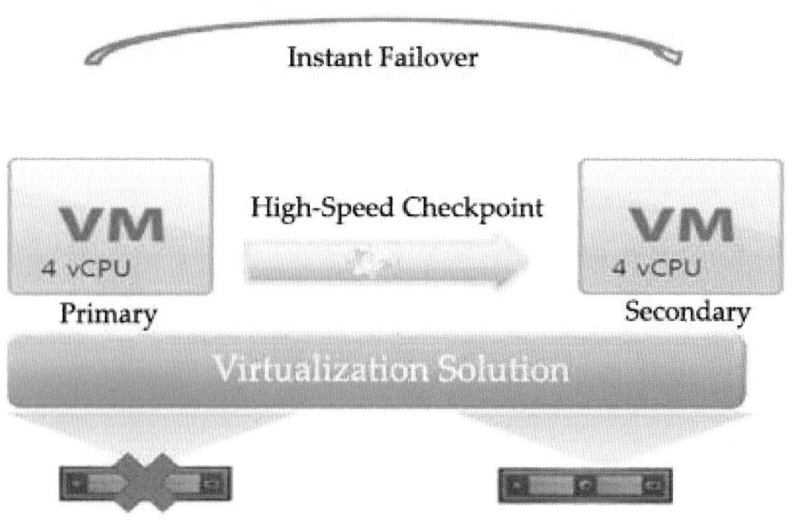

Figure 2-22 Disaster recovery logic of Virtualization solution

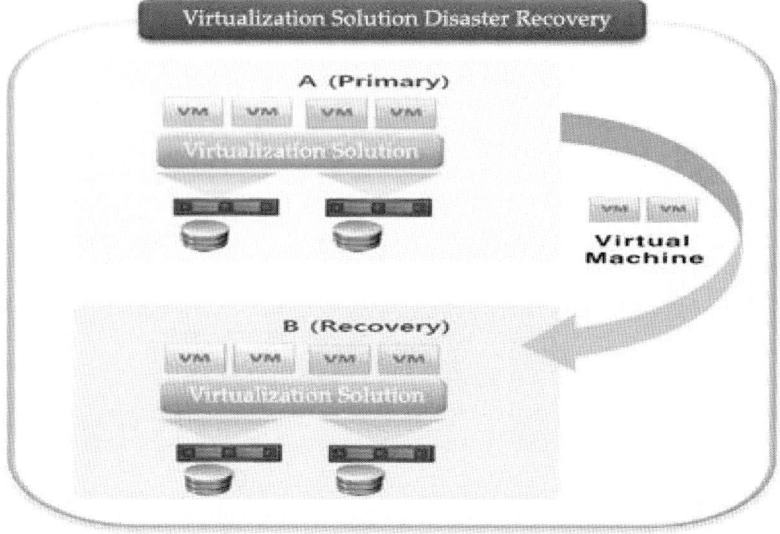

Third, security management becomes complicated due to the dynamic life cycle of virtual machines. Virtual machines can be created, stopped, restarted, copied, and deleted easily, and can be moved in real time between different physical hosts, that is, virtualization systems. A virtual machine can be moved to different physical hosts in real time by using the Live Migration function, and when the virtual machine is restarted after a pause, it can be restarted on a different physical host according to the system settings.

This provides the possibility that a virtual machine that is vulnerable to security or already infected with malicious code can move to another physical host without restrictions because no security patch is applied. This characteristic is accompanied by another vulnerability compared to the security management in the existing static IT environment. Therefore, a virtualization environment must consider the dynamic lifecycle of each virtual machine to manage the security status of the virtual machine's life cycle, including its current status and movement path.

Regarding this virtualization concept, I introduce the case of virtualization in Internet of Things environment as well as computer virtualization in my patent.

The title of this patent is a location-based service using a virtual beacon device and a linked information system (Patent 1). It is an invention for providing various information system services by configuring a location-based service and a linked information system through the connection of other information systems using the virtualization method and the virtualized beacon.

For virtualization of beacon, first, a description of frequency is required. Frequency is usually expressed as angular frequency (ω), radians per second (in radians/second), or f - hertz (Hz). It can also be expressed in BPM (beats per minute) and RPM (revolutions per minute). The relationship between the angular frequencies ω (rad/sec) and f (Hz) is given by the following formula: $\omega = 2\pi f$. Frequency is also related to phase (φ), which is the waveform offset of a particular point at the initial time (t0), expressed in Degrees or radians. Taking a sine wave as an example, the waveform function consists of amplitude A, angular frequency ω, and phase φ. The present invention utilizes these frequency characteristics and various service characteristics according to frequency bands and provides services using the same frequency network such as a WIFI network frequency, a base station carrier frequency, and an Internet network. Using these frequency characteristics, the beacon frequency is input in advance on the location-based map regardless of the band, and when you go to the area, the beacon frequency is applied to the other existing frequencies along with the frequency of the basic characteristics. It is a technology for providing a virtual beacon device by modulating in such a manner as to receive a beacon frequency using the physical characteristics of the frequency.

In addition, it is an invention related to a method of providing various services in connection with an information system associated with a location-based service using such a virtual beacon device.

As a background technology of the present invention, a Bluetooth radio frequency is used, and the Bluetooth frequency is located in the ISM band 2.4 GHz band that can be used worldwide. Although there is a slight difference in each country, most countries in the United States and Europe use a frequency band of 83.5 MHz and use 79 channels with a space of 1 MHz each. However, Japan, Spain, and France use 23 fewer channels with a space of 1 MHz each. Until now, Japan had allocated a frequency of 23 MHz to Bluetooth, but in October 1999, Japan's MPT announced to expand to 2400 ~ 2483.5 MHz. Bluetooth frequency protocol is divided into RF defining the physical layer, baseband defining hopping patterns, link manager defining packet composition and HID and RFCOMM defining the interface between L2CAP and the host system above it. In addition, frame configuration on the upper level of the baseband, error control, authentication, encryption, etc. are defined here. Voice CODEC adopts CSVD and log PCM of 64kbps. The protocol stack of TCP/IP is mounted over the L2CAP. As interfaces with the host, USB and EIA-232 are installed.

In mobile communication, multiple access technology is used to accommodate multiple users in one frequency band. However, even if multiple access is used, more than a certain amount of user access at the same time, channel saturation will occur, and normal service will be difficult.

In mobile communication, a large area is divided into small cells in order to use limited frequency resources more efficiently, and a base station located in the middle of the cell provides a service using a specific frequency. The frequency utilization efficiency is increased.

In general, four types of frequencies are used for mobile communication services.

It can be seen that adjacent cells use different frequencies to avoid problems caused by frequency interference, while reusing the same frequency in distant cells.

By configuring the cell in this way, it is possible to service a vast area with a limited number of frequencies.

Here, the maximum amount of calls that a cell can handle is constant. A cell can be thought of as an electromagnetic wave of the same intensity and becomes a circle around the base station on a plane.

In reality, it has a polygonal shape DEU to division adjustment according to the radio wave intensity with the adjacent cell.

Reducing the radius of a cell in half reduces its area by 1/4.

Therefore, if the cell size is reduced by half number of cells is placed in the same area by four times, and the amount of call that can be accommodated is also increased by four times.

By using this, it is possible to reduce the size of cells in a place with a large amount of call, and the cells appropriately arranged by enlarging the cell size in a place with a small amount of call.

The type of cell actually used are a mega cell(a wide range cell used for satellite communication, etc. with a radius of 100 - 500 km), and a macro cell(a cell used in suburban areas with few mobile communication subscribers with a radius of 35 km), Micro Cell(a cell with a radius of 0.5 km - 1 km, and its main propagation path is the distance that the mobile communication antenna can be seen with the naked eyes; the small radius of the cell causes a diversity effect in which radio waves are received by the antenna through multiple paths.), and Pico Cell(A cell within a radius of 50 m, which is placed in dense urban areas and underground.)

One cell can be further subdivided into sectors. A case in which the entire cell is serviced through one antenna is referred to as an omni-directional cell, and a case in which a specific area is divided into sectors using a plurality of antennas is referred to as a directional cell. Currently, most cells are designed as directional cells to increase cell capacity and improve call quality.

And when explaining the frequency of Bluetooth, the modulation method of the Bluetooth frequency uses a method called GFSK with a transmission rate of 1Mbps. It is a modulation method that uses a modulator with a filter with Gaussian characteristics in front of FSK modulation.

The goal is to limit power consumption to 30 µA in standard mode and 8 to 30 mA during transmission. In addition, Bluetooth uses a frequency hopping method, which is a type of spectrum spreading method to reduce interference with other devices. This method prevents interference by a fixed transmission frequency, changing a random frequency every one time slot. In the case of Bluetooth, the 1 Time Slot is 625 µs, and frequency hopping occurs 1600 times per second.

Basically, 1 Hopping slot (625 µs = 1/1600 sec) is used as a unit to transmit and receive TDD (Time Division Duplex). The throughput of the data transmission is unidirectional/asymmetric and is up to 721kbps. In data transmission and reception, the Master always uses the even-numbered slot and the Slave always uses the odd-numbered slot.

Slots may be reserved for synchronization packets. Each packet is carried at a different hopping frequency. A packet usually covers one slot but can be expanded to cover up to five slots.

Bluetooth can support one asynchronous data channel, up to three voice channels at the same time, or support asynchronous data and synchronous voice simultaneously. Each voice channel supports a synchronous (voice) link of 64 Kbps. The asynchronous channel can support an asymmetric link up to 721 Kbps in one direction and up to 56.7 Kbps in the reverse direction, or it can support a symmetric link of 432.6 Kbps. By utilizing the frequency technology of the mobile communication base station and the characteristics of the Bluetooth frequency, a virtual beacon device can be created and recognized to build a location-based service and a linked information system. As a problem to be solved, the present invention uses the frequency of the base station to match the virtual area to the virtual area, the virtual beacon, and the real space, and designates the real space area as the virtual space area to apply the coordinate values of the virtual beacon to the virtual space. By constructing a virtual beacon service, the frame is reprocessed in the stage of generating the signal frequency of the virtual beacon to increase the accuracy and performance of the virtual beacon location and create a server that receives it and analyzes information about the beacon signal through the server. And the task to be solved by the present invention is to create a method of constructing various types of location-based information systems by reprocessing them into user and administrator applications to provide services, and by linking the servers providing the same with other information systems. As a component, an access point of a virtual beacon for each information source is placed, the ID of the virtual beacon signal is received and the location and user information are provided from the server to another linked server, and the information system receiving the information has each characteristic. The present invention is to make the flow of information flow back to the existing virtual beacon system after going through the logic of the appropriate information system.

As a solution of the present invention, various service characteristics are used according to frequency characteristics and frequency bands and virtual beacons are installed using all communication networks using frequencies such as a WIFI network frequency, a base station carrier frequency, and an Internet network. It aims to provide information system services using beacons. Utilizing the characteristics of frequencies used for all communications, the virtual beacon frequency is input on the location-based map in advance regardless of the band. It is a technology that provides a virtual beacon device by receiving a virtual beacon frequency by using the physical characteristics of the frequency by modulating and demodulating it using a frequency hopping method. It is an invention related to a method of interworking with various services.

The present invention sets up a virtual space and a virtual beacon installation area using the concept of Bluetooth frequency communication, and builds a certain service using it. And it is a characteristic of the present invention to describe the technology of constructing various virtual beacon-based location-based information systems through the connection of specific methods and logic by utilizing other existing information systems and virtual beacon information systems.

As an effect of the invention, the present invention provides a beacon-related service, that is, an indoor location-based service and an information provision service through various signal devices, through a specific hardware for a beacon called a beacon, a virtual beacon device without specific hardware (beacon device) in a specific place. It is possible to secure technology to provide various location-based services and information provision services using it. That is, the beacon service that used to provide information system service based on hardware is set up as a virtual beacon and recognized and used as a reference point to provide information system-related services. Using these virtual beacons, beacon devices for countless spaces can be manufactured and installed one by one, or hardware costs and maintenance costs such as battery replacement can be eliminated. Indoor location service and specific information provision service can be configured. In other words, in the past, detailed information about daily life and the space where users or objects are physically located could not be provided through physical restrictions. Although it was possible to acquire or experience information about it only by locating other sensors there, the present invention provides a service using internal location information on an area where radio waves or frequencies are covered, that is, where humans cannot reach. It is the biggest feature of the invention.

As a specific content for carrying out the invention, it is based on information and communication engineering to provide various information system services by composing a location-based service and a linked information system through a method of virtualizing the function of a beacon in the form of hardware using the communication method of Bluetooth 4.0. It extracts various location-based information through frame reprocessing of the Bluetooth wireless communication protocol, processes it through a server, and communicates with other information systems. It is an invention that includes a method of linking an original and unique location-based information system that provides services to users through a user's smart device or terminal in connection with other information systems.

To illustrate the drawing in detail, for example,

Drawing 1 is a diagram of the structure of a virtual beacon. When the frequency signal of the base station number 100 is received, it is divided into a signal of the PICO cell unit in number 101, and a specific identity is assigned to the signal of the smallest unit of 102 to be selected, and the signal is assigned a number order and the given sequence number is converted into a Cell of Location sector as the minimum unit for physical space. This converted cell is converted into the No. 103 Cell of map, which divides the map of physical space into the form of the smallest unit of Cell. The cell of the minimum unit divided in this way displays the position of the virtual beacon in the form of ON/OFF through each flag value. That is, ON becomes 1 and OFF becomes 0. That is, the physical space is divided into the smallest units of the Cell, the cell in which the virtual beacon is located has a flag value of 1, and the area where the virtual beacon does not have a flag value of 0, so the space where the virtual beacon is located and the space where it is not located are separated. In other words, the flag value is used to create, modify, and delete the location of the virtual beacon in the virtual space. The flag value of No. 104 can always be controlled by an application in user mode through a connection with the cell of map No. 103 and the virtual beacon Access point of map No. 109

In addition, the flag values of No. 104 are also linked with the beacon signal generated through the Beacon Signal Generator of No. 105. The signal from the beacon is a value generated and passed on by the software itself. As in No. 106, the hopping key value, Mac Address, and DLC (Device Location Code)are the main value, and the UUID, Major, Minor, Tx-power and RSSI values output from the general hardware type beacon are also output. The virtual beacon signals generated from the beacon signal generator of No. 105 are received by the application of the user's smartphone device as the Virtual Beacon Coordinate Value of No. 110 which is the virtual beacon coordinate value. As described above, the Pico Cell Signal received at No. 101 is received in the Original Base Station Signal as in No. 107 in the case of a communication frequency and used for communication, and for other purposes, it is used for other purposes. In No. 108, in the Map information insert & Modify application area, user creation and modification of Cell of Map No. 103 is shown. In other words, it shows that the user can measure the basic cell of map form or modify it in an arbitrary unique map form. In this way, using the frequency of the commonly received base station (communication, academic, research), it is possible to divide it into the smallest unit area, and assign a number to it. When a Cell-type Map is created based on the assigned number and the location of the virtual beacon is defined with the flag value, it generates a code through pairing with the virtual beacon signal frequency generated by the virtual beacon signal generator, passes through the application processing areas of No. 108, No. 109, and No. 110. Here, No. 112 is a virtual beacon manager, which is an application area that controls virtual beacons, and modifies information values (UUID, Major, Minor, Tx-power, RSSI, etc.) for virtual beacon signals that are created and generated in a virtual environment. It serves to monitor the operation or state of the beacon cell.

Here, to explain the essential content of this invention, first, this provides a beacon service capable of creating a virtual space and virtual beacon based on a frequency of a base station received by a smart device, installing an indoor location-based service and an information provision service. Also, as shown in FIG. 1, it provides a beacon service capable of providing an indoor location-based service and information provision service by creating and virtual installation of a virtual space and a virtual beacon in the area after hardware location of the described beacon manager. That is, virtual beacons can be created and maintained through two path methods.

Based on the user application area of No. 111, the virtual beacon can query the beacon information through CMS (Contents Management Server) of No. 113 and push the previously registered beacon information back to the user application. It manages each virtual beacon device through a real beacon manager and a virtual beacon manager and provides information system services linked to various systems through No. 115 linked information systems (CRM, SCM, AMS, KMS, etc.).

FIG. 2 is a diagram showing how to receive a base station signal as a base station signal, distribute it to cells, and match it with a beacon signal. No. 201 represents the range of the mega cell of the base station and s the base station signal range with a radius of 100 to 500 km, and No. 202 represents the cell with a range of 35 km as the base station signal range of the macro cell stage. No. 203 is the base station signal range of the microcell and indicates the base station signal range of 0.5Km to 1Km. Pico Cell No. 206 has a signal range of a base station with a radius of 50 Meters, which is consistent with the general signal range of a basic hardware beacon. In general, a Pico Cell is the most suitable to define the signal range as a sector and use that region, but it is also possible to define the No. 202 macro cell or No. 203 micro cell as a virtual beacon signal region by defining a sector unit.

The sector area defined by dividing No. 205 is combined as Pairing Code, which is defined by combining with Beacon signal and ID value of each cell.

That is, the identity values (03, 0303, 0308, 03030801) of each cell of No. 201, No. 202, No. 203, and No. 206 generate the pairing code with AP values obtained from the values of virtual beacons in the virtual space through the information of the virtual beacon signal No. 204. Generate code.

FIG. 3 is a diagram showing how to connect the Pico cell unit of the Pico cell base station with virtual beacons. As in No. 302, the Access Point value of the Virtual Beacon Signal is specified through the hopping key value generated through the virtual beacon signal generator No. 301, the unique MAC address, and DLC(Device Location Code) value of the device. The AP values designated in this way are paired by generating a pairing code in a matrix structure with the virtual base station signal range Cell of the actual minimum unit of the sector. To explain this pairing again, it means that the area specified by the actual frequency of the base station is matched with the area for the virtual beacon. That is, when the virtual area and the area covered by the actual frequency match, the location of the beacon in the virtual area is specified through the virtual beacon information, and the value is matched through the flag value displayed in the cell of the sector.

FIG. 4 is a diagram explaining in detail how the virtual space and the real space described in FIG. 3 form a matrix in pairs as a pairing code matrix between the virtual space and the real space.

The Beacon Signal Generator Code of No. 401 represents the beacon signal generator. Based on the base station signal received through the basic communication protocol of No. 402, the Bluetooth signal of No. 403 is combined to create a unique beacon signal No. 404, and through it, the general beacon signal value of No. 405 is generated. Among the beacon signals generated from the virtual beacon signal generator, the hopping key value is an algorithm key value for modulation and demodulation of the virtual beacon signal, and represents the characteristic that distinguishes the types of virtual beacon signals. A unique value is assigned to indicate the characteristic. In addition, DLC serves to specify the location of a device on a communication network and indicates where a virtual beacon is located in a virtual space. That is, these values are divided into cells through the frequency of the actual base station, and the matching key is generated through the actual space to which the identity value is assigned and the value of flag No. 406. This matching key value becomes the pairing code. In other words, it is divided into Cells managed by the base station signal and matched with each other through the Hopping Key value, Mac Address, and DLC value of the virtual beacon in the real space and virtual space to which the identity is given, and the virtual beacon created through the virtual space in the real space is actually where it is located in the space is indicated through the Flag value so that the real beacon can be recognized as if it were in a specific place in the real space.

The flag value is matched with the identity of a specific cell of the Cell of the map numbered 407. If a virtual beacon exists, the flag value has a value of 1, and if it does not exist, the flag value has a value of 0.

FIG. 5 is a diagram showing the structure of a Beacon Signal Generator virtual beacon signal generator. No. 501 and No. 502 are base station signals received from various base stations (broadcasting, mobile communication, research, military, satellite, etc. according to each country's frequency operation policy). For example, as in No. 503, the Bluetooth frequency protocol is applied in the manner of demodulation and modulation to create a Bluetooth signal frequency as in No. 505. The virtual beacon signals created in this way are stored in each field value of the database with the hopping key value, the Mac address, and the DLC value as main values, as in No. 509. The virtual beacon signals stored in this way designate the Access Point as the Cell Identity values and Flag values in the real space of the frequency range received from the real base station.

As a frequency derived by demodulating and modulating the general base station frequency and Bluetooth protocol frequency in FIG 5, when the communication signal constants $Vc(t) = VcCOS(2\pi fct + \theta)$ and $fi(t) = 1/2\pi * d\theta i(t)/dt = fc$ are defaulted, the modulation method is $2fc = 2Vc(t) = 2(Vm)/Vc) = m$ and the demodulation method is configured so that $fc = Vc(t) = Vm/Vc = 2m$. The frequency generated through demodulation and modulation of this frequency has characteristics as a Bluetooth frequency by applying the Hopping method. The type of method applying the hopping method is defined as a hopping key value, which is a key value defining the characteristics of the beacon signal generated as a virtual beacon signal. It can also be used as a key value that can separate the original base station frequency from the virtual beacon signal. That is, the frequency of the virtual beacon demodulated and modulated based on the base station-based frequency signal goes through an encryption process with the hopping key value and cannot return to the original base station frequency form without this hopping key value.

The Hopping Key value can be used when using a virtual beacon signal in a section where encryption is required for security and can also be used to encrypt frequency data.

FIG. 6 is a cell of the map and Coordinate Value. It is a diagram showing the form of specifying the location of a virtual beacon as a coordinate value on a map for an area through information obtained by matching the range of the real area space parsed from the base station frequency with the virtual space and the virtual beacon and through the flag value set.

The pairing code matrix No. 601 places the virtual beacon in the real space matched to the virtual space by matching the flag value set through the virtual space and virtual beacon information to 0 or 1, mainly by matching the value to the coordinate value of the real area. The virtual beacon location is specified in the designated real area from the indicated Cell of the map, that is, the Cell of the location sector, which is the base station signal frequency. The virtual beacon specified in this way has the same phase as an actual hardware beacon installed in the real area and is a form of receiving the virtual beacon signal in the user's application.

The virtual beacon indicated by the black dot in FIG. 6 is located in the area indicated by a dotted line virtually designated in the drawing of the real area and the area indicated by the installed virtual specified dotted line.

FIG. 7 is a view for explaining the detailed function of the DLC of the beacon signal generated through the beacon signal generator No. 105 in the Virtual Beacon Architecture of FIG. 1, the Bluetooth Frame DLC Bluetooth frame device location code. DLC area is added separately in the general beacon signal frame, and the location of the beacon device in its own virtual space is specified through this area. No. 701 has a movement value, a time value, etc. as a flag value of the beacon signal generation step and is a different concept from the flag value of the pairing code matrix of the present invention. The DLC value, which combines the location-related constant information of the virtual beacon in the virtual space, is 1 or 0 depending on whether the location is moved, 1 or 0 depending on whether the location is stopped, 1 or 0 depending on whether the location range is changed, 1 or 0 depending on whether the location coordinate value is changed, 1 or 0 depending on whether the existing current time has been changed, 1 or 0 depending on whether the current time has been changed, 1 and 0 depending on whether the time range has been changed, 1 or 0 depending on whether the error range is over, and 1 or 0 depending on whether the security code is applied. This DLC value is sent to the CMS server DLC calculator, and the CMS server converts the current virtual beacon position into an information value by referring to the DLC value. This information value is converted into values such as the current virtual beacon's status, distance, location, movement value, time, error tolerance, and security.

FIG. 8 is a view for explaining the virtual beacon processing method of the Virtual Beacon Process. The application program receiving the base station signal No. 801 recognizes the real space No. 802 in the form of a Cell of Location Sector and creates a Cell of map No. 803. Here, identity is given to the Pico Cell unit signal of No. 807 for each cell unit, and the real space is divided in the form of the smallest cell. Through the flag value, the identity of each cell is created as a pairing code. Here, the user can directly input or modify information in the Cell of the map through the Map information insert & Modify area in parallel, thereby improving the accuracy and reliability of the Map. Since the original base station signal is received through No. 812 as the first base station signal to arrive, the smartphone will be used for communication on the frequency of the communication base station. can be received simultaneously in parallel.

That is, the virtual beacon frequency of No. 805 generated based on the received base station frequency is placed on the map calculated through the virtual area, virtual beacon, and real frequency area specified through No.

801, No. 802, No. 803, and No. 804 described above. They generate a continuous virtual beacon frequency as shown in No. 805 and receive Virtual Beacon Coordinate Values in the real spatial domains converted to the virtual domain through No. 806. No. 811 indicates the virtual beacon manager, and the virtual beacon manager controls the status or activation of a virtual beacon specified in a specific cell in the virtual area. Here, the virtual beacon access point of the map, which is the position of the virtual beacon on the virtual area map, can be controlled through the virtual beacon manager, and this virtual beacon manager can be replaced with a physical device of hardware. In other words, the virtual space and virtual beacon control the real space, and the virtual beacon manager is used, but by installing only one beacon manager device in the real space, it can be configured to control the virtual beacons as if the existing virtual space and virtual beacon exist.

In this case, the actual hardware beacon manager specifies and activates the virtual area and virtual beacon and can communicate directly with the CMS through the Internet. It has the advantage of being directly applied to the drawing.

FIG. 9 is a diagram showing the description of all information-linked information systems using the virtual beacon.

Like No. 901 and No. 902, the real space is specified as a virtual space, a virtual beacon device is placed there, and the coordinate value is defined as a Virtual Beacon Access Point. The virtual beacon defined in this way continues to broadcast the Virtual Beacon ID periodically. The broadcast frequency is linked to the integrated management system of No. 910 through the administrator mode of No. 904 at the user application level and the user mode of No. 905 at the user application stage, and with the AP Device Control at No. 909 through the Parameter Calculator and Flag values at No. 908.

No. 906 indicates the beacon manager of both hardware or software, which communicates with the virtual beacon device to set the location of the virtual beacon through the Connect Module and sets the logical battery level of the virtual beacon and activation and deactivation control and the value of each Control beacon parameter. From No. 901 to No. 909 express the structure of the virtual beacon system, and based on this, various information systems with virtual beacons can be configured by linking the integrated information system of No. 910, the virtual beacon server CMS of No. 908, Parameter Calculator of No. 908, flag values, and the META Flag Database of No. 915.

No. 912 Location Database, No. 913 Information Database, and No. 914 Identify Database of No. 916 are exchange databases of other linked information systems that are linked with the virtual beacon service area.

Through this, it has a structure that is linked with the No. 907 database of the virtual beacon service and the 908 parameter and flag.

As described above, the virtual beacon considers the real area as a virtual real area by using the commonly received base station (bands such as broadcasting, mobile communication, research, military, satellite, etc.) frequency according to each country's frequency operation policy. In addition, it is the core of the present invention to create an integrated virtual information system by linking the base service with the information providing service and other systems, by creating a virtual space and virtual beacon signal, matching the two, setting a virtual beacon at a specific point in the area where the virtual and real are matched, and receiving the virtual beacon signal through the location.

That is, as described above, this invention is not a simple virtual beacon-based information system construction methodology, but a virtual beacon-based real space converted into a virtual space and is an invention for arranging the virtual beacon device in the virtual space again and establishing a linked information system with various information functions. It is basically a virtual beacon-based customer management system, a virtual beacon-based disaster evacuation system, a virtual beacon-based access management system, a virtual beacon-based asset management system, and a virtual beacon-based advertisement platform. This invention is based on a cloud-type virtual Internet of Things and virtual information system in which things and the Internet are completely combined without adding new hardware devices by linking all objects to existing information systems without physical equipment or space constraints.

As described above, the virtual beacon considers the real area as a virtual real area by using the commonly received base station (bands such as broadcasting, mobile communication, research, military, satellite, etc.) frequency according to each country's frequency operation policy. In addition, a virtual beacon signal is made and the two are matched, a virtual beacon is set at a specific point in the area where the virtual and real are matched, and a virtual beacon signal is received through it, which is a general beacon service for the real space area. It is the core of the present invention to create an integrated virtual information system by linking the location-based service, the information providing service, and other systems.

To summarize this invention, when a frequency signal of a base station is received, it is divided into a signal of a PICO cell unit in No. 101, a specific identity is assigned to it, and the base station signal of the smallest unit of No. 102 is selected and a number sequence is assigned to it. And the given sequence number is converted into a Cell of Location sector as the minimum unit for physical space. This converted cell is converted into the No. 103 Cell of map, which divides the map of physical space into the form of the smallest unit of Cell. The cell of the minimum unit divided in this way displays the position of the virtual beacon in the form of ON/OFF through each flag value. That is, ON becomes 1 and OFF becomes 0. That is, the physical space is divided into the smallest unit of Cell, and the cell in which the virtual beacon is located has a flag value of 1, and the area where the virtual beacon does not have a flag value is 0, so the space where the virtual beacon is located and a space where the virtual beacon is not located exist separately. That is, the flag value is used to create, modify, and delete the location of the virtual beacon in the virtual space. The flag value of No. 104 can always be controlled by the application through the connection of map No. 103 and the virtual beacon Access point of map No. 109 in user mode.

Also, the flag values of No. 104 are linked with the beacon signal generated through the Beacon Signal Generator of No. 105. The signal from the beacon is a value generated and passed on by the software itself. As in No. 106, the hopping key value, Mac Address, and DLC (Device Location) Code) is the main value, and UUID, Major, Minor, Tx-power and RSSI values output from general hardware type beacons are also output. The virtual beacon signals generated from the beacon signal generator of No. 105 are received by the application of the user's smartphone device as the Virtual Beacon Coordinate Value of No. 110, that is, the virtual beacon coordinate value. As described above, the Pico Cell Signal received at No. 101 like No. 107 is received as an Original Base Station Signal and used for communication if it is a communication frequency, and if it is for other purposes, it is used for other purposes. In No. 108, in the Map information insert & Modify application area, user creation and modification of Cell of Map No. 103 is shown. In other words, it shows that the user can measure the basic cell of map form or modify it in an arbitrary unique map form. In this way, using the frequency of the commonly received base station (for communication, academic, research), it is divided into the smallest unit area, and the number is assigned to it. When a Cell-type Map is created based on the assigned number and the location of the virtual beacon is defined with the flag value, it generates a code through pairing with the virtual beacon signal frequency generated through the virtual beacon signal generator, passes through the application processing areas of No. 108, No. 109, and No. 110. Here, No. 112 is a virtual beacon manager, which is an application area that controls virtual beacons, and modifies information values (UUID, Major, Minor, Tx-power, RSSI etc.) for virtual beacon signals that are created and generated in a virtual environment. It serves to monitor the operation or state of the beacon cell.

Here, to explain the essential content of this invention, first, this provides a beacon service capable of creating a virtual space and virtual beacon based on a frequency of a base station received by a smart device, installing an indoor location-based service and an information provision service. Also, as shown in FIG. 1, it provides a beacon service capable of an indoor location-based service and information provision service by creating and virtual installation of a virtual space and a virtual Beacon in the area after hardware location of the described beacon manager. That is, the virtual beacon can generate and maintain beacons through two path methods.

Based on the user application area of No. 111, the virtual beacon can query about the beacon information through CMS (Contents Management Server) of No. 113 and pushes the previously registered beacon information back to the user application. to manage each virtual beacon device through the real beacon manager and the virtual beacon manager.

Information system services linked to various systems can be provided through the 115 linked information system (CRM, SCM, AMS, KMS, etc.).

The identity values (03, 0303, 0308, 03030801) of each cell of No. 201, No. 202, No. 203, and No. 206 generate the pairing code with the AP values obtained from the virtual beacon values in the virtual space through the information of the virtual beacon signal No. 204.

As in No. 302, the Access Point value of the Virtual Beacon Signal is specified through the Hopping Key value generated through the virtual beacon signal generator of No. 301, the unique Mac Address of the device, and the Device Location Code (DLC) value.

The AP values designated in this way are paired by creating a pairing code in a matrix structure with the virtual base station signal range Cell of the actual minimum unit of the sector.

This means that the area specified by the actual frequency of the base station is matched with the area for the virtual beacon. That is, when the virtual area and the area covered by the actual frequency match, the location of the beacon in the virtual area is specified through the virtual beacon information, and the value is matched through the flag value displayed in the cell of the sector.

The Beacon Signal Generator Code of No. 401 represents the beacon signal generator. Based on the base station signal received through the basic communication protocol of No. 402, the Bluetooth signal of No. 403 is combined to create a unique beacon signal No. 404, and through it, the general beacon signal value of No. 405 is generated. Among the beacon signals generated from the virtual beacon signal generator, the hopping key value is an algorithm key value for modulation and demodulation of the virtual beacon signal and represents the characteristic that distinguishes the types of virtual beacon signals. A unique value is assigned to indicate the characteristic. In addition, DLC serves to specify the location of a device on a communication network and indicates where a virtual beacon is located in a virtual space. That is, these values are divided into cells through the frequency of the actual base station, and the matching key is generated through the real space to which the identity value is assigned and the value of flag No. 406. This matching key value becomes the pairing code. In other words, it is divided into Cells controlled by the base station signal and matched with each other through the Hopping Key value, Mac Address, and DLC value of the virtual beacon in the real space and virtual space to which the identity is given, and the virtual beacon created through the virtual space in the real space is actually where it is located in the space is indicated through the Flag value so that the real beacon can be recognized as if it were in a specific place in the real space.

The flag value is matched with the identity of a specific cell of the Cell of the map numbered 407. If a virtual beacon exists, the flag value has a value of 1, and if it does not exist, the flag value has a value of 0.

For base station signals received from various base stations (broadcasting, mobile communication, research, military, satellite, etc. according to each country's frequency operation policy), apply the Bluetooth frequency protocol as in No. 503 by demodulation and modulation as in No. 505. Creates a Bluetooth signal frequency. The virtual beacon signals created in this way are stored in each field value of the database with the hopping key value, Mac address, and DLC value as main values as shown in No. 509. The virtual beacon signals stored in this way designate the Access Point with the Cell Identity values and Flag values of the real space in the frequency range received from the real base station.

As a frequency derived by demodulating and modulating the general base station frequency and Bluetooth protocol frequency in FIG. 5, when the communication signal constants $Vc(t)= VcCOS (2\pi fct+ \theta)$ and $fi(t)= 1/2\pi*d\theta i(t)/dt=fc$ are defaulted, the modulation method is $2fc=2Vc(t)=2(Vm/Vc)=m$ and the demodulation method is configured so that $fc=Vc(t)=Vm/Vc=2m$. The frequency generated through demodulation and modulation of this frequency has characteristics as a Bluetooth frequency by applying the Hopping method. The type of method applying the hopping method is defined as a hopping key value, which is a key value defining the characteristics of the beacon signal generated as a virtual beacon signal. It can also be used as a key value that can separate the original base station frequency from the virtual beacon signal. That is, the frequency of the virtual beacon demodulated and modulated based on the base station-based frequency signal is encrypted with the hopping key value, and without this hopping key value, it cannot return to the original base station frequency form.

The Hopping Key value can be used when using a virtual beacon signal in a section where encryption is required for security and can also be used to encrypt frequency data.

The pairing code matrix No. 601 places the virtual beacon in the real space matched to the virtual space by matching the flag value set through the virtual space and the virtual beacon information to 0 or 1, mainly by matching the value to the coordinate value of the real area. The virtual beacon location is specified in the designated real area from the indicated Cell of the map, that is, the Cell of the location sector, which is the base station signal frequency. The virtual beacon specified in this way has the same phase as the actual hardware beacon installed in the real area, and the virtual beacon signal is received in the user's application.

The Virtual Beacon indicated by the black dots in FIG. 6 is located in the area indicated by a dotted line virtually designated in the drawing of the real area, but when accepted by the user's smartphone, it is displayed as the actual hardware beacon is installed in the actual area.

No. 703 indicates the protocol configuration of a general beacon signal. A DLC area is added separately in the general beacon signal frame, and the location of the beacon device in its own virtual space is specified through this area. No. 701 has a movement value, a time value, etc. as a flag value of the beacon signal generation step and has a different concept from the flag value of the pairing code matrix of the present invention. The DLC value, which combines the constant information related to the location of the virtual beacon in the virtual space, is 1 or 0 depending on whether the place is moved or not, 1 or 0 depending on whether the place is stopped, 1 or 0 depending on whether the location range is changed, and whether the location coordinate value is changed. The value is given as 1 or 0 depending on whether the existing current time is changed or not, 1 or 0 depending on whether the current time is changed, 1 and 0 depending on whether the time range is changed, 1 or 0 depending on whether the error range is over, and 1 or 0 depending on whether the security code is applied. This DLC value is sent to the CMS server DLC calculator, and the CMS server converts the current virtual beacon position into an information value by referring to the DLC value. This information value is converted into values such as the current virtual beacon's status, distance, location, movement value, time, error tolerance, and security. The application program receiving the base station signal recognizes the real space of No. 802 as a Cell of Location Sector type and creates a Cell of Map No. 803. Here, identity is given to the Pico Cell unit signal of No. 807 for each cell unit, and the real space is divided in the form of the smallest cell. Through the flag value, the identity of each cell is created as a pairing code. Here, the user can directly input or modify information in the Cell of the map through the Map information insert & Modify area in parallel, thereby improving the accuracy and reliability of the Map. Since the original base station signal is received through No. 812 as base station signal that arrives first, the smartphone will be used for communication at the frequency of the communication base station. Services can be received in parallel at the same time.

That is, the virtual beacon frequency of No. 805 generated based on the received base station frequency is placed on the map calculated through the virtual area, virtual beacon, and real frequency area specified through No.801, No. 802, No. 803, and No. 804 described above, and the virtual beacon is placed on this virtual beacon. They generate a continuous virtual beacon frequency as shown in No. 805 and receive Virtual Beacon Coordinate Values in the real space domains converted to the virtual domain through No. 806. No. 811 indicates the virtual beacon manager. The virtual beacon manager controls the status or activation of the virtual beacon specified in a specific cell in the virtual area. Here, the virtual beacon access point of the map, that is, the location of the virtual beacon on the virtual area map, can be controlled through the virtual beacon manager, and this virtual beacon manager can be replaced with a physical device of hardware. That is, virtual space and virtual beacon control the real space and use a virtual beacon manager, but installing only one beacon manager device in the real space can be configured to control virtual beacons as if existing virtual space and virtual beacon exist.

In this case, the actual hardware beacon manager performs the role of specifying and activating the virtual area and virtual beacon and can communicate directly with the CMS. It has the advantage of being directly applied to the drawing.

Like No. 901 and No. 902, the real space is specified as a virtual space, a virtual beacon device is placed there, and the coordinate value is defined as a Virtual Beacon Access Point. The virtual beacon defined in this way continues to broadcast the Virtual Beacon ID periodically. The broadcast frequency is linked to the integrated management system of 910 through the administrator mode of No. 904 at the user application level and the user mode of No. 905 at the user application stage, and with the AP Device Control at 909 through the Parameter Calculator and Flag values at No. 908.

No. 906 indicates the beacon manager of both hardware or software and sets the location of the virtual beacon through the Connect Module through communication with the virtual beacon device, checks the logical battery level of the virtual beacon, and controls activation and inactivation, and each Controls beacon parameter values. Numbers 901 to 909 express the structure of the virtual beacon system, and as described in number 910, it is linked with the integrated information system as described in number 910. A variety of information systems to which virtual beacons are applied can be configured by linking the parameter calculator No. Location Database No. 912, Information Database No. 913, and Identify Database No. 914 of No. 916 are exchange databases of other linked information systems that are linked to the virtual beacon service area, and through this, they are linked with database No. 907 and No. 908 Parameter and Flag of the virtual beacon service.

As described above, the virtual beacon considers the real area as a virtual real area by using the generally received base station (bands such as broadcasting, mobile communication, research, military, satellite, etc.) frequency according to each country's frequency operation policy. In addition, a virtual space and virtual beacon signal are made to match the two, and a virtual beacon is set at a specific point in the area where the virtual and the real are matched, and the application receives the virtual beacon signal through it. It is the core of the present invention to create an integrated beacon-based virtual information system and an information system linked thereto through the beacon service, which is a location-based service, an information providing service, and linkage with other systems. The following is a diagram (Patent 1) of a location-based service and a linked information system using a virtual beacon device.

Drawing 1 (Patent 1)

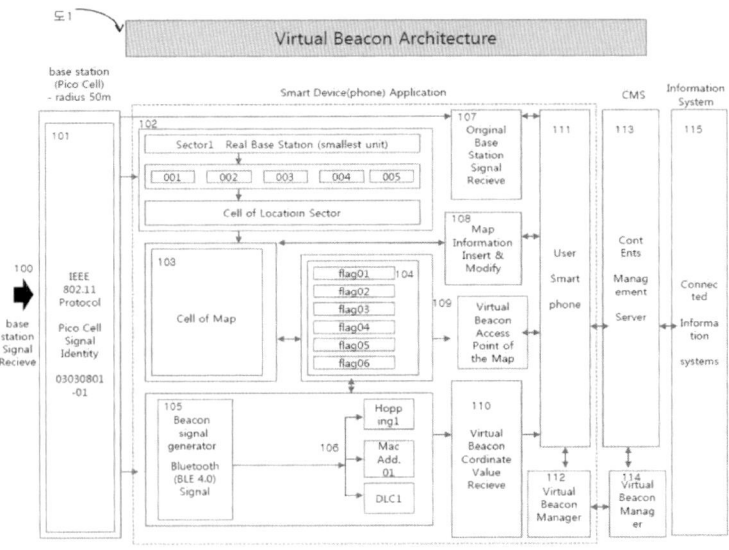

Drawing 2 (Patent 1)

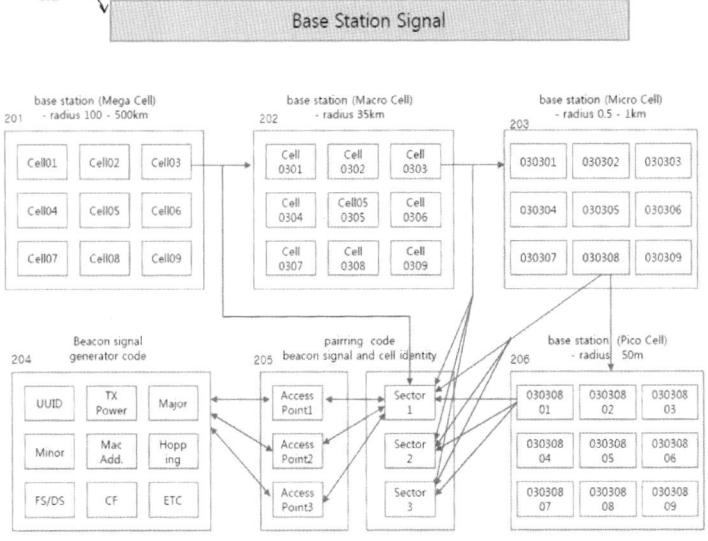

Drawing 3 (Patent 1)

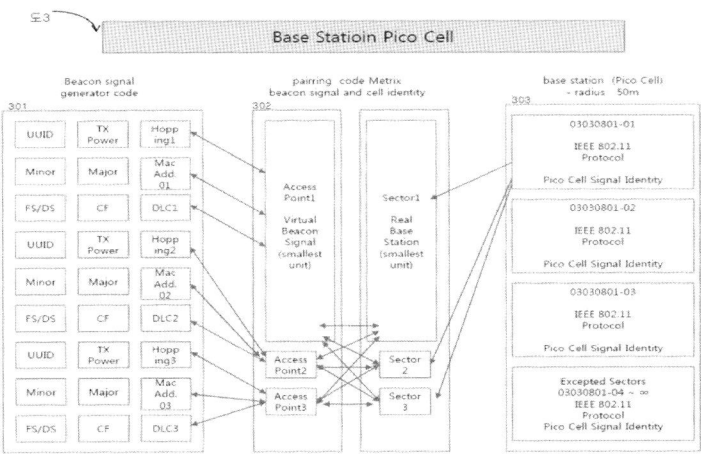

Drawing 4 (Patent 1)

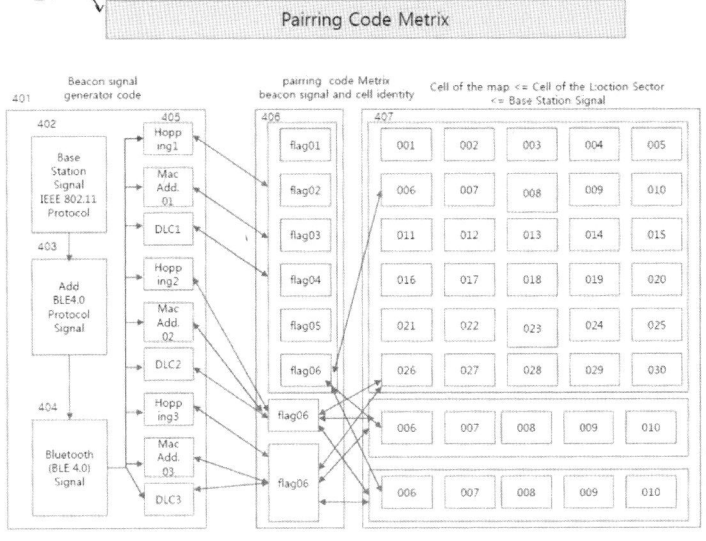

Drawing 5 (Patent 1)

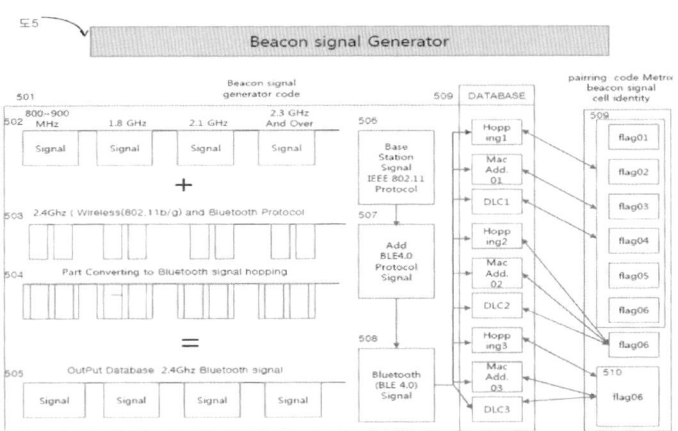

Drawing 6 (Patent 1)

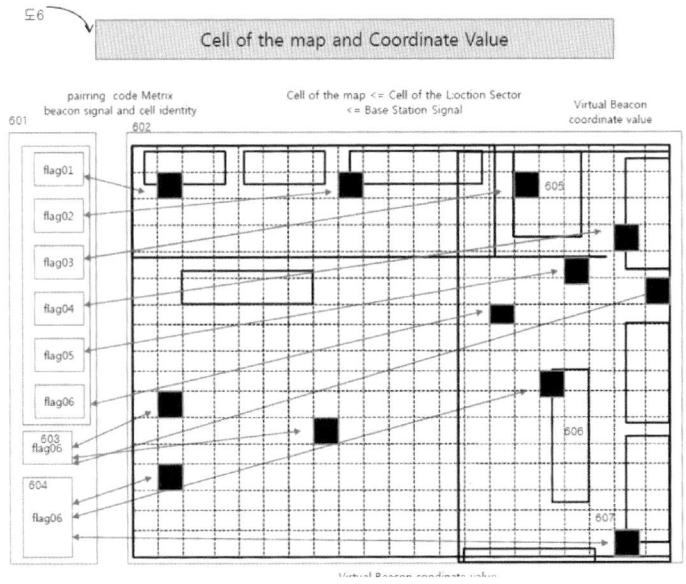

Drawing 7 (Patent 1)

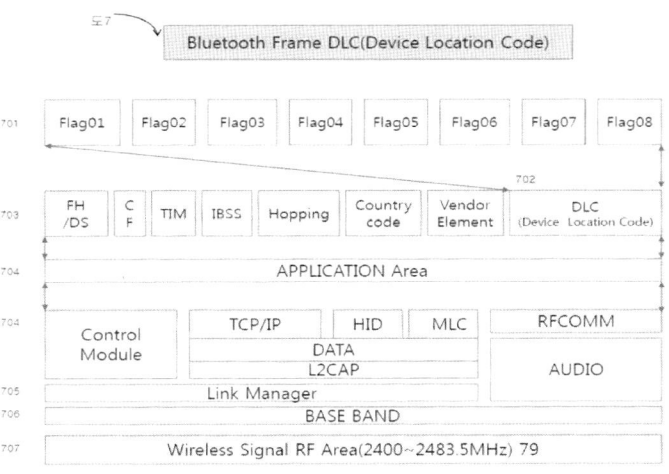

Drawing 8 (Patent 1)

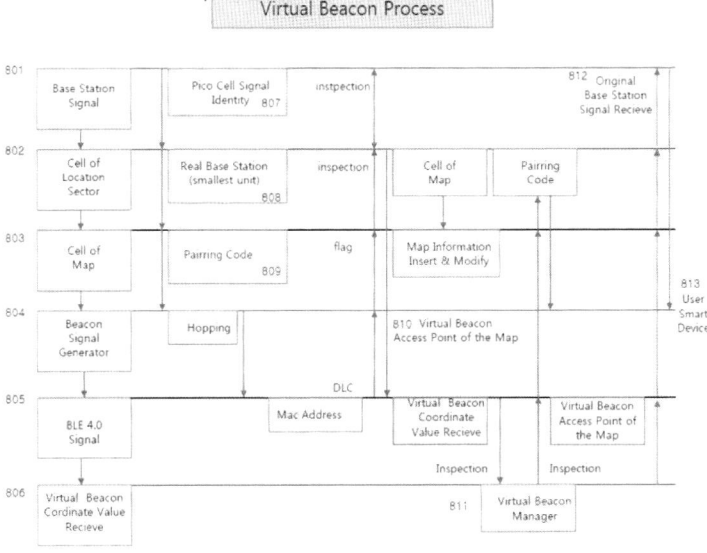

Drawing 9 (Patent 1)

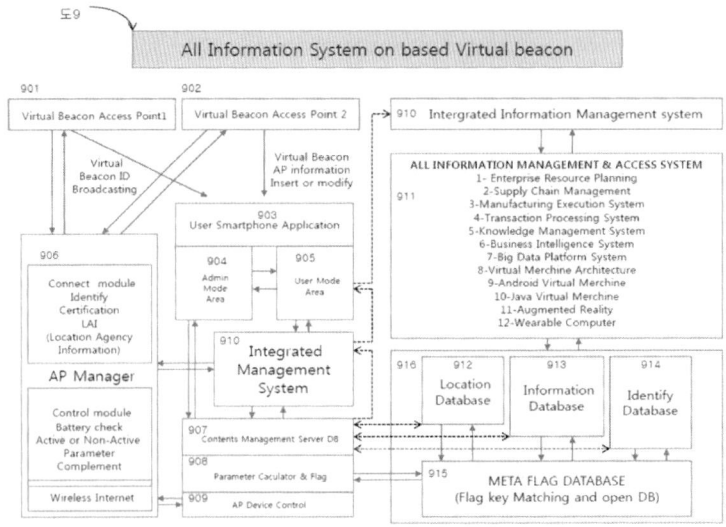

Drawing Abstract (Patent 1)

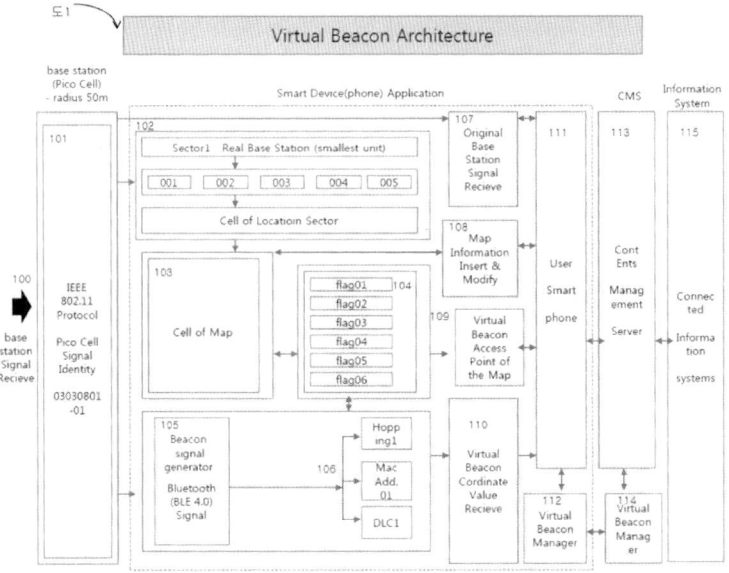

In general, virtualization solutions, or virtualization software, can be divided into three types as follows. The first is the virtualization of the host, which is to run the Guest OS based on the host OS. Types include VM Workstation, VMware Server, VMware Player, MS Virtual Server, Virtual PC, Virtual Box, and Parallels Workstation.

The advantage is that there are no restrictions on the host operating system because it emulates virtual hardware, but the disadvantage is that the overhead can be large because the OS is placed on top of the OS.

Second, there is a hypervisor virtualization solution, which is a method of installing and using a hypervisor in hardware without a host OS.

There are Xen, MS hyper-V, citrix, KVM, etc., and there is little overhead because there is no separate host OS, and it has the advantage of being able to use resources efficiently because it directly controls the hardware. Since there is no management function for it, a computer or console for management is required and the hypervisor virtualization solution is further classified into Full-Virtualization or Hardware Virtual Machine and Para-Virtualization as follows.

(1) Full-Virtualization

Full virtualization is a method of completely virtualizing hardware, also called Hardware Virtual Machine.

When the hypervisor is driven, a management virtual machine called DOM0 is executed, hardware access of all virtual machines is made through DOM0, and DOM0 intervenes for all commands.

In other words, the hypervisor can understand the commands issued by each OS, whatever the virtualized OS.

For example, when you give a command called Add in Windows, ADD in Linux, or add in Mac, the hypervisor translates "add" and executes the command. A hypervisor is not only responsible for this translation role, but also

Figure 2-23 The first core attribute of Virtualization solution

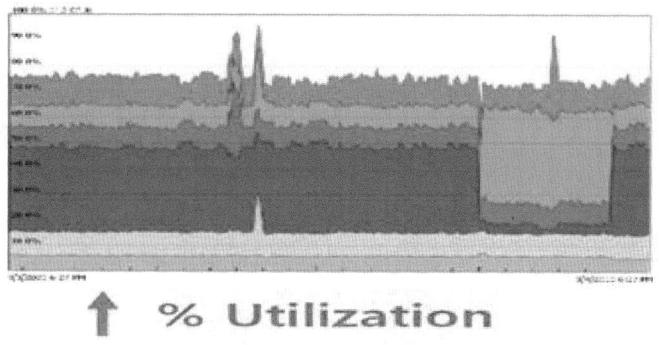

Figure 2-24 The second key attribute of Virtualization solution

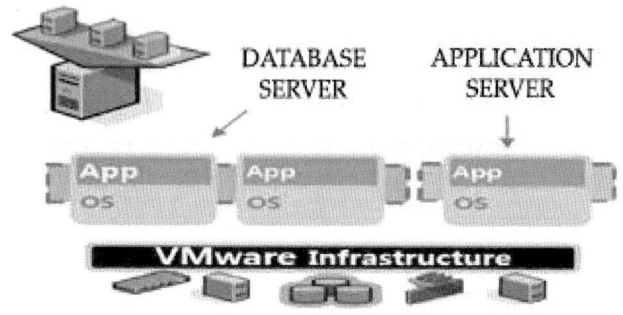

Figure 2-25 Central management solution of Virtualization system

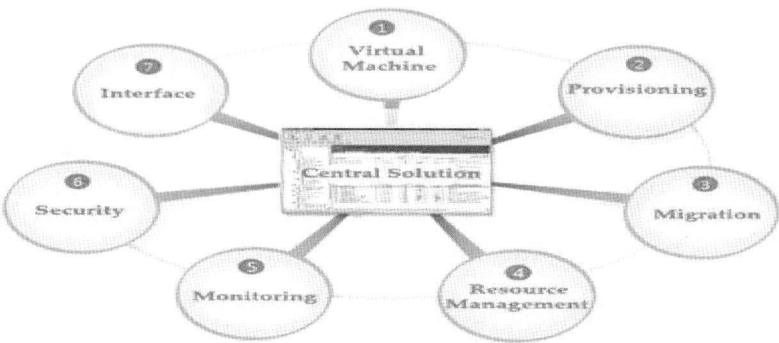

for allocating resources to virtualized OSs.

Since the hardware is completely virtualized, there is an advantage that the Guest OS operating system does not need to be modified. However, the performance is relatively slow because the hypervisor mediates all commands.

(2) Para-Virtualization

Unlike full virtualization, paravirtualization does not completely virtualize hardware.

To solve the problem of performance degradation, which is the biggest drawback of full virtualization, a request can be sent directly to the hypervisor through an interface called Hyper Call.

In other words, each virtualized OS has a different translator. The translator translates different commands issued by different OSs as "add".

It has the advantage of faster performance than full virtualization, which requests all commands to the hypervisor through DOM0, and the disadvantage is that kernel of each OS needs to be modified to make a hyper call request to the hypervisor, and Sime-virtualization is not easy to use unless it is open-source.

(3) Container Virtualization.

Container management software is installed on the host OS, and containers are logically divided and used. Since a container is composed of libraries and applications for application operation, each can be used as an individual server. Container virtualization has the advantage of being light and fast due to low overhead.

As seen above, the hypervisor is a very important concept of virtualization. It is no exaggeration to say that is the concept of virtualization. Therefore, if we describe the hypervisor in more detail, it can be said that it is a logical platform for running multiple operating systems simultaneously on the host computer. It is also called virtual machine monitor

Figure 2-26 Gartner Comparison Table by Virtualization solution

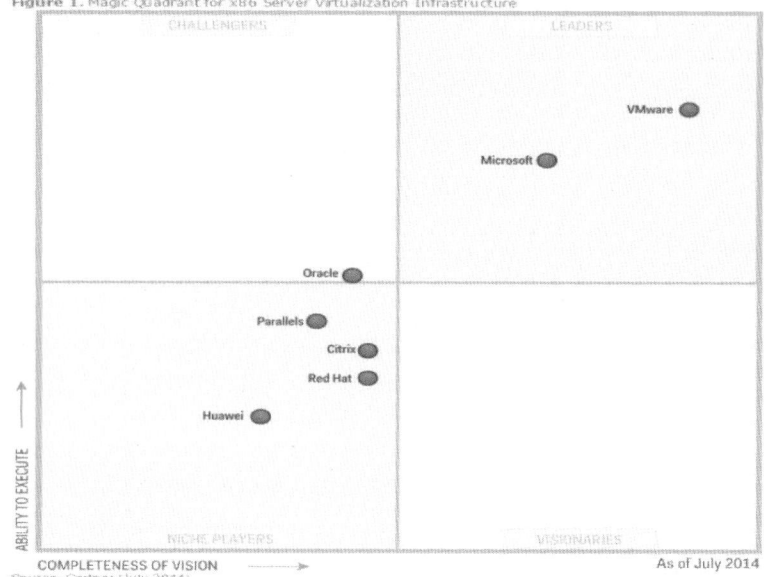

Figure 2-27 Performance comparison graph of Virtualization

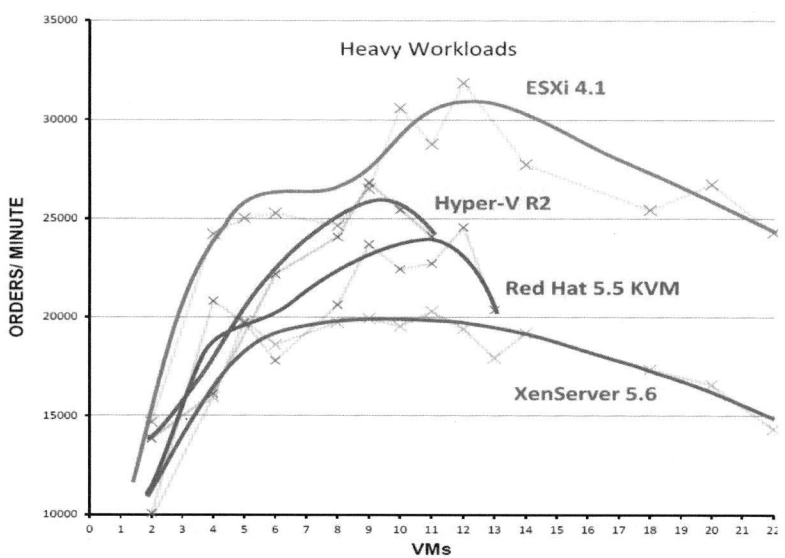

Figure 2-28 Organize supported OS by Virtualization solution

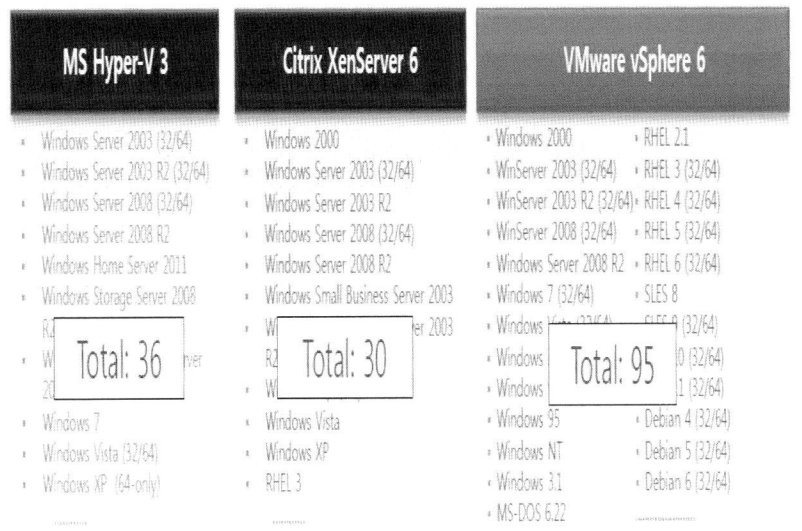

Figure 2-29 Business efficiency increase graph of Virtualization

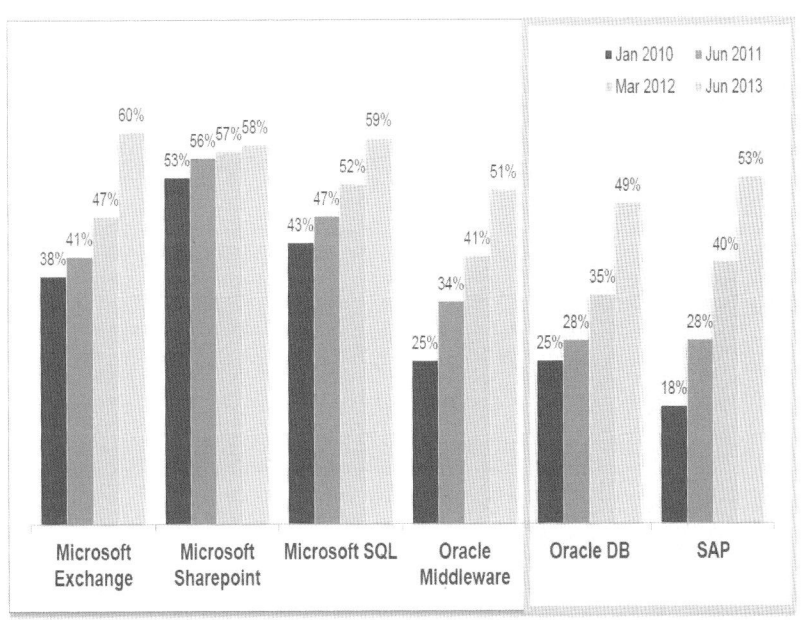

or virtual machine manager and is often abbreviated as VMM.

Recently, virtual machines have appeared a lot in embedded systems such as mobile phones. This is what facilitates the virtualization of IoT services. Embedded virtualization started with the maintenance of API of Real-Time operating system to provide a high-level operating system interface such as Linux or Windows to program application programs for ordinary smartphones. The low-level Real Time operating system environment needed to be maintained continuously to support the existing functions, and it is now used.

Therefore, the hypervisor used for embedded must meet real-time performance, and it is difficult to be compatible with the hypervisor used in other high-level areas. Therefore, in embedded systems with limited resources, especially in battery-powered mobile systems, there is a problem of small memory size and low overhead. While x86 architecture is common in the PC field, a wide variety of architectures are used in the Embedded field. Memory protection is required to support virtualization, and most microprocessors do not, because normal user mode and administrator mode are distinguished. Therefore, architectures such as x86, MIPS, ARM, and PowerPC that are widely used for embedded systems from middleware to high-end levels continue to evolve. Manufacturers of embedded systems usually have their own operating system source code and there is little need for full virtualization. On the other hand, the high performance of paravirtualization led to the choice of virtualization technology, and ARM recently added support for full virtualization with its Trust Zone technology. The first commercial mobile embedded system hypervisor sold was OKL4 used in Toshiba mobile phones, a microkernel commercial version of the L4 switch that supports x86, ARM and MIPS processors. Another embedded system is TRANGO, which supports ARM, MIPS, and PowerPC.

In other words, virtualization technology has only maintained its legacy since the advent of the first computer and is meeting explosive needs with the advent of the Fourth Industrial Revolution. Now, there is no place where virtualization technology is not applied to general PCs, corporate workstations, supercomputers in research labs, and smartphones used by ordinary people. This virtualization technology is playing the role of a medium for realizing the Internet of Things, Big Data, and artificial intelligence, and will be an field where infinite technological advancement and development are expected in the future.

2.3 Virtual Currency and Financial Security System

Strictly speaking, cryptocurrency is another word that intersects cryptocurrency, digital money, and electronic money.

Bitcoin, for example, is a cryptocurrency, a digital currency, and a virtual currency. And it is a currency that uses blockchain technology. However, if the application is used and the fee is exchanged in Ethereum, this can be game money. Virtual Currency refers to digital or electronic money used in electronic form in a specific virtual community connected through a network without physical objects such as banknotes or coins.

Figure 2-30 Wallet to store cryptocurrencies

Figure 2-31 Arbitrage for cryptocurrency trading

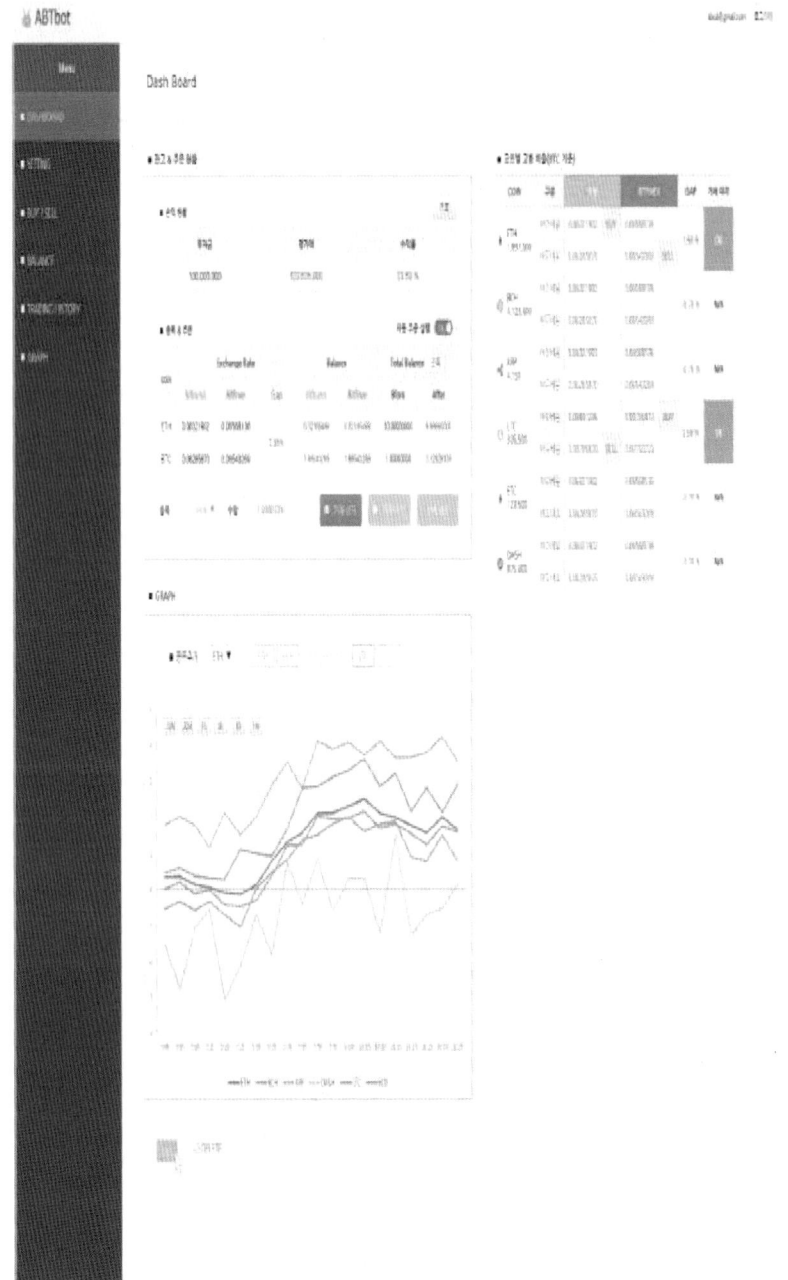

Figure 2-32 Auto Trading cryptocurrency

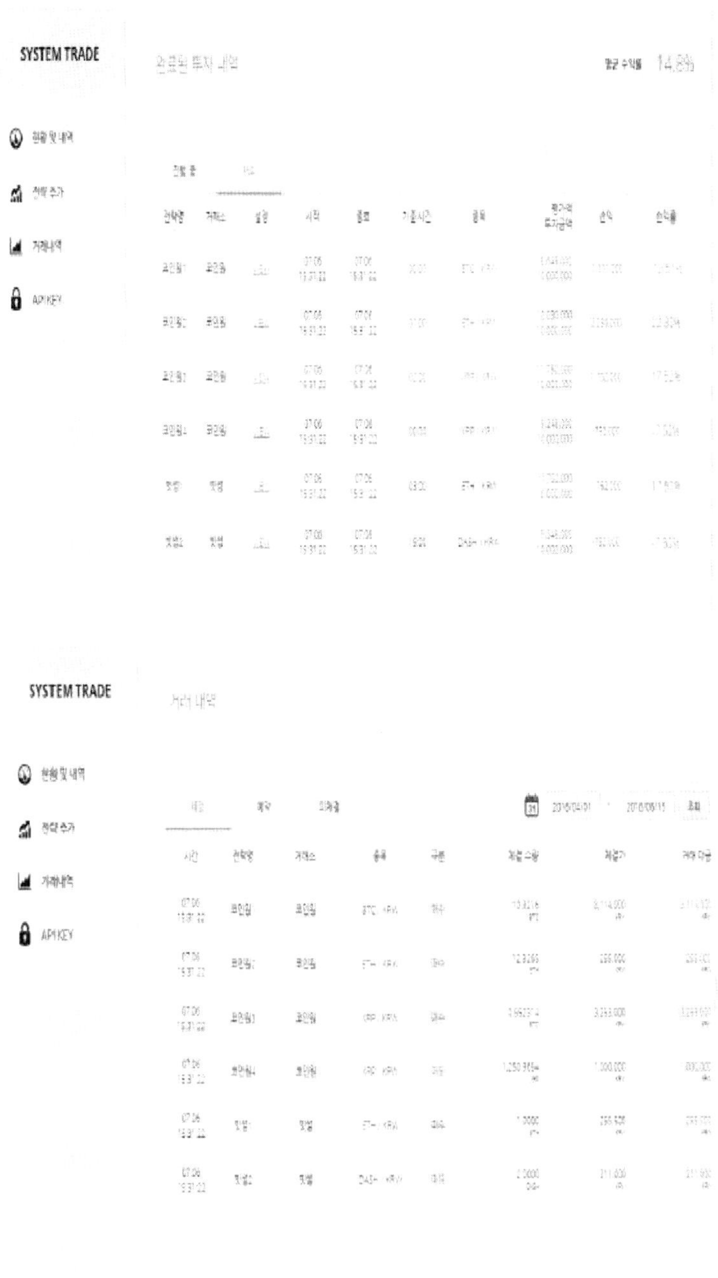

Figure 2-33 Investment amount in the cryptocurrency market

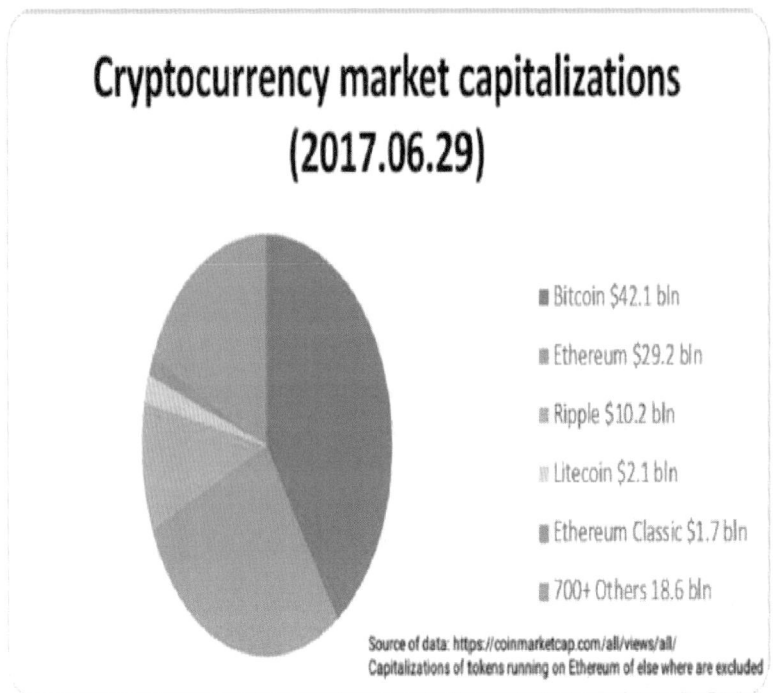

Therefore, cryptocurrency can be seen as a kind of virtual currency. However, if the European Central Bank or the US Treasury strictly applies the definition of cryptocurrency, few virtual currencies can be called cryptocurrency. That's why the U.S. Department of the Treasury's Financial Crimes Enforcement Unit (FinCEN) does not call virtual currencies cryptocurrency.

However, as shown in [Figure 2-33], interest in the current virtual currency market is very hot. As of 2017, $42.1 billion of Bitcoin was invested, and $29.2 billion of Ethereum exceeded $103.9 billion of the total virtual currency market. Converted to Korean won, it is a huge amount exceeding 120 trillion won.

What is the difference between virtual currency and cryptocurrency? According to the definitions made by the European Central Bank, the US

Department of the Treasury, and the European Banking Authority, virtual currency is a type of digital currency that is not controlled by the government, and it is issued and managed by developers and use the payment method only in a specific virtual community. According to this definition, most cryptocurrencies are both digital and virtual currencies. However, although Bitcoin, which is received as a payment method at many online and offline stores, is a digital currency, but it is not a virtual currency. Also, since most cryptocurrencies are not issued by developers, most cryptocurrencies are not virtual currencies in terms of issuance.

The U.S. Department of the Treasury's Financial Crimes Enforcement Unit (FinCEN) uses the term 'virtual currency' to mean "a means of exchange that works like legal money in some circumstances but does not have all the characteristics of real money." Except for electronic gift certificates, the word 'virtual currency' is not used when referring to cryptocurrencies such as Bitcoin Ethereum, and Ripple.

Here, virtual currency or digital currency includes all online payment methods that can be paid in virtual space, such as Kakao Pay or Samsung Pay. The fact that virtual currency, digital currency, or cryptocurrency can use blockchain technology or be used in the online space can be the biggest advantage in the era of preparing for the Fourth Industrial Revolution.

You will be able to understand the concept of virtual currency more easily through my patent.

The name of this invention is a method of a virtual currency and payment system using a frequency (Patent 2).

In the description of the technical field, this invention relates to a technology for implementing a virtual currency and a payment system using frequencies scattered in space, and a method for configuring the system. Cryptocurrency is a type of electronic money that remains in the form of information on a computer, etc. and is traded only on the internet without real things.

It refers to money traded online without real money such as banknotes or coins. In foreign countries, it was called digital currency or virtual currency because it was invisible and expressed on the computer in the beginning, but recently, it is called cryptocurrency, which means money using encryption technology, and the government uses the term "virtual currency." Unlike ordinary currencies issued by governments or central banks, cryptocurrencies are valued according to rules set by the person who first invented it. In addition, since it is distributed based on blockchain technology, the government or central bank does not manage transaction details and does not guarantee the value or payment.

In the background, virtual currency is usually given value as a currency when the values existing on each computer in the network are connected in one block unit using blockchain technology and the blocks are combined into one item. However, this invention deals with a new type of virtual currency production method that combines frequencies scattered in space to form a virtual currency configuration and a method of configuring a payment system through it.

This invention is a method of using frequencies scattered in space in a blockchain technology used in a computer database. First, a description of frequencies scattered in space is required. The frequency is usually expressed in angular frequency (ω), radians per second (in radians/second), or f - Hertz (Hz). It can also be expressed in BPM (beats per minute) and RPM (revolutions per minute). The relationship between the angular frequencies ω (rad/sec) and f (Hz) is as follows: $\omega = 2\pi f$ Frequency is also related to phase (φ), which is also the waveform offset of a particular point at initial time (t0), expressed in degrees or radians.

This invention uses these frequency characteristics and various service characteristics according to frequency bands, and provides services using the same frequency network, such as the WIFI network frequency, the base station carrier frequency, and the Internet network. By giving each unique value, encryption can be performed on the currency. In the existing wireless communication, the transmitting and the receiving sides are configured and communicated in a mutually agreed manner based on a predetermined protocol. Like this, the value stored in each PC also has a specific identity through a specific value of the frequency of the virtual currency. The encryption method using this is a key feature of the virtual currency configuration of the present invention.

This invention provides a virtual currency and payment service to PC and smartphone users based on frequency technology, describes a detailed method of constructing a system that interworks with each other, and describes a system for using it. Its core contents are non-contact and non-face-to-face contact through the virtual currency created by the present invention for a store or product in a store, mart, department store, or in a transaction between individuals. It describes the configuration of a system that allows users to pay directly with a smartphone without having to go to the cash register using the monetary value of the current cryptocurrency or to pay directly with smartphones when exchanging money between individuals. For example, you can order and pay on the spot without entering the store, check the value of virtual currency and make another transaction.

As described above, the core of this invention is to describe the logic, process, and method of constructing a system that enables non-visit, contactless, and non-face-to-face payments for the products. I want as virtual currency directly through applications on PCs or smartphones in the transaction between stores or individuals.

As a means of solving the problem, in this invention, by using the frequency technology and its other form of virtual currency, the virtual currency that has not been used or tested in the past is entered as a virtual currency in the smart device, and the amount is used as the virtual currency. It is possible to create a chargeable virtual currency by inserting the information as a token and then updating the information using the broadcast transmission frequency, and by using it, it is possible to implement a system in which money transactions between stores and individuals are possible.

For this, it is necessary to reprocess the frame for the VMK value in the signal frequency reception stage to increase the value, money, and security performance, and to utilize the smartphone and application that receives it.

Since virtual currency is created based on frequency, it is necessary to create a medium that transmits and receives data to and from a server with a database for frequency manipulation, and it is necessary to create a server that updates the record by storing and updating the total value of the virtual currency.

It analyzes and reprocesses the signal of the value of the virtual currency received through the server and is in charge of linking with the existing general software payment systems in connection with a payment agency, bank, or credit card company. The biggest feature of this invention is to describe that virtual currency is regarded as a key value through the broadcasting of the entire frequency, and the logic and process that constitutes the payment service providing system using it, and the method thereof.

As an effect of the invention, this invention does not constitute a virtual currency by mining or storing block values in the user's computer like the existing virtual currency but creates cryptocurrency that cannot be forged because the frequency in space is used as the key value of the virtual currency. That is, the value of the frequency existing in all spaces on the earth, such as the ground, the basement, and the inside of a building, can serve as an ID. This is because frequencies scattered in space can be changed due to the expansion of base stations or additional communication networks, but the frequency map value created by mapping the space has a unique ID.

For example, if a virtual currency contains a location-based frequency KEY value, the virtual currency is encrypted differently according to the user's location in the payment service for all amounts that occur in people's daily lives, so it can provide an important security function that distinguishes the current owner of the actual currency. When this invention is commercialized, monetary transactions or virtual currency transactions between individuals that existed only in computers are encrypted based on location, and can be changed in value, so virtual currency transactions can be made only by transmitting and receiving frequencies between each other. What used to be a virtual currency transaction through the exchange of computer codes becomes a currency transaction through the exchange of frequencies, and deposits, withdrawals, and transfers are possible through each smartphone, so a new form of electronic money and payment system can be configured.

The present invention is not a conventional cash or NFC card contact method, but a method of generating and exchanging virtual currency by generating a frequency through a smartphone or PC and increasing portability, convenience, and security. It is an invention related to a method of configuring a payment system linked thereto.

The frequency has quite a variety of forms, in the case of RF, anyone can generate it in an application with just a small battery in everyday life. However, if the value is converted into the coordinate value of the natural system based on the location and the value is included, a unique value that does not exist anywhere else can be created. It is the core of this invention to convert its unique value into the security, portability, and convenience of virtual currency. The frequency generated by the electronic device can adjust the broadcasting distance, for example, RF can adjust the broadcast distance from 10M to 100M or more. I would like to explain how to create a new code by inserting a unique value of location value into the code that fits the characteristics of this frequency and use it as the key value of virtual currency. In detail, the smart device or the electronic device that reprocesses frequency frames to broadcasts identification information and receives it acquires VMK information (Money Value Code) included in the frame of the frequency, inserts it into the existing virtual currency and payment system, calculates the VMK deduction amount, re-recognizes the embedded VMK, updates the database, and reuses the VMK. In other words, the VMK value only holds the unique ID of the electronic money, and the VMK value of the electronic money is stored in the server in the form of a database twice, and its update is performed by the smart device that received the signal and the command is given.

Existing virtual currency utilizes blockchain technology that becomes one complete code when code values are finally combined through each PC, and the exchange operates a server that manages the information of the complete code. This invention is an invention that can satisfy the portability, security, and scalability of transactions while using the network configuration of the existing virtual currency as it is.

In other words, the VMK signal is a value included in the frequency signal, and the electronic device receives the signal in the form of an ID specifying the value of the virtual currency through the application and defines the value of the virtual currency (the owner of the smartphone is the owner of the virtual currency), the store and the product price information as Pairring1. Again, payment information grouped into Pairing is approved through a payment agency or payment approval company, and the result information is matched with the customer user's VMK information and stored.

Another feature of the frequency virtual currency of the present invention is that it does not pair with any terminal. In other words, the frequency of virtual currency is mapped with the location value and the value fluctuates, so it can operate only when there is a transaction or update. Therefore, the value of the virtual currency stored in the electronic device does not change unless it is traded or updated, but the value changes continuously. For example, like the server where the Zone file of the Internet domain name is stored, the value of the amount for the value of one virtual currency is included in the frequency. It becomes a form of cryptocurrency that is one step higher in portability and security than the blockchain technology included in the existing pc and combined.

Various big data such as artificial intelligence and blockchain technology and combination technologies using them are being invented, but virtual currency obtained from sensors in the natural world does not exist. This is because natural sensors have a fixed value but always express a variable value and have a unique value.

That is, as in the present invention, the frequency virtual currency, which has the KEY value of the virtual currency in the frequency and the value of the amount only in the application, has the advantage of being able to use the existing infrastructure by installing a frequency cryptocurrency application on a smartphone when making payments. The VMK value of the frequency virtual currency is processed in the database of the software application server, and if it is necessary to link with an existing account and card, the payment system logic is used through the Payment Gateway. Otherwise, the payment process can be completed by the software application server.

This invention is a form of recognizing remittance and payment systems that did not exist before as an Access Point value of a virtual currency having a value of money using a frequency signal that exists in the natural world and updating the value of the money in the database of the server to create a new value and to make transactions between each other.

To explain in detail using drawings,

Drawing 1 expresses the principle of operation of frequency virtual currency, and the signal generated by reprocessing the frequency of the smartphone application is classified into a Money value, creation time, use range, creation position, extinction position, charging record, extinction time, and security key values as shown in 101.

The money value is the virtual currency value and is not the same as the actual value. It just means the serial number of the frequency cryptocurrency. It becomes the serial number of paper money, and through this, it is matched with the actual value of the server. The generation time, usage level, generation location, etc. are calculated in the server through the frequency information signal part of 103 and frequency parsing and recalculation. In the software application installed on the smart device, after parsing the frequency received from 101, the present value of VMK is re-recognized as shown in 104, and after re-recognized the current value of VMK Money, information about extinction or recharging, and the security key value as shown in 105, it will be updated in the VMK Money Database matched with the security key value.

After that process, in 106, when another additional transaction occurs, the process proceeds from 101 to 106 again based on the updated VMK information.

The infrastructural device classification of the frequency virtual currency payment system is that 101 is the stage that broadcasts the frequency of the virtual currency, 103 is the software application of the smartphone or PC that received the signal, and from 104, the application server stage of this frequency virtual currency is processed, and the update cycle ends at the application stage of the smartphone.

As described above, the broadcast frequency consists of these steps: VMK has a total of eight data values; each of the eight data values consists of a value, time, area, location 1, location 2, history, generation period, and security key; the transmitted frequency updates the VMK of the application;

The updated VMK is transferred from the smartphone to the smartphone and from the PC to the PC.

The transferred VMK value is updated and consists of a step of updating the VMK of the virtual currency of the application stage.

Drawing 2 shows a frequency of virtual currency flow chart. In 201, a smartphone or PC generates a frequency signal and broadcasts a VMK signal together, and in 202, a signal receiver such as a smartphone or PC receives the signal. Parsing and calculations for VMK are performed in the software application installed on the smartphone in 203, and the database is updated on the server of 204 and, if necessary, goes through the Payment Gateway at 205 to link with the existing payment system, and finally at 206, the frequency of virtual currency VMK is updated in real time and is continuously used for other transactions as a virtual currency.

In detail, the frequency signal broadcast from 201 broadcasts the VMK Code together, and the signal receiver of 202 re-recognizes the current value through the validity and value VMK serial number, and update payment information. That is, if the amount of VMK of person A is 5VMK and the amount of VMK for goods or services purchased by person A is considered to be 2VMK, the VMK value is reset to 3VMK, and the value of VMK code is reset to 3VMK.

That is, the reset VMK value is transferred to the serial code through the VMK Main Database, and the payment level is also updated.

If it is necessary to link with an existing account, payment can be performed together through the payment gateway by moving from the revalued amount of a bank or credit card company.

Since the above process is carried out within the information communication network, it is a payment flow that can be processed within 1 second. In the case of RF, the frequency broadcasting cycle is possible from 1 to 100 times per second, and the Internet packet transmission rate is several times per second. Since it can process up to several Mbytes per second, data transfer with VMK values can process all processes in a very short time, and additional or multiple transactions in parallel are possible. The above is a step of broadcasting a frequency by a smartphone or PC; another smart phone or PC receiving the frequency; Calculating the amount of the received frequency acting as VMK in the virtual currency included in the application; Calculating an amount by including the transmitted frequency as VMK in the virtual currency included in the application; Transmitting the VMK value of the virtual currency to a database of Payment Gateway, which is a payment server; and receiving the VMK value by the sending smartphone and the receiving smartphone to update the amount of virtual currency.

Drawing 3 shows the principle of operation of the frequency virtual currency payment system. Devices installed with frequency virtual currency applications of 300 and 301 continuously broadcast frequency signals including VMK signals. The frequency signal broadcast in this way is received through the signal receiver of the user's smartphone, etc., and the application installed in my terminal first classifies the frequency signal through parsing, and then recognize as ID value using the serial number of the existing VMK, query the server, perform parsing and calculation with the frequency signal corresponding to the transaction, and update the server's database. As shown in 306, the updated VMK value is re-recognized for VMK Money current value, expired or recharge information and termination, and the security key value, and then updated with the amount value in the VMK Money DB matched with the security key value. At this time, when linking with credit card or other payment method, not with frequency virtual currency only, it is linked to a bank or credit card company through a payment agency of 302 and VAN company. It is possible to proceed in various ways as shown through 302 to 303 and 305.

In other words, when purchasing a specific product using frequency virtual currency, it is possible to inquire the amount of the current account through the credit card or bank and proceed with the payment by linking together based on the database value in the VMK zone file.

That is, when a frequency signal is generated, the frequency virtual currency requires the actual value of the Zone file (the actual value of the VMK existing in the server) indicating the value of the electronic money, and according to the response, the amount of the application installed in the smartphone is stored. It becomes the form in which the actual payment is made as it is determined and updated.

Drawing 4 shows the configuration diagram of the frequency virtual currency payment system.

Frequency Signal, which is used as the virtual currency of 401, continuously broadcasts the VMK information it has during transaction. The broadcast VMK information is received through 403 to the terminal of a smartphone that can be within 100M or more, and the received VMK value is based on the amount value of the VMK value of the server through the software application of 407. It performs transaction calculations and updates the database. In other words, if a transaction occurs, it is a new type of payment method for virtual currency that is different from the method of sending and receiving each other using paper money or using other short-distance communication means such as NFC. It is characterized by a payment method that can replace credit cards, cash, and other monetary verification methods just by generating a frequency. In 407, 408, and 411, the software application has a common server and database, which updates, calculates, and stores the value of VMK. It will go through the payment Gateway server and database of 412 if they need to be linked with the existing payment method, and as shown in 413 and 417, it is linked to a payment agency, bank, or credit card company to update the database of the software application server. This process includes the steps of a smartphone or PC broadcasting a frequency; A receiving step of receiving a frequency signal of a base station or electromagnetic wave by entering a smart phone in a situation in which an application is executed in a specific space; Calculating the amount of the received frequency as a KEY to the virtual currency included in the application; Calculating the amount of the transmitted frequency is included as a KEY in the virtual currency included in the application; transmitting the KEY value of the virtual currency to a database of Payment Gateway, which is a payment server; The sending smartphone and the receiving smartphone receive the KEY value and include the step of updating the amount of virtual currency.

Drawing 5 is a diagram showing a frequency configuration diagram of a frequency virtual currency.

Basically, the frequency protocol has a structure from 502 to 510. It broadcasts radio frequency RF (Radio Frequency). It includes the basic data area of the Control module 505 on top of the link manager area of 508 through the base band of 509 and TCP/IP, HID, MLC area for communication. It is divided into areas such as FH/DS, CD, TIM, and IBSS in the application area of 503. Among these subdivided areas, there is basically a buffer area, but nothing is defined. This area is reset to VMK (Money Value Code) area at the application level. The reset application area is included in the existing frequency and broadcast as one package frequency. This area is defined by subdividing it into Code values of VMK01~VMK08 like 501. As shown in FIG. 1, the broadcast frequency virtual currency value is separated again into a value having 8 pieces of information through parsing at the application stage of the received terminal.

The steps of creating a VMK having 8 types of information in the buffer area of the frame of the frequency is as follows: The data insertion step in the buffer area of the frequency signal; the mapping step of the inserted data and the frequency; A modulation step for the mapped frequency; a step of broadcasting a frequency containing VMK information.

As described with the above drawings, frequency virtual currency and payment systems basically regard frequencies that are continuously broadcast based on spatial frequencies as virtual currency, and are installed on smartphones, PCs, POS terminals, etc. that have received signals from them.

It is a trading system that uses the VMK signal, or the serial number of the virtual currency as a recognition value using a software application, checks the actual value of the virtual currency on the server, parses the product or the value to be moved through it, and recalculates the value of the amount.

The biggest feature of the present invention is that in the application step, only the serial number including the value of the amount and the location value is recognized in different manner from existing NFC, Bluetooth pairing payment, and online financial transaction, and then the actual value of the amount is located. The difference is that the application server handles input and output according to the value and that pairing is never performed between electronic devices and terminals.

Cryptocurrency is a payment system that can satisfy portability, convenience, and security at the same time by having the location value included in the VMK with the value that existed only in the PC. The biggest feature and core of this invention is that it can have a convenient function as money in that all payments can be made by installing only an application on a smartphone without the need to carry paper bills.

This invention is not a conventional cash or NFC-type card contact method, but a method of generating a frequency through a smartphone or PC and using it to generate and exchange virtual currency and increase portability, convenience, and security. It is an invention related to a method of configuring a payment system linked thereto.

The frequency has quite a variety of forms, but in the case of RF, anyone can generate it in an application with just a small battery in everyday life. However, if the value is converted into the coordinate value of the natural system based on the location and the value is included, a unique value that does not exist anywhere else can be created. It is the core of this invention to convert its unique value into the security, portability, and convenience of virtual currency. The frequency generated by the electronic device can adjust the broadcasting distance, for example, RF can adjust the broadcast distance from 10M to 100M or more. I would like to explain how to create a new code by inserting a unique value of location value into the code that fits the characteristics of this frequency and use it as the key value of virtual currency. In detail, the smart device or the electronic device that reprocesses frequency frames to broadcasts identification information and receives it acquires VMK information (Money Value Code) included in the frame of the frequency, inserts it into the existing virtual currency and payment system, calculates the VMK deduction amount, re-recognizes the embedded VMK, updates the database, and reuses the VMK. In other words, the VMK value only holds the unique ID of the electronic money, and the VMK value of the electronic money is stored in the server in the form of a database, and its update is performed by the smart device receiving the signal and the command is given.

Existing virtual currency utilizes blockchain technology that becomes one complete code when code values are finally combined through each PC, and the exchange operates a server that manages the information of the complete code. This invention is an invention that can satisfy the portability, security, and scalability of transactions while using the network configuration of the existing virtual currency as it is. In other words, the VMK signal is a value included in the frequency signal, and the electronic device receives the signal in the form of an ID specifying the value of the virtual currency through the application, and through it, the owner, store, and product price information of the value are defined as Pairing1. After the payment information is paired again, it is approved through the payment agency or payment approval company, and the result information is matched with the customer user's VMK information and stored.

Another feature of the frequency virtual currency of the present invention is that it does not pair with any terminal. In other words, the frequency of virtual currency is mapped with the location value and the value fluctuates, so it can only operate when there is a transaction or update. Therefore, the value of the virtual currency stored in the electronic device does not change unless it is traded or updated, but the value changes continuously. For example, like the server where the Zone file of the Internet domain name is stored, the value of the amount for the value of one virtual currency is included in the frequency. It becomes a form of cryptocurrency that is one step higher in portability and security than the blockchain technology included in the existing pc and combined. Various big data such as artificial intelligence and blockchain technology and combination technologies using it are being invented, but virtual currency obtained from sensors in the natural world does not exist. This is because natural sensors have a fixed value, but always express a variable value and have a unique value.

That is, as in the present invention, the frequency virtual currency which the KEY value of the virtual currency exists in the frequency and the value of the amount exists only in the application stage is a necessary component when performing remittance, collection, and payment. It has the advantage of being able to use the existing infrastructure as it is if it is installed. The VMK value of frequency virtual currency is processed in the database of the software application server, and if it is necessary to link with an existing account and card, the payment system logic is used through the Payment Gateway. Otherwise, the payment can be completed by the software application server. Following is a diagram (Patent 2) of a method of cryptocurrency and payment system using frequency.

Drawing 1 (Patent 2)

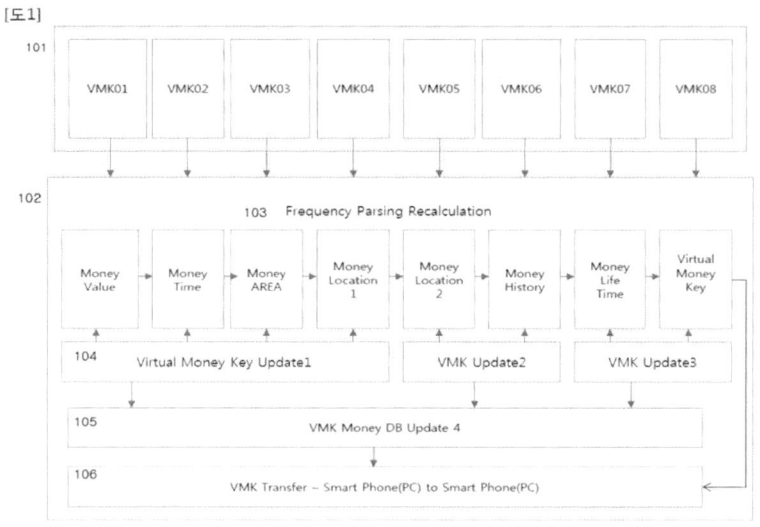

Drawing 2 (Patent 2)

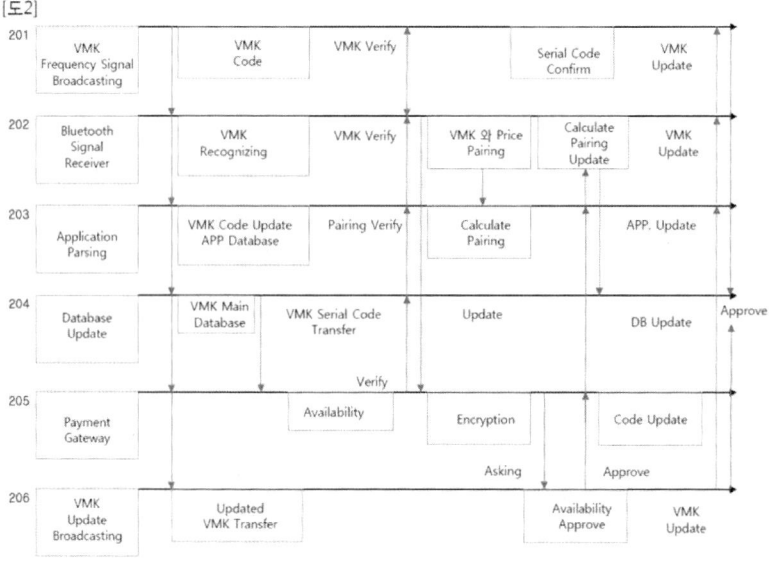

Drawing 3 (Patent 2)

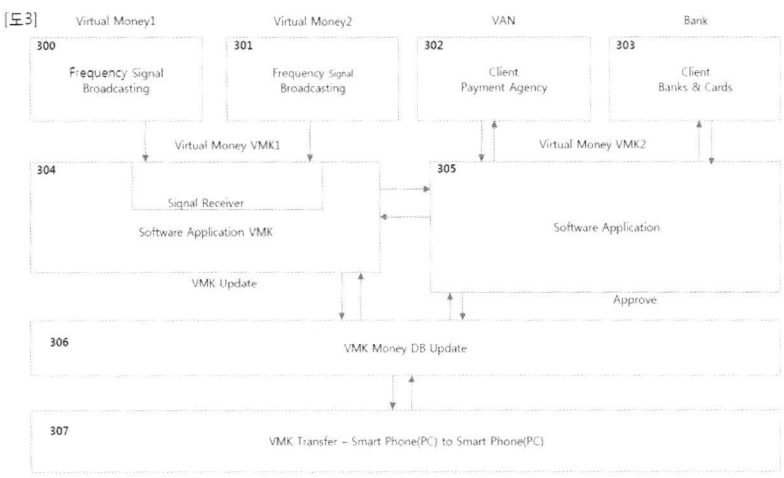

Drawing 4 (Patent 2)

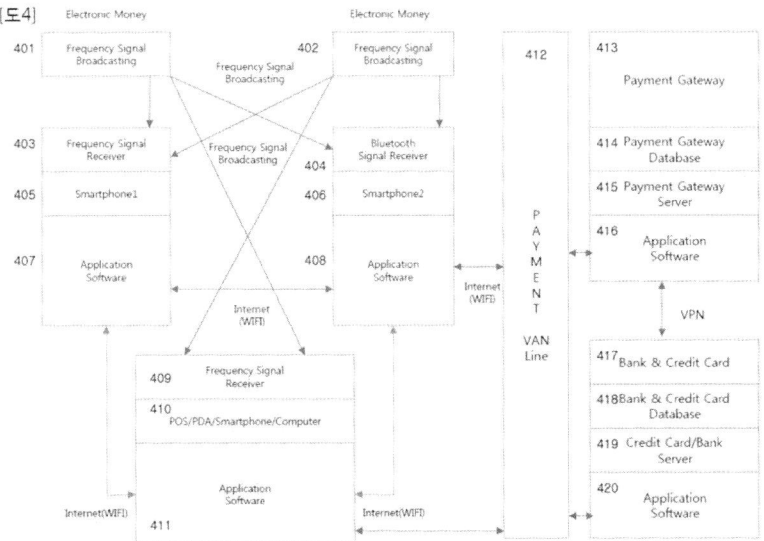

Drawing 5 (Patent 2)

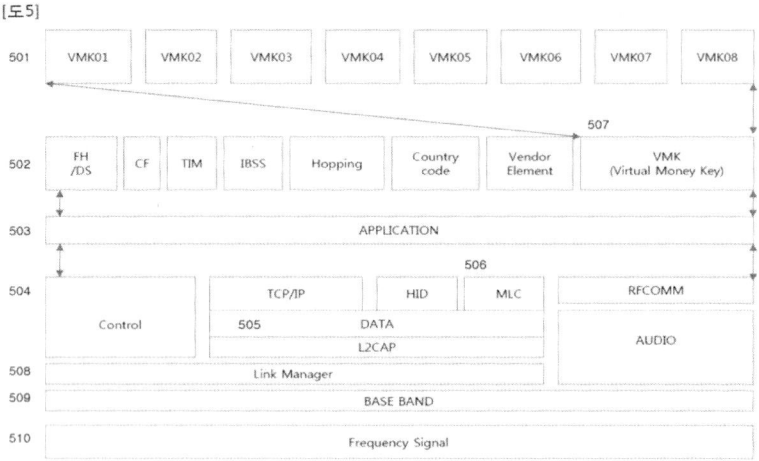

Drawing Abstract (Patent 2)

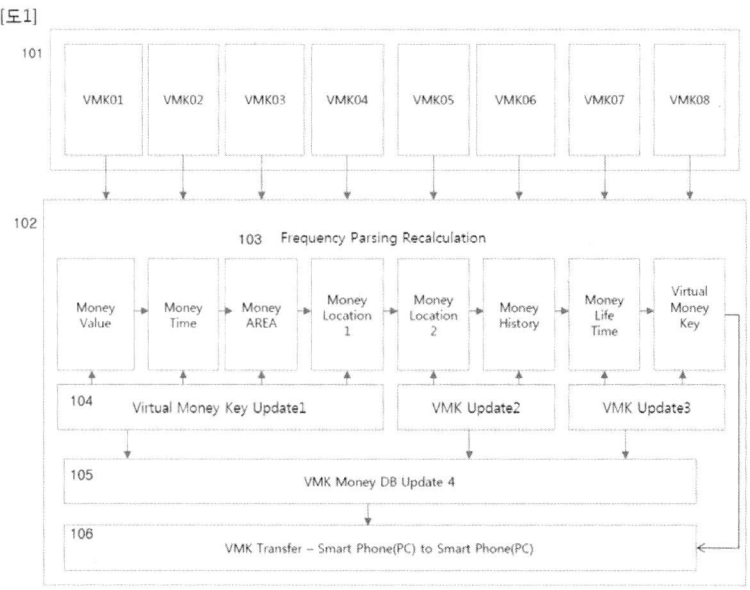

As discussed earlier, blockchain technology has played a role in attaching wings to the previously used virtualization technology. Since most virtual currencies on the market, such as Bitcoin and Ethereum, which are a kind of cryptocurrency, use blockchain technology, it is necessary to understand virtualization technology before understanding blockchain technology.

Virtualization technology is a kind of tool concept that increases the utilization rate of existing resources. Similarly, the blockchain technology can be said to have added logic for information integrity to this virtualization technology. Ultimately, the collection, distribution, and dissemination of information have been fully explained through the description of big data. However, in terms of information integrity, it proves that virtualization can only have reliability when it meets blockchain technology.

With the advent of blockchain, which was created through the development of virtualization technology, and the emergence of virtual currency, which is a virtual solution, again through the blockchain technology, it has a cyclic structure. This is because the technical circulation of information inevitably aims for information integrity, that is, reliability. The reliability of such information is directly linked to the security of the information system. Blockchain was born because of security, and security is the most important key to ultimately determining its value in virtual currency created through the blockchain

In this concept, security can be an important keyword to maintain and develop information systems. In this regard, the information system in the future should be the definitive edition of the Fourth Industrial Revolution, which includes security, virtualization technology, blockchain technology, and virtual currency technology, especially for financial information systems. The most important and risky field in information system security is the financial security system. What makes our free economic system work properly is that there is finance that guarantees reliability, and the financial system can provide the greatest security issue.

Figure 2-34 Financial Security Control Center Operation System

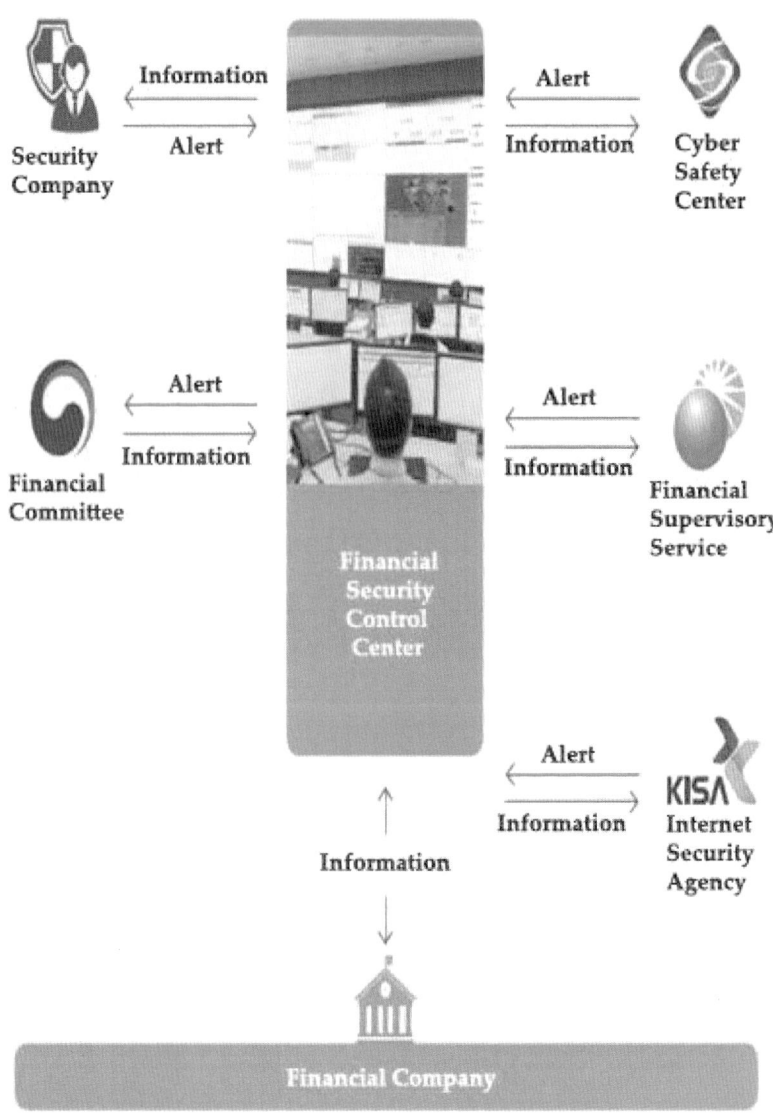

In Korea, there was also a fraud case in which virtual currency was sold under the pretext of salvaging a treasure ship. The following is a part of the newspaper article content. "Amid the ongoing investigation into allegations of investment fraud involving the salvage of the so-called Donskoi of Russia, it has been confirmed that over 200 people have been arrested over the past year for investment fraud related to cryptocurrency. In addition, since 2016, the amount of fraudulent damage related to cryptocurrencies has been reported to exceed KRW 593.8 billion. It is pointed out that the continuing fraudulent activity is clouding the waters of the cryptocurrency and blockchain industry." And "the virtual currency they sold through large-scale investment briefing sessions and 12 sub-exchanges in Gangnam and Daejeon in Korea, for the first time in the world, has a serial number, and the market price never goes down and only rises, so there is no loss of principal. As electronic money certified by the Bank of Korea, the Korea Financial Supervisory Service, and the Fair Trade Commission, it can be used like cash at banks, shopping malls, and game companies. " There are fraud cases that deceived investors with these lies.

Existing banks and financial institutions cannot be free from the trend of having a fence called a financial security system.

Shinhan Bank of Korea conducted a risk management-based early response system construction project for about 6 months from January to June 2010, integrating an early warning system and response process computerization for early detection and response of infringement attempts and the information system constant vulnerability inspection system to strengthen the prevention of intrusion accidents into one frame.

In addition, through this, Shinhan Bank significantly strengthened monitoring of not only known network intrusion patterns for internal networks and Internet service networks, but also overall network traffic, so that new intrusions that could not be detected in existing intrusion detection systems or Distributed DoS (DDOS) response systems, etc. Automated detection of tangible and small-scale Distributed DoS (DDOS) attack traffic is now possible. In addition, depending on the type and risk level of the detected intrusion attempt, through a predefined incident response process, the information security officer can share the dedicated situation monitoring screen optimized for the requirements of the relevant department and management to effectively respond jointly.

In addition, it was possible to conduct a regular vulnerability check for the overall information system, build a database of the inspection results, and establish a systematic response plan according to the risk level of the information system.

Figure 2-35 Fintech service development progress

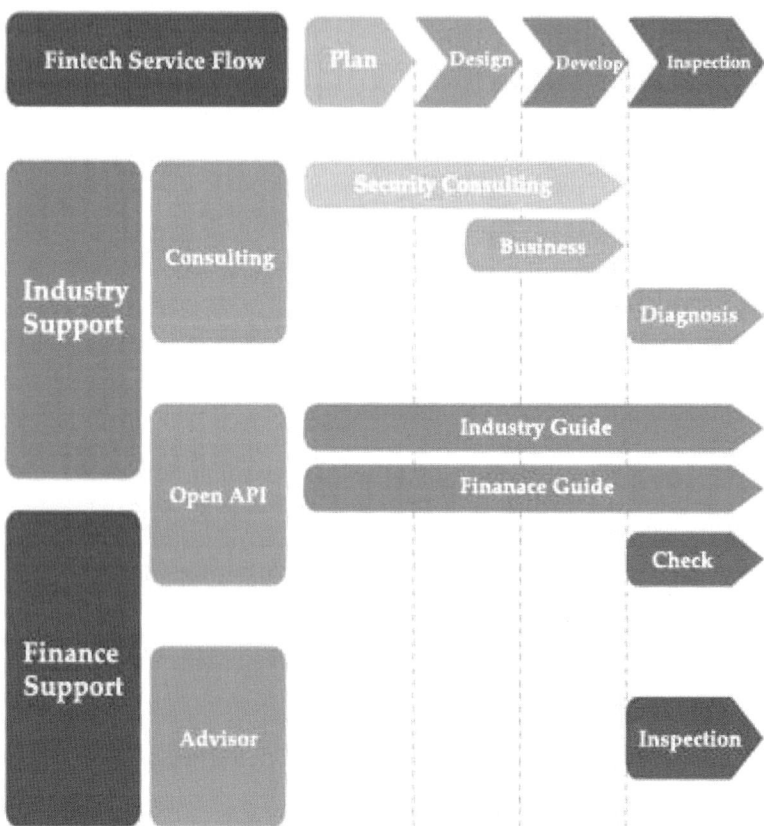

Shinhan Bank said, "We plan to expand the established system to the entire information security area to build an internal information leakage system based on risk management in the same frame, and to expand and apply it to the group in the future to use it to enhance the security level of all group companies." said.

This is part of the countermeasures against intentional crimes that frequently exploit loopholes in the financial security system.

In modern times, electronic financial services including internet banking have become a daily life as a convenient means of financial transaction, and their importance is increasing. As a side effect of this, infringement accidents such as user error, leakage of electronic financial access media through hacking of financial institutions, shopping malls, and portals, and abnormal payment or Internet banking transfer accidents are also increasing. Korea's financial sector, centered on the Financial Supervisory Service, establishes comprehensive electronic financial security measures and enforces the Electronic Financial Transactions Act, making it mandatory to provide various security programs to prevent hacking of customer PCs, differentiating transfer limits according to security levels, and establishing an integrated OTP authentication system in the financial sector. We are making active efforts to prevent electronic financial infringement accidents.

 Recently, new cyber fraud techniques such as Phishing or Pharming, or highly intelligent hacking tools developed by overseas professional hackers have been used to disable security programs and leak customer information, or to leak customer information, such as general portal sites, web hard disks, web mails, etc. It is not possible to completely block new financial security breaches such as leaking internet banking access media of customers registered on internet sites through hacking of internet banking and causing internet banking breaches. In the event of an intrusion, the need to significantly strengthen the existing security system, such as establishing a traceability system to identify the cause and arrest criminals, is emerging. In other words, as the Internet and virtual currency are created and financial security systems through more advanced information systems develop day by day, hacking or fraud or hacking using the weaknesses of the financial security system occurs in proportion to that.

Therefore, in the era of the Fourth Industrial Revolution, the development of a new and convenient financial system and the development of a security system to operate it must be done in parallel. The financial system to which the technology of the Fourth Industrial Revolution is applied is now called fintech in other words.

FinTech is a compound word for finance and technology, and collectively refers to changes in financial services and industries based on advanced information technologies such as mobile, big data, and SNS. As a change in financial services, technology-based financial service innovation that provides financial services differentiated from existing financial techniques by utilizing new IT technology is representative. Recent examples include mobile banking and app cards. As a change in the industry, there is a phenomenon in which innovative non-financial companies use their technology to provide financial services such as payment and settlement directly to users, such as Apple Pay and Alipay. In other words, virtual currency using blockchain is also a kind of fintech. In other words, the combination of Fintech and security is the financial security system.

The five fields below are where technology is most concentrated in Fintech.

First, payment and remittance fintech is an account that confirms the identity and saves money, a tool for depositing and withdrawing money, and a system for securely exchanging money between different parties.

Second, borrowing and lending fintech is used by consumer institutions to raise money from depositors and provide credit to borrowers.

Figure 2-36 Fintech field belonging to financial security system

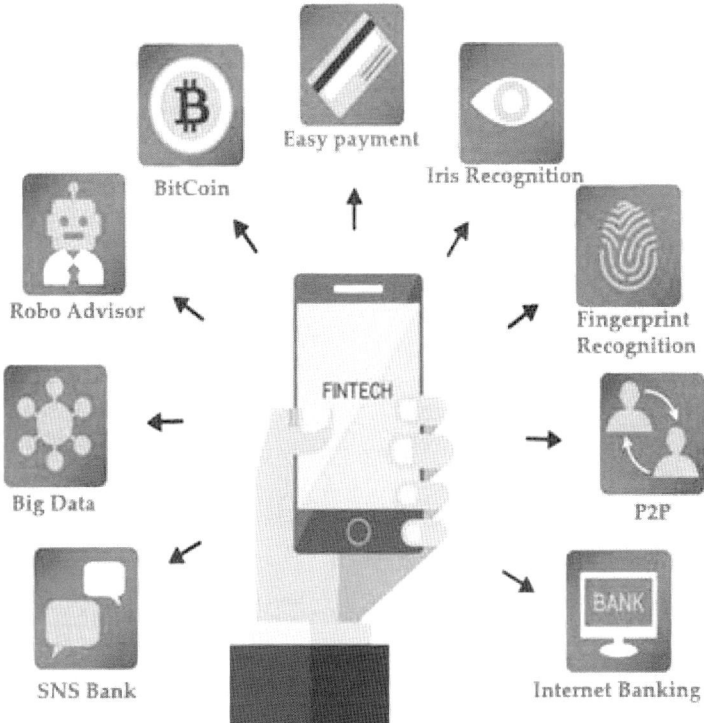

Third, asset management fintech refers to advisors, brokers, and investment managers who advise and execute financial investments and transactions related to retirement and real estate planning.

Fourth, insurance Fintech includes not only life insurance but also non-life insurance and auto insurance.

Fifth currency Fintech is a store, account unit, and exchange medium backed by national values, and can be applied to US dollars or euros.

The grafting of information system technology to the above five fintech patterns will become a tool to realize fintech. It is the financial security system that applies security to these tools. Therefore, as described above, all technologies in the Fourth Industrial Revolution should always be considered in pair with security.

This is because fintech technology with weak security cannot be applied to real life, and even if applied, it will quickly become obsolete.

In other words, we must not forget that the realization of the successful technology of the Fourth Industrial Revolution is innovation with security in mind.

Part 3 Big Data Business

3.1 Mobile Communication Technology and IoT

Big data goes hand in hand with mobile communication technology. In particular, the information system that produces big data in Korea is dominated by three telecommunication companies, and it is difficult to utilize big data without utilizing the infrastructure. This is not much different from the US or Europe.

The reason for this can be found in the fact that all three telecommunication companies are running ISP (Internet Service Provider) business.

The commonly known G in 1G stands for Generation. The first-generation mobile communication service was an analog-based technology that transmits the human voice as an electrical signal, so noise and confusion were severe and only voice could be used. Motorola's DynaTAC, announced as the first personal mobile phone in 1983, was as big as a brick at a construction site, so it was also called a brick phone. Motorola developed the world's first mobile phone, the DynaTAC 8000X, and it is the world's first commercial mobile phone that Motorola released after 15 years of research and investment of 100 million dollars. It weighs 794g, is 33cm in length, and has 30 minutes of continuous talk time. although it is quite insufficient in specifications compared to current ones, it was the world's first handset and the price was close to US$4,000.

The first-generation mobile phone, which was similar in size to the KPRC-6A radio used in the military, had a greater meaning in that it could make calls while moving rather than its size. This is because it was not easy to imagine making a phone call on the move before. Along with the first-generation mobile phone, a car phone, which is hardly considered a complete mobile phone, also appeared. The car phone, which was usually installed on the console between the driver's seat and the passenger's seat, had a limitation in that it could not be brought out of the car as the electric wire was connected to the car body, but it had the advantage of not having to worry about the battery like a mobile phone and having better call performance.

Among large first-generation mobile phones, some models could optionally purchase a booster that can be used as a car phone in the vehicle.

The car phone was also not a phone that anyone could use, as it would cost millions of won at the time including the cost of the device and installation.

Figure 3-1 The world's first mobile phone

In the first generation of mobile phones, Motorola was almost the dominant company in the world. The MicroTAC, released in the late '80s, was the first flip-type mobile phone, and it has a much smaller and thinner design compared to the DynaTAC, making it feel like a true mobile phone. The first mobile phone in Korea was the SH-100, released by Samsung in time for the opening ceremony of the 1988 Olympic Games. With a large bar-type design, this device began to be sold on the market in 1989, about a year later. The first generation of mobile communication started in Korea in 1984. At that time, a company called Korea Mobile Telecommunication Service started the car phone service, and the cell phone service started in 1988 with the 24th Seoul Olympics. Korea Mobile Telecom changed its name to SK Telecom in 1997. In Korea, the mobile communication technology changed from analog to digital in 1996, and the generation of mobile communication was replaced.

Figure 3-2 Mobile communication technology by generation

Technology	1G	2G/2.5G	3G	4G	5G
Bandwidth	2kbps	14-64kbps	2mbps	200mbps	>1gbps
Technology	Analog cellular	Digital cellular	Broadbandwidth/ CDMA/IP Technology	Unified IP and seamless combo of LAN/WAN/WLAN	4G+WWWW
Service	Mobile telephony	Digital voice, Short messaging	Integrated high quality audio, video and data	Dynamic information access, variable devices	Dynamic information access, variable devices with AI capabilities
Multiplexing	FDMA	TDMA/CDMA	CDMA	CDMA	CDMA
Switching	Circuit	Circuit/ circuit for access network and air interface	Packet except for air interface	All packet	All packet
Core Network	PSTN	PSTN	Packet network	Internet	Internet
Handoff	Horizontal	Horizontal	Horizontal	Horizontal & Vertical	Horizontal & Vertical

A characteristic of the second generation mobile communication is that voice signals are converted into digital signals, which are divided into GSM and

CDMA. Using Qualcomm's Code Division Multiple Access (CDMA) method of the U.S., mobile phone manufacturers paid Qualcomm a fee, so each device had a small Qualcomm sticker attached to it. Another characteristic of the second generation is that it started to support data transmission such as text as well as voice as digital communication methods were used. In the second generation, 800 MHz was used initially, and a PCS using a frequency of 1.7 GHz was introduced in 1997. The PCS service was started by Korea Telecom Freetel (now KT) and LG Telecom. The so-called cellular, which uses the 800 MHz band, and the PCS, which uses the 1.7 GHz band, have different characteristics because the frequency bands used are different. In general, since the attenuation increases with distance as the frequency increases, the area that one base station can cover is larger forcellular with a lower frequency than for a PCS. Also, the higher the frequency, the higher the diffraction loss of radio waves. For this reason, although cellular communication performance was superior to the PCS, the PCS was able to provide services at a much lower cost than cellular, and thus secured many users. CDMA technology continued to develop into CDMA2000 and CDMA2000 EV-DO.

Figure 3-3 Characteristics of mobile communication by generation

Generation	1G	2G	3G	4G	5G
Speed	14Kbps	144Kbps	14Mbps	75Mbps	20Gbps
Function	Voice	Voice+Messages	Voice+Data	Data+Movie	Realize
Time	Before 1990	In the 1990s	In the 2000s	In the 2010s	After 2020

KT terminated the 2G service first for inefficient network maintenance cost and frequency use for next-generation services, and SKT and LG Telecom maintained the service after that but ended the service shortly thereafter. Motorola's Startac can be the first thing that comes to mind as a representative mobile phone of the 2G era. Motorola, which introduced the world's first flip-type phone with Micro Tac (a small cover is attached to the button of the phone only to prevent the phone button from being pressed incorrectly during normal movement), released the Startac, which occupied the title of the first foldable phone (the screen and button of the phone are half-folded). Startac gained worldwide popularity for its innovative design, as well as its excellent call sensitivity and completely new attempts in many areas, such as being able to be worn around the waist using a clip.

Figure 3-4 Frequency usage by generation in mobile communication

Generation	Frequency / Wave Length	BandWidth
2G	800MHz(10MHz), 1.8GHz(20MHz)	30MHz
3G	2.1GHz(40MHz)	40MHz
4G	800MHz(50MHz), 900MHz(20MHz), 1.8GHz(90MHz), 2.1GHz(80MHz), 2.6GHz(100MHz)	340MHz
5G	3.5GHz(280MHz), 28GHz(2400MHz)	2680MHz

Figure 3-5 The 3rd generation mobile communication technology

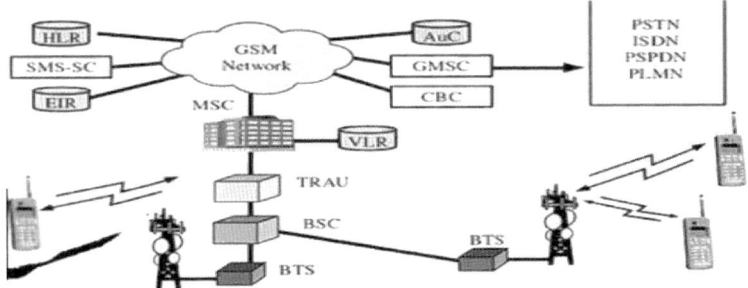

At that time, Nokia, which was leading the mobile phone market together with Motorola, made a unique type of phone called a slide phone, among which the model named Nokia 8110 became as global as the movie "The Matrix" a box office hit worldwide, as it emerged as an important prop in the movie. The device that topped off the end of 2G is the Motorola's RAZR. When

Motorola released the RAZR in 2004, Motorola quickly regained its former reputation. RAZR, with its thin and beautiful design, was used by global celebrities such as movie stars at the time and gained explosive popularity around the world.

In the 2G mobile phone market, many additional functions are added to the device. Away from the days when only voice calls and text messages were possible and only monophonic ringtones sounded, the camera function, mp3 playback, colorful chord ringtones, and games began to enter the phone. Its personality began to change to a smart device with various functions.

Figure 3-6 Mobile terminal connection status

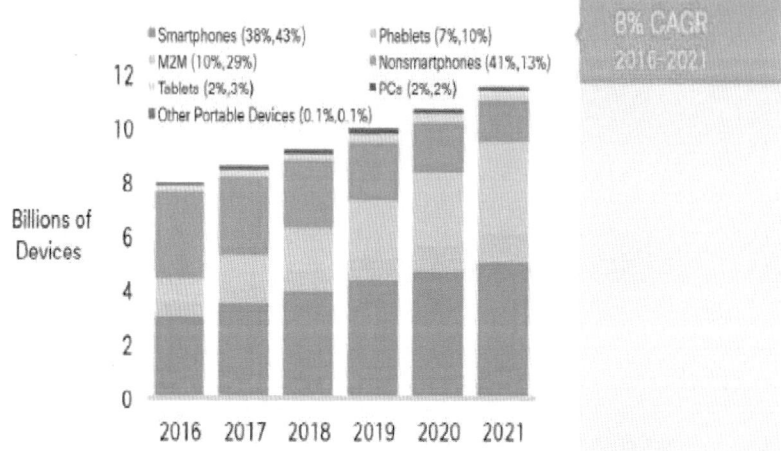

3G supports 2G voice and text transmission with a transmission speed of up to 2Mbps, and multimedia communication functions such as video are added. In Korea, it started in 2002, and SK Telecom, KT, and LG Telecom competed with each other by launching T, Show, and Oz, respectively. It can be said that competition for content on mobile phones began from this time, and competition between telecommunication companies for the preoccupation of consumers with the current smartphone application has begun.

The largest feature of 3G is that it started using a small chip called USIM.

Figure 3-7 Location tracking technology

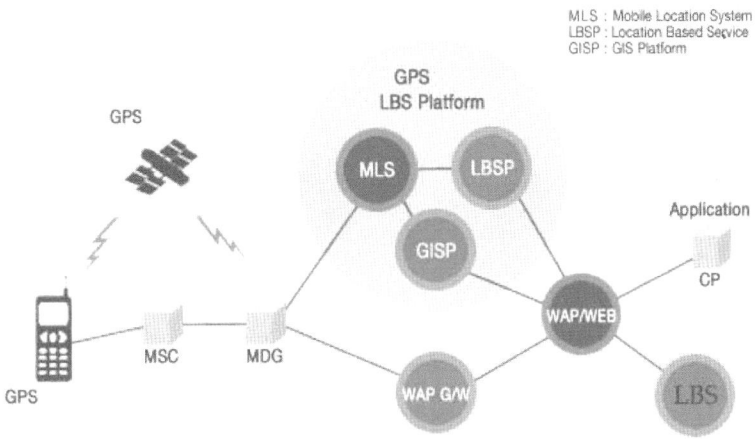

In the past, the user's mobile phone information was stored in the mobile phone device, so to change the device, information such as the line number had to be stored in the new device through the procedure called device change. In 3G, even if you change the SIM, you can use a new device as soon as you move the SIM. Since it has been taken for granted that line information is stored in the device, the emergence of the SIM was quite confusing in the beginning, and as the compensation policies of telecommunication companies competed with each other, it was also difficult to freely change the device, which is the original purpose of the SIM. This phenomenon has improved a lot in the present where 5G is the mainstream, so you can use a telecom operator anywhere in the world by activating a SIM. Therefore, it is now possible to conveniently use a local mobile operator without roaming separately.

The third generation used Wideband Code Division Multiple Access (WCDMA) technology and had a speed of about 1.9 Mbps. Later, with the advent of HSPA technology, the communication speed increased to 5.8 Mbps in the upward direction and 14.4 Mbps in the downward direction, which continued to develop into HSPA+.

Nowadays, smartphones are so widespread that even the elderly in their eighties or elementary school students have them, but if you go back 15 years and remember 3G, you used a SIM in a foldable feature phone.

It is from this 3G that the history of smartphones begins. When smartphones first came out, a lot of people said that there was no reason to use a smartphone because a feature phone with many functions already existed. But now, as almost 90% of people use smartphones, technology has evolved society.

In 3G, Apple's iPhone is a representative product that has opened up the era of smartphones. Some people say that the first smartphone was introduced by IBM in 1992 as Simon, but the true beginning of the smartphone was the advent of Apple's iPhone.

There is no doubt that Apple's iPhone, which provided the standard for touch screens, applications, and the App Store ecosystem, is the representative device of the early smartphone. The iPhone did not get much response when the first model was introduced, but in 2008, the iPhone, which used 3G communication network and used the same App Store as the current iPhone, gained tremendous popularity, resulting in a tremendous development in the smartphone market.

Samsung's Galaxy-S series is a leading 3G smartphone of a Korean company. The Galaxy-S series also surpassed 100 million units in cumulative sales less than three years after the first model Galaxy-S was released. After that, 5G has been commercialized from Galaxy-S1 to Galaxy-S10 and Galaxy-S20. Korea, which has few industrial resources of natural resources, has developed a technology-intensive industry for a long time, as has been the case in the mobile communication market. Samsung smartphones had the highest market share in the global mobile communications market, which led to the development of communication technology.

The same goes for 4G services. Korea's 4G service began in July 2011 when LG

Uplus and SK Telecom competitively launched the service. 4G LTE (Long Term Evolution), launched in Korea, provides download speeds of up to 75 Mbps and upload speeds of up to 37.5 Mbps. When the LTE service was first introduced, it was said that it was not true 4G due to speed problems. Since 4G is a standard with data transfer rates of 1 Gbps in a stationary state and 100 Mbps in high-speed movement, LTE, which provides a much lower speed than this, was not 4G. However, as the International Telecommunication Union (ITU) announced in December 2010 that 4G could be viewed as a technology that was significantly more advanced than the technology commonly referred to as 3G for the term concept of 4G, LTE was included in the category of 4G. Before that, only WiMAX2 (LTE-Advanced and Worldwide Interoperability for Microwave Access) was recognized as 4G. At that time, even if LTE did not deliver the speed of true 4G, the speed of LTE was a leap forward, which was increased by 7 times upward and 5 times downward compared to 3G. In addition, since it is a technology developed from WCDMA, it has the advantage that it is easy to link or improve with the 3G communication network that has been established.

After LTE in 4G, LTE-A was developed. LTE-A is the very LTE-Advanced that the ITU officially recognized as 4G from the beginning. For LTE-A, SK Telecom started commercial service for the first time in the world, and the upload speed was 37.5 Mbps, the same as LTE, but the download speed was significantly increased to 150 Mbps, twice that of LTE. LG UPLUS, which started LTE-A service after that, came out with a differentiation of 100% LTE. Unlike its competitors, it used LTE network for both voice and data. Since SK Telecome used WCDMA network for voice and LTE network only for data, LG UPLUS took this as a marketing point and advocated true LTE. However, LG UPLUS did not have a WCDMA network, soto use voice as its CDMA network, it is necessary to add a CDMA chip in addition to the LTE chip. LG UPLUS adopted a method of processing both voice and data through a LTE network to solve this hassle.

Briefly describing WCDMA, you need to understand the CDMA system before WCDMA. CDMA is a U.S. standard technology used in digital automotive mobile phones using spread-band technology, and users can distinguish them using a pseudo-noise code called a user communication channel PN.

The developed form of it is Wide Band CDMA, which has superior bandwidth efficiency per 1 MHz bandwidth compared to CDMA and is advantageous in terms of subscriber capacity.

Almost all smartphones on the market these days are 5G-enabled models, and 4G is now slowly disappearing from history.

LTE is a technology that uses two frequency bands. In the past, when using only one frequency, there was a problem that the speed decreased when there were more users. However, if you prepare two frequencies at the same time and select one of the two frequencies according to the degree of user crowding, the bottleneck will be reduced and the overall speed will increase. This technology is called Multi-Carrier. In LTE advertisements, traffic control by increasing the number of channels when users are flocking like this has been seen a lot. While LTE is a method in which two frequency bands are prepared and distributed according to the situation, LTE-A is a method to increase speed by combining two roads and using carrier aggregation technology that uses all the bandwidth. In theory, carrier aggregation technology can bundle up to five frequency bands and use up to 100 MHz of bandwidth, but LTE-A serviced in Korea uses two frequency bands together. Now, after passing 4G, 5G is finally commercialized, and the public is receiving mobile communication services through 5G service.

5G mobile communication is a wireless network technology that has been adopted since 2018, and uses Millimeter waves frequencies operating at 26, 28, 38, and 60 GHz. 3GPP of December 2017 is the most common definition of

5G. Some prefer the more stringent ITU IMT-2020 definition, but it only includes a much faster high-frequency band.

Figure 3-8 Comparison of the 4th and the 5th generation mobile

Performance Index	4G	5G
Maximum Transmission Speed	1Gbps	20Gbps
Feeling Speed	10Mbps	100Mbps
Connected Maximum Machines	105/km2	106/km2
Delay Transmission Time	10ms	1ms
High Spped Movement	350km/h	500km/h

5GTF (5G Technology Forum) was established and led by Verizon operator in the U.S. at the end of 2015. KT and SKT of Korea and Docomo of Japan joined the 5GTF. 5GTF announced the trial standard for None Mobility products as the first stage of 5G technology, Verizon started the 5G CPE (Customer Premises Equipment) pilot service in February 2017, and launched the world's first 5G wireless mobile communication for commercialization on December 1, 2018. 5G networks use millimeter waves to realize broadband. Due to the straightness of millimeter waves, collisions and dispersion can occur in the presence of obstacles. However, it is necessary to use millimeter waves or very high frequencies to provide a broadband service above 1G speed, so a method is needed to prevent the millimeter waves from being damaged in the middle. In other words, there is no choice but to build a small network that consists of cells in a short distance

Figure 3-9 Trend of global 5G market size

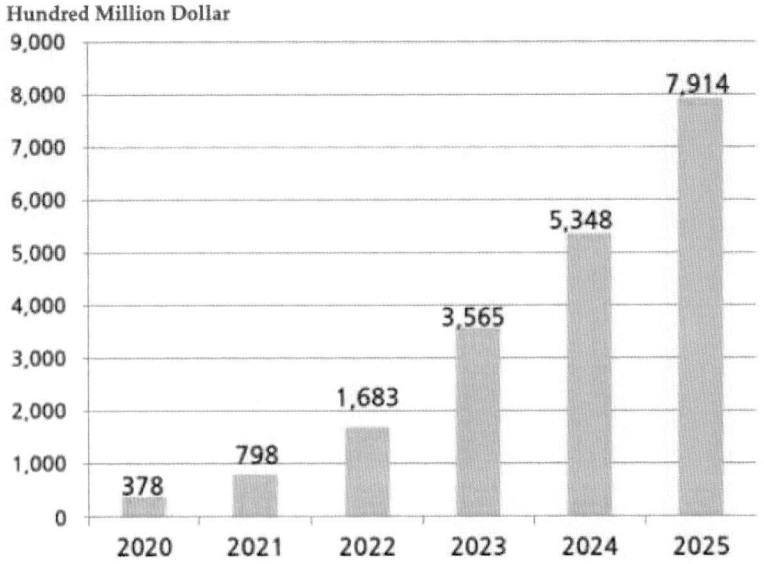

so that the connection to the 5G network is not cut off. To make the cell size smaller, the cells are usually configured in a small size at a distance of about 250-300 m. There are multiple and numerous antennas in these areas, which are called 5G fixed radio services. In other words, in order to provide 5G services with stable quality, it is essential to install more base stations when moving from 3G to 4G.

The 5G mobile network should be constructed based on the existing 4G network infrastructure, but due to the characteristics of the frequency spectrum corresponding to 30 GHz-300 GHz of millimeter waves, it can transmit only a short distance, so a short-range small cell station of about 250-300 m can only be placed in the 5G standard design method. Since the possibility of radio wave blocking by such physical obstacles is always present, there is also a task to solve the technical problem of millimeter waves with strong straightness.

Figure 3-10 Global service change trend through 5G

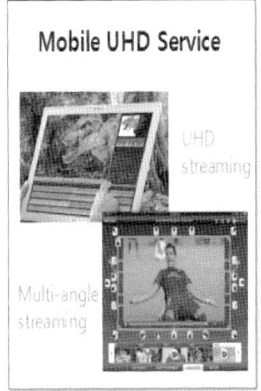

5G can be redefined as millimeter waves. Millimeter waves are extremely directional, propagated in narrow beams, and are usually blocked by solid objects such as walls inside or outside buildings. Because of this, most of the radio applications for Millimeter waves are line-of-sight (electromagnetic waves or sound waves propagated in a straight line). The effective distance for any given application depends on how clear the expected path between the endpoints is, the transmit power applied, and the type and configuration of the antenna used. In general, it is also possible to use technologies such as directional antennas, MIMO, beam forming, and beam steering through the Active Antenna System, which can increase throughput and extend distance.

Directional parabolic antennas used for connection are usually very small, because of the small wavelength involved.

Figure 3-11 Service usage by frequency band

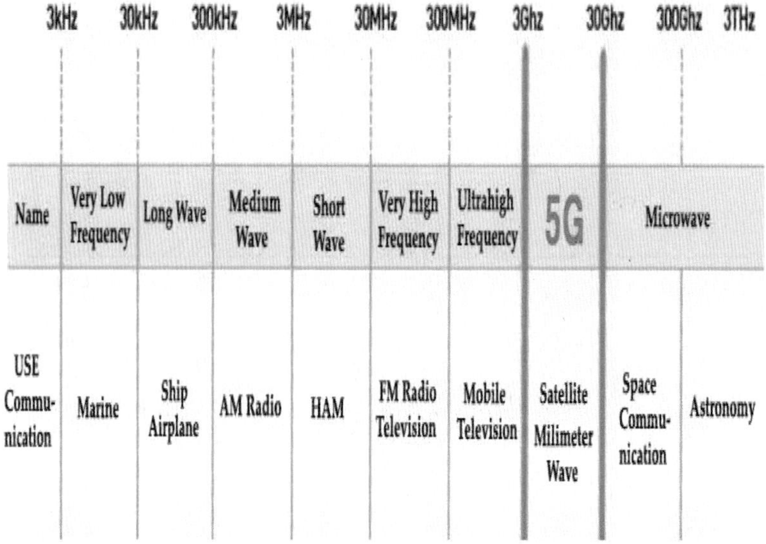

Frequency	3kHz	30kHz	300kHz	3MHz	30MHz	300MHz	3Ghz	30Ghz	300Ghz	3THz
Name	Very Low Frequency	Long Wave	Medium Wave	Short Wave	Very High Frequency	Ultrahigh Frequency	5G		Microwave	
USE	Commu-nication	Marine	Ship Airplane	AM Radio	HAM	FM Radio Television	Mobile Television	Satellite Milimeter Wave	Space Commu-nication	Astronomy

Even at the frequency of ordinary millimeter waves, there is a limit to the fundamental physical properties of the wavelength, such as frequency propagation. At several millimeter wave frequencies, signal attenuation can be addressed with amplification techniques. However, since the 60 GHz band is an oxygen-absorption frequency, it is not easy to respond to attenuation. This is because oxygen in the air is the point in the electromagnetic wave spectrum where radio waves are attenuated. This can be supplemented by deploying multiple nodes with a short distance between nodes, but also has the advantage of improving overall capacity through frequency reuse. Usually, by using a narrow beam spectrum and a directional antenna, it is expected that interference or distortion with other connections on the same frequency nearby can be resolved.

Figure 3-12 Usage by band of electromagnetic waves

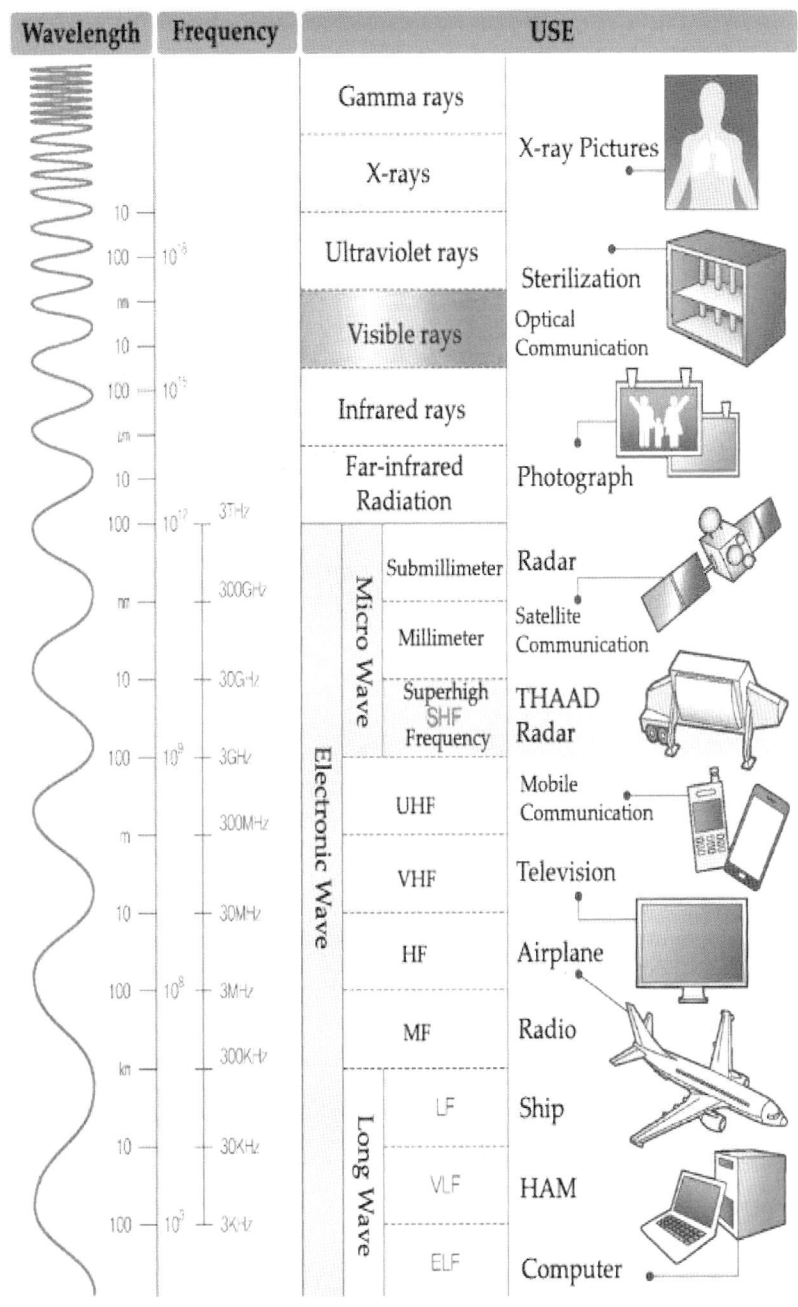

171

Figure 3-13 Changes in frequency usage from 3G to 5G

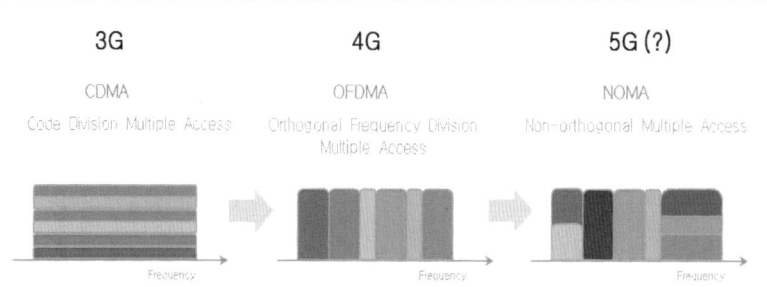

Other millimeter wave bands also exhibit varying degrees of atmospheric attenuation, but most are only slightly affected. In particular, 20~50GHz, 70~90GHz, and 120~160GHz are correct, but when a specific band and an appropriate application field are fused, the limitations of millimeter waves can be overcome and interference or distortion is expected to be reduced.

In addition, the narrow beam spectrum of millimeter waves has limited distances and the interconnection part of the call has advantages in terms of security and communication integrity. However, encryption must be applied to all connected wireless links. Currently, most commercial millimeter waves wireless link products support encryption.

Conventional millimeter waves have been mainly used in fixed wireless communication applications. The two end points of a certain link are fixed points. In the future, the various applications of the mesh technique that binds wireless communication into a network will increase significantly, which will provide maximum flexibility and range of application in any network configuration. In other words, the network becomes flexible. Millimeter waves wireless communication was once a method used for space and terrestrial fixed communication but is now adopted in 5G as an efficient way to solve the network volume problem.

Figure 3-14 5G's main technical features

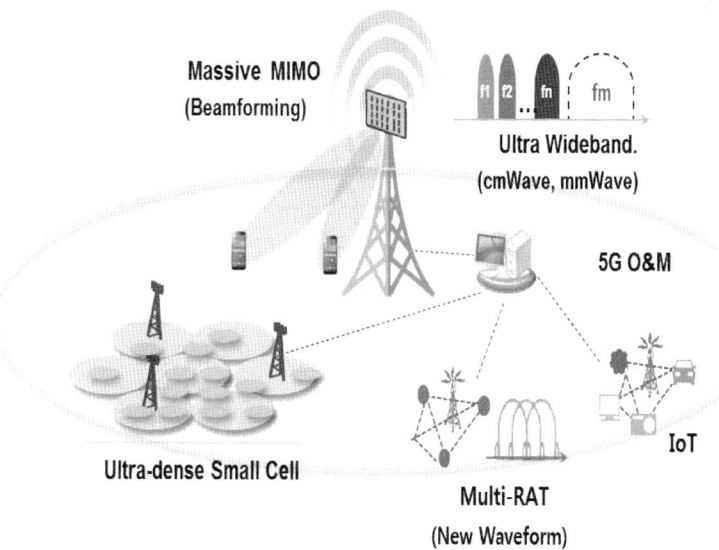

In general, in the case of corporate wireless communication networks, in order to achieve the maximum effect in establishing a wireless network using millimeter waves, it is necessary to upgrade the inside of a building, wiring, and Ethernet switches. However, Millimeter waves will be used more and more because they provide a much larger frequency volume and can provide much higher throughput when needed.

Millimeter waves or Extremely High Frequency (EHF) wavelengths occupy the relatively unused electromagnetic spectrum of 30 GHz to 300 GHz, so application technologies are expected to develop together in the future.

The Internet of Things and 5G have a very close relationship. 5G's Electromagnetic Spectrum can be said to be a highway on which wireless communication operates. Each path can transmit traffic at different rates, and the higher the frequency, the more information it can transmit. It has more throughput than the increasingly congested Wi-Fi band below 6GHz. Therefore, it can have a higher overall carrying capacity.

Figure 3-15 5G technology evolution direction

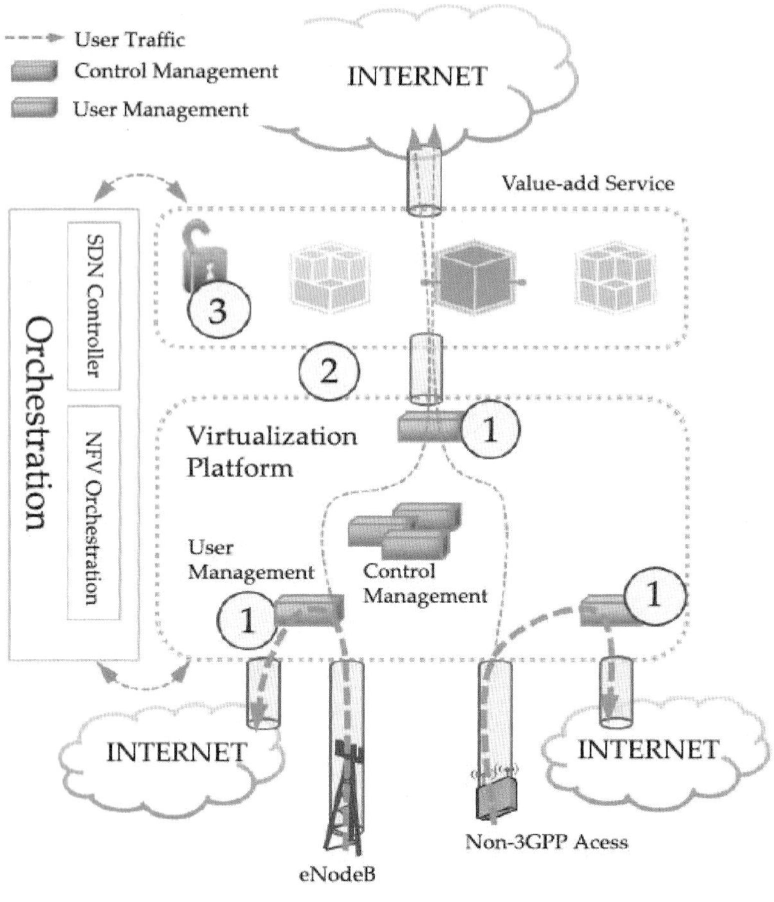

In the future, there are various technological changes in 5G. As shown in ① in [Figure 3-15] above, when designing the transportation infrastructure, it is necessary to minimize the bottleneck section by using a flat network structure that occurs for structural reasons of the infrastructure. Similarly, since the current 4G network with a hierarchical structure has a structure in which traffic is gathered in one upper section and becomes a bottleneck, it must evolve into a flat network structure that can efficiently distribute the explosive data and deliver the traffic. These flat networks are more suitable for services that require short responses because they reduce the time data stays in the network as a result.

As indicated by ② in [Figure 3-15] above, equipment such as toll gates, cameras, and traffic information collection devices installed in the transportation infrastructure and used for various services and overall infrastructure operation are installed and operated integrated with the road. If the environment changes and the equipment has to be replaced, upgraded, or moved to another location, a considerable exchange, upgrade, dismantling, or reinstallation cost is incurred. In the 5G environment, it is expected that various environmental changes will occur, such as the emergence of new network functions and services and changes in the communication paradigm. Accordingly, virtualization of network functions will proceed, which separates only S/W functions from existing H/W and enables quick, flexible, and cost-effective installation, update, removal, and reinstallation of network functions. By modularizing the functions, it will be possible to select and use only the necessary detailed functions within one S/W. Virtualization and modularization of network functions will make cost-effective and flexible use of the overall S/W and detailed functions depending on time, place, and situation according to dynamic demand.

As indicated by ③ in [Figure 3-15], transportation infrastructure equipment and services are generally proposed, installed, and operated by transportation infrastructure managers. Likewise, network functions and services have also been proposed, installed, and operated by network operators. While this operation method has the advantage of being more conservative and security-enhanced, it has become a stumbling block in introducing and supporting innovative services that are rapidly generated by the needs of various industries in the network. However, as network separation and security functions through virtualization are strengthened, the network is gradually opened to third-party service providers, thereby promoting the introduction of new and innovative services, and improving the quality of services at the same time. Therefore, in the era of the Fourth Industrial Revolution, the evolution into an open network is expected.

Millimeter Waves technology, the main technology of 5G, has been expensive and difficult to use easily. This is because it was limited to limited fields such as Radio Astronomy, Microwave Remote Sensing, and Terrestrial Fixed Communications.

Figure 3-16 5G high-capacity multi-antenna technology

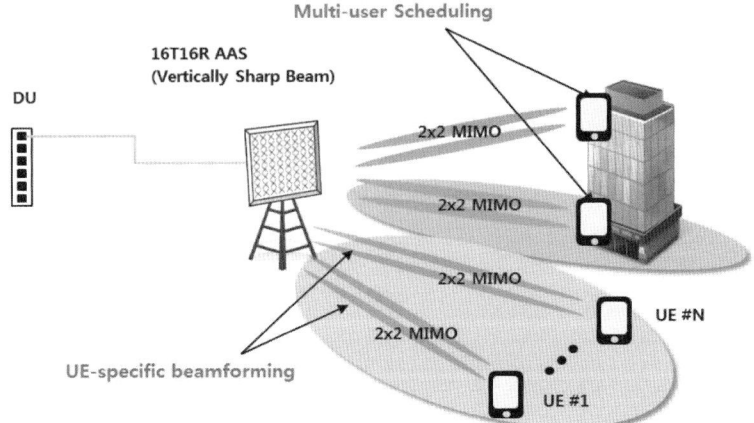

The IEEE wireless personal network standard 802.15.3c, 802.11.ad WIFI standard, and the future 802.11ay standard all use the 60GHz band. Due to the limited object penetration and distance and direction of millimeter wave signals, the field of wireless communication applications has generally been limited to indoor and open office environments where straight waves can be guaranteed, but in the future, general access wireless communication applications using 802.11ad will become common and many existing microwave and Millimeter waves solutions will evolve over time into inexpensive P2P, P2MP and Mesh solutions based on 802.11ad components.

Figure 3-17 Required technology for 5G performance

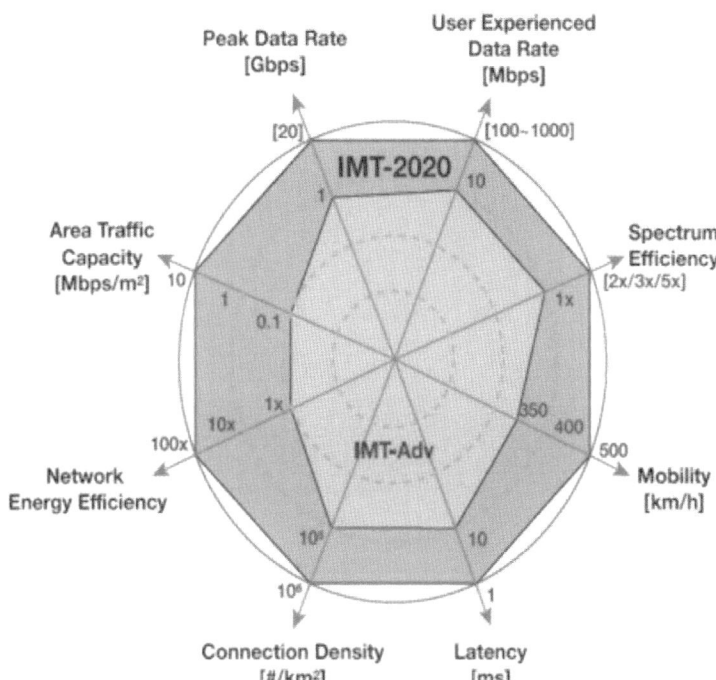

The millimeter waves component is expected to be applied to various IoT solutions in the future. This is because so many IoT solutions are composed of data clusters, which will be suitable for short-range and the wireless communication network mesh methodology.

In conclusion, 5G mobile communication technology will become an essential infrastructure technology to properly implement big data and artificial intelligence, which are the core technologies of the Fourth Industrial Revolution. In other words, it is the same principle that no matter how good food is, you cannot eat it unless you bring it to your mouth. No matter how well artificial intelligence is designed with an algorithm, if the network that brings and distributes big data in the right place at the right time does not support the speed and environment, it is like the proper algorithm cannot be applied.

Figure 3-18 Next-generation network configuration centered on 5G

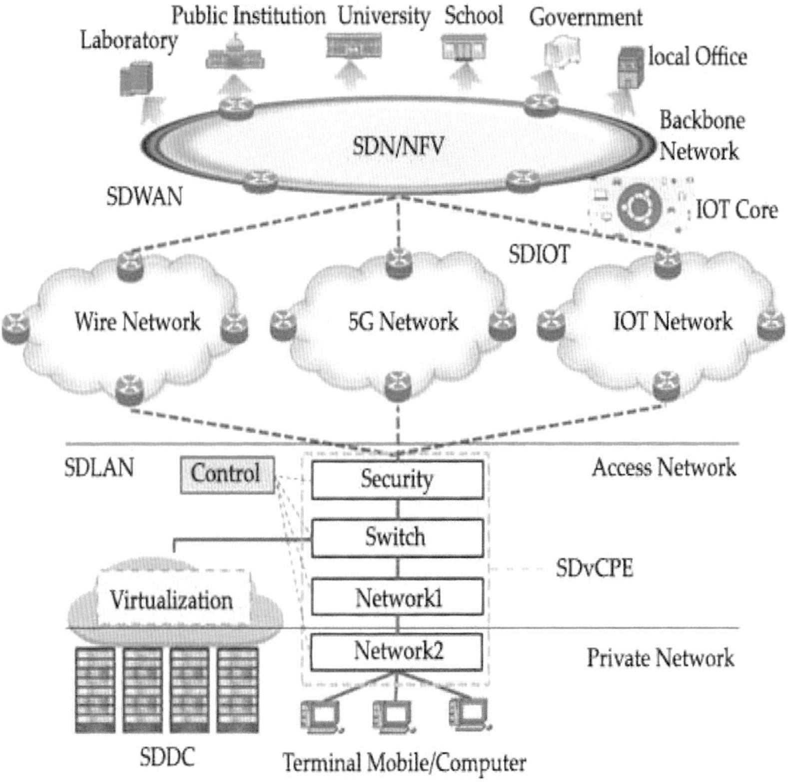

As shown in [Figure 3-18] above, the outline of the next-generation national network, the hyper-connected network, was announced. It is characterized by applying software-based technologies such as software-defined local area network (SDLAN) and software-defined Internet of Things (SDIoT) to the entire network.

In a word, this next-generation network can be referred to as an intelligent hyper-connected network, and mainly includes SDIoT, software-defined data center (SDDC), software-defined long-distance communication network (SDWAN), and network service virtualization (SDvCPE).

Figure 3-19 SD-IOT for Next-generation network hyper connection

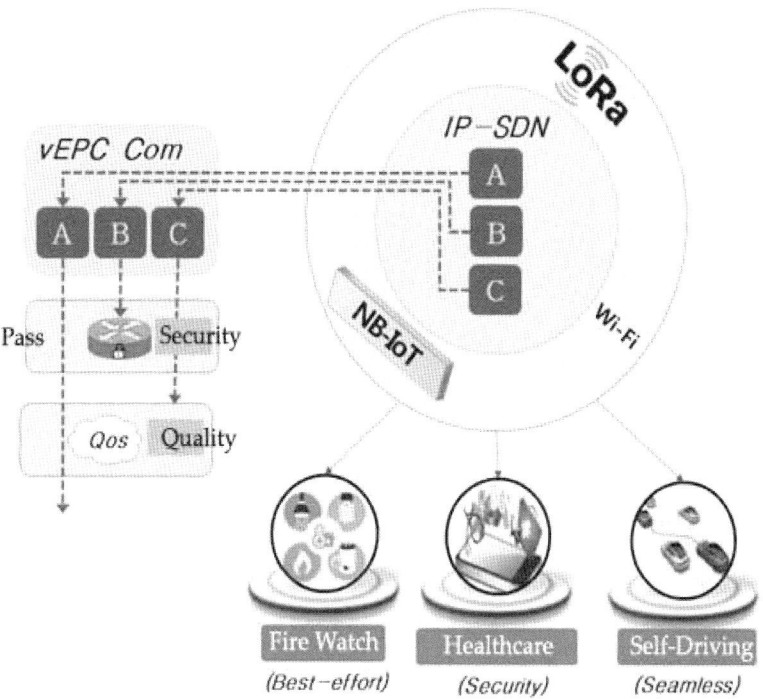

The mobile communication technology examined as described above has developed in connection with the use of Internet of Things (IoT) services and, furthermore, big data, artificial intelligence, and the Internet of All Things, as smartphones are used as mobile communication terminals from a form that simply played the role of a phone while moving..

In particular, 5G can provide a key role in IoT services, and it is mainly provided as a location-based service in our real life. The most well-known is car navigation, and the expanded form applies to autonomous vehicles and autonomous flying drones. This is because a proper Internet of Everything service becomes possible when a large amount of data moves quickly in real time and a managed environment is established. Representative examples of sensor data utilization through such a network

Figure 3-20 Internet of Things service application main screen

are solutions that allow users to identify or track the location of themselves or various objects through their terminals.

Location-based service using a Bluetooth frequency, a location-based service using the Earth's magnetic field sensor of a smartphone, and a location-based service using a Wi-Fi signal are frequently emerging these days.

According to my current research, location-based services using short-distance mobile communication technology have successfully settled in the market in the early stages of location-based services using frequencies of NFC and RFID, and in the future, location-based services using cloud computing and various contactless communications will be available and expected to be popular.

In particular, the Internet of Things (IoT) is the field that I have most experienced while working in related fields for 20 years. It means that the three main components, humans, things, and services, cooperate in a distributed environment without human intervention to form an intelligent relationship. In other words, if a smartphone connects people to people, the Internet of Things connects people and all things to exchange information.

Technologies required for this Internet of Things include Sensor Networking technology, which serves as a channel for communication between objects and for acquiring information from the surrounding environment. In addition, wired and wireless communication and network infrastructure are required, which means all wired and wireless networks that can connect services between people and people, people and things, and things and things. An interface technology is also required, which can be defined as a technology to provide Internet of Things services to people.

Smart cars, smart homes, and wearable devices are representative IoT services that can be seen around us. There are also diapers, syringes, and medicine bottles with the Internet of Things (IoT) functions that are commonly seen these days.

Figure 3-21 The concept of IoT service

The IoT also introduced the concept of eye-to-eye communication. It is a kind of line-of-sight communication concept that allows you to select a person want to talk to on the smartphone screen and send a call or message without knowing the other person's phone number. In conclusion, the development of mobile communication technology is connected to the Internet of Things, the Internet of Everything, big data, and artificial intelligence.

3.2 Internet of Things Business

IoT technology is deeply related to global energy utilization. Low-power technology is the most popular technology among IoT technologies. The ultimate goal is to create maximum energy efficiency through minimum electricity consumption. For example, in the case of Bluetooth technology, it was used only for simple earphones or short-distance communication until low-power technology was introduced. However, with the introduction of low-power technology from Bluetooth 4.0, it has established itself as a barometer of IoT technology by securing a two-year operating period through coin batteries. In the case of a beacon, a coin battery the size of a small coin can serve as a sensor for two years, so it is currently being used in many IoT-related businesses.

In other words, the beginning of IoT technology can be said to have started in terms of energy utilization. From an energy perspective, electricity costs are accelerating worldwide due to the depletion of petroleum resources, aging and shutdown of nuclear power plants, increased demand for electricity in emerging countries, and increased energy consumption. At the national level, the lack of electricity reserve ratio has emerged as an important problem, and problems such as blackouts, cyclic blackouts, and electricity rate hikes are pointed out, but fundamental measures have not been taken. In most enterprises, factories, and buildings, infrastructure, and energy costs account for a large portion, but in most places, the relationship between energy costs and business cannot be comprehensively assessed and the rising energy cost expenditures cannot be managed. Nowadays, the Internet of Things (IoT) is widely used to reduce energy.

Figure 3-22 The barometer beacon of the Internet of Things

Based on the Fourth Industrial Revolution technology, the method of reducing energy costs can be summarized as follows.

First, energy bills can be dramatically reduced if energy consumption is effectively managed. It is important to efficiently manage the areas with a high proportion of energy use.

Second, diversifying energy sources can help reduce costs.

There are different ways to reduce energy costs depending on the type of energy used, such as electricity, water, or gas. Sometimes changing the type of energy used can help reduce energy costs.

Third, managing energy usage time can also be a way to reduce energy costs. Electricity rates vary widely depending on usage time. One way to reduce energy costs is to be aware of the hourly electricity rate system and real-time electricity rates and to change the electricity usage pattern of the workplace.

Nowadays, many companies provide integrated energy optimization systems for energy cost management using IoT technology.

Existing energy cost management has been done by reducing energy consumption. However, it is difficult to reduce costs just by reducing energy consumption itself, and it also conflicts with the efficient operation of the company. The Energy Optimization System (EOS) provided by IT companies these days provides an energy management platform that monitors the company's energy usage in real time and optimizes usage patterns through self-learning to save energy and minimize costs and risks. This is an example of the energy management area being combined with IoT technology.

These days, the Energy Optimization System built with IoT technology has the following characteristics. Overall, based on data collected through real-time energy usage monitoring, we realize optimal energy use management and a comfortable environment through usage and cost prediction, energy tracking, and optimal and integrated operation algorithms through system tracking. All these functions are serviced based on the cloud server, so it is easy to manage energy categories and is optimized to reduce facility and service operating costs.

Internet of Things-based energy consumption measurement, environmental measurement, and facility control technologies strengthen the company's energy management competitiveness by reducing installation and operation costs and reduce the burden of system introduction by minimizing installation time and process. The building information is modeled, and the building information system linkage technology pursues the unification and efficiency of construction and operation data by making building information a database during the design and construction stages. In addition, these days, energy management technology is being improved through big data analysis in the energy field.

The characteristics of the Energy Optimization System to which the Internet of Things is applied can be summarized as follows.

First, the energy usage status informs the detailed and integrated energy usage by area, use, and facility in real-time through energy monitoring and environmental measurement.

Second, energy usage information prediction or analysis predicts future energy consumption based on the measured usage information and analyzes savings points. In addition, it enables efficient facility management by diagnosing performance degradation or failure through energy consumption analysis of facilities.

Third, security and disaster prevention strengthen the security of a building by identifying the number of occupants and locations by area and provide data that helps save lives in preparation for disaster situations. In addition, by analyzing excessive energy consumption areas and diagnosing abnormal consumption patterns, it is possible to prepare in advance for various disasters such as short circuits and fires.

Fourth, system notification improves customer convenience in system management by arranging essential matters that managers need to know, such as abnormal situations in the energy management system.

Fifth, the energy report provides an integrated report that summarizes essential information customers need to know about energy use by period.

As discussed above, energy optimization methods in modern times show a tendency to develop mainly in connection with information technology and IoT solutions. In conclusion, it is also connected to the solution of carbon neutrality, a global issue. Another important issue for IoT business is the battery problem. All devices in the world cannot operate without power. Likewise, electronic sensors used in the Internet of Things also require batteries. Therefore, the most important part in the sensor design of electronic circuits is how to efficiently use power in each module and increase the efficiency always arises as a problem. In the location-based service using

Bluetooth's low power technology, which I am researching, battery efficiency and lifespan are recognized as the most important key words of the service. I have studied various IoT platform technologies using low energy technology, and representative ones are RFID, Beacon, ZigBee, and WIFI. Among them, a beacon using a low-power module is the most popular these days and has many applications in the future. In particular, in terms of energy efficiency, it is an example to install a beacon in a specific place, acquire data about that location, and use them as big data for an energy optimization solution.

One of the IoT solutions I developed was a solution that could identify or manage the location of users or various energy-efficient objects through terminals, i.e., smartphones.

The most emerging these days are location-based services using Bluetooth frequency, one of the mobile communication technologies, location-based services using smartphones, and location-based services using Wi-Fi signals. According to my research, location-based services using NFC and RFID frequencies were successfully established in the market in the early stages of location-based services using short-distance mobile communication technology, and location-based services using cloud computing and various contactless communications are expected to be in the spotlight in the future.

For example, power device management or energy efficiency service can be provided through sensor communication through an object located in the air. I will explain this in more detail through my patent.

The title of the invention is a location and link information service (Patent 3) using a beacon that is located or moving in the air.

The present invention is based on information and communication engineering, and the frequency of Bluetooth is 2400-2483.5 MHz, which can be used to implement various personalized services. It describes a method of constructing a system that provides various personal services through smart devices within the range of the frequency from the beacon by allowing them to stay or move in the air through drones, kites, or balloons, instead of attaching or fixing the beacon's access point to the ground.

Taking the drawing as an example to describe in detail, beacons floating in the air continuously broadcast a Bluetooth signal. The position of the beacon floating in the air has a basic primary position value through the GPS value and is corrected to a secondary position value through a smart device with the application of the smart device installed on the ground. Here, as in 106 and 107, the smart device serving as the AP Manager on the ground and the smart device receiving the service may or may not be the same. In other words, some smart devices on the ground perform the role of AP Managers, but if the real-time correction value according to the location falls within the error range, the AP Manager mode is automatically switched to the User mode. That is, from the user's smart device perspective, the first GPS map location value is received through a flying beacon floating in the air, and the second correction value is determined through the smartphone secondarily.

The correction method is to correct the map value, the distance value of the smartphone, and the signal strength measurement value with the positioning algorithm, and the error can be corrected within 1M.

That is, a beacon floating in the air can be fixed or moved in real time. It receives the primary position value as a GPS value and specifies the position range of the flying beacon through a smart device that receives the beacon frequency and specifies the location of the user's smart device.

A beacon floating in the air continuously broadcasts Bluetooth Wavelength, and when a smart device is located within that range, it receives various information such as Tx-power, Major, Minor, and Mac Address like 204. This is calculated as the unique position value of the beacon, and it plays a role in correcting the position value by matching it with the GPS map through the GPS module built into the existing smartphone. The corrected location data is sent to the Contents Management Server, which is transmitted through the Internet network. The corrected location value sent to the server in this way gets the message ID of the location, which has a unique message ID value for each user. This unique message ID is matched with each smartphone user ID, and it is possible to provide a specific unique message to a specific user in a specific location along the movement path of the matched ID. That is, like 201, this message becomes a location-based service of the user and a specific information-providing service that can be received only at that specific location.

The 306 AP Manager is physically included in the smart device and controls the activation and deactivation of the beacon floating in the air and the battery status by software. After the position and status values are corrected, the process daemon is killed. It means a module that continuously turns on and off the process, and it is controlled through communication with the server, which can be managed using the Internet network. The Bluetooth signal coming into the user's smartphone is divided into a location service module of 304 and an information provision service module of 305, which can be managed through the integrated management system of No. 310.

The values returned from each module provide the location and information provision service to users within the exact range where the specific flying beacon is located in a specific location.

When the flying beacon of 400 in Drawing 4 is in Position1, x1, y1, and z1 operate at the position closest to User Position1. However, as shown in 401, when the flying beacon is in Position2, x1, y1, and z1 are the same, but it is closest to User Position2 and matches it. That is, the coordinate value of the flying beacon has a three-dimensional position value accompanying the user's position. GPS takes the location value on the map through the absolute location of the flying beacon and the user's smartphone, and the flying beacon and the user's smartphone take each other's three-dimensional location value based on the distance between them. This means that matching occurs only when the absolute value of the user's smartphone is within the absolute value of the position value of the flying beacon captured by GPS.

The location of the user's smartphone can be specified on the map within the range of the flying beacon through the flying beacon. The user's smartphone, whose location is specified on the map of the flying beacon in this way, can provide both the location-based service and the information provision service to the user through the integrated management system of 410, and the accuracy can be implemented within 1 meter.

Instead of measuring the distance between the user's smartphone and the person on the ground with the location value of the flying beacon floating in the air, the range of the flying beacon is mapped when the flying beacon and the user's smartphone are included as an intersection within the GPS range and it is implemented in a way that inversely corrects the user's smartphone's response within that range. This is internally a method in which GPS, flying beacons, and the user's smartphone form a triangle to extract the closest mathematically value, which is equivalent to the theory that the intersection of lines descending vertically from a certain vertex is located at the exact center of the equilateral triangle. That is, a line starting from three different points represents the size of the map, and the intersection point represents the location of the user's smartphone. In detail, each vertex of the equilateral triangle is divided into GPS position value, flying beacon position value, and user's smartphone position value. This is because each value is the intersection.

Drawing 5 is showing a service flow of a flying beacon.

A Bluetooth signal from a beacon placed in the air, such as in the 501, is continuously broadcast periodically. As in 502, the broadcast signal is given the position value of the GPS primarily. The given location value identifies whether the location of the user's smartphone is included in the range of the flying beacon through Inspection. The location on the user's smartphone identified in this way is specified through the GPS location value and the location value of the flying beacon, and more accurate location of the user or information based on that location is provided to the smartphone user.

503 represents the Contents Management Server providing the information provision service. Each message ID is verified for the information corresponding to the location through map pairing, and this message validates again whether the user is authenticated and correctly located. All these processes are controlled by Flag values, and Flag Result and Flag Transfer of 505 show how these Flag values are authenticated and exchanged. As in 506, the verified message enables the user's smartphone to receive information and location services that match the location.

Drawing 6 is showing a service configuration diagram of a flying beacon.

When a smartphone user of 601 enters position 1 located within the signal range of the flying beacon, the user can receive location-based information provision service within that range. If the user's position is moved to Position2, the user's position is also located in Position2 and is included in the range of Position2 of the flying beacon. In this way, even if the user goes to Position3 or Position4the first mapping is done through the GPS within that range of the flight beacon always floating in the air, and the range of the signal is converted to the map by the flying beacon. The area converted into this map becomes the same as if the user exists on the map of a specific space, and the location of the user's smartphone located in it is identified using the beacon placed in a specific place in a specific indoor space, and location-based service is provided through it. If a user enters an indoor space that disappears within the range of GPS, it can be replaced with a case where a flying beacon is floating indoors after first mapping with the final GPS value. That is, just as the user's location is determined by mapping the area that receives the signal of the beacon floating in the air outdoors, the final GPS value is used as the primary value even when the user enters the room from the outdoors, and when the second correction value, the flying beacon, enters a room, the room can also be converted into a map of a flying beacon.

In other words, the core of the present invention is to provide a location-based service to users within the corresponding range on a map by floating and moving a beacon, which was fixed in a specific space and used only as an identification value of a specific fixed connection point.

In summary, as described above, the present invention is not a location providing service that installs a beacon at a fixed location in a specific space, obtains a fixed value, and calculates a location within that range through it, but uses a device such as a drone, a kite, or a balloon that can be located in the air for the beacon to stay or move in the air, first maps the area where the signal arrives through GPS, and secondarily maps the designated space through the flying beacon installed in the air. This mapped space forms the intersection of the vertices of an equilateral triangle by using the user's smartphone as the third access point. The intersection points on the map of the space formed in this way is obtained through the application installed on the user's smartphone, and the location becomes the point where the user's smartphone is located in the first specified space.

The user's smartphone also functions as a hardware management function of the access point of the flying beacon, and the process is activated when the user's location is within the frequency reach of the flying beacon. After a certain period, the data is stored in the DB, and the user's smartphone again operates in pure application user mode.

What is necessary to practically apply the present invention is to configure the above detailed invention process in software and then hang the beacon on a drone, kite, or balloon to position it in the air. In other words, the existing location service using a beacon simply installs a beacon in a specific space and maps the map of the space with information such as the signal strength of the beacon to provide the location service to the user's smartphone entering the space. A key advantage of the present invention is that the flying beacon can provide a location area recognition service while moving to multiple areas with just one beacon.

In other words, the flying beacon does not provide a fixed access point in space but converts the space covered by the frequency domain into an area that can provide a single location service. It has the advantage of being able to expand the scope of the service to an infinite space.

The above is the main content of the present invention, and the flying beacon places a beacon in a specific space and the air, thereby converting all the areas within the frequency range into a Map and providing location services for all people and objects entering the frequency area. It is also meaningful in that it can transform an infinite space into an area that can provide location services by moving a beacon floating in the air.

The following is a detailed drawing of the Flying Beacon patent, which is an extension of the IoT-based location-based service.

Drawing 1 (Patent 3)

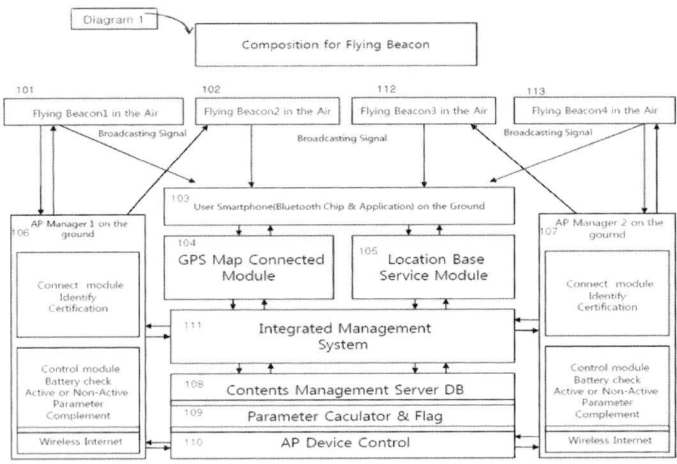

Drawing 2 (Patent 3)

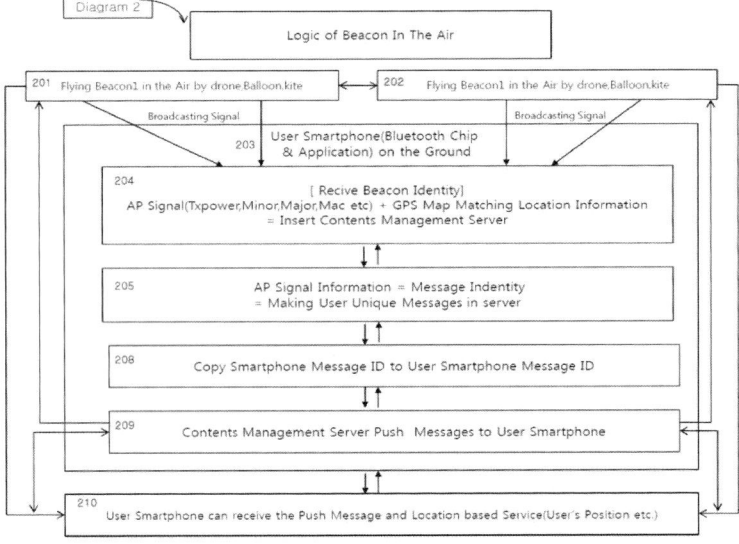

Drawing 3 (Patent 3)

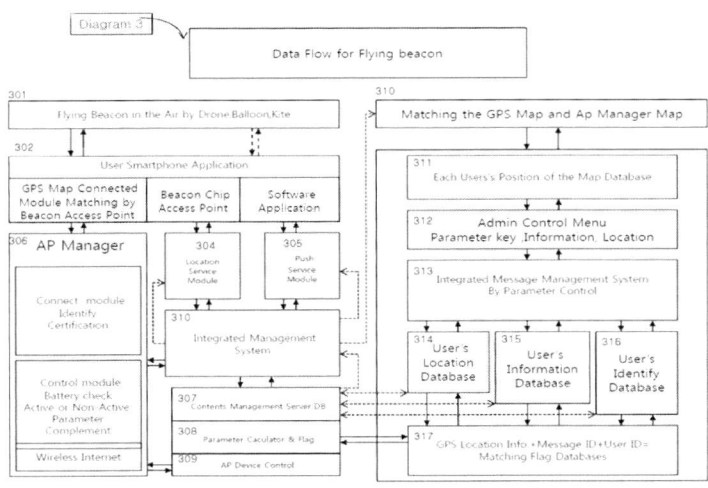

Drawing 4 (Patent 3)

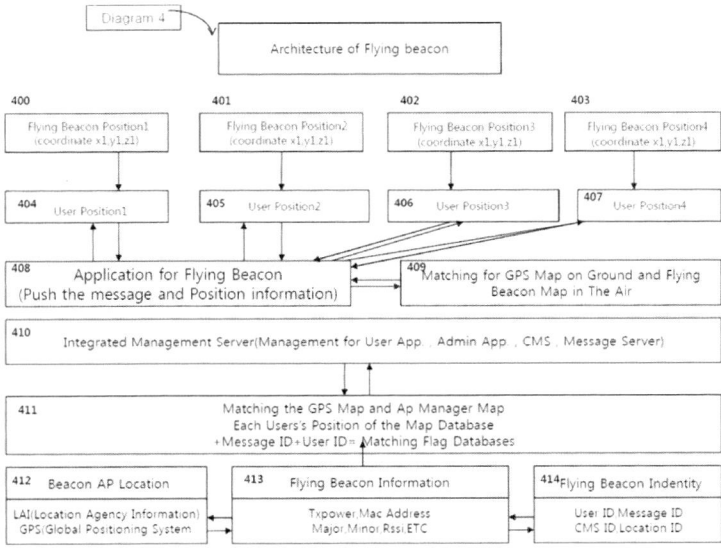

Drawing 5 (Patent 3)

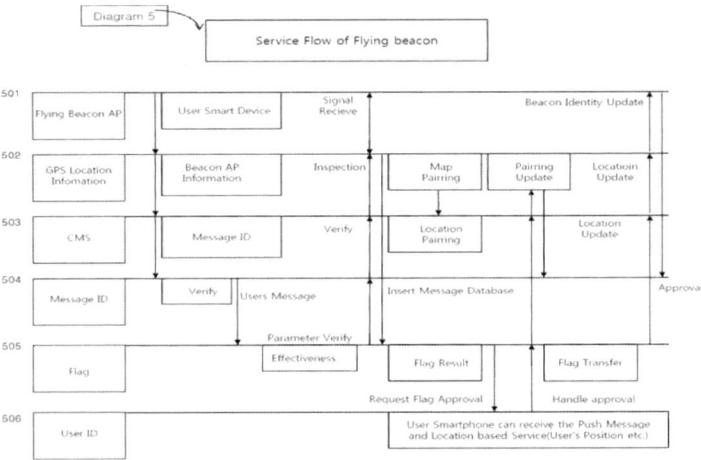

Drawing 6 (Patent 3)

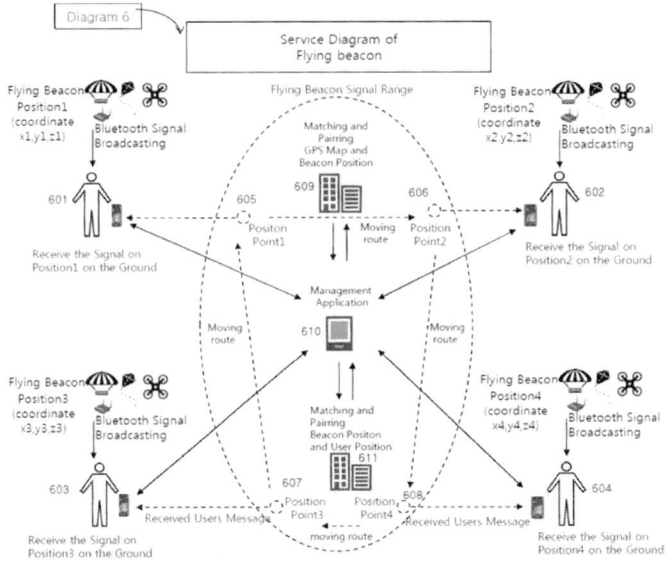

Michael Porter of the United States said that the first wave of the 1960s and 1970s, the era of automation, and the 1980s and 1990s, the second wave that can be accessed and connected anywhere cheaply due to the rise of the Internet, have passed, and today, it has completely entered the era of the Third Wave, where IT has become a core of the product itself. In the era of the third wave, IT technology has become the core technology of products as the function and performance of the product itself have been dramatically improved through the connectivity of sensor => processor => software => product.

Figure 3-23 Changing the size of the IoT business

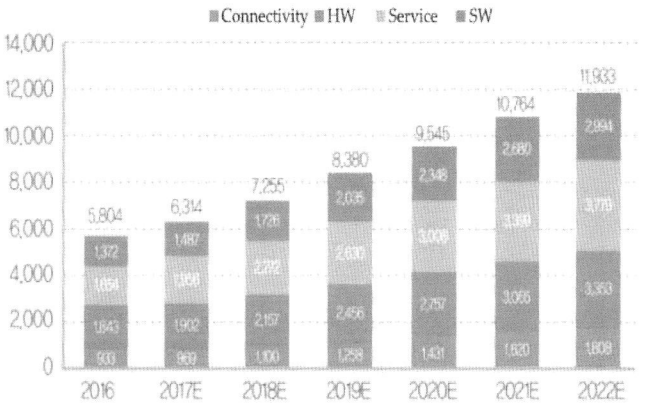

In the present era, where the Third Industrial Revolution and the Fourth Industrial Revolution exist at the intersection, the functions of smart and connected products are increasing, changing the competitive structure within the industry, and making the boundaries between industries unclear. In this industry trend, the Internet of Things (IoT) expands industry boundaries and changes existing businesses. A company that simply produced agricultural machinery called cultivators has developed into a company with a comprehensive agricultural machinery system that monitors and controls data and agricultural machinery through smart cultivators and Smart and

Connected cultivators. It shows the evolutionary process of changing into a farm management system by linking the weather information system, agricultural machinery system, irrigation system, and sowing optimization system into one. A manufacturer that simply manufactures cultivators is expanding into a farm management system business through the Internet of Things. This is consistent with the platform business, which is the direction of intensive change in the Fourth Industrial Revolution.

Figure 3-24 The concept of Internet of Things business

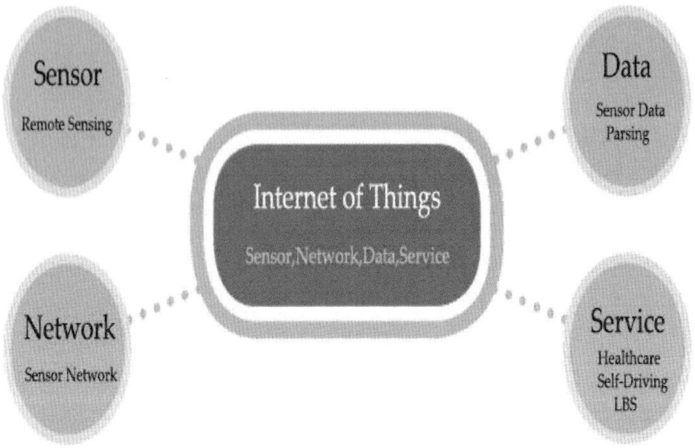

In the era to come, a company that develops and sells products can develop into a company that makes a management system through an IoT product. Taking the home appliance manufacturer as an example, it will produce smarter and connected products from simple home appliances, and it will develop into a business that provides a system for monitoring and controlling these smart home appliances. Ultimately, the business may be upgraded to managing the entire house through a smart home system. If developed further, it could become a smart city builder. As the Internet of Things (IoT)

era spreads, the opportunities for companies to change from existing businesses to new ones are expanding.

For example, IBM's Watson IoT is a representative data analysis platform that analyzes data acquired through IoT devices based on artificial intelligence. IBM provides Watson IoT Platform to operators who have big data or need data analysis, and operators can provide IoT services using Watson IoT Platform.

Figure 3-25 IBM Watson Internet of Things Platform

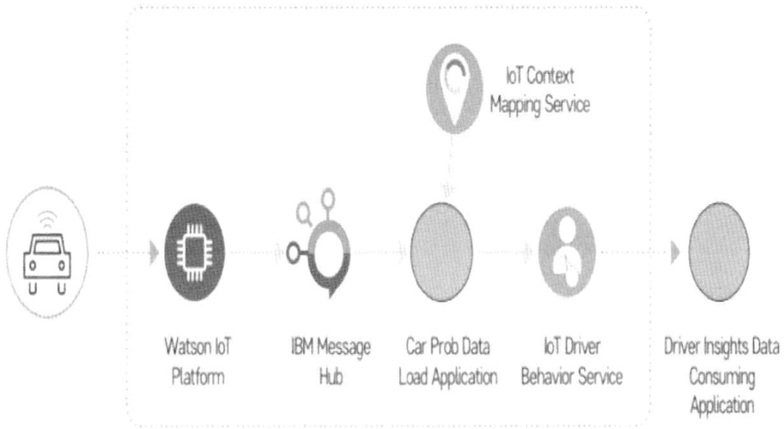

Watson IoT started with data analysis in the medical industry and is being applied to various industries such as machinery, automobiles, logistics, security, finance, healthcare, and robot applications.

In other words, the Internet of Things plays a role in opening opportunities for companies to do platform business.

In general, IoT platforms are classified into four categories: device platform, network platform, data analysis platform, and service platform.

A device platform is a hardware resource provided by a device and a platform that uses these hardware resources, and includes an operating system (OS), open-source hardware including sensors and software, sensors and actuators that are interlocked with hardware, and a network platform is a device-to-device connection platform that defines the IoT communication protocol that supports various standards and non-standards.

The data analysis platform is a platform that collects, stores, and analyzes data obtained from various devices, and the service platform is a platform that supports the easy creation and execution of various application services, and implements and distributes applications that support the distribution of IoT services. For example, in major advanced countries, the environment for the full-scale spread of 5G is being created along with the construction of 5G networks. First, the 5G communication network is expected to make a decisive contribution to the spread of IoT services due to its super-fast speed. It is easy to implement ultra-high-definition (4K) images or VR and AR contents because it is possible to transmit and receive large amounts of data at a data transfer rate of up to 20GB per second, which is 20 times faster than 4G.

Figure 3-26 IoT Platform and 5G

5G has a response speed of less than 0.001 seconds, which is 10 times faster than 4G, making it possible to stably implement remote services such as autonomous driving and remote control, where real-time response speed is important.

Second, the characteristic of hyper-connectivity is realized. Since simultaneous access to more than 1 million devices per square kilometer, it is suitable for implementing IoT services that require real-time data transmission and reception with multiple devices.

Third, the characteristic of the hyper era is established. Not only Korea, but also the United States and China have allocated or plan to allocate 5G frequencies, and plan to provide commercial 5G services by mid-2020 at the latest. For reference, in the U.S., after Verizon conducted a 5G trial service in 2017, AT&T and T-Mobile also plan to start a 5G commercial service in 2020. In Korea, 5G frequency allocation was completed in June 2018, and since KT demonstrated the 5G pilot service at the Pyeong-Chang Olympics in February, the three telecommunication companies have been investing in 5G since 2019 and have been providing 5G services in major cities since March 2019.

In other words, the Internet of Things business will become a barometer of the Fourth Industrial Revolution that realizes ultra-high speed, hyper-connectivity, and the hyper era.

3.3 Big Data Production and Technology

The world today is a world of data. Just as trees in the Amazon jungle produce oxygen, people now live in data, locate in data, and produce data.

When you think about the house where you live your daily life, household appliances generate data through the remote control and operate using it. They are designed to be improved to a better environment according to the operating time, location, and environment. In the space where we live, location information is recorded minute by minute through satellites or various radio base stations, and more accurate location is being identified, which is also done through big data.

Google has been collecting personal location information for a long time and has been using it for better quality services. However, in recent years, such location data is recognized as personal information and is controlled and managed by the relevant laws and regulations. Everything is data. In other words, it is not unreasonable to think that modern human life begins with data and ends with data. Like the concept of big data described above, a huge amount of data can be called big data, as well as raw materials that can process data and make it meaningful and useful, that is, oxygen that makes up the air can be defined as big data.

Let's see what meaningful and useful data will be. Companies typically use big data to predict customer needs in advance. They are building predictive models for the development of new products and services by classifying key attributes of previous and current products and services and modeling the relationship between these attributes and the commercial success of those products and services.

Figure 3-27 The principle of AlphaGo using big data

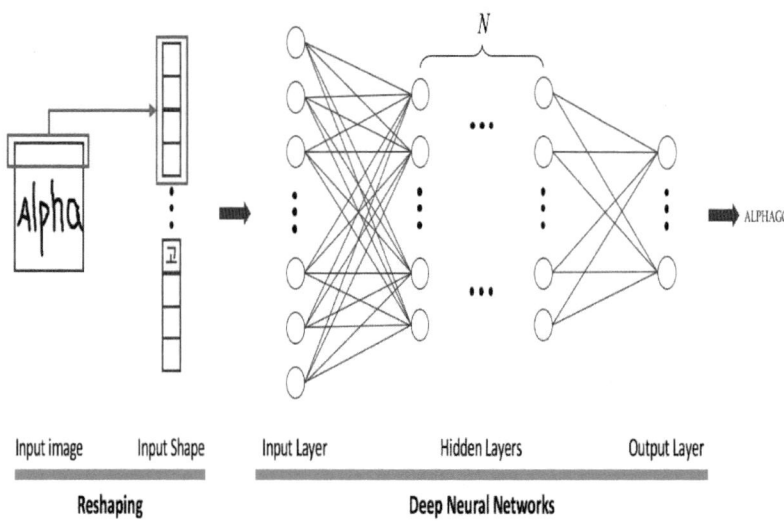

In particular, online-based companies such as Facebook, Google, and Twitter, and information and communication-based companies such as Samsung Electronics, Sony, and Ericsson plan, produce and release new products using data and analysis results collected from the test market and initial store launches.

In other words, predictive maintenance is a factor that can predict equipment failure. In addition to structured data such as equipment production year, manufacturer, and equipment model, it can be deeply hidden in unstructured data including millions of log entries, sensor data, error messages, and engine temperature.

By analyzing the indicators of potential problems before they happen, companies can make the most cost-effective maintenance while maximizing component and equipment uptime.

These days, the market is moving in a form that places great importance on customer experience.

Figure 3-28 VR Glass to improve user experience

It is necessary to analyze the customer experience from a clearer perspective than ever. By using big data, it is possible to improve the interaction environment and maximize value by collecting data from various sources such as social networking activity records, web visit records, and call logs. In addition, by providing customized services, it is possible to reduce customer churn and proactively respond to business-related issues.

Machine learning is a hot topic these days due to AlphaGo, artificial intelligence that won the game of Go against Sedol Lee. One of the factors in the popularity of artificial intelligence technology is data, especially big data. We can now teach machines instead of programming them. This is because there is big data available to train machine learning models.

Figure 3-29 Artificial intelligence implementation process

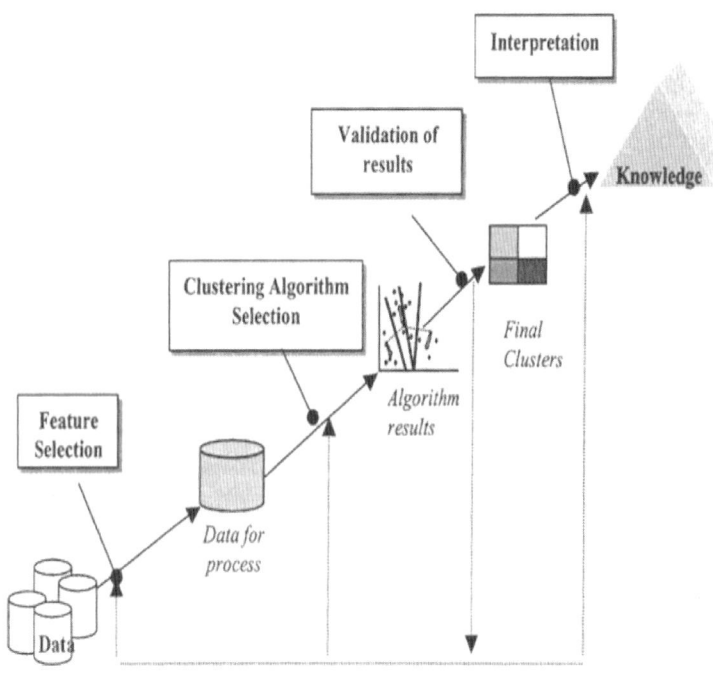

Operational efficiency may not always be an important factor in AI technology, but it is clear that big data has the greatest impact. By using big data, it is possible to reduce the occurrence of problems and predict future requirements in advance by analyzing and evaluating various factors such as the production process for a certain result, customer feedback, and profit. It can also be used to effectively make decisions about current market demands. In other words, Big Data can study the interdependence between humans, institutions, companies, and processes and find new ways to utilize the analysis information obtained through this study, which is artificial intelligence. A to Z of business operations leads to data, just as effectively establishing financial and planning-related decisions using data analysis information and providing new products and services by examining market trends and customer requirements. A slight application of the phrase "All roads lead to Rome." Can create the sentence "All business operations lead data." As such, it is difficult to create a first-class company these days by excluding data and big data from corporate operations.

Figure 3-30 Qualcomm's Internet of Things Big Data Platform

Let's look at an example of using data in the past.

In the 2008 U.S. Presidential Election, U.S. Presidential candidate Barack Obama developed a "voter-tailored election strategy" by securing and analyzing various types of voter databases. At that time, the Obama camp went beyond classifying voters based on basic personal information such as race, religion, age, household type, and consumption level, and used phone calls, individual visits, or social media to determine voter preferences, such as whether they voted in the past, magazines they subscribe to, and drinks they drink. The collected data was sent to the Obama camp headquarters, and with the help of the VoteBuilder system, which integrated and managed the voter database online, voter propensity analysis, undecided voter selection, and voting prediction for voters were performed. By creating a voter map based on such big data and developing a campaign tailored to voters, the Obama camp was able to hold cost-effective elections using big data and eventually became the president of the United States.

Figure 3-31 Big data production by Vote Builder

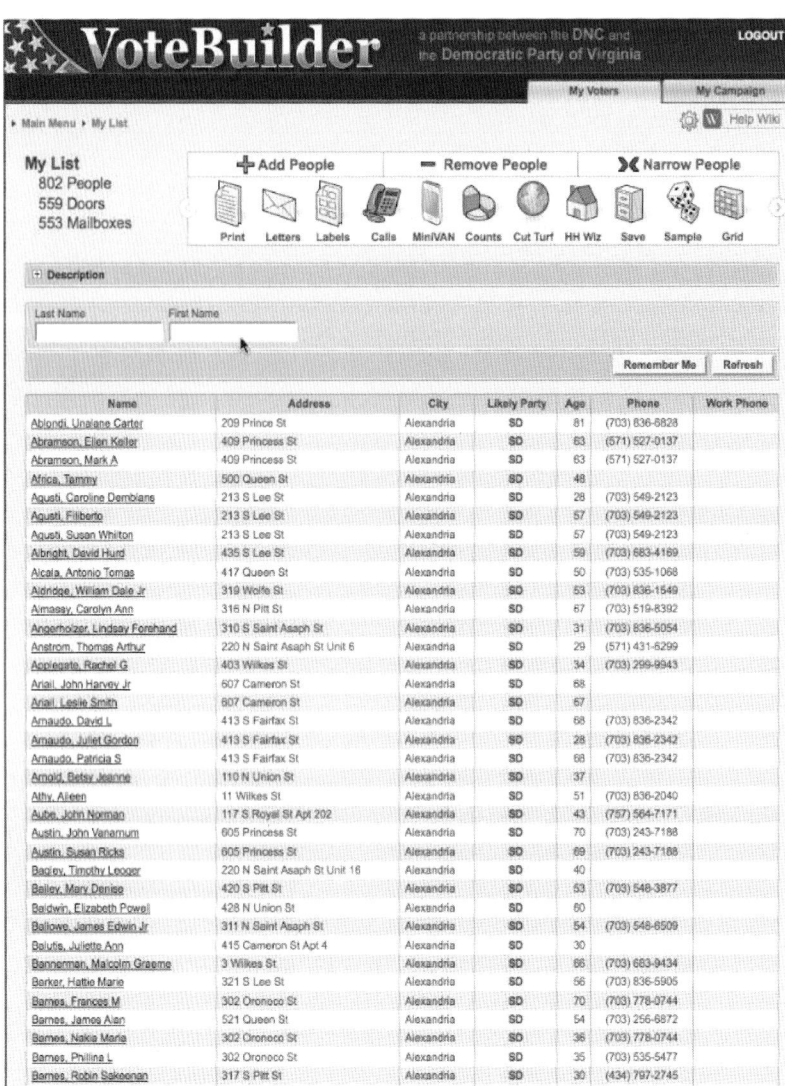

In the era of the Fourth Industrial Revolution, the importance of big data is expanding even more in its influence on politics. For example, how many politicians do not use Facebook or Twitter, whether in Korea, the United States or Europe? How many politicians do not conduct polls on the disposition or distribution of voters, and how many of them form public opinion through Facebook or Twitter?

It's safe to say that it's almost non-existent now. In the end, these social networking activities are the same as creating new big data based on the information obtained through big data. In other words, in the era of the Fourth Industrial Revolution, most of what connects and defines human society will be stored as big data and used as big data, and the utilized big data will be used again as new big data.

3.4 Big Data Business

There is no place where big data is not utilized in all fields from business activities to production, distribution, and marketing. Even in politics, the importance of big data is growing to the point that it is impossible to properly conduct politics without big data. This is because, when you know the tendencies of the voters, you can make promises, and you can conduct proper politics only when you know the public sentiment that the voters want. In particular, opinion polls are closely related to politics. This manipulation of public opinion by big data is a big national issue and plays an important role in determining the direction of politics and elections. Since the 19th general election in Korea, the National Election Commission of Korea has allowed election campaigns on the Internet, including social networks, at all times. As a result, election-related data on social media was amplified, and the political parties that confirmed the importance of social network services in the 2010 Korean 5th local election and the 2011 Korean by-election also reflected the SNS (Social Network Service) competency index in the nomination screening. It focused on the use of social networks, that is, the use of data. In addition, public opinion polling organizations conducted SNS opinion analysis using big data technology to compensate for the large difference in the actual voting results from the results of the 5th local election in 2010 and the by-election in 2011 predicted by the existing poll method. However, since the majority of SNS users are concentrated in their 20s and 30s in the metropolitan area, SNS analysis of the 19th general election in Korea using big data revealed limitations of expression limited to the metropolitan area. Since then, with the continuous development of data utilization technology, big data is actively used to improve the accuracy of elections, voting propensity, and public opinion polls of people in different environments across the country.

Figure 3-32 Big data market analysis (service, software, and hardware)

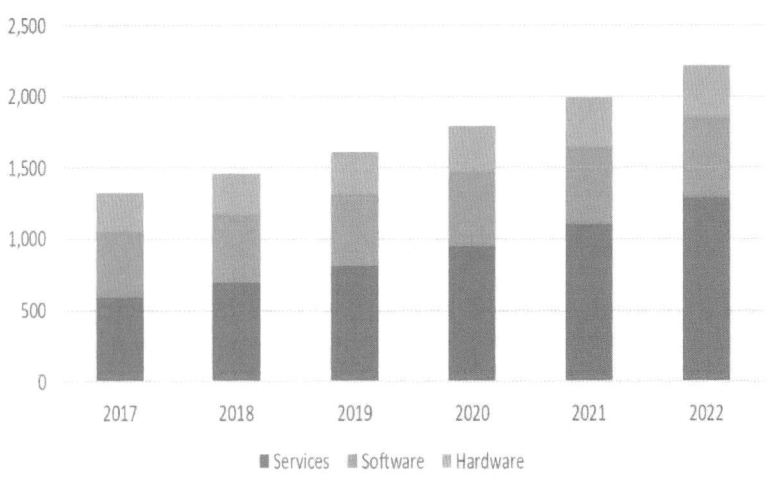

Figure 3-33 Predictive delivery system using Amazon's big data

Amazon.com plans to ship you things before you even buy them. Using predictive analytics, the online retailer will guesstimate your next purchase.

Let's look at the use cases of big data in online companies.

Amazon in the U.S. records all customers' purchase histories in a database and analyzes the records to understand consumers' consumption preferences and interests. By utilizing such big data, Amazon displays recommended products for each customer. It identifies the tendency of each customer and automatically presents the product that is considered to match it to each customer by focusing on the e-mail and website. In the same way as Amazon's recommended product display, Google and Facebook are also increasing the use of big data, such as providing customized advertisements to users by processing users' search conditions and use of unstructured data such as photos and videos in real-time. Many of Korea's famous shopping malls use IP to select products viewed by users and keep them as cookies to analyze consumer purchasing patterns and improve purchase rates by providing recommended products or advertising to the same user.

Figure 3-34 Business use cases of big data

SORT	Company	BigData USE
Customer & Experience	Aviva Life Insurance	Providing customer-tailored insurance products
	Southwest Airlines	Personalized advertising
	Target	Customer-tailored product promotion
Process & Efficiency	DHL	Logistics Efficiency and Investment Reference
	Zara	Efficient logistics and delivery network operation
	Google	Optimizing data center performance
New Value Proportion	Amazon	Predictive delivery before customer order
	General Electronics	Realization of Smart Factory with Industrial Internet
	Fujitsu	Provision of big data analysis solution for agriculture

Looking at the use of data in sports, this field is also very actively using big data.

For example, there is the Money Ball theory, which is a kind of game theory that thoroughly analyzes game data and places players in the right place based on only the data to increase the win rate. This is derived from the case where Billy Beane, the owner of Oakland Athletics, a major league baseball player in the United States, achieved the most effect with the minimum cost despite the low subsidy for the 25th in the league. Billy Beane transformed the team from the bottom to the postseason for four straight years and set a new record for winning the first 20 streaks in the major leagues.

Figure 3-35 The Money Ball of Soccer Evolved with Big Data

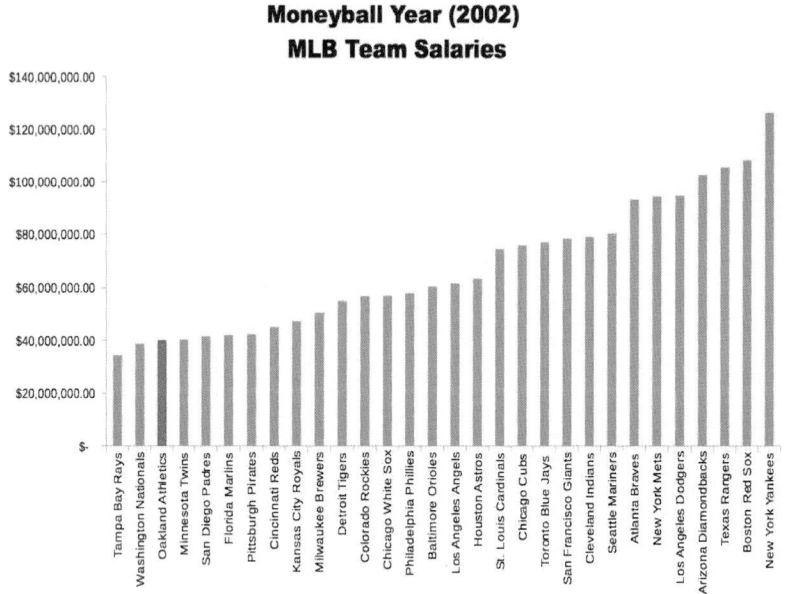

In 2003, The Wall Street Journal in the United States selected Billy Bean along with Warren Buffett and Alan Greenspan as one of the 30 power elites who have the greatest impact on the American economy. In recent years, with the development of science and technology and camera technology, more sophisticated data collection has become possible, but at that time, the trajectory of the pitch, the grip of the pitcher, the direction of the batted ball, and the movement of the fielder were already made with big data. This is an example of using big data in baseball games through the collection, analysis and utilization of not only existing structured data but also unstructured data. Baseball is more fun if you watch it not only by the player's name, but by the team's win rate or a number that indicates the player's performance. The on-base percentage is the ratio of the number of times a batter has successfully stepped on the base, including walks that are not recognized as batting averages, the slugging percentage is the ratio calculated using the total base stepped on for each stroke, indicating how strong the hitting power is, and all are ratios using big data.

Figure 3-36 Money Ball Theory

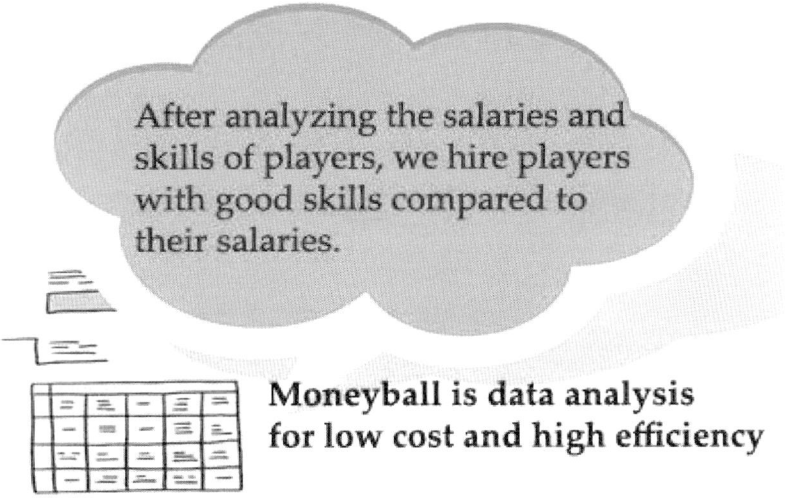

After analyzing the salaries and skills of players, we hire players with good skills compared to their salaries.

Moneyball is data analysis for low cost and high efficiency

These days, the Money Ball theory is widely used not only in sports but also in the national defense budget, welfare budgeting, and various government agencies' plans. In other words, the economy can succeed only with big data. If we take soccer as an example, as we know well these days, VAR is judged on average 2-3 times per match. That is, in the case of an ambiguous judgment that cannot be grasped by the human eye, the image data recorded through

Figure 3-37 Application of Money Ball Theory - Defense Budget

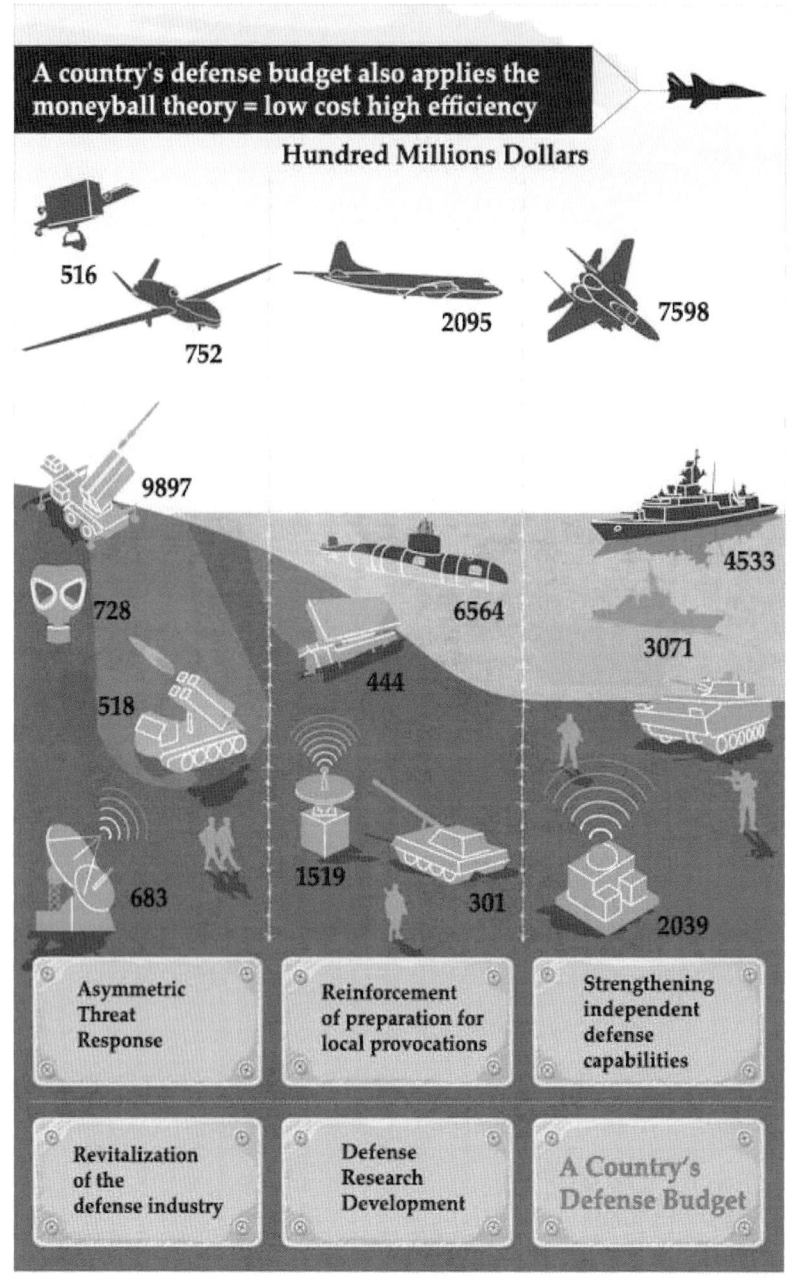

the camera is utilized to provide a source from which many people can make a judgment at once again. In other words, a device was prepared to reduce later judgment disputes and suspicions by judging a visual scene passed by one judge by personal memory judgment by a large number of people viewing the VAR image data at once. Data is no longer a means to assist people in their abilities but has the power to make the impossible possible with their abilities. With such data, a market economy and the Fourth Industrial Revolution began.

Figure 3-38 Aircraft flight information stored as big data

Living in the modern age, we utilize and produce big data at every moment. Whether we drive a car or fly an airplane, we are now receiving information about the speed, location, and status of cars and planes. Without this information, in other words, without data, you cannot drive a car or operate an airplane. Likewise, unlike the society of the past, in modern society, it is difficult to lead a social life and maintain a job without such information. It also makes it difficult to lead a daily life. All this information related to human life can be called data in other words, and with this data, we are advancing into the era of the Fourth Industrial Revolution.

3.5 The Future of Big Data

The future is the world of big data. In other words, information is property. It is because those who have information can get an opportunity ahead of others, and those who produce information are the ones who can lead others.

Figure 3-39 Gartner's Analysis of Big Data Usage Purposes

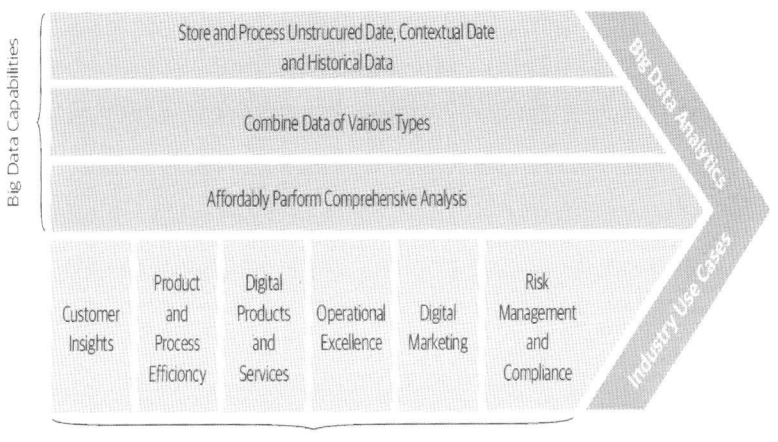

As shown in [Figure 3-39] above, Gartner of the United States divided the main purposes of big data analysis into six categories through The Big Data Value Model. These include Customer Insight, Product & Process Efficiency, Digital Marketing, Products & Service, Operational Excellence, and Digital Marketing.

Based on this, the main purpose of big data analysis was regrouped into customer relationship management, change of experience, improvement of internal process efficiency, and creation of new value, and examples of big data use by major companies were examined.

Aviva insurance company in the UK provides customized insurance products based on the driver's driving pattern. Rate My Drive, a pay-as-you-drive product that calculates, received a good response from customers.

Figure 3-40 America's leading low-cost airline

Southwest Airlines of the United States provides different advertisements for each passenger on the screens of airplane seats. After analyzing the shopping habits and purchasing patterns of aircraft passengers stored in the DB, it provides optimized advertisements for each passenger.

DHL in the United States analyzes daily delivery information and uses it to identify the flow and pattern of consumers' use of logistics services. At the same time, unnecessary fuel consumption is minimized. In addition, the analysis results of the data obtained in this way are used to predict the increase in demand for logistics services and to make investment decisions for the expansion of logistics centers and the addition of delivery vehicles.

ZARA, a Spanish clothing company, uses big data analysis to analyze the sales status of stores around the world in real time, and then builds a logistics network that can supply high-demand clothing in real time, reducing inventory burden and maximizing sales.

Google analyzes a vast amount of operational data on the usage time and energy consumption of data center servers and other equipment and operates two indicators that have a trade-off relationship: data center performance and energy consumption in an optimal state.

The use of big data is not only in business and sports but also in politics. Therefore, all modern politicians are providing information to many people using various big data production tools such as Facebook, Twitter, and YouTube.

Figure 3-41 US President Trump's Twitter Politics

It is because they know well that the production of such information is the way to become a political leader.

In particular, these days, one-person broadcasting through YouTube almost exceeds the information production capacity of general mass media.

One-person YouTube broadcasting, such asshowing ordinary individuals eating food, expressing their political views, showing off their singing skills, or showing individual talents, is currently in its heyday

Some people make enough money to make a living on YouTube alone. Of course, that kind of income can be earned because so many people watch

YouTube broadcast.

It is expected that the production and consumption of big data in personal broadcasting media will increase exponentially in the future.

In other words, in modern times, human life itself is the production and consumption of information, and information is money and the economy. This information is gathered as data, which means the production of big data. In other words, information is data, and data is information. The Fourth Industrial Revolution, which begins with such big data, is making all standards of human life go through data. Therefore, the Fourth Industrial Revolution is a technological society that can only be born from information and the data that composes it. The Fourth Industrial Revolution that starts from these data is connected with artificial intelligence as described above, connected with mechanical engineering and developed into robotics and unmanned transportation means (unmanned aerial vehicle and unmanned vehicle). Along with the development of information and communication technology, the Internet of Things and the Internet of Everything are realized. 3D printers are made through material physics technology, and nanotechnology is realized through ultra-fine integration technology.

Part 4 Artificial Intelligence and Robots

4.1 Artificial Intelligence on The Internet of Things

As we enter the era of the Fourth Industrial Revolution, continuous investment in artificial intelligence is increasing, and along with the development of mass new products and the increase in corporate content production, artificial intelligence has begun to affect the Internet of Things. A typical example of this is the Artificial Internet of Things (AIoT).

Figure 4-1 Examples of Intelligent Internet of Thing

Sort		Explanation	Example
Cloud Intelligence	Intelligent Cloud Platform	Cognitive and machine learning such as vision and language	Amazon Alexa
	Intelligent IoT Platform	Providing intelligent IOT by adding cognitive and analysis functions	Artificial Intelligence Home appliances
Object Intelligence	Intelligent Engine Object Mounted	Equipped with an intelligence engine to provide cognitive and thinking functions	MIT Baxter Robot
	Leverage Intelligent Tools	Utilizing data analysis tools in the Internet of Things	IBM Quark

According to the 2017 Global Internet of Things Outlook report published by IDC Future Scape, by early 2020, more than 40% of the data generated by the Internet of Things will be stored at the edge of the network for processing and analysis. It is also predicted that effective IoT technologies will be combined with streaming analytics and machine learning.

Therefore, in order to effectively operate IoT applications, an analysis-oriented, data-based enterprise technology system is required. For example, a company can replace a regular maintenance system that maintains objects such as devices, machines, and equipment on a predetermined date and time with predictive maintenance based on data analysis. Through this, it is possible to obtain effects such as cost reduction and downtime prevention by identifying and responding to the possibility of failure in advance. Analysis through such big data will gradually be applied less in data centers and clouds, and more in network edges and contact points. Streaming data is analyzed and moved to the right location. As such, streaming analysis provides the right distribution of system resources in the right place.

Figure 4-2 Intelligent IoT Platforms

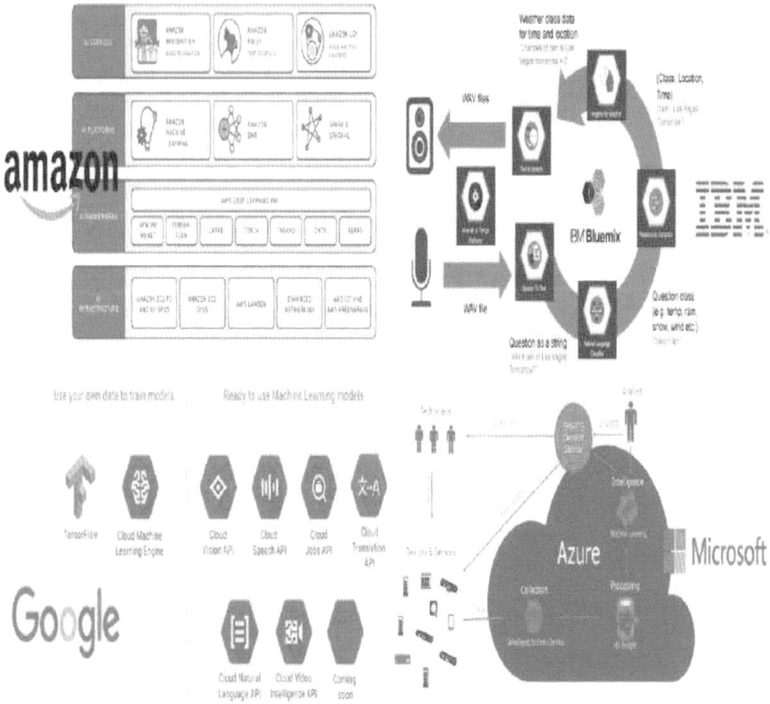

Artificial intelligence systems can also be referred to as computerized systems that make decisions or perform tasks, such as human processing.

In particular, the current artificial intelligence has evolved into machine learning, and is the best advanced analysis tool for optimization.

Artificial intelligence is defined in the encyclopedia as the artificial implementation of some or all of human intelligence.

Figure 4-3 The advent of artificial intelligence

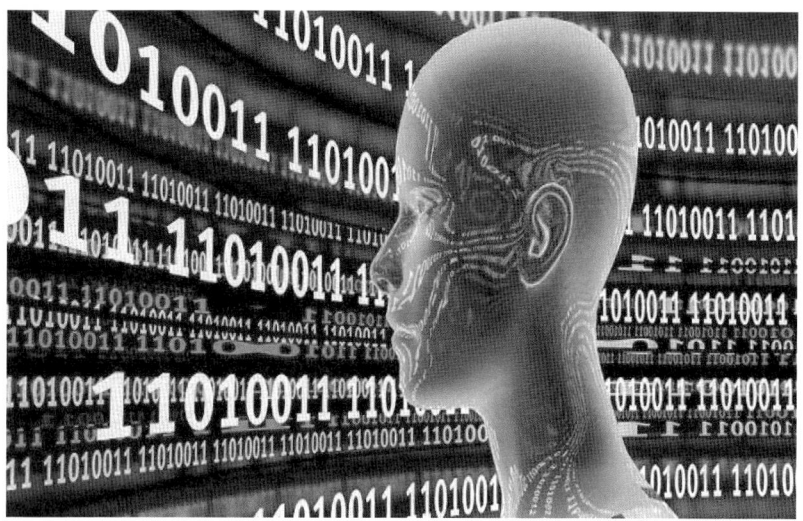

The term artificial intelligence was first used by John McCarthy in 1956 in Dartmouth, USA, at a conference held by Marvin Minsky and Claude Shannon, who made significant contributions to artificial intelligence and information processing theory. However, the concept of artificial intelligence itself existed long before that. For example, Alan Turing proposed the feasibility of thinking machine and the Turing test in 1950, and the world's first neural network model was proposed in 1943. And, of course, not only the United States but also the Soviet Union were interested in this matter, as Anatoly Kitov suggested in his book "Red Book", "National Planned Economy Network-Centered Control System", which aims to pursue a better planned economic system and society through computer networks. This was further improved by the Soviet computer engineer Viktor Glushkov, the OGAS, or National Automated System for Computation and Information Processing program.

If you trace the history of artificial intelligence further back to the early 20th century, it was already born from the 17th to the 18th century, but at this time, it was staying at the level of a philosophical debate about the relationship between the brain and the mind rather than AI itself. At that time, there was no information processing system other than the human brain. For reference, as shown in [Figure 4-4] above, the human brain consists of 100 billion neurons and 100 trillion synapsis. They are connected through electrical signals between them, and it constitutes an information processing system. However, as computers began to develop in earnest from the mid-20th century, it was suggested that it would be possible to make brains with computers and make them do what we do, and many people agreed, and artificial intelligence finally entered the realm of science.

Even the mid-20th century, artificial intelligence research was a fairly innovative research that was able to solve problems that only humans could do, such as natural language processing and solving complex mathematical problems, with computers. Naturally, the AI industry was already a field with a large market value, forming a $1 billion market in 1980.

In 1969, when Marvin Minsky and Seymour Papert published a book "Perceptrons" the popularity of artificial intelligence waned for a while in the 1970s due to the limitations of single-layer neural networks, ,but interest began to grow again with the introduction of multi-layer neural networks in 1980.

Although there have been many studies on the growth of the backpropagation algorithm and the expert system presented in 1974, and the study of neural network theory resumed in 1980, the growth was still sluggish, causing great disappointment. While there were fields with tangible

Figure 4-4 The human brain, the motif of artificial intelligence

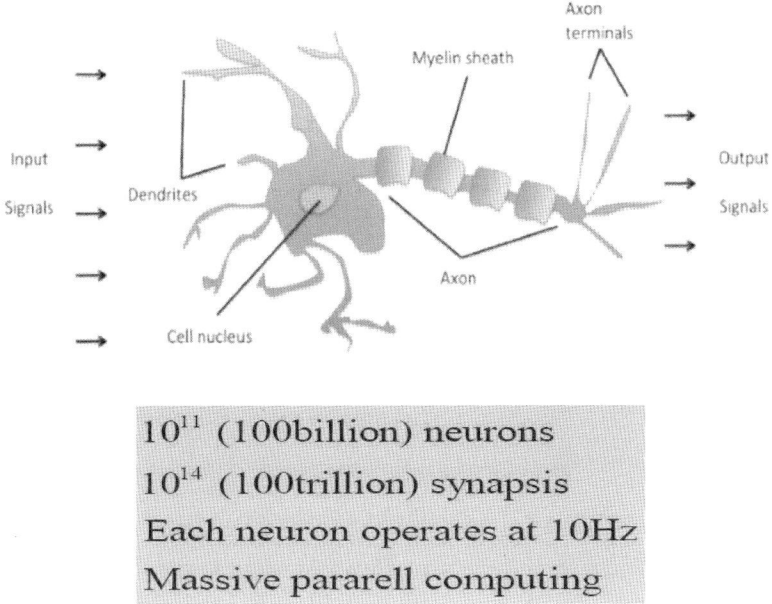

10^{11} (100billion) neurons
10^{14} (100trillion) synapsis
Each neuron operates at 10Hz
Massive pararell computing

Figure 4-5 Comparison of human brain and artificial intelligence

Biological neuron and Perceptrons

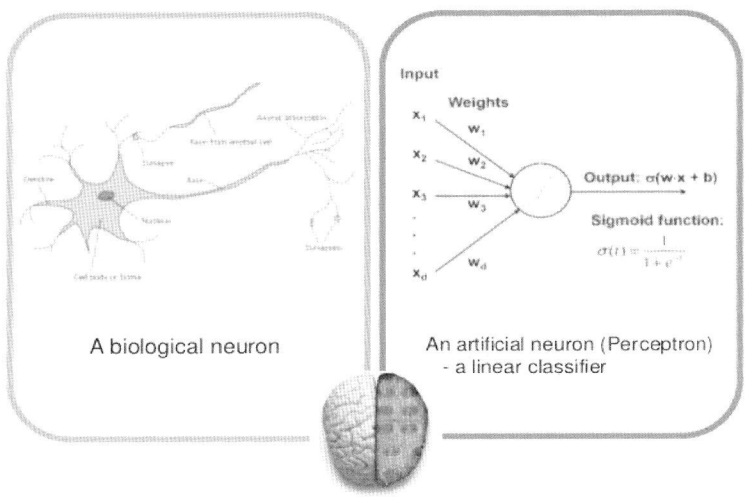

achievements such as text recognition and voice recognition, there were many cases where the goal was not achieved, such as the failure of the development of interactive artificial intelligence, etc. It is difficult to say that many artificial intelligences that came out after 2010 can even talk to humans. For this reason, since 1990, the goal of artificial intelligence has changed from the vaguely broad goal of realizing human intelligence to a more cautious and narrower field centered on problem solving and business, and only then can it become a more successful field with the development of hardware that appeared in the time. Since the 21st century, deep learning papers were published by Professor Geoffrey Hinton in 2006, making learning methods possible for problems that were considered impossible, and already in some fields, results that exceed the human level are appearing one after another. The current AI technology in 2020 has a higher face recognition rate or better object recognition compared to human cognitive ability and there is a growing perception that artificial intelligence can surpass human abilities at a rapid pace. As shown in [Figure 4-7], human intelligence for information processing is overtaken by artificial intelligence at a certain point since the early 2000s. In other words, the information processing ability, excluding emotions and the other five senses, already shows a much higher performance of artificial intelligence. Looking briefly artificial intelligence technology, first of all, machine learning serves to provide algorithms that turn data into actionable knowledge and help us understand the meaning of the data in the world.

In addition, machine learning can be widely used in spam email filtering, targeted advertising, classifying customers based on consumer behavior, forecasting weather and climate change, preventing fraudulent card use, estimating money loss due to typhoons and natural disasters, predicting election results, automatic driving, home or building energy use optimization, crime prevention, and disease diagnosis.

Figure 4-6 History of artificial intelligence

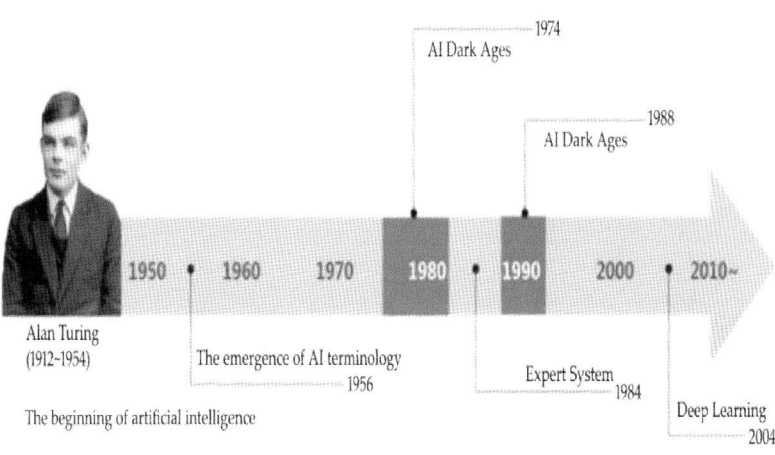

Figure 4-7 The singularity of artificial intelligence and the intelligence

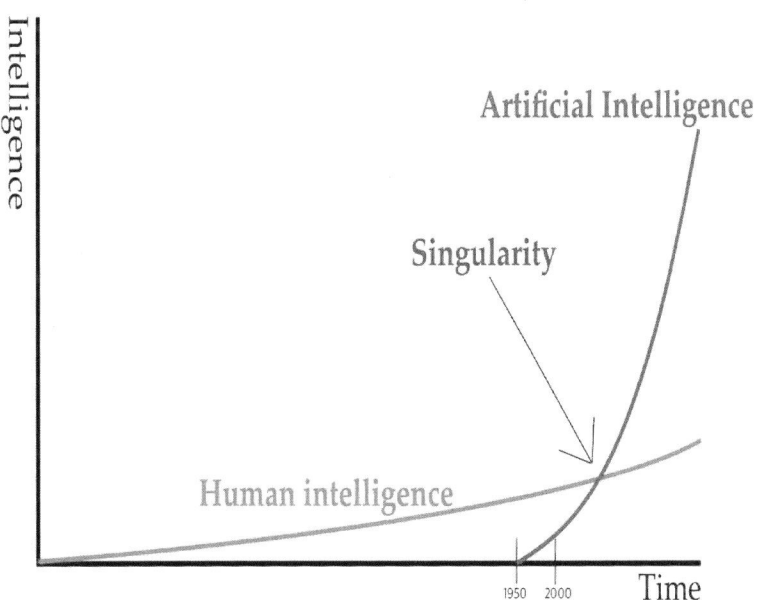

Artificial Intelligence of Things (AIOT) can be said to be the goal for the ultimate industrial future of the Internet of Things.

In general, the conditions for Smart + Connected IoT, the evolutionary direction of the Internet of Things, to become an intelligent Internet of Things are as follows.

The Internet of Things consists of a physical element, a smart element, and a connection element. Physical elements refer to mechanical and electrical components, and smart elements include sensors, processors, storage, and software. And the connection elements correspond to ports, antennas, protocols, and the like.

In the Internet of Things, the physical element of a connected device is amplified by the smart element, and the smart element is amplified by the connected element.

If Smart + Connected things are to meet the conditions of the Intelligent Internet of Things, they must be able to perform decisions and actions that humans can make. In other words, because general IoT devices only provide a control function through an application or a user basic setting learning function, strictly speaking, they are not intelligent IoT devices.

For example, a home heating device with only a temperature setting function is not an artificial intelligence system.

Conversely, autonomous vehicles can be said to be artificial intelligence. This is because self-driving cars drive on the road for the driver. If the vehicle is connected to other vehicles or the Internet environment, it can become a vehicle in the form of an intelligent IoT.

As shown in [Figure 4-8], it can be seen that the current Internet of Things (IoT) mainly requires automatic setting and autonomous control in order to become a complete intelligent Internet of Things.

In general, if it has its own aggregation, distribution, and decision making, it can be called artificial intelligence. For example, if there is aggregation, distribution, and decision through autonomous algorithms such as autonomous blade angle adjustment of wind turbines, autonomous flight, accommodation rebooking or recommendation functions, facial recognition, translation, and loan approval tasks, it is called artificial intelligence.

Figure 4-8 Analysis of current issues and necessary technologies of IoT

Analysis of Current Issues	Necessary Skills
Efficient operation method of IoT technology	Automatic setting, Autonomous control, Optimal operation
Provides uninterrupted service even when the Internet is disconnected	Continuous operation equipment technology in case of internet disconnection
Convergence of artificial intelligence technology and the Internet of Things	Intelligent technology of the Internet of Things
Minimize human intervention and make decisions through machine learning	Automating and intelligentizing the movement of things

As mentioned above, the Internet of Things includes connectivity elements. Connectivity enables monitoring, control, and optimization through smart elements such as sensors, processors, storage, and software in products and devices.

In general, connectivity alone cannot progress learning, but it provides the foundation for that learning. When many IoT applications transmit data to the cloud or data center, data are analyzed, modeled, aggregated, distributed, and determined, and the results are obtained through this. After extraction, the corrected result is transmitted to the device.

In other words, the ability to change and adapt to behavior over time is the same as a person's ability to personalize and collective intelligence. So, just like humans, devices that learn by themselves and learn from other devices can be considered artificial intelligence.

To This day, we often learn from group information that is not tailored to each individual.

Figure 4-9 Home appliances with Intelligent IoT

Home Appliances	IOT-based service	Functions of home appliances equipped with artificial intelligence
Air Conditioner	Automatic on/off through human body detection	Technology that sends air only to a space where there are people
Refrigerator	Check food types and expiration dates	Recognizing user behavior, saving energy and managing food condition
Robotic Vacuum	Remote cleaning control	Recognize and remember obstacles to control behavior in advance
Washing Machine	Remote laundry control	Autonomous behavior of the laundry function according to the weather and customer habits

Figure 4-10 Intelligent IoT device

For example, when a camera installed around a soccer stadium where artificial intelligence is applied adjusts the aperture according to the lighting, it automatically learns not to reflect the weather environment more than 10 meters away through big data calculations using artificial intelligence. The same is true for vehicles approaching the highway accident area to understand the traffic situation on their own and to drive on the bypass road on their own.

Even if there is no accident, a system that guides people to the place with the lowest probability of an accident through a traffic accident prediction system has emerged these days. It is the Internet of Things using the learning ability of artificial intelligence, that is, the Intelligent Internet of Things.

In other words, the opportunity of the IoT is to promote learning and personalization at the same time. Everyone wants to be provided with a customized experience that reflects their habits, patterns, and preferences.

Therefore, intelligent IoT systems can be easily operated by artificial intelligence systems such as systems developed based on reinforcement learning.

Without an automated system with the flexibility to optimize itself for thousands of scenarios, it is difficult to achieve a high degree of personalization.

As seen in the artificial intelligence Go player AlphaGo software, the artificial intelligence trains the algorithm to present the best number to win out of hundreds of thousands of different numbers in Go. Adjusting the blade angle of a cooler and wind turbine for control, supplying the most appropriate light, nutrients and moisture to plants, and distributing feed through big data learning about the growth of animals or plants on the farm, and nurses in hospitals or nursing homes. Instead, it would also be possible to train big data to dispense a dose or give an injection to a patient on time. In this way, the intelligent IoT system can be converted into an artificial intelligence system based on reinforcement learning of big data, so that the existing information system can be operated more efficiently and easily.

4.2 Artificial Intelligence with Big Data

4.2.1 Pattern Recognition and Artificial Intelligence

The Deep Learning and Pattern Recognition are the most talked about among people when applying artificial intelligence algorithms through big data. Strictly speaking, pattern recognition is one of the problems belonging to the fields of cognitive science and artificial intelligence. Cognitive science refers to a comprehensive interdisciplinary scientific field that deals with problems of intelligence and cognition using psychology, computer science, artificial intelligence, neurobiology and linguistics, and philosophy. Artificial intelligence refers to a technology that implements the ability to perceive external objects, and the ability to understand syntactic patterns such as natural language in computer programs.

Research on artificial intelligence is currently developing in the field of information systems based on artificial intelligence called intelligent systems. In the information age, intelligent systems are being applied to the expression and processing of information, as well as to properly process a large number of easily obtainable data. Pattern recognition mainly deals with the problem of recognizing aggregated objects, which is a practical implementation problem of artificial intelligence using an engineering approach. Pattern recognition can be defined as a field of artificial intelligence that deals with the problem of recognizing a certain object by a mechanical device capable of calculation.

In general, cognitive abilities are considered to be a basic property of humans as well as other living organisms. Humans are awake and engage in cognitive activity at every moment of life. Humans recognize objects around then, and then move and act in relation to them. For example, commuting to school or work, working, and socializing with people are all cognitive activities.

Figure 4-11 Cognitive transmission process in the human brain

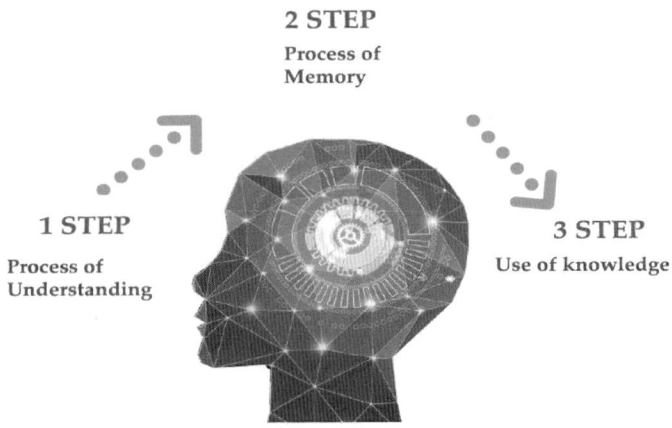

Humans can see and understand handwritten characters, symbols, pictures, etc., and can also analyze the contents of documents. You can also distinguish the difference between an angry gesture and a smiling expression. Since humans have excellent pattern recognition ability, it can be said to be a very multidimensional information system.

One pattern depicts an object. Human recognition behavior can be classified into two main types according to the properties of the target pattern to be recognized. One is the recognition of a concrete item, and the other is the recognition of an abstract item. Humans can recognize surrounding texts, pictures, music, and various types of objects, which is called sensory perception. This includes recognizing visual and auditory patterns. This recognition process involves the identification and classification of spatial and temporal patterns. On the other hand, you can infer an answer to a point or problem with your eyes closed and your ears covered. This process of recognizing abstract items is called conceptual recognition as opposed to visual or auditory pattern recognition.

Figure 4-12 Pattern classification for objects to be recognized

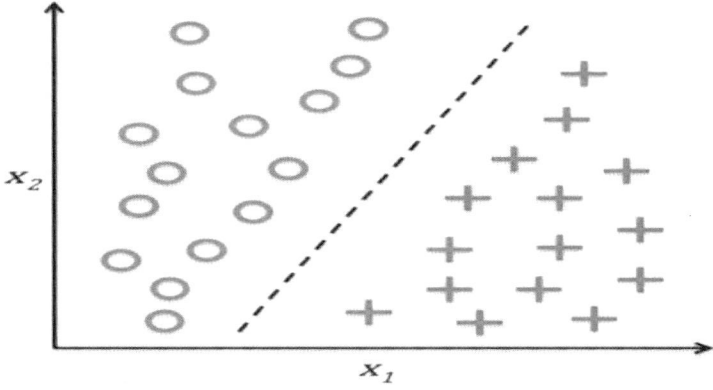

Figure 4-13 Pattern classification based on the human brain

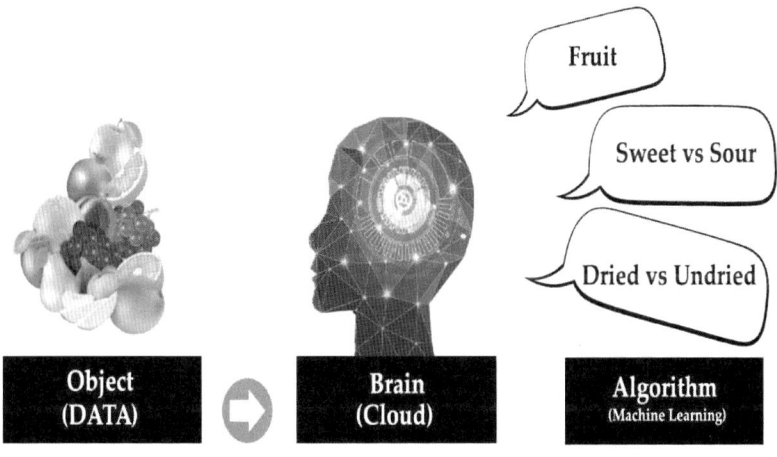

In general, artificial intelligence pattern recognition and sensory recognition is mainly dealt with. Here, when defining an object to be recognized, spatial patterns include text, fingerprints, astronomical maps, objects, and pictures, and temporal patterns include voice, waveform, electrocardiogram, and time series data. Human perception of specific patterns can be regarded as a psychophysiological problem related to the relationship between humans and physical stimuli. Humans associate detected patterns with general concepts or clues derived from past experiences through inductive reasoning. Indeed, the recognition problem can be viewed as estimating the relative likelihood of associating input data with one of a known statistical population. At this time, the statistical population depends on past experiences and forms clues and prior information necessary for recognition. Thus, the pattern recognition problem can be considered not to discriminate input data among individual patterns, but to discriminate input data among populations by searching for features or unchanging attributes among members of the population.

Figure 4-14 A network that mimics the human brain (Perceptron)

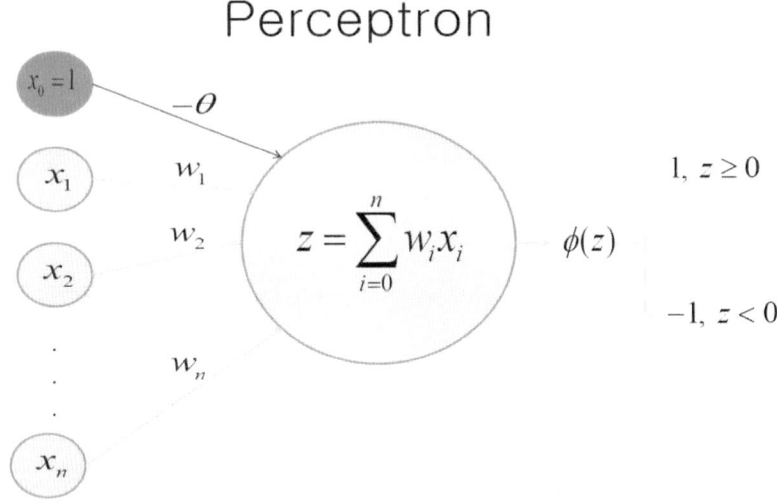

From a logical point of view, research on the pattern recognition problem can be divided into two main categories. One is to study the pattern recognition ability of humans and other organisms, and the other is to develop theories and techniques for designing devices capable of performing a given recognition task in a specific application field. The first mainly applies to fields of metaphysics such as natural sciences, social sciences, and biology, and the second corresponds to information science, which is metaphysical knowledge such as engineering or science.

Figure 4-15 The principle of artificial intelligence

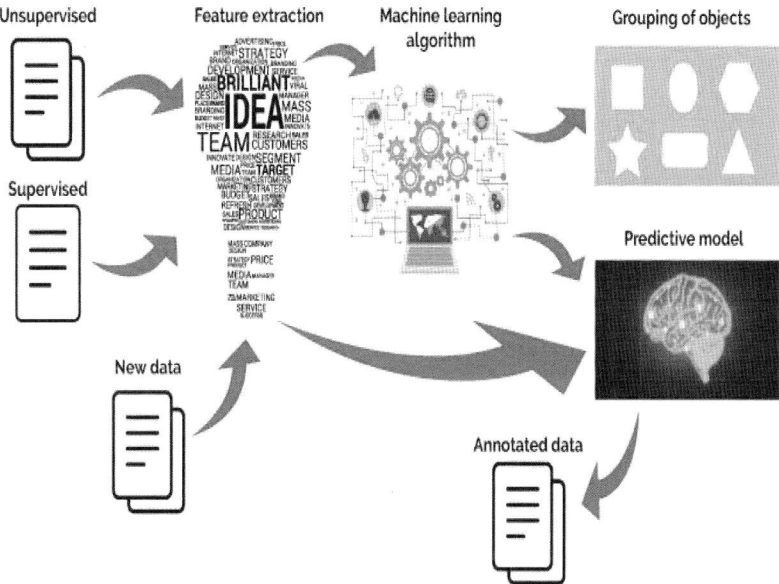

Pattern recognition in artificial intelligence can be said to be the second category of information science.

In general, pattern recognition can be defined as extracting important features or attributes from data and classifying input data into identifiable classes.

For example, weather forecasting can be treated as a pattern recognition problem. The recognition system extracts important features from the weather data received as input, interprets the weather data, and then makes a weather forecast based on the extracted features. A medical diagnosis can also be treated as a pattern recognition problem. A certain symptom serves as input data to the recognition system, and the recognition system identifies the disease by analyzing the symptom, which is the input data. The character recognition system is a pattern recognition system that accepts an optical signal as input data and identifies the characteristics of the character. In the speech recognition system, the name of the pronounced word is identified based on the waveform of the sound received as input data.

Figure 4-16 Perceptron Hidden Layer

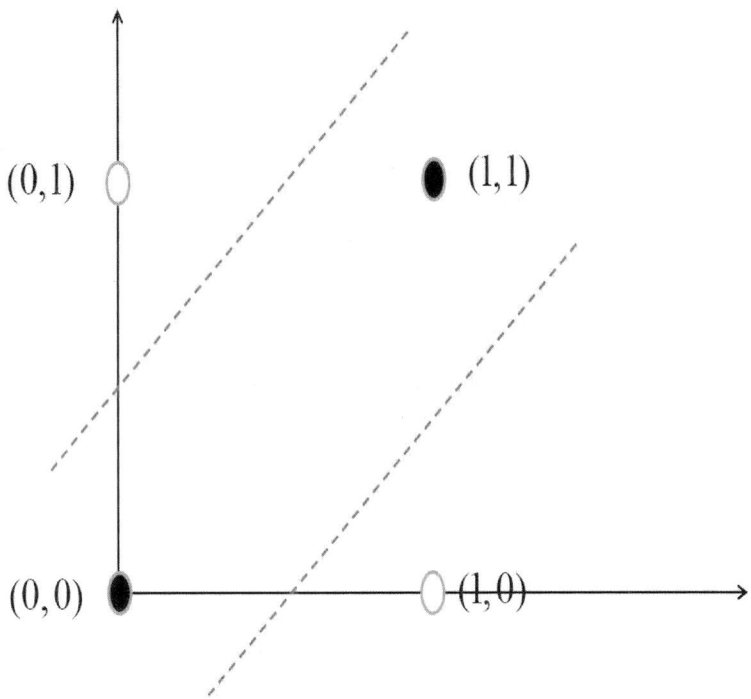

In general, the pattern vector in pattern recognition includes all available measurement information about the pattern. Measuring objects belonging to an arbitrary pattern class can be regarded as an encoding process in which symbols belonging to an alphabet set are assigned to the characteristics of each pattern. When generating information in the form of real numbers through measurement, it is often used to regard one pattern vector as a point in the N-dimensional Euclidean space. A set of patterns belonging to the same class corresponds to a set of points scattered within an arbitrary area of the measurement space.

Figure 4-17 Perceptron Hidden Layer position

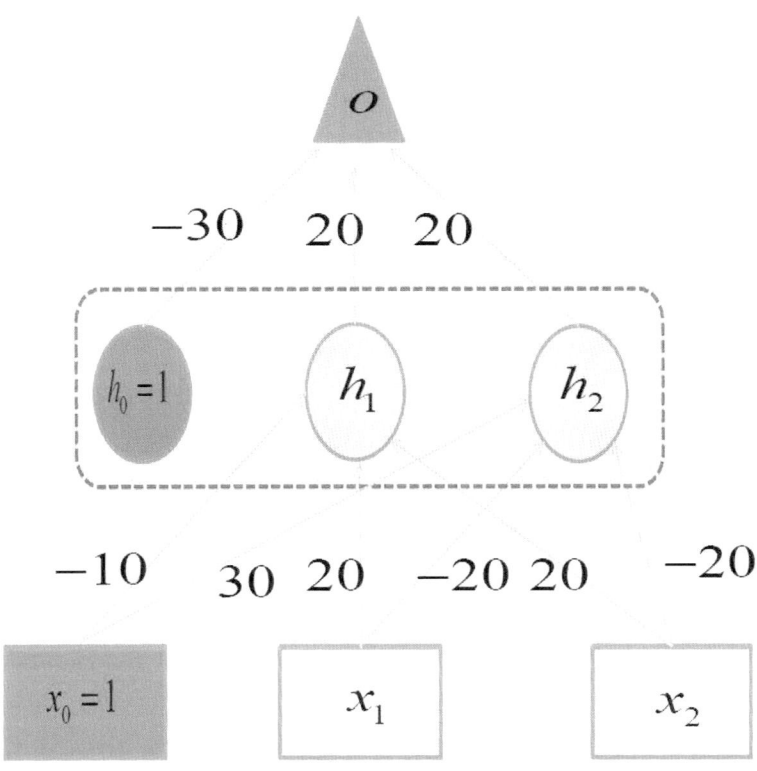

The pattern vector may be regarded as one coordinate point in two-dimensional coordinates. When a pattern is divided into two classes, it may form a set separate from each other due to the properties of the measured values. However, in real data, it is not always possible to adhere to a metric that results in a neatly separated set.

In general, when designing a pattern recognition system, an important problem is always the problem of extracting features or properties of the received input data and the problem of reducing the order of the pattern vector. These problems can usually be called preprocessing and feature extraction problems.

Figure 4-18 LNS as an AI Network (Perceptron) Exception

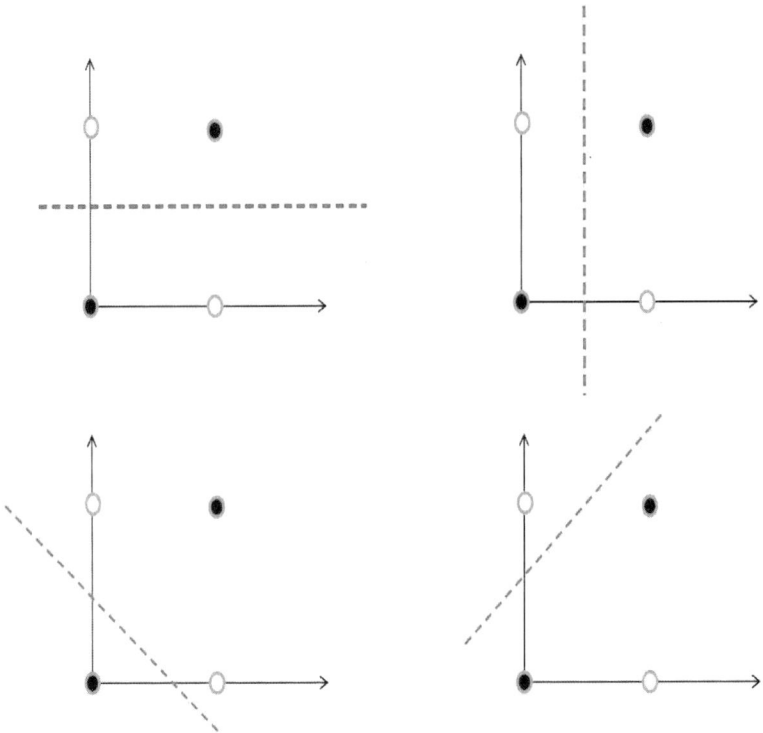

For example, in speech recognition, vowels and similar vowels can be distinguished from fricatives and other consonants by measuring the energy distribution for a frequency within a frequency band. Characteristics commonly used in speech recognition include the duration of a sound, the ratio of energy in various frequency bands, the position of the peak or formant in the frequency band, and the movement of these peaks in time.

First, a characteristic is found to recognize a pattern, and that is the key value for recognizing the pattern. This refers to the method of pattern recognition, which will be explained later, but the method of pattern recognition varies depending on whether there is a target feature or not, and the AI application algorithm is also different.

A characteristic of a pattern in a normal population is an attribute that indicates the common characteristics of all patterns belonging to that class. Such features are called intra set features, and conversely, features that indicate differences between pattern classes are called intra set features. Certain elements within a set that are common to all pattern classes under consideration can be ignored because they are information that cannot be used to distinguish between classes. Feature extraction is considered an important problem in the design of pattern recognition systems. From the perspective of big data, this is directly related to the data mining technique for data, that is, the tagging method. If it is possible to determine a complete set of distinct features between each pattern class from the measured data, the difficulty of pattern recognition and classification will be greatly reduced. In this case, the automatic recognition process can be simplified with a simple matching process or a table lookup structure. However, in most pattern recognition problems that arise in practice, it is usually impossible or very difficult to determine a complete set of distinct features.

Another problem that arises when designing a pattern recognition system is selecting an optimal decision procedure.

After expressing the observed data from the pattern to be recognized in the form of pattern points or measurement vectors in the pattern space, it is necessary to determine which pattern class this data belongs to.

The design concept of pattern recognition can come from how to specify and define a class of patterns. If several basic possibilities have been derived through experience, it is possible to use the member list concept as a method for designing a pattern recognition system when a certain pattern class can be specified as a list of members of that class. If a class of patterns can be characterized as common characteristics shared by all its members, then the concept of common characteristics can be used as a method for designing pattern recognition systems. If a certain pattern class shows clustering characteristics in the pattern space, a pattern recognition system can be designed based on the clustering concept, and the design concept can be divided into three categories as follows.

First, the concept of a member list is a list of members and specifying one pattern class enables automatic pattern recognition with Template Matching. A set of patterns belonging to the same pattern class is stored in the pattern recognition system. When an unknown input pattern is given to the system, it is compared with the stored patterns one by one. When the input pattern matches one of the stored patterns belonging to the pattern class, the pattern recognition system classifies the input pattern as a component of the pattern class. For example, if characters composed of different typefaces are all stored in a pattern recognition system, they can be recognized as a member roster approach unless they are distorted due to contamination by writing on transparent paper, etc. With this simple concept, it is possible to design a direct recognition structure that satisfies the purpose of any application. The member roster approach can classify near-perfect patterns if a near-perfect pattern sample is used.

Second, the concept of common characteristics is a common characteristic that all components have and classifying pattern classes enables automatic pattern recognition that finds and processes similar characteristics. The basic assumption of this method is that patterns belonging to the same class have some common characteristic or attribute indicating similarity. For example, after storing common characteristics within the pattern recognition system, new patterns are accepted and classified as patterns with similar characteristics. Therefore, the main problem in this method is to determine common characteristics from a finite set of sample patterns.

This concept is superior to the member roster approach in several respects. The memory space required to store features for one pattern class is much smaller than the memory space needed to store features for all patterns belonging to that class. In one pattern class, since the characteristics do not change, it is possible to allow variations in individual patterns by comparing the characteristics. On the other hand, in circular registration, severe pattern deformation is not allowed. If all the features for a class can be determined from the sample pattern, the recognition process can be reduced to simply feature matching.

Third, the concept of clustering is that when a component of a pattern belonging to an arbitrary class is a vector composed of real numbers, the pattern class can be specifically identified as a clustering characteristic in the pattern space. In the design of the pattern recognition system based on this general concept, various pattern clusters can be represented in the form of relative geometrical arrangements. A simple recognition structure such as a minimum distance classifier can also be used if a class can be specifically identified based on a characteristic located far away between clusters. However, when clusters overlap, a technique of partitioning the pattern space must be used. The phenomenon of cluster overlap is mostly due to a lack of observed information or contamination of data. Therefore, the degree of overlap can be minimized by increasing the quantity and quality of the measured values calculated for one type of pattern.

As discussed above, when designing a pattern recognition system, three methods can be used methodologically: member list, common characteristics, and cluster.

In general, when designing a pattern recognition system in an AI system, it is meaningful and important to make the most of the available data. It is desirable to use a priori information to obtain good performance. This preemptive experience information is an essential element in constructing an effective pattern recognition system.

Figure 4-19 Clustering of radio frequency training data

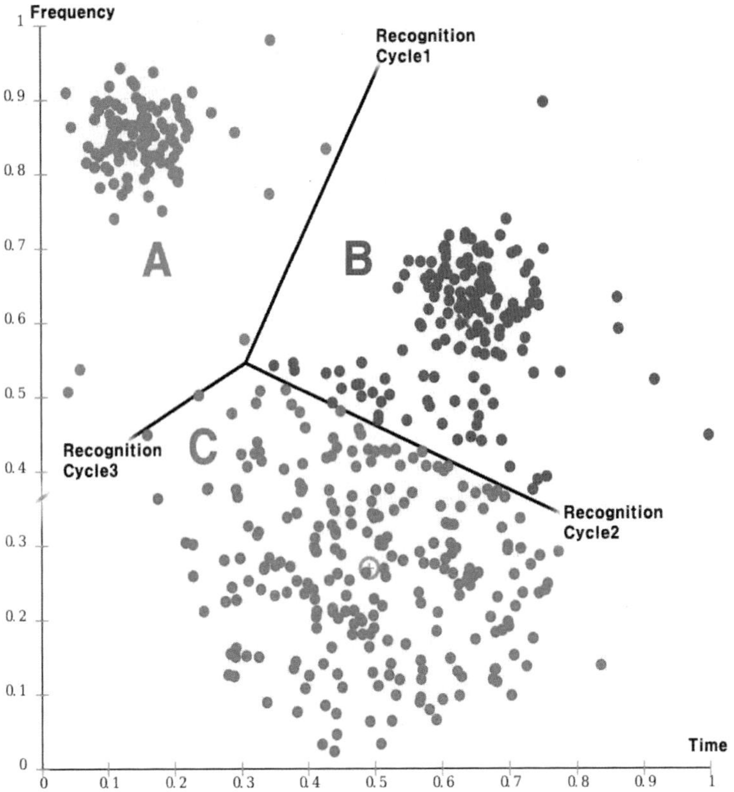

A typical set of patterns whose properties or structures are known is called a training set.

In a general sense, the training set provides the meaningful information needed to decide whether to output the input data. In artificial intelligence or pattern recognition, training is often associated with or considered to be equivalent to learning. This training set is used when the recognition system learns appropriate information such as statistical parameters, key features, or basic structures.

Figure 4-20 Recognition, classification, and clustering

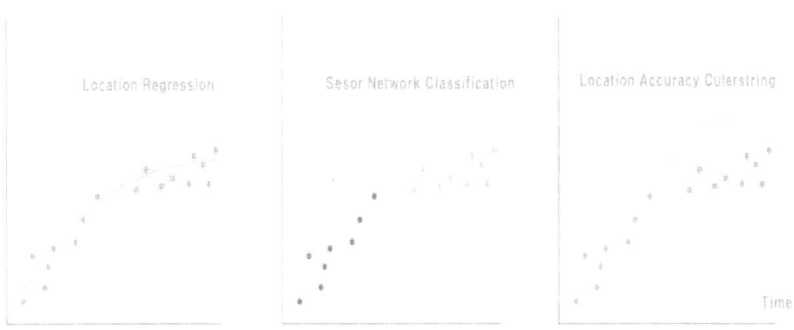

Learning in the realm of artificial intelligence has more general implications, similar to the self-adaptation process seen in humans.

The learning system of artificial intelligence can be applied to its internal structure in order to get a better evaluation based on the previous quantified performance.

Usually, the performance of an AI system can be evaluated as the difference between the expected system output and the actual system output. This general learning concept is also related to a pattern recognition technique based on error correction used when developing a linear decision function in statistical pattern recognition or a generalized delta rule in pattern recognition using a neural network.

These two techniques are typical Gradient Descent techniques, and the recognition system is modified according to the results of each experiment or iteration.

In the era of the Fourth Industrial Revolution, artificial intelligence pattern recognition can be applied in various ways. There is an inherent and quantified statistical basis for the generation of a certain pattern, or the structure inherent in the pattern provides basic information for recognition.

Figure 4-21 Optimization for data recognition

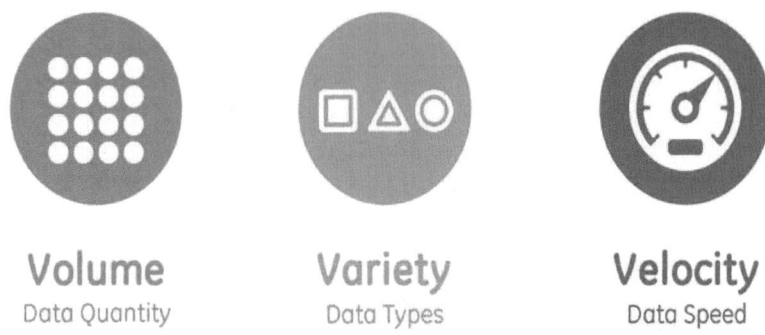

In artificial intelligence, particularly pattern recognition, a given problem can be answered by one or more different approaches.

As shown in [Figure 4-21] above, when trying to solve a problem in general, an important guideline is to use the most appropriate tool for the task. In general, in artificial intelligence, optimization for data recognition is exactly that. In other words, to obtain the highest performance in pattern recognition, each optimized approach is the most appropriate approach to the target.

For the successful design of an artificial intelligence pattern recognition system, there are the following principles.

In general, designing a pattern recognition system that sets an automatic approach rather than suggesting the most appropriate approach to a target is complex, repetitive, and requires a lot of interaction.

However, it is thought that a more systematic design is possible if the design proceeds as follows.

The first step is to examine the patterns under consideration to find features. Not only the similarity or dissimilarity within and between patterns, but also the quantifiable pattern structure and probabilistic specific erasure are investigated. At this stage, the deformability or invariance of the pattern and the definition of the source point for the possibility of contamination should be considered at this point.

Figure 4-22 Setting patterns in real-world data

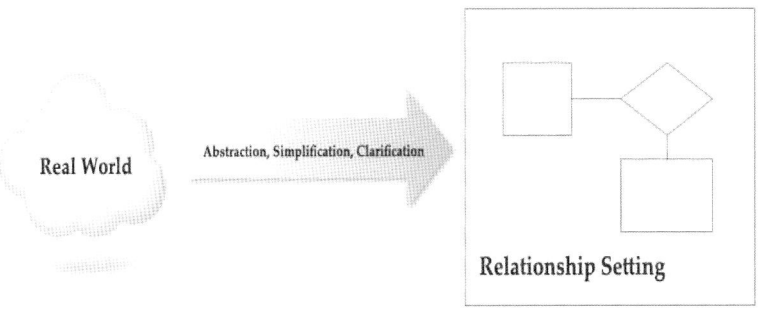

Establishing a relationship for the purpose of use based on stored knowledge

The second step is to determine whether the feature or measurement data can actually be used.

The third step is to consider the system's expected performance and constraints on computational resources. There is no way to verify if I write an algorithm that can be calculated only at the supercomputer level when my computer resources are at the workstation level. Again, the pattern recognition of artificial intelligence is a repetition of training, that is, learning and evaluation. This is because performance is improved through the repetition of such a loop.

Fourth, the availability of training (learning) data should be considered. Data that cannot be used continuously cannot have value as learning data.

The fifth step is to consider whether to use an appropriate and proven pattern recognition technique. Since many people have already tried to verify the algorithm for mathematical statistical pattern recognition, syntactic pattern recognition, and clustering, the quality of performance can be expected to some extent, resulting in some integrity of data contamination.

The sixth step is to simulate the pattern recognition system. Through simulation, it is necessary to check whether the experiment has errors in the model, grammar, and network structure. In the seventh step, the algorithm learns using the tagged data. In the eighth step, the simulation proceeds again. This is to verify the adequacy of the algorithm.

Finally, as described above, the learning of artificial intelligence is an iteration from the first stage to the eighth stage. The learning of artificial intelligence is training, and it is the repetition of learning and evaluation. This is because performance is improved through the repetition of such a loop.

If pattern recognition is used as the main engine when designing artificial intelligence, the structure for pattern recognition can consist of a feature extractor and a classifier. A feature extractor is a device that converts a pattern to be recognized into a pattern vector value. A classifier is a device that assigns each input to one of a finite number of classes by calculating a set of decision functions. An error occurs when assigning a pattern that does not belong to a pattern to a pattern. The pattern classifier means that it has the probability of making fewer errors than the error probability it will make, and it can be defined as a better pattern classifier with a smaller error probability than the previous pattern classifier. Usually, the output of the feature extractor represents N measurements of the actual pattern. As described above, pattern recognition, the most basic concept of artificial intelligence, extracts the characteristics of clustering, learns performance through training on the extracted target feature or non-target feature, and provides the desired result through repeated evaluation of the evaluated performance. Since this series of processes is learning that takes place in a machine, not in a human brain, we call it machine learning.

Figure 4-23 Artificial intelligence, machine learning, deep learning

Artificial Intelligence

It is a technology that realizes certain intellectual abilities of the human brain, such as thinking and learning, through a computer.

Machine Learning

A methodology that expresses the performance of an electronic calculator that learns by itself and improves the quality of the desired result

Deep Learning

It is one of several algorithms in machine learning as an algorithm that replicates the logic that processes the electrical signals of the human brain.

Let's take a look at the principles of machine learning logic. First, the learning of machine learning takes place through the four-step process of first data storage, second abstraction, third generalization, and fourth evaluation.

Figure 4-24 4 stages of machine learning

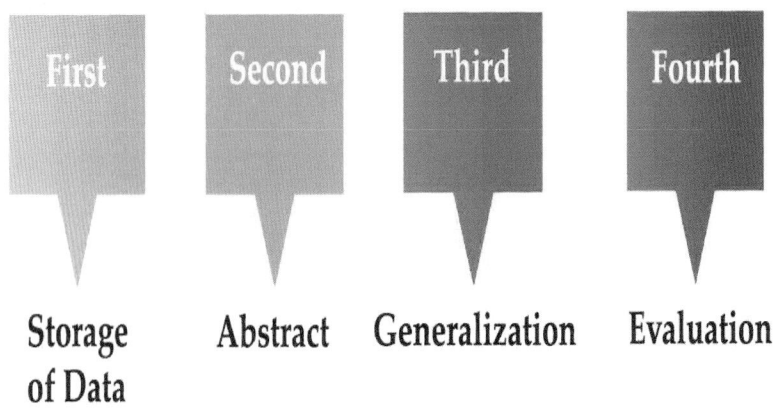

First, the storage of data provides the necessary factual basis for inference, and all machine learning starts with data.

Second, abstraction is to transform the stored data into a more comprehensive form and concept, and to summarize the stored data using a model to specifically describe the pattern hidden in the data. As a representative form of the model, it refers to the division of data into relational pictures such as mathematical equations, tree diagrams, graphs, logical rules, and homogeneous groups.

What comes out of the abstraction process is training, which is a process of fitting a model to a data set, and the source information contained in the data is converted into an abstract form by the trained model. The trained model can uncover previously unknown relationships that were already in the data. This is the reason for machine learning and the purpose of using artificial intelligence technology.

Figure 4-25 Data storage among the 4 stages

| First Storage of Data | Second Abstract | Third Generalization | Fourth Evaluation |

It provides the necessary factual basis for inference, and all machine learning starts with data.

Third, generalization is the process of transforming abstracted knowledge so that it can be applied to future tasks that are similar to but not identical to those experienced in the past by creating knowledge and reasoning that can cope with new situations using abstracted data. Among the patterns discovered through the learning process, the task of leaving only those most suitable for future tasks is performed in the generalization process.

Figure 4-26 Abstraction among the 4 stages

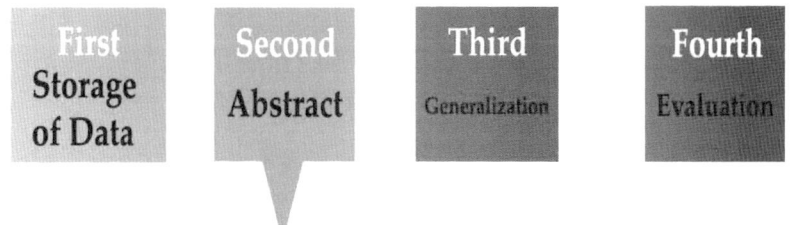

Transforms stored data into comprehensive forms and concepts, and summarizes them using a model.

Fourth, the evaluation aims to measure the utility of the learned knowledge and provide information on future improvements by providing a feedback system.

For reference, over-fitting is a model that over-fits a model that showed excellent performance in the training process of artificial intelligence but not in the evaluation process of the training data. It means that the model loses its generalization ability by reflecting even the noise contained in the training data into the model, and thus the model does not respond properly to test data not experienced in the training process.

If you understand the algorithms of machine learning, let's look at the types of machine learning.

Machine learning can be classified into the following types.

First, supervised learning is an algorithm that finds a function that outputs a suitable target feature when inputting a specific feature set through optimization. This is mainly used to construct the predictive model, and the target feature must be specified as a method for modeling by discovering the relationship between the target feature (prediction target) and other features. It is mainly used for classification and numeric prediction. Existing algorithms that are already available are Near least Neighbor, Naive Bayes, Decision Tree, Classification Rule Learners, Linear Regression, Regression Tree, Model Tree, Neural Networks, Support Vector Machines, and more.

Second. unsupervised learning is mainly used when the target feature is not available. Learning is made based on the similarity or distance between examples, and it is used to construct a descriptive model. It is suitable for the task of obtaining intuition by newly summarizing data in an interesting way. It is mainly used for pattern detection and clustering. Existing algorithms that have already been published include Association Rules and k-means clustering.

Third, semi-supervised learning is used when most of the examples do not contain the target feature, but only some of them. It is mainly used when it contains a lot of information about which classification the data belongs to. It is mainly used for Classification and Clustering.

Figure 4-27 Generalization of the 4 stages

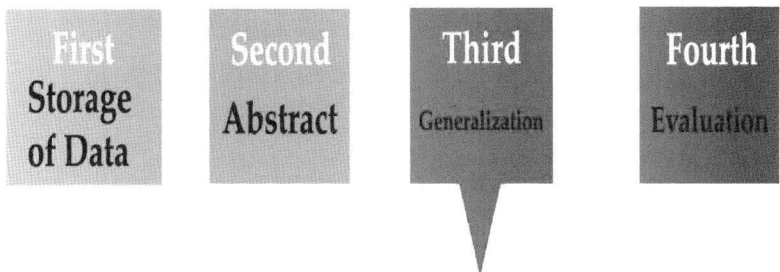

Among the patterns discovered through the learning process, the task of leaving only those most suitable for future tasks is performed in the generalization process.

Figure 4-28 Evaluation of the 4 stages

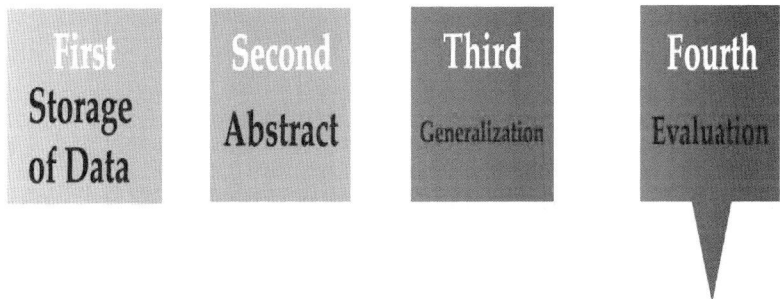

It measures the utility of the learned knowledge, provides a feedback system, and presents standards for future improvement.

Fourth, Reinforcement Learning aims to discover how to maximize rewards through trial and error by learning what actions to take to maximize rewards for results. It is characterized by the fact that the current action affects not only the reward of the next action but also the situation, affecting all subsequent rewards.

This is usually appropriate if it is currently impossible to obtain the data needed for learning of if the data changes rapidly, and continuous learning is required through a given environment until all cases are experienced. It is mainly used for classification and control.

Figure 4-29 Deep Learning Algorithm Flowchart

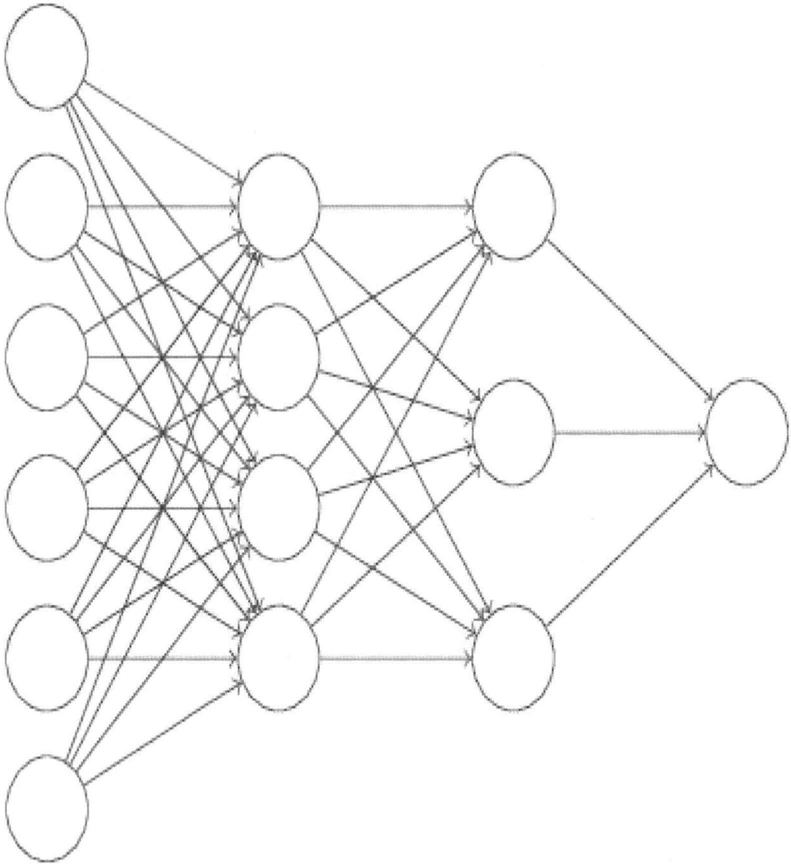

Fifth, Meta-Learning (Ensemble Learning) is an algorithm created by combining the learning results of several types of machine learning algorithms. Algorithms already available include Bagging, Boosting, and Random Forest.

In general, artificial intelligence technology, or machine learning, is widely used for the following purposes.

Figure 4-30 Data Architecture in Machine Learning

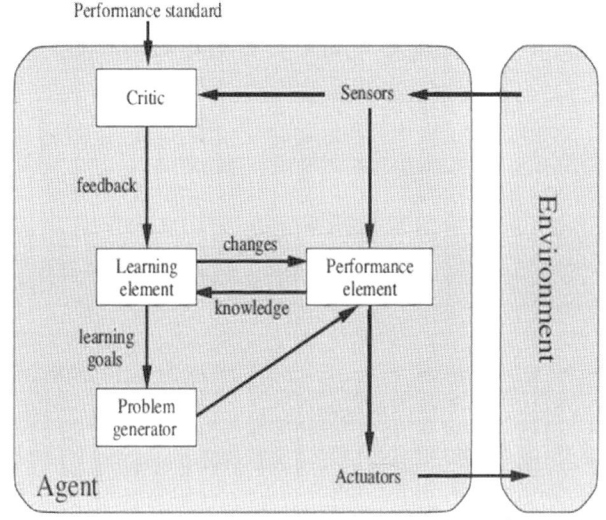

First, it is used for classification (classification) such as spam mail filtering, cancer diagnosis, sports competition prediction, election result prediction, and loan review.

Second, it is used for predicting monetary loss due to natural disasters and weather forecasting Numeric Prediction.

Third, it is used for pattern detection such as market basket analysis, credit card fraud detection, genetic disease diagnosis, crime prevention, and automatic driving.

Fourth, it is used for clustering for customer classification for target marketing.

Nearleast Neighbor algorithm, which is an algorithm already shown in Supervised Learning, is an algorithm premised on the proposition that similar entities have similar properties. For example, birdscan be grouped into similar properties in that they have wings. If you list several animals and check that they have wings, that individual is most likely to be a bird among animals.

Figure 4-31 Errors in generalization of objects to be recognized

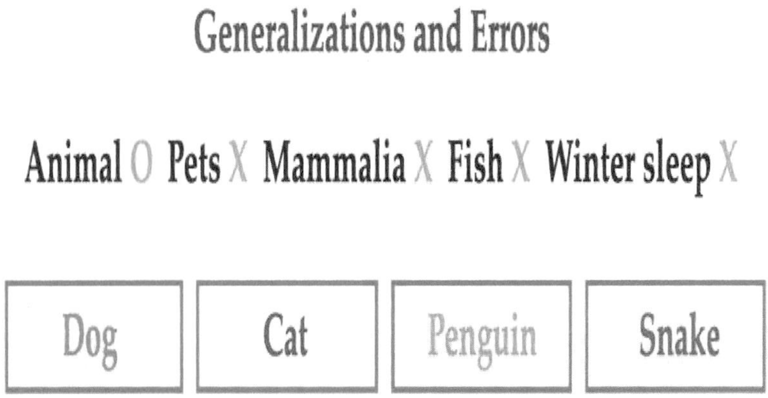

Generalizations and Errors

Animal O Pets X Mammalia X Fish X Winter sleep X

| Dog | Cat | Penguin | Snake |

A method of grouping similar properties is called generalization, and there is always a generalization error in this generalization. For example, dogs, cats, penguins, and snakes are all animals, but they may or may not be pets. Some are also mammals, but there are also reptiles like snakes. They are all animals, but of course they are not fish. Snakes hibernate, but not the rest. As such, errors of generalization must be considered from the design stage of artificial intelligence. The Nearleast Neighbor algorithm is a method that learns based on the closest properties of a specific entity.

KNN (K-Nearest Neighbors) is the most used among the well-known Nearest Neighbor algorithms.

KNN determines the classification of this sample by determining which classification the K objects most similar to the sample to be classified belong to, and the properties of the sample are recognized as spatial coordinates. Also, the similarity between two individuals p and q is measured by Euclidean Distance.

Figure 4-32 Classification of objects to be recognized

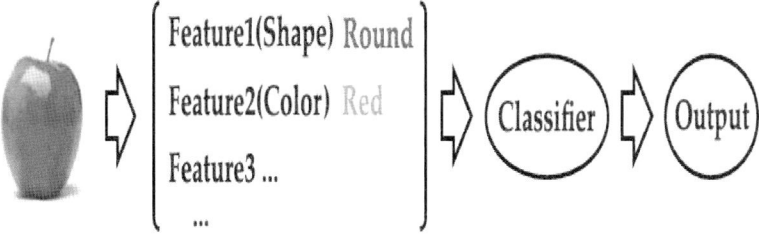

Figure 4-33 Euclidean equation

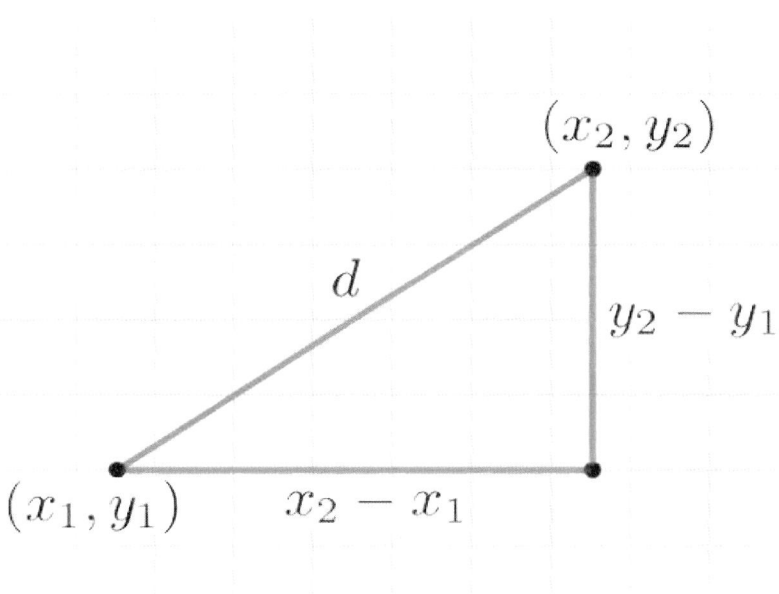

The Euclidean distance is a commonly used method to calculate the distance between two points. Euclidean space can be defined using this distance, and the norm corresponding to this distance is called the Euclidean norm. In simple terms, if we have a point x = (x1, x2, ~ n to the nth power) and y = (y1, y2, ~ y to the nth power) expressed in a Cartesian coordinate system, we can

use the two Euclidean norms to find two points (x1, y1) =p, (x2, y2)=q
Calculating the distance d is as follows.

$$d = \| p - qvert \| = \sqrt{(p-q).(q-p)} = \sqrt{\| pvert \|^2 + \| qvert \|^2 - 2p.q}$$

Clustering in machine learning, as discussed earlier, is an unsupervised machine learning technique that groups data together with similar items to form a cluster.

Clustering is primarily used for knowledge discovery rather than prediction, as it can provide insight into the natural clusters found in data, and we may not know what we are looking for.

The principle of cluster classification is to divide and group items that are very similar to items belonging to the same cluster and very different from items belonging to different clusters. The basic definition is to divide the data so that the associated elements belong to the same cluster.

Therefore, clustering has usefulness because it can match complex and diverse data into a small number of groups. It provides insight that can reveal patterns of how items included in data are intertwined with each other. Simply put, it can be said that a large data set is simplified into a small number of categories. If we look at the difference between Clustering and Classification, which is easy to confuse concepts, Clustering is an Unsupervised Classification. That is, clusters classified by clustering have no intrinsic meaning, and only show how the samples included in the data are related to each other, but do not provide an interpretation of the meaning of each cluster.

A concept often used in machine learning is a decision tree, which uses a tree structure to model the relationship between input variables (features) and output variables (potential outcomes).

If we look at the actual use of decision trees around us as an example, it is widely used in personal credit evaluations of credit information companies, customer satisfaction surveys, and diagnosis of disease states. Taking personal credit rating as an example, credit rating can be said to be a value calculated from such a decision tree concept.

Figure 4-34 Evaluation of Machine Learning

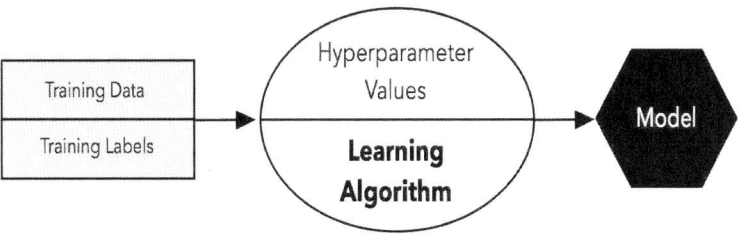

The basic principle of the Decision Tree is Divide and Conquer in computer algorithms. In other words, after dividing the data into subsets, each subset is repeatedly partitioned into smaller subsets. When the elements in the subset are homogeneous or the termination condition is satisfied, the partitioning stops.

The condition for terminating the division is when there are no more divisions left or when the decision tree reaches a predetermined size.

Figure 4-35 Decision Tree in Machine Learning

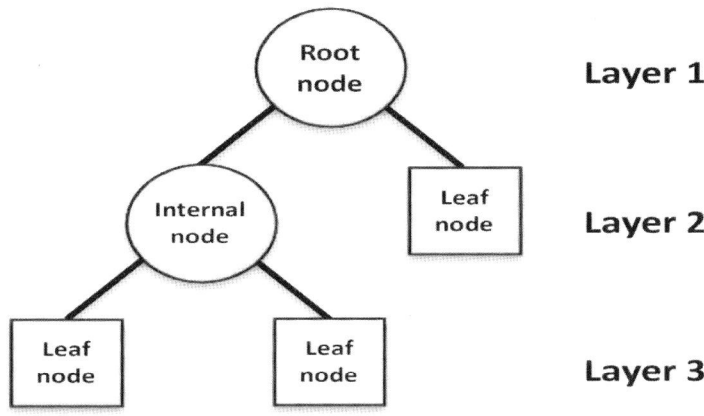

In this case, the value for determining the optimal partition has the following criteria.

It is necessary to partition the data to include only the individuals belonging to a single taxonomy so that the divided subsets become the divided subsets because purity indicates the degree of homogeneity of the individuals belonging to the subset.

Therefore, a subset consisting only of individuals belonging to a single taxon is called pure.

Here comes the concept of entropy, a representative method of measuring purity. It is a concept created in information theory and represents the degree of disorder in a set of several individuals belonging to various taxonomic groups.

A set with high entropy is a case in which little information about the entities belonging to the set is provided because there is no clear commonality. After all, it consists of very diverse entities.

Decision Tree pursues partitioning in the direction of reducing entropy and ultimately aims to increase homogeneity within individual sets of partitioned subsets.

Here, entropy is measured in bits as a data quantification standard. If a set can be divided into only two groups, the entropy range of this set is 0 and 1, and if the set can be divided into N groups, the entropy range is 0 and N.

In other words, when entropy is minimum, the set is said to be completely homogeneous, and when entropy is maximum, the set can be said to have maximum diversity.

As for entropy, the higher the information gain of a certain property, the more homogeneous subset can be obtained when data is divided based on the property.

Here, the maximum information gain is the entropy before division.

In other words, if the entropy becomes zero after division, this means that completely homogeneous subsets are obtained due to this division.

In entropy calculation, properties that are the basis of division of Numeric Features are nominal variables, but in Decision Tree,

even if the properties are numerical, not nominal, they can be divided using information gain, which is calculated by dividing them into two groups below and above this value based on a specific value.

Figure 4-36 Numeric Features Sample

Factor	Mean	SD	Min	Max
LE_1	84.34	0.3524	30.90	97.98
LE_2	76.58	0.5283	13.05	98.50
LE_3	83.56	0.3397	39.00	98.05
LE_4	87.02	0.1590	45.63	95.38
LE_5	84.33	0.3615	35.93	97.93
LE_6	87.05	0.1705	45.88	96.13
LE_7	89.72	0.1582	46.50	98.88
LE_8	89.15	0.1859	47.00	97.25
FB_3	42.60	0.0742	30	64
FB_4	2.57	0.0273	1	5

In general, by experimenting with various reference values, the number that can obtain the highest information gain is used as the standard for division.

The size of the decision tree can be infinitely large as described above. This is because it continues to partition into smaller and smaller subsets until each individual has been completely classified or there are no more properties to partition. Therefore, if the decision tree is excessively large, overestimation occurs on the training data. To prevent such overestimation, the generalization ability of the model can be increased by reducing the size of the decision tree. Here, generalization ability is the ability to make appropriate conclusions even on new data after the model has been trained.

In other words, pruning is early stopping (pre-pruning), and splitting stops when decisions are made more than a certain number of times or the number of entities included in the decision node is too small. This has the advantage of preventing wastage due to excessive segmentation, and also has the disadvantage that there is no way to know in advance whether a subtle but very important attribute is omitted from the segmentation criterion.

In addition to the algorithms of basic artificial intelligence and machine learning above, there is slightly applied machine learning, an example of which is an algorithm called Naive Bayes. It is an algorithm that measures the probability of event A occurring, or the conditional probability under the premise that event B occurred, and is a classifier made based on the Bayes probability theory.

The era of the Fourth Industrial Revolution also includes innovation and integration of these artificial intelligence algorithms. However, the library or platform combination that engineers and researchers often talk about is not an algorithm, but an application method.

4.2.2 Distributed Processing System and AI

Artificial intelligence is a game of probability. 100% conclusions are rare in this world. This is because there is always an environment variable of time in every event, and there are many other variables.

Machine learning provides algorithms that turn data into actionable knowledge and serves to help us understand the meaning of the data in our world. In addition, current machine learning is already used in countless modern human life to filter spam emails, classify customers based on consumer behavior for targeted advertising, forecast weather and climate changes, prevent card fraud, estimate money loss due to typhoons and natural disasters, predict election results, automatically drive, optimize home and building energy use, prevent crime, and diagnose diseases, etc. Big data basically means a lot of data that can be used. Artificial intelligence needs to be trained on such a large amount of data. A resource distribution policy different from the existing small-capacity data is required.

So, what emerged is the use of distributed computing.

Distributed computing is a field of computer science that studies distributed systems. It is a distributed processing model that attempts to solve huge computational problems using the processing power of several computers connected to the Internet. In general, the idea of utilizing the processing resources of idle personal computers appeared when ARPANET, also known as the dawn of the Internet, first appeared in the early 1970s. Several programs such as Creeper and Reaper appeared, and with the popularization of the Internet, RSA Data Security started the Distributed.net project in 1997, involving about 300,000 users, and decrypted DES 64-bit encryption.

Figure 4-37 Large-capacity deep learning

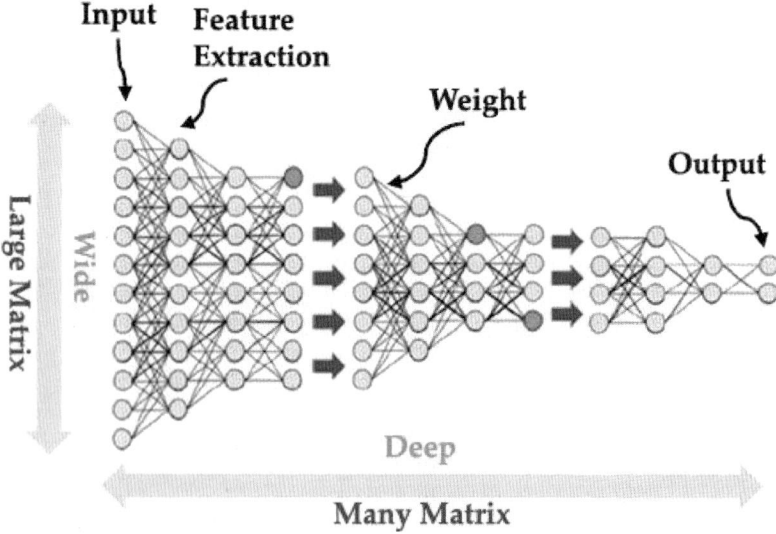

Looking at the trend of overseas distributed computing projects, various countries such as the United States, England, Germany, and others are showing interest in projects based on distributed computing, and projects are underway in various application fields such as biofield, meteorology, artificial intelligence, mathematics, and cryptography.

Among them, the most popular and successful is the well-known SETI@Home (Search for Extraterrestrial Intelligence) project. SETI@Home started the project in earnest in 1999, and as of 2020, more than 10 million users are participating. Distributed processing systems are also widely used in space astronomy.

In addition, Stanford University and Oxford University in the UK are playing a pivotal role in the @Home project, and related companies such as Entropia, United Devices, and Parabon are typically intensively carrying out projects in the bio field.

Figure 4-38 Data parallel processing

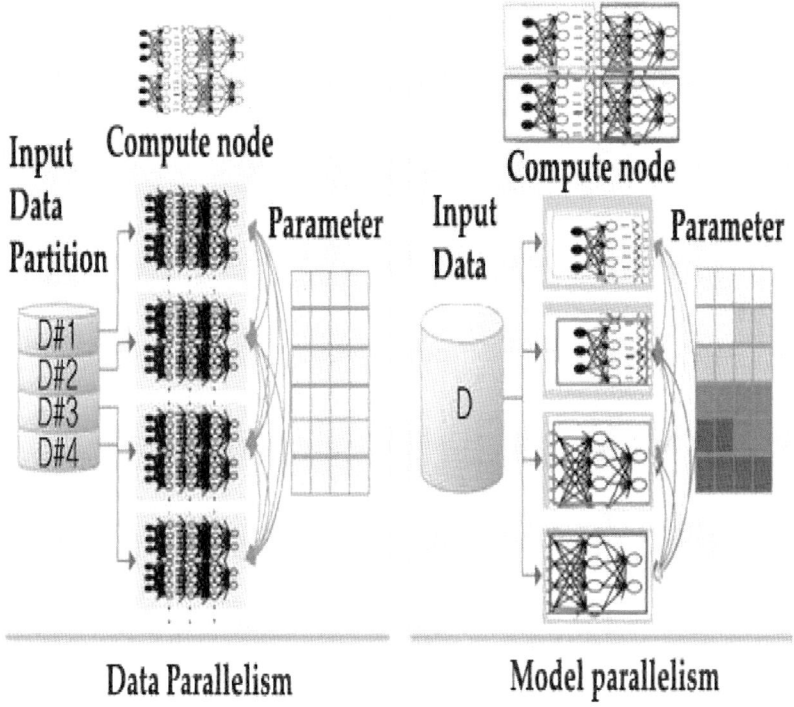

A distributed system is a group of computers in a network that have a common goal for working. Parallel computing, parallel computing, and distributed computing have a lot of overlap and there is no clear difference between them. The same goes for multiprocessor computing.

Grid computing is a field of distributed parallel computing that is being actively researched in recent years. It refers to performing high-level computational work or large-capacity processing by configuring. In other words, it refers to a next-generation digital neural network service that maximizes computational power by connecting all computers through a single high-speed network. Virtually connecting multiple computers to perform computational tasks jointly is also called distributed computing.

Figure 4-39 Distributed processing system configuration diagram

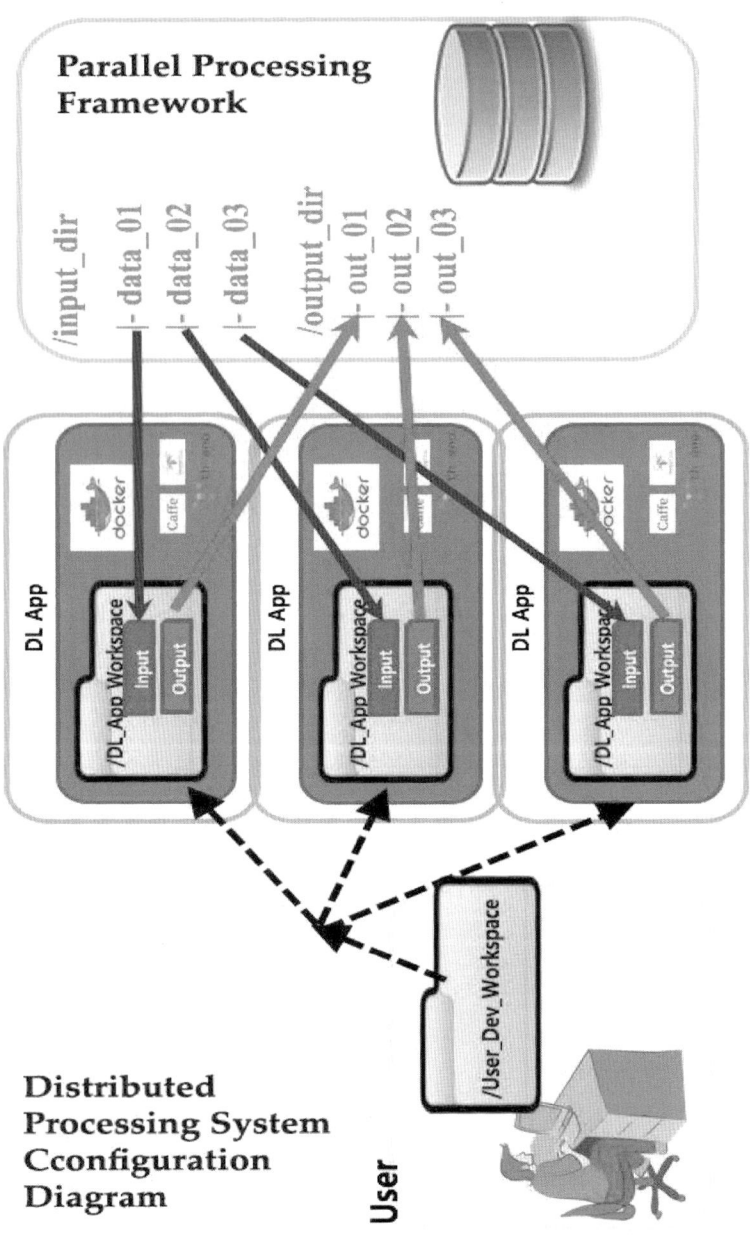

Grid computing can be seen as an extended concept of cluster computing in that it divides large data operations into small operations and distributes them to several small computers. Due to the connection, various standard protocols that were not considered in cluster computing are required, and it is different from cluster computing in that it connects various platforms with each other.

Hadoop is a popular system configuration for deep learning in distributed processing systems these days.

Hadoop (High-Availability Distributed Object-Oriented Platform, Hadoop) is a freeware Java software framework that supports distributed applications running on large computer clusters capable of processing large amounts of data. Hadoop was originally developed in 2006 by Doug Cutting and Mike Cafarella. At the time, Doug Cutting was working at Yahoo, but later moved to the Apache Foundation and developed open software. Hadoop was developed as a system corresponding to the structure after Google's Distributed File System (GFS) paper was published. Hadoop's logo is a yellow baby elephant because Doug Cutting named it Hadoop after the toy elephant his child used to play with. Therefore, the elephant is sometimes considered an animal that symbolizes Big Data.

Hadoop consists of a common package, which includes the Hadoop File System (HDFS), OS level abstractions, and MapReduce engine. It consists of scripts to start Hadoop, source codes, and related materials.

A small Hadoop cluster consists of one master and several worker nodes. Master nodes are composed of Job Tracker, Task Tracker, Name Node, and Data Node. Worker Node operates as Data Node and Task Tracker. Hadoop requires Java Runtime Environment 1.6 or higher. Generally, scripts for startup and shutdown use SSH to configure settings between nodes in the cluster. The Hadoop File System (HDFS) is managed through a Name Node dedicated server for managing the file system index.

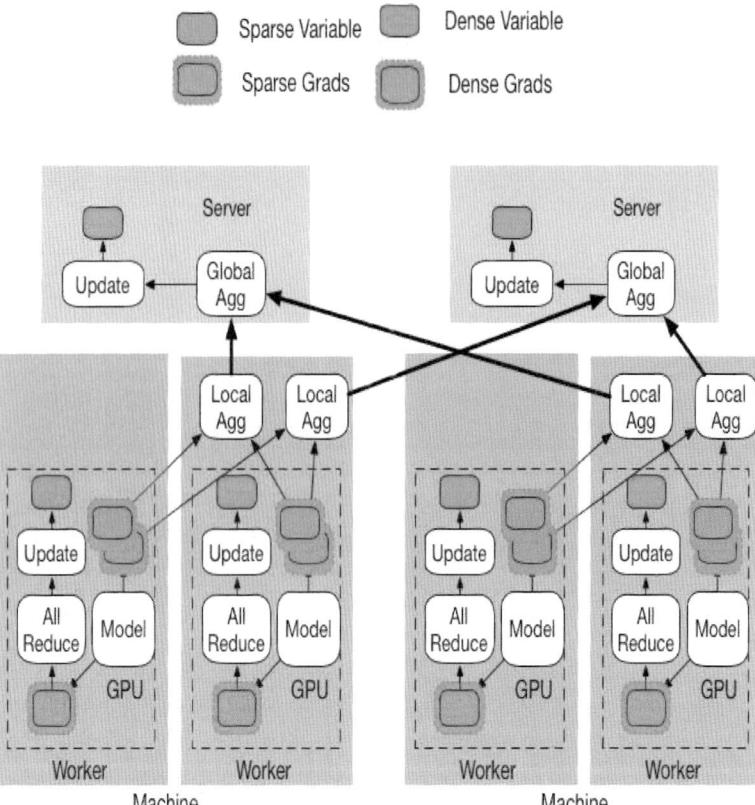

Figure 4-40 Deep Learning Model Distributed Learning System

It is a distributed extended file system written in Java language for the framework. HDFS divides and stores large files on multiple machines and acquires stability against data loss by storing data redundantly on multiple servers. Therefore, there is an advantage that the host does not need to use a distributed storage method such as RAID.

Hadoop File System (HDFS) has a Master and Slave structure like a general PC. HDFS cluster consists of one Name Node and a master server that manages the file system and controls client access. In addition, there is one Data Node in each node of the cluster, and this Data Node manages storage added to the node whenever it is executed. HDFS exposes namespaces to allow user data to be stored in files. Internally, a file is divided into one or more blocks, and these blocks are stored in Data Nodes. The Name Node manages the file system such as Open, Close, and Rename of files and directories. In addition, it determines the matching of data nodes and blocks. The Data Node is responsible for the Read and Write functions requested by the client of the file system and performs functions such as creation, deletion, and duplication in the Name Node.

From the user's point of view, there is no significant difference from the general personal computer's file system structure. Although the internally operating logic is a distributed processing system, the user interface makes it look like a central processing system for the convenience of users.

In particular, Hadoop File System (HDFS) uses Java language, so it has the advantage of being able to run Data Node or Name Node software on any computer running Java.

These distributed processing systems and artificial intelligence technologies that need to learn large-capacity big data are inevitably bound to each other. In particular, in the case of deep learning, most learn a distributed processing system rather than a central processing system.

Using deep learning technology, the machine learns tens of millions of images to recognize objects and learns thousands of hours of voice data to understand human speech. Therefore, distributed processing technology to efficiently use multiple computers is essential for deep learning.

Deep learning AlphaGo, which has recently become an issue among people, is a Go game program using Convolutional Neural Net, that is, a deep learning technique called CNN and a Monte Carlo search technique.

It was executed in a distributed processing system using 1,920 CPUs and 280 General-Purpose computing on Graphics Processing Units (GPGPUs) when playing against a Korean professional Go player Sedol Lee. AlphaGo's victory was due not only to its excellent artificial intelligence algorithms but also to

Figure 4-41 Distributed processing system IBM WORKLOAD

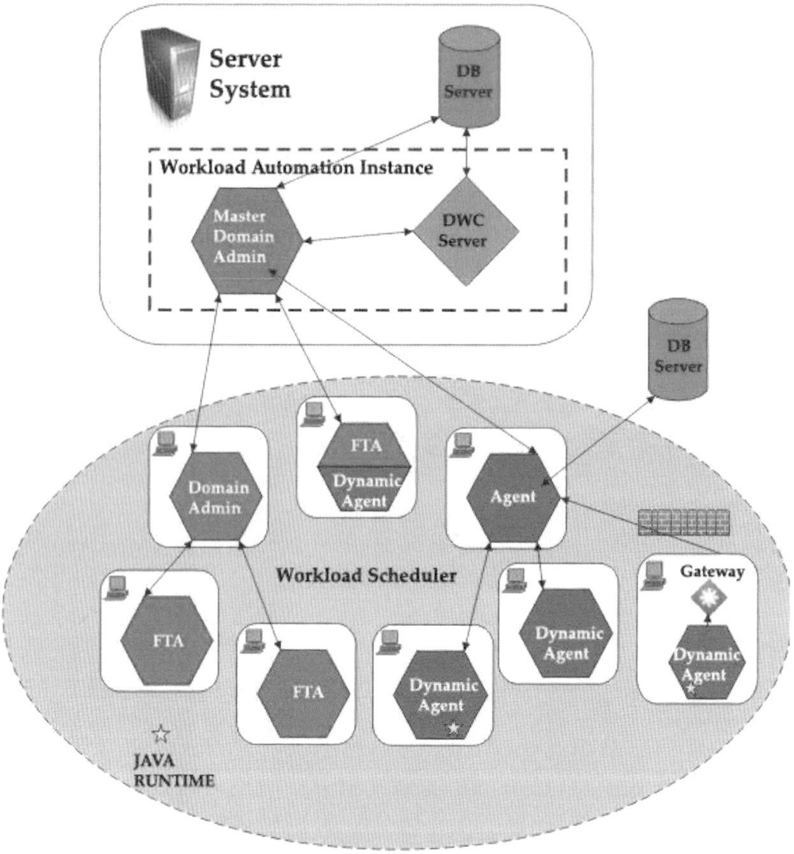

a thousand computers that could completed calculations in a short time and respond within a set time. However, Demis Hassabis of Google DeepMind, who developed AlphaGo, said that if the capacity of computer resources was increased, the performance of AlphaGo was rather poor, so the capacity of computer resources was not increased unconditionally. This means that performing tasks quickly does not necessarily depend on a large amount of computing resources, but on how efficiently they are used according to the needs of the applications. In general, deep learning technology analysis is largely divided into training and inference. Training is the process of learning a model through input data, and inference is the process of performing services such as recognition of the learned model. Deep learning training is synonymous with learning. Learning is a computationally intensive process with many repetitions, and the development of distributed parallel processing technology is essential due to the problem of taking a long time to process.

Deep learning is an artificial neural network-based machine learning method that mimics human biological neurons and enables machines to learn.

As an example of distributed parallel processing technology, Microsoft trained its model for speech recognition (Context-Dependent DNN-HMM) in 2012, which took 17.8 days to train the Fisher's data set with one computer equipped with 4 GPGPU, and in the same year, Google took a week to model and train 10 million CNN videos with1,000 computers with 16,000 CPU cores. The use of GPGPU has gradually spread, and in 2013, Stanford University reported that it took 3 days with 98,304 GPGPU cores on 16 computers to learn 10 million images with a CNN model. Baidu of China, developed a supercomputer for image recognition, Minwa, in 2015, and said that it took 8.6 hours to reach 80% accuracy by training 512×512 pixel images with a CNN model with 92,160 GPGPU cores on 32 computers.

This is an example that shows that the revolutionary development of distributed troop processing technology coincides with the development of artificial intelligence technology.

As the size of the deep learning model increases and the amount of input data increases to increase the accuracy of data recognition, many computers are needed, and an efficient distributed processing system is essential.

The deep learning distributed processing techniques known so far are divided into three main categories. The first is a technology to extend the big data distributed processing framework to deep learning distributed processing, the second is a technology to extend the existing machine learning framework, and the third is a technology to newly develop a distributed processing framework for deep learning.

If we look at deep learning a little more here, training using deep learning is basically the repetition of the Feed Forward process and the Back Propagation process. That is, deep learning training is a repetition of the feed forward process of calculating feature values and objective functions from the input layer to the output layer through several hidden layers, and the back-propagation process of modifying weights from the output layer through several hidden layers to the input layer by reflecting errors (the difference between the feed forward result and the correct answer). Weights modified during training are repeatedly updated until errors are minimized. In distributed processing, all computers must share weights and parameters of deep learning. Here, parallel processing methods of distributed data and models, parameter sharing techniques, communication protocols, and synchronization problems arise. Resolving these problems is the core of deep learning distributed processing technology. In general, when training with a distributed processing system in deep learning, training acceleration is attempted through distributed parallelism. There are two methods of this method: data parallelism and model parallelism. Data Parallelism is a method in which multiple computers train by dividing the input data set to be learned, and Model Parallelism is a method in which multiple computers train by dividing a deep learning model. As a framework of a distributed processing system for deep learning, there are Petuum, etc. Petuum is an open-source distributed machine learning framework developed by Carnegie Mellon University and Intel Lab. In addition to deep learning libraries such as DNN and CNN, Petuum supports more than 10 machine learning libraries such as Latent Dirichlet Allocation (LDA), MedLDA, sparse coding, and k-means. It also supports distributed execution on individual clusters and clouds such as Amazon EC2 or Google GCE and provides distributed programming tools for running machine learning that support big data and large-scale models.

Figure 4-42 PETUUM Distributed Processing Architecture

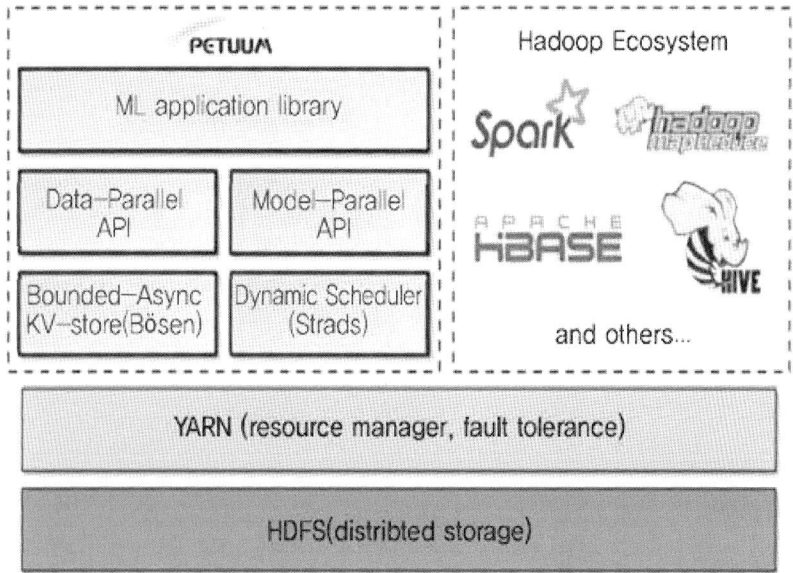

Figure 4-43 PETUUM Distributed processing logic

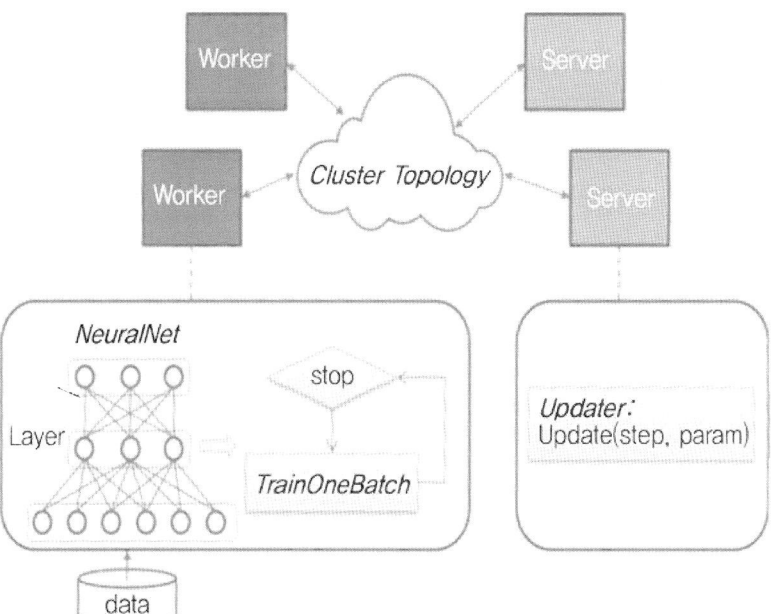

Programmers who perform development on their own can use this distributed processing machine learning framework when developing deep learning algorithms.

As seen above, distributed processing systems have a close relationship with artificial intelligence, especially deep learning, and it can be seen that it is difficult to improve the performance of artificial intelligence technology without implementing a high-performance distributed processing system.

Deep learning, also known as AlphaGo, starts with the basic concept of artificial intelligence to train and evaluate. The most basic thing to know is to understand the four learning methods of artificial intelligence, namely, training methods.

Figure 4-44 Reinforcement learning through four-step

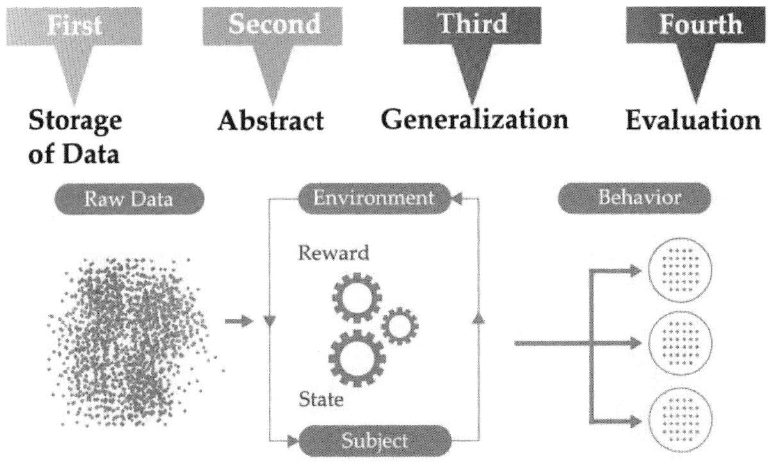

Therefore, if we rearrange the machine learning of artificial intelligence, it is achieved through the four-step process of first data storage, second abstraction, third generalization, and fourth evaluation.

First, the storage of data provides the necessary factual basis for inference, and all machine learning starts with data.

Second, an abstraction transforms the stored data into a more comprehensive form and concept, and summarizes the stored data using a model to specifically describe the pattern hidden in the data. As a representative form of the model, it refers to the division of data into relational pictures such as mathematical equations, tree diagrams, graphs, logical rules, and homogeneous groups. What comes out of the abstraction process is training, which is a process of fitting a model to a data set, and the source information contained in the data is converted into an abstract form by the trained model. The trained model can uncover previously unknown relationships that were already in the data.

This is the purpose of using artificial intelligence technology.

Third, generalization is the process of transforming abstracted knowledge so that it can be applied to future tasks that are similar to but not identical to those experienced in the past by creating knowledge and reasoning that can cope with new situations using abstracted data. Among the patterns discovered through the learning process, the task of leaving only those most suitable for future tasks is performed in the generalization process.

Fourth, an evaluation aims to measure the utility of the learned knowledge and provide information on future improvements by providing a feedback system.

For reference, in the concept of artificial intelligence, over-fitting is a model that over-fits a model that showed excellent performance in the training process of artificial intelligence but did not perform well in the evaluation process of the training data, as opposed to optimizing the training data. It means that the model cannot properly respond to the test data that it has not experienced in the training process because it loses its ability to generalize by reflecting even unnecessary data in the model.

4.2.3 AI in 5G communication network

The International Consumer Electronics Show (CES), where you can read the world's new trends in information and communication technology, opens in Las Vegas in early January every year. Smart home, smart city, autonomous driving technology, and robotics based on 5G mobile communication and artificial intelligence, which have been commercialized in Korea, have emerged as hot topics in 2020. About 4,400 companies from 155 countries around the world participated and 19,21 products in 33 fields were exhibited. There are over 180,000 visitors from all over the world.

The biggest topic in 2020 at the International Consumer Electronics Show (CES) is 5G mobile communication. 5G mobile communication, characterized by high speed, ultra-low latency, and ultra-connectivity, has attracted attention because it can be used in all industrial fields. For this reason, mobile communication technology was usually covered at the Mobile World Congress (MWC) held in Spain at the end of February every year, but 2 out of 7 keynote speeches at CES 2020 are related to 5G mobile communication. It can be easily explained with big data to explain what kind of correlation there is between the 5G communication network and artificial intelligence. For example, without data, you cannot study, work, or store knowledge. Of course, we cannot create the Internet of Things or artificial intelligence, and we cannot develop the technologies corresponding to all Fourth Industrial Revolutions.

In particular, artificial intelligence platforms based on 5G communication networks are receiving new attention. LG Electronics introduced the evolution of its proprietary artificial intelligence platform ThinQ. LG

Electronics emphasized the expansion of the user experience, active product management, and the provision of optimal services for each situation as the strengths of ThinQ.

Figure 4-45 CES First

Samsung Electronics also exhibited its own artificial intelligence platform, New Bixby. Smart View, which connects TVs, refrigerators, and lights through the Galaxy Home and Family Hub, an artificial intelligence speaker, as well as links with mobile devices, was also introduced.

The evolution of Amazon's Alexa and Google Assistant, which are far away from Korean companies in the field of artificial intelligence platforms, also attracted everyone's attention. LG Electronics introduced a smart TV linked with Alexa for the first time this time. The world's data is expected to increase tenfold to 44 trillion gigabytes by 2020. However, this is also difficult to see as an accurate prediction. Even now, the field of application of the Internet of Things (AIOT) is expanding and the sensor market is growing explosively because the data is also likely to increase on a larger scale.

Figure 4-46 CES Second

According to The Mobile Economy Asia Pacific 2018 published by the GSMA, the Asia-Pacific region will become the world's largest 5G network area by 2025, led by China, Japan, Korea, and Australia. expected to do When commercial 5G networks are launched in the Asia-Pacific market in 2020, it is reported that Asia is expected to create 675 million 5G connections by 2025, accounting for more than half of global 5G connections.

As such, the 5G communication network will smoothly provide different services to various types of users and devices with high speed, low latency, and high reliability, and will act as the most basic infrastructure necessary to implement the distributed processing system described above.

Figure 4-47 CES Third

Just as a distributed processing system is emerging as an infrastructure that implements artificial intelligence, accurate AI training data can be extracted only when the 5G communication network that connects such distributed processing systems is functioning properly. In addition, such a 5G communication network will be able to provide a customized distributed processing system that is optimally configured for specific applications such as artificial intelligence within a range that does not affect the performance of a wide range of networks.

The ITU (International Telecommunication Union ITU-T 13 Research Group) also has established a 5G artificial intelligence (machine learning) network standardization group (Focus Group on Machine Learning for Future Networks including 5G) in the telecommunication sector for Standardization of Artificial Intelligence Network Technology for 5G

Figure 4-48 CES Four

The three Korean telecommunication companies, which have commercialized 5G for the first time in the world, regard artificial intelligence as the future driver and are aggressively attacking the market by reorganizing their organizations for artificial intelligence.

Artificial intelligence basically uses big data as a raw material. It is widely applied from smart speakers and home appliances equipped with the well-known AI voice assistant platform such as Alexa and Google Assistant, to smart homes, robots and cars, and digital twins (virtual models that are equally expressed on physical objects and computers and a concept created by GE), and smart cities. Many economists predict that the year 2025 will be the year when AI technology will be widely applied and yield results. In fact, AI-

Figure 4-49 CES Five

related technologies are taking the best position every year in Hyper Cycle, a visual tool of Gartner in the US to express the maturity of a specific technology. In artificial intelligence technology, above all else, the data loaded on the sensor is very important.

In other words, data is the most important component of the Fourth Industrial Revolution and can be regarded as oxygen in terms of air. Just as humans cannot survive without oxygen, the technologies of the Fourth Industrial Revolution cannot exist without data.

In this Fourth Industrial Revolution, data such as oxygen must be collectively classified and transported to the right place to have a form that can be processed as meaningful and useful data. cannot distribute Only 5G technology can provide the speed and bandwidth needed to run these AI algorithms. Therefore, the development of artificial intelligence technology can only be properly implemented when a smooth foundation of a 5G transmission network is provided along with big data.

By 2025, the number of sensors that will fill people's daily lives is expected to reach 10 trillion. The most important data technology in artificial intelligence is also growing rapidly. According to DELL EMC, a company specializing in computer data storage, the annual data generated from 4.4 trillion gigabytes in 2013 is expected to increase tenfold to 44 trillion gigabytes in 2020. However, this is also difficult to see as an accurate prediction. Even now, the IoT application area is expanding, and the sensor market is growing explosively because the data is also likely to increase on a larger scale. As a result, the time at which the technological maturity of artificial intelligence arrives has accelerated.

In other words, most of the basic technologies of artificial intelligence are in line with the characteristics of 5G communication networks: ultra-high speed, ultra-low latency, and hyper-connection. The 5G communication network can act as a driving force that can influence the development of artificial intelligence technology.

Today is the era of the Fourth Industrial Revolution. All technologies are converging in all directions, all connections are being tied together, and the speed has long exceeded human cognition.

In the era of the Fourth Industrial Revolution, with the commercialization of 5G communication networks, competition among countries around the world over artificial intelligence technology is getting fiercer than ever before, and the level of the finished product is developing day by day. Therefore, soon, autonomous judgment robots and autonomous vehicles that are implemented as a distributed processing system using a 5G communication network and are equipped with artificial intelligence technology will coexist with us.

4.3 Artificial intelligence and robot technology

4.3.1 Atom and Mazinger Jet and Terminator

In general, robots using artificial power may operate instead of human or together. Typically, robots are designed to do what their creators planned.

If we look at the etymology of the term robot, it was written in a play published in 1920 by the Czechoslovak playwright Karel Capek, and it came to be commonly used. ROBOTA, which means "labor" in Czech, is the etymology.

For reference, when defining a robot, the three principles regarding the behavior of a robot to define a robot as proposed in the novel iRobot published by Isaac Asimov in 1950 are as follows.

The first law is that robots must not harm humans and must not neglect humans in danger.

The second law is that robots must obey human commands. However, there are exceptions when the first rule is violated.

The third law is that a robot must protect itself. However, there are exceptions when the 1st and 2nd laws are violated.

Therefore, if the military robot has an attack function, it will violate the first principle. In other words, the robot is the crystallization of mechanical engineering for humans made with a human motif.

In general, many tasks that have been done by humans are now being replaced by robots. There are many monotonous repetitive tasks, tedious tasks, and unpleasant tasks in industrial sites, and these tasks are particularly suitable for entrusting robots. Screwing, welding and painting car bodies in an assembly plant are good examples. Robots can do better than humans for these kinds of tasks because the robot can always continue to work with a certain level of precision and accuracy and never tire. Therefore, the quality of the product is always constant, and besides, there is no need to take a break, so a large number of products can be made.

Figure 4-50 History of robots

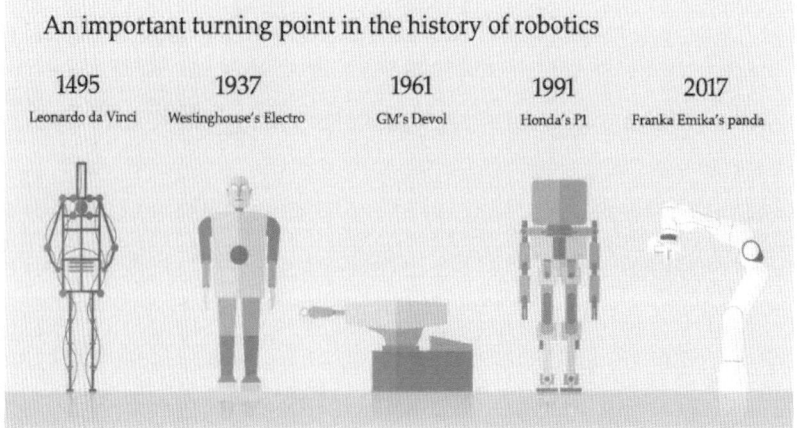

Robots can also take over dangerous tasks. It is possible to handle radioactive materials or toxic chemicals in nuclear power plants without wearing protective clothing, and to work in environments that are too hot or too cold for humans. Robots can also be used in places where human life may be at risk. Searching for explosives, depriving bombs, for example, and working in outer space are among them. These days, robots are especially ideal for working in outer space. Robots are also used to repair or maintain satellites orbiting the earth, and robots are naturally used to fly to distant celestial bodies for exploration and discovery purposes, such as the US space probes Voyager 1 and Voyager 2 in the United States. Renowned space exploration columnist Carl Sagan asked NASA to photograph the Earth by turning the camera once toward Earth before Voyager left the solar system. And when he saw the image of the Earth filmed by the robot arm of the Voyager, he said this.

Figure 4-51 Spaceship's robot Arm

A pale blue dot that looks smaller than a single piece of dust is the Earth where we humans live. He emphasized how small the earth is in the vast universe and how small the humans living on it are, and said that we should live beautifully recognizing that humans are members of a family who live together in a very small house called the Earth, loving and caring for each other rather than hate, envy, and fight such small beings.

Perhaps this profound and philosophical saying came about because there were robots and robotic arms mounted on spaceships.

Robots are being used a lot around us living in modern times. In general, more and more robots are being used to help with housework, and it is expected to be used a lot in caring for people with physical disabilities in the future. Robotic nursing assistants will help people with disabilities or those who have weakened due to old age to live independently from their families and avoid having to be hospitalized. In reality, robots that can be closely combined with human life as described above appeared in the 19th century in the era of the Fourth Industrial Revolution and became a daily routine of human life in the 20th century. Looking at the development of robots in each country, in the United States, there is a thought that robots may threaten mankind in the future rather than machines that help people in life. Also, military robots mainly used for military purposes, such as unmanned aerial vehicles, are the most developed.

Han can not only communicate with people, but also recognize their facial expressions, gender, and age. The most surprising thing about Han is that he can make human-like facial expressions.

The United States is the originator of industrial robots. It ranks second in the world in terms of market size and the world's first robot leader in the field of source technology such as artificial intelligence. The use of robot technology in space, defense, and medical fields is outstanding, and robot research is conducted at Carnegie Institute of Technology's RI Lab, MIT's AI Lab, NASA's JPL Lab, Sandia National Lab, Stanford University's SRI Lab, and US Defense Research Institute DARPA. Representative companies include iRobot, which produces the world's first cleaning robot, Roomba, Boston Dynamics, which has recently become famous for its Big Dog, and Intuitive Surgical of Da Vinci Systems, the world's number one surgical robot company. Microsoft is also showing great interest in advancing into the robot industry by developing Robotic Studio, a software development environment. As a society, there is the IEEE Robot and Automation academic conference where world-class robot authorities gather to present and discuss research results every year. The U.S. government also focused its national resources on R&D in the robotics field to the extent that the National Innovation Council (NIC) in July 2008 selected service robots as the six disruptive technologies that will change the national map 25 years later.

Figure 4-52 Robot arm with tactile sensor developed by MIT

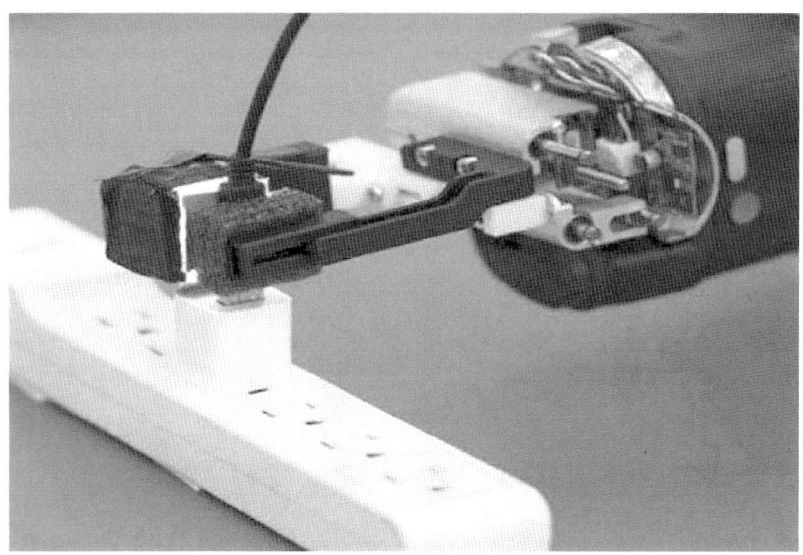

Figure 4-53 The battle robot from the movie Terminator

Figure 4-54 T800 in the movie Terminator

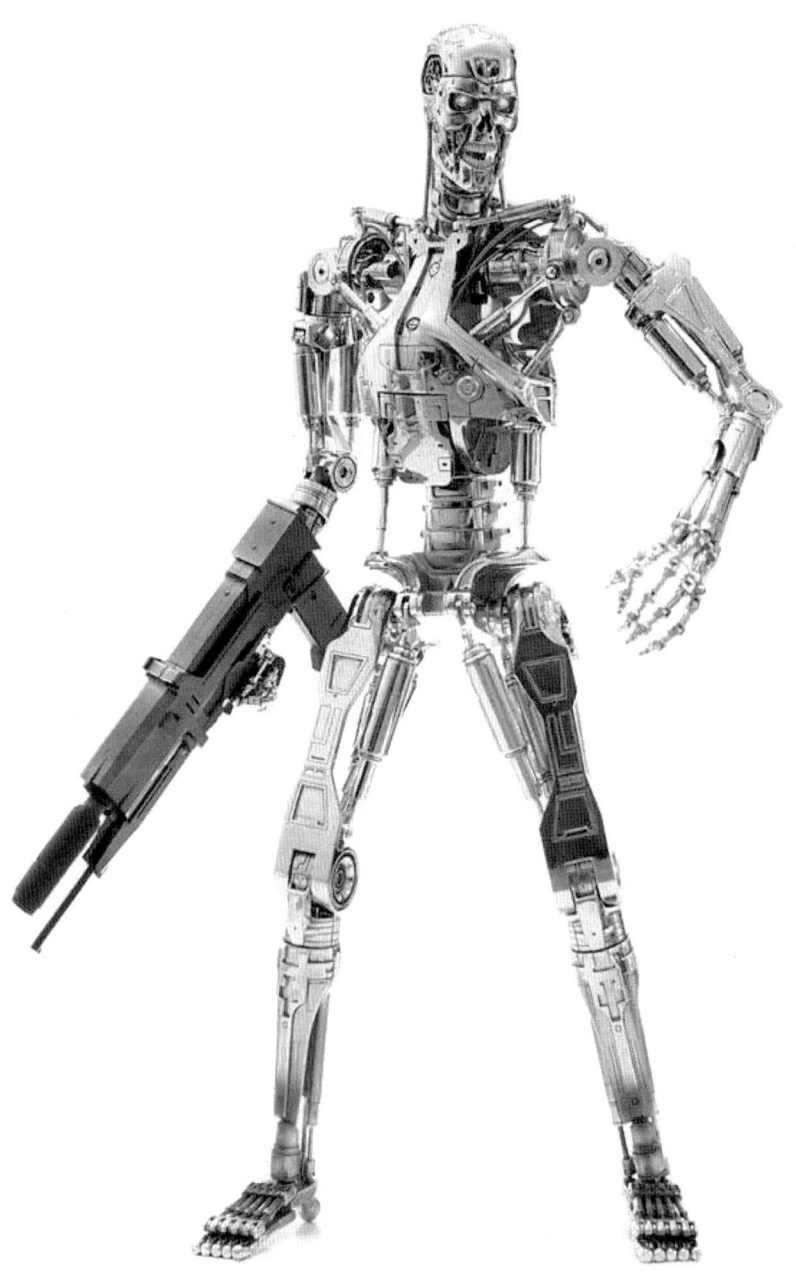

Figure 4-55 Robot with autonomous intelligence

Figure 4-56 Humanoid Robot

Japan, which has developed after the United States in the field of robots, developed humanoid robots such as Asimo, pet robots such as Sony's AIBO, and industrial robots, as well as robots close to human form. Robot manga such as Atom and Gundam were also made in Japan. Japan is the world's No. 1 robot powerhouse in terms of the size of the market where industrial robots (Unimation's PUMA) invented in the United States were fully industrialized. Mitsubishi Heavy Industries, Hitachi, Yaskawa, and Nagasaki Heavy Industries, the world's leading industrial robot manufacturers, are forming the robot industry. In particular, it has global competitiveness in the parts industry such as industrial motors, precision reducers such as harmonic drives, and robot sensors such as encoders and CCD cameras. With the advent of the humanoid robot Asimo announced by Honda in 1997, the era of intelligent robots was ushered in, and with the advent of the pet robot Aibo and the dancing robot Curio announced by Sony in 2000, the service robot industry began in earnest. In Robodex, held every two years, robot-related large companies and small and medium-sized enterprises (SMEs) are exhibiting innovative service robots. The Japanese government is also fostering the service robot industry as a national core industry as part of its "Made in Japan" strategy.

In China, there is a tendency to think of robots as human-controlled puppets rather than machines that help industries or homes. However, in 2000, an upright walking robot named Predecessor was developed, and due to the pipe-shaped part installed between the legs of the predecessor, an animation called Predecessor, the Ultimate Heavy Weapons Weapon, was released in Japan, and exploded in popularity as a cartoon character.

In the Joseon Dynasty, Korea manufactured water clocks, Jagyeongnu and Okru, in which various puppets were operated by the power of water. In the early days, Korea manufactured machinery necessary for industry and

Figure 4-57 Japanese Manga and Robot Industry - Mazinger Jet

Figure 4-58 Japanese Manga and Robot Industry - Atom

economy, and recently, it has been working hard to develop humanoid robots. Europe has traditionally been a developed region for the dairy industry and welfare industry. As for robots, research on agricultural robots and silver welfare robots is in full swing. Germany and Sweden are powerful industrial robots, such as Germany's KUKA robot and Sweden's ABB, and France is also strengthening its investment in service robots such as educational robots. In Germany, research on original technologies such as the Smart Robot Hand of the German Aerospace Center's DLR Research Center is also active.

Robots are no longer the objects of the future in cartoons or science fiction movies. In the era of the Fourth Industrial Revolution, robots will become a necessity that is closely related to our lives, like a kind of companion animal that exists with us.

If artificial intelligence is made with the human brain as a motif, then the robot is made with the human body as a motif. Just as artificial intelligence has surpassed the ability of the human brain, the day will come shortly for robots to surpass the physical ability of humans.

It is expected to be a technological innovation that can be experienced in reality closer to the space for us living the era of the Forth Industrial Revolution.

4.3.2 From Robot Vacuums to Spaceships

Is there any house without a robot vacuum cleaner in the house these days? Robots are always right next to us, small or large.

If we classify these familiar robots by technology, they can be classified into a total of four technologies. The first is operation control technology, the second is autonomous movement technology, the third is object recognition technology, and the fourth is location recognition technology. With only four key technologies of such a robot, it is possible to make a robot once. Among them, operation control technology, which is the most important element of a robot, is one of the four key technologies of intelligent robot technology, and it is a technology to hold objects and handle them freely. The operation control function is the most powerful function that differentiates a robot from a computer. Looking at the example of a silver robot that assists the elderly at home, various services such as assisting the elderly, running errands, and housekeeping services are expected to become possible depending on the realization of operation control technology. When viewed as 100, this technology remains at the level of around 60 globally (handling index for a 4-year-old) and is the most robot-like challenger technology that all robot researchers constantly challenge. The human five-finger smart hand technology is representative, and Germany's DLR hand is considered to be the most advanced.

Humanoid robots are equipped with human-like tactile and force sensors and have object-handling capabilities to the extent of cutting fruit with a paring knife. For this technology to be implemented, many original technologies such as a new material actuator, multi-hand mechanism design, multi-axis coordinated control, force angle control, and learning-type grip control must be secured. However, given the development trend of new materials, next-generation computers, semiconductor integration technology, and artificial intelligence technology, it is unlikely that these technologies will become a reality in the next 20 years. Robot technology, which will come realistically within 20 years, seems to be an operation control technology that has a tidying function that overcomes the limitations of existing robot vacuum cleaners.

Figure 4-59 Cotton candy making robot exhibited at CES

The cleaning robots we are most familiar with currently rely only on suction ability. Therefore, it has the decisive disadvantage of not being able to clean the corner well. The tidying robot with a manipulator has the shape of the current industrial robot arm and has both arms of a lightweight structure. One arm has a vacuum inhaler, sucking up dust from every nook and cranny, and the other arm is expected to function to remove cluttered light clothes and tissues.

An autonomous movement technology is a technology that can move freely and is classified into movement mechanisms such as wheel type, quadrupedal type, and bipedal type. In the case of the wheel type, path planning, and control technology, and the case of the quadruped type, the technology that can move and balance on an outdoor flat such as the Big Dog in the United States is the core technology. In the case of the two-legged type, as Asimo and Hubo show, it is a technology that realizes a human gait pattern. Currently, in the case of the four-legged type, it seems that it has reached the level of 90 (movement index like that of a donkey), and in the case of the two-legged type, it is judged to have stayed at the level of 50 (the movement index of a 5-year-old who has just learned to walk). In the case of Asimo, it is possible to climb stairs and run at a speed of 5 km/h, but like Korea's HUBO, even a slight protrusion (edge of a carpet, etc.) is not detected and falls.

Autonomous movement technology is largely composed of technology that moves along a path, such as mechanical positioning technology and autonomous path planning collision avoidance. If only the current sensor information is provided in real-time, it is not difficult to implement a route planning unit such as collision avoidance. The problem is that it is necessary to add a separate mechanism, such as climbing a threshold and stairs, suitable for a person's living space.

Object recognition technology is one of the four key technologies of intelligent robots. Based on the knowledge information learned in advance, it is a technology to view an image of an object and find out three-dimensional spatial information such as the type, size, direction, and location of the object in real-time. am. Unlike the previous two technologies, it is a challenge not only in the field of robotics but also in the field of computer science as a whole. It is a very difficult technology that requires high-level artificial intelligence to unravel the secret. Currently, ER of the United States has commercialized the most advanced object recognition software, but the recognition rate is judged to be still at the level of 50 (infant level recognition index). In the field of robots, it is necessary to specialize in recognition functions while moving and apply them to errands robots that classify specific items in the house and deliver them to the owner. Like humans, the technology to discriminate objects with two eyes is a high-level technology that is difficult to reproduce perfectly even after 20 years. Therefore, object recognition suitable for robots will be in the form of a three-dimensional application of measurement technology such as a laser spatial sensor rather than a camera. That is, it is possible to scan the floor to determine foreign substances, and determine the type of object with a simple three-dimensional model.

Location-aware technology is a technology in which a machine perceives space by itself. It is based on artificial intelligence technology. As a second-generation cognitive technology along with object recognition, it is a core technology for realizing the autonomous movement function of robots. Various approaches such as sensor-based, mark-based, and stereo vision-based location recognition technology are being studied. Currently,

Figure 4-60 Robot with optical sensor

location recognition technology is being applied in various fields under the name of location-based service, and the most actively researched area is location-based technology using radio frequencies existing in space.

The most widely used and easily recognized technology is GPS. Usually, the location can be measured through the GPS chip embedded in the wireless terminal. In this case, the wireless terminal receives signals from a plurality of GPS satellites and directly handles the entire positioning function of calculating position coordinates from the signals and can inquire various information using the coordinates as input values through a mobile communication network.

However, it is difficult to directly perform satellite signal reception and coordinate calculation functions due to low power and low computational performance problems in the current mobile communication network terminals. Accordingly, a variety of mixed positioning methods have been devised to calculate location coordinates in a complex manner by using the GPS signal as an auxiliary and adding the distance relationship and radio wave state measurement values of adjacent mobile communication base stations, and this is called A-GPS (Assisted GPS). In this case, the radio location method and the trilateration method are used to calculate the location relationship based on the radio wave conditions between multiple adjacent base stations and the terminal.

In addition, depending on the type of mobile communication service provider and location information service, a single base station reference location inquiry method may be used instead of using a method of calculating a location relationship between a plurality of base stations and terminals. Because the mobile communication network always performs base station-based terminal mobility management due to its characteristics, this method is a method that can provide a location-based service without adding a separate positioning system and without a location calculation load when requesting a location.

As for the accuracy of the location measurement, GPS and its equivalent satellite-based location measurement method have the highest accuracy, and the base station-based method has the lowest accuracy because it can measure only regional divisions, not latitude and longitude coordinates.

It is not always possible to implement location-based services using only one of these methods. Since various terminals with different positioning performances are distributed in the current mobile communication network, common mobile carriers provide location-based services by mixing GPS, A-GPS, or base station-based methods. In addition, the flow of identifying the location of a user or thing in an area other than the mobile communication network and reflecting it in the service continues to increase. Research and industrialization of user location recognition technology based on IP address in a new standard mobile network environment such as a mobile network using wireless LAN or WIBRO or a wired Internet environment is in progress. Also, many other positioning technologies are emerging, which are methods that use radio frequencies such as Bluetooth, ZIGBEE, and WIFI.

Basically, there is a case where the positioning technology using a sensor that generates or receives a wireless signal and the technology for machine learning using the positioning data are fused. First, as a positioning technology, several techniques for positioning a location using radio frequency or radio waves in a specific space have been developed in various ways. In a space beyond the range of GPS, that is, a location tracking technology using a wireless signal in a place where there are many undergrounds, indoor, and buildings has been proposed in various ways.

WSN(Wireless Sensor Network) is a basic technology of pervasive computing, and a new concept of information and communication technology that can implement various services by collecting and analyzing information transmitted from various sensors using a wireless network is developing.

In addition, as a positioning technology, various location recognition services are used through GPS (Global Positioning System) and GIS (Geographic Information System), and location tracking using ultrasound, RF, and image processing is being studied indoors. The GPS method has limitations in that it cannot be used indoors because it receives signals from satellites, and there are many limitations in indoor positioning, including multi-path problems, recognition distance, and range. The general positioning technology is a method of measuring the arrival time of radio waves to obtain a location, a method of measuring the time of arrival (TOA) between a terminal and a base station, and the relative difference TDOA (Time of arrival) between radio waves from two base stations Difference of Arrival) was used as a measurement value. In addition, a passive positioning system such as Cricket calculates the distance between each beacon and the receiver using RF and ultrasonic signals transmitted from three or more beacons fixedly attached to the inside of the building. However, as the distance from each fixed transmitter becomes closer or farther according to the movement of the receiver, distortion always occurs due to changes in frequency intensity or angle, and errors due to the Doppler effect of frequency always occur. For reference, the Doppler effect refers to a phenomenon in which the frequency and wavelength of a wave change according to the relative speed of the wave source and the observer. In a wave moving through a medium like sound, the effect changes depending on the relative speed of the observer and the wave source to the medium. In other words, if we look at the positioning technology using a radio frequency in terms of principle, there is a positioning technique in which sensors that generate or receive frequency signals, such as various radio signals (mobile, broadcasting frequency, base station frequency, other communication frequencies, RF, Bluetooth, FID, Zigbee, and UWB), are viewed as objects of positioning and values of positions. It generally uses a beacon or a mobile device as a device that broadcasts or receives a frequency. The radio signals from these mobile devices are converted into a position value of a three-dimensional map at the receiving end, the position value is parsed through an application at the receiving end, and positioning is performed using the parsed frequency data. If the various parameter values used for positioning are fused using big data in this way, a location prediction system can also be created. And there is HRI technology, which is an interface technology between humans and machines, such as artificial emotion technology to understand emotions, bio-interface technology, and gesture recognition to find out human intentions. It is the most ultimately implemented technology that combines artificial intelligence technology and BT technology. This technology is one of the most difficult technologies at a level that has not yet passed the beginner's stage. If this technology is unleashed, a full-fledged robot age is expected to open. In addition, sensor and actuator technology is a technology that is included when classified into five technologies that make up a robot. It is a technology that implements various materials such as artificial eyes, micromotors, tactile sensors, artificial skin, micromotors, artificial muscles, and mechatronics fusion technology.

Figure 4-61 Increasing trend by use of robot industry

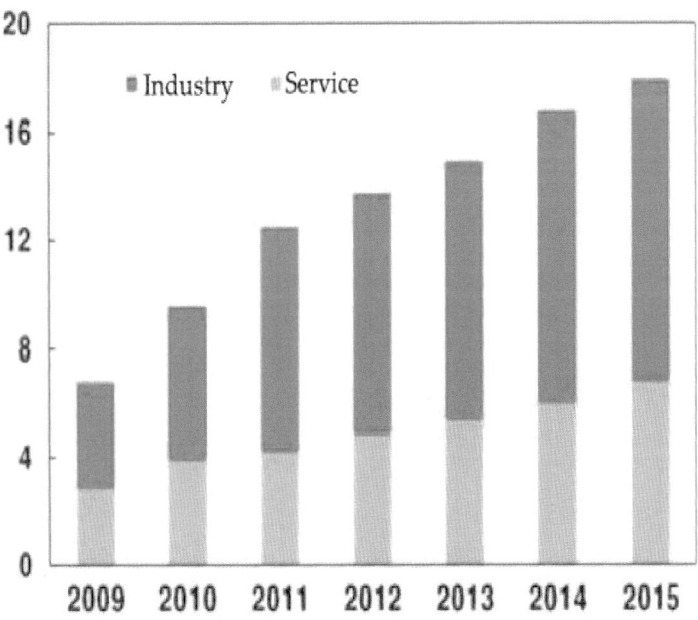

Currently, research on sensor technology based on MEMS (Miniature Mechatronics) technology, manipulation for humanoid robots, and artificial muscles required for movement technology is in full swing.

The robot industry refers to an industry that manufactures, sells, and services finished robot products or robot parts. Its characteristics are both characteristics of the mechanical industry such as the automobile industry, and the IT industry such as the PC and semiconductor industry, due to the nature of the mechatronics of the intelligent robot itself.

A robot is not simply composed of a single chip like a semiconductor, nor is it a static system like a PC. Rather, it is closer to a car in that it operates in the outside world. However, while having the characteristics of the exterior of the automobile industry, the classification is classified as an IT industry. The reason is that two of the three major functions of robots (intelligence, information, and control), intelligence and information, are IT technologies. Therefore, it can be said that the robot industry is an MT industry based on IT technology, that is, an industry that combines IT and MT.

Figure 4-62 Increasing trend by user in the robot industry

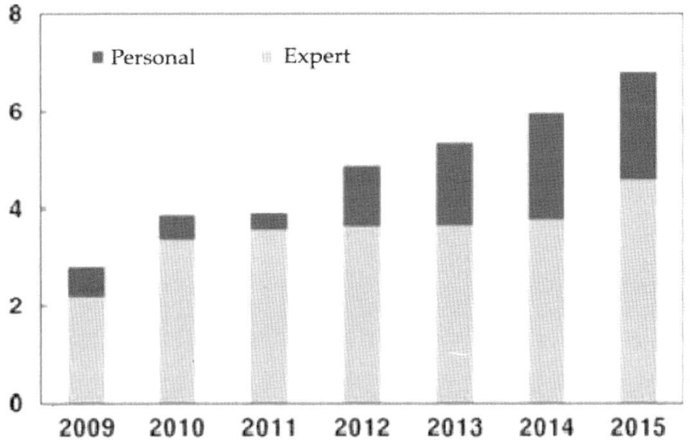

Figure 4-63 Robot industry market size and forecast by service

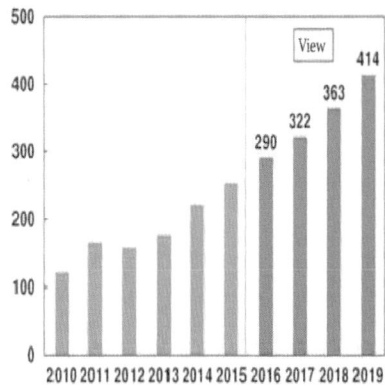
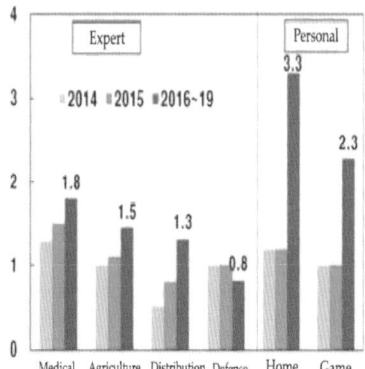

The robot industry develops from robotics, which is the science and technology of robots. Robotics engineers design, manufacture, or work with applications of robots. Robotics requires knowledge in various fields such as electronics, mechanics, and software and mechanical engineering, and is supported by various types of knowledge in various related fields.

Each year, the United Nations Economic Association (UNECE) and the Mitsubishi Economic Research Institute (MERI) publish reports on the size of the global market and forecasts. According to the report, it is expected that all industries will be robotized within the next year, and the robot industry is expected to become the core of national competitiveness, not just one industry, as only a country with an edge in the robot industry survives in the era of future technological competition. As seen above, almost all countries around the world are concentrating their national capabilities on developing robots that are more useful for human life. The direction of robots developed in line with the global development trend of these robots results in one direction. It is an intelligent robot. In the future, intelligent robots are expected to dominate the robots in the era of the Fourth Industrial Revolution.

Strictly speaking, in terms of mechanical engineering, the 3D printer that is closest to the robot field among the technologies of the Fourth Industrial

Revolution is manufacturing, not printing. Therefore, although there are some errors to call it a printer, it is accepted that it belongs to the category of a printer because the operating mechanism and the basic logic of exporting data from a computer to a real medium are similar to a printer.

Existing CNC machining is also included in the category of a printer by dictionary definition because it can extract the output directly from the 3D model, but 3D printing usually refers to additive manufacturing, which is the shape that is made by stacking up, not the conventional subtractive manufacturing, that is, the shape made by cutting. A hybrid method that mixes both is included in the 3D printer.

3D printing technology was a printing technology called Rapid Prototyping. In 1981, a patent was applied for by Dr. Hideo Kodama of the Industrial Research Institute in Nagoya, Japan, but the patent was canceled because the description could not be written within the one-year deadline.

In 1986, the first patent for a 3D printer was given to Chuck Hull, who built a photocurable additive manufacturing (SLA) machine. Then, in 1988, two years after the establishment of the 3D System, a 3D printer was commercialized for the first time in the world.

In 1987, Carl Deckard, who was a college student at the University of Texas in Austin, USA, with the help of Professor Joe Beaman, obtained a patent for a 3D printer using the Selective Laser Sintering (SLS) method in 1989. The principle of operation was to spread the adhesive in the desired shape on the plastic powder and then blow off the remaining powder, which can be said to be the beginning of the current SLS method. This patent was later commercialized by DTM, and the company was then acquired by 3D System. In 1989, a patent for the FDM (Fused Deposition Modeling) method was also applied for, which was acquired by Scott Crump, and after that, Stratasys was established and commercialized for the first time in 1991. The company is currently the world's number 1 manufacturer of 3D printers. For reference, to avoid trademark disputes, FDM is called FFF (Fused Filament Fabrication).

3D printers have been known to the public for a while since they got their name, but it has been quite some time since they were introduced into the actual field. Originally called Rapid Prototype, it was mainly used by companies to make prototypes. Up to this point, it took 12-24 hours to produce one item, and the cost was quite high, so it was not suitable for general use.

The time when 3D printers became known and familiar to the public was when the FDM (Fused Deposition Modeling) method, which had a relatively low production cost and short production time, was commercialized.

A 3D printer consists of three main steps as follows.

The first is the 3D modeling stage, which includes the process of scanning the object.

In general, it can be produced from 2D photos taken, and preparing a geometric modeling process through computer graphics is similar to a modeling technique such as sculpture. Models that can be made with a 3D printer are created with a 3D scanner, an ordinary digital camera, or a computer-specific design program (CAD) created using photogrammetry software. A CAD-generated model can reduce errors during production and can be corrected while checking the design before the model is printed.

3D scanning is the process of creating a digital model by collecting the shape or appearance of an actual object as digital data. A CAD model can be produced by STL (Stereolithography), which produces a 3D model by shining light. However, stereolithography (STL) is not suitable for additive manufacturing because the number of surfaces involved creates a systematic classification and part and grid structures with large file sizes. So, a new CAD file format, Additive Manufacturing Facility (AMF), an additive manufacturing file format, was introduced in 2011.

The second is the error correction step for 3D printing.

In the STL (Stereolithography = Standard Triangulated Language) generation step, a step known as Repair fixes these problems in the original model. If there is an error when uploading the file to the slicer program for 3D printing, the error is corrected and the file to be printed is completed.

The slicer program makes a G-code by converting the model into thin layers and then attaching it differently for each type of printer. This G-code file can be printed with 3D printer client software.

Printer resolution indicates layer thickness and XY resolution in dots per inch (DPI) or micrometers (μm). Some machines can print a single layer as thin as 16μm (1,600 DPI), but a typical single layer is about 100μm (250 DPI) thick (XY resolution is comparable to that of a laser printer). These particles (3D dots) are about 50 to 100μm (510 to 250 DPI) in diameter. At these printer resolutions, a net of 0.01 to 0.03 mm and a line length of 0.016 mm or less produce optimal STL (Standard Triangulated Language) results for a given model file.

Using a high resolution is to create large files without increasing the print quality of the print and making the model can take hours to days depending on the method used, the complexity, and the size of the model. Still, the stacking method is highly dependent on the type of machine used and the size and number of models being produced at the same time.

3D printers in this way help designers and prototyping teams create basic models. In the normal additive manufacturing method, all layered structures are unavoidably warped at bent or inclined parts. This effect is highly dependent on the orientation of the part surface within the fabrication process.

The third is the post-processing step for the output from the 3D printer.

Usually, 3D printer technology creates a three-dimensional shape, so the support is often made together during the manufacturing process. These supports can be removed mechanically or melted after printing is complete.

All commercial metal 3D printers involve cutting out the metal support after printing, and if the material is a metal such as aluminum or iron, surface modification is a finishing step in fabrication.

The most necessary to understand a 3D printer is how to print the model. It is close to two dimensions that we simply print text or pictures on paper with a printer because there is no need for height and density. However, 3D fritting is three-dimensional, and the direction angle is 360 degrees multiplied by 360 degrees.

Figure 4-64 3D printer principle

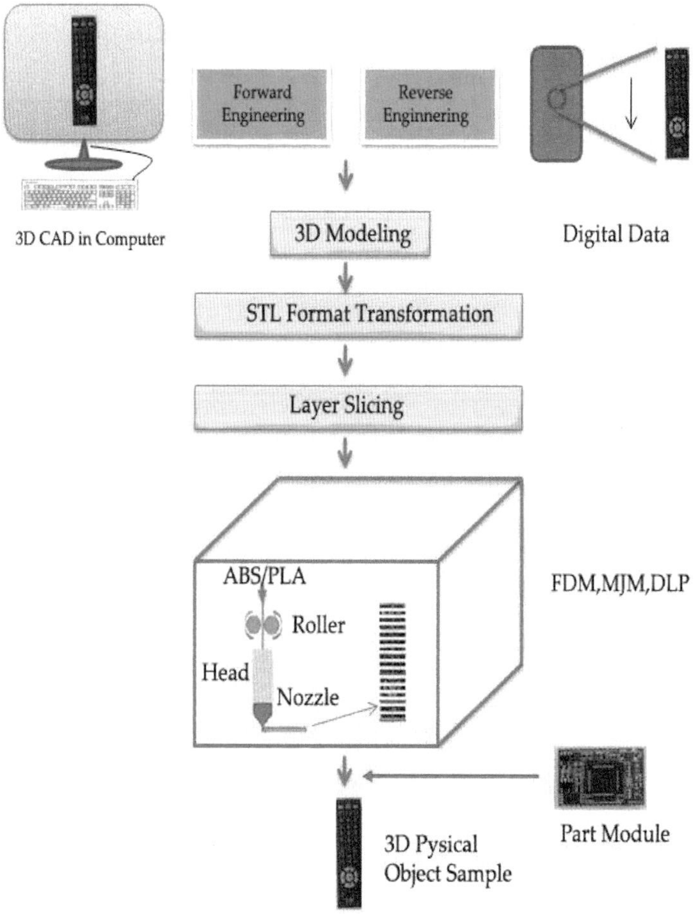

Therefore, the key is how to combine the width, length, and height. This can be easily seen from the output method of the 3D printer.

The first method is to sculpt a large chunk of raw material using a blade. The quality of the finished product is high, but the coloring work must be carried out separately, it consumes a lot of material due to the principle of operation of cutting it from a lump, and it has disadvantages that it is difficult to manufacture objects with many bends such as cups and pipes. This is usually called a 4-axis or 5-axis machine, which is included in the category of CNC (Computer Numerical Control) rather than a 3D printer. This is because the 5-axis machine is completely different from conventional 3D printers. What the 5-axis processing machine and general 3D printer have in common is that three-dimensional modeling is free. The 5-axis machining machine has already been commercialized and widely used in industrial fields, and it is not a new technology.

General CNC (Computer Numerical Control) processing does not fall into the category of three-dimensional printing, but there are many similarities to 3D printers in operation. This is because the original 3D printer was designed with these mechanical engineering elements as motifs.

The second method is called Additive Manufacturing, which is a common 3D printer method. In other words, there are "Printing layer by layer" and "Printing point by point" methods, in which media are stacked layer by layer to form. It is classified according to the operation method or material, and the biggest advantage is that it can be stacked to implement a very sophisticated structure inside. In the case of CNC (Computer Numerical Control) machining, there is a need for space for the end mill to enter somehow. In other words, it is almost impossible to design a structure with a narrow entrance but a wide inside or an elaborately divided inside. However, Additive Manufacturing is a very good approach, except that some supports need to be removed at the finishing stage.

Most of us know that 3D printers are prototyping using plastic materials, but the biggest advantage of 3D printer technology is that there are almost no restrictions on output materials. In other words, if the properties of materials, whether metal or organic, are used well, any material can be used to make the desired model and even a product.

At the CES exhibition in Las Vegas in 2019, even a car that can be sold with a 3D printer has been released.

In general, 3D printing technology using metal has been used for a long time. This is an application of a technology called Laser Cladding, which sprays metal powder through a nozzle, melts it with a laser, and laminates it to a uniform thickness. In general, this technology was used more for damage repair of metal work than for product production. For example, if there is slight damage to a metal mold for plastic injection or a metal turbine component, this technology fills in only the damaged area and restores it to its original state by post-processing am. By applying this technology, it is possible to make a three-dimensional shape with metal while continuously stacking it so that it has a certain shape. In October 2013, there was an article that the European Space Agency had made metal parts that could be used on a spacecraft with a 3D printer, and on November 7, 2013, a company called Solid Concepts in Texas announced that it had built metal pistols with 3D printers and fired more than a dozen guns without problems.

In March 2014, Joris Laarman and ACOTECH jointly developed a product called MX3D-Metal, which is a method of making metal products by welding in the air.

In August 2014, NASA announced that it had successfully tested the combustion of rocket engine parts made with a metal 3D printer.

The parts originally made by assembling 163 small parts were produced using only parts printed with two 3D printers. During the experiment, pressure close to 100 atmospheres and heat of over 3000 degrees were applied, but it

Figure 4-65 Rocket engine test made with 3D printer

was said to have successfully withstood it.

Bugatti Chiron, a luxury car produced since January 2018, is said to have the world's first 3D-printed titanium brake caliper. Titanium is a typical metal with strong tensile and cutting strength, and it means that the method of accumulating metal with 3D printer technology is more efficient than cutting with CNC (Computer Numerical Control) processing. As an example, the titanium brake caliper used in conventional luxury passenger cars had a problem of poor performance due to its simple structure or weak strength by combining several parts, but the calliper produced using a 3D printer uses fewer parts and the structure is complicated, so the performance is good and the strength is secured.

In October 2018, the U.S. Navy stated that the nuclear aircraft carrier Harry S. Truman would be equipped with metal 3D-printed parts for 12 months of operational testing.

As described above, 3D printers use more than 300 materials as of 2018, and there are over 30,000 spray nozzles that eject them. Beyond plastic, it can also make food, build houses by injecting concrete, and print metal parts. Also, with the development of bio 3D printer technology these days, artificial organs can be printed.

There is a lot of news in a newspaper that a 3D printer made an artificial organ and transplanted it to a patient, and the results were very good. If these 3D printers become popular like cars and smartphones and the era comes when anyone can make and use the things they need, this will surely accelerate the development of the Fourth Industrial Revolution (using a whip to make a running horse run faster).

Currently, NASA in the United States is researching how to put a lot of 3D printers and powdered materials in order to repair parts that are broken when flying to very distant places such as space travel. This is because you don't know which part will break, so it is more efficient to load a 3D printer and make the broken parts than to load a lot of spare parts. Now, when traveling in space, we take space food or finished products, but in the future, we may come to an era where we only take very finely compressed ingredients and print out the dishes with a 3D printer to consume.

Also, there is an opinion that the ultimate product of a 3D printer is a three-dimensional form, so there is an opinion that higher-quality prints are more likely to be produced in space without gravity than on the earth where gravity acts. Although it is a reasonable opinion, it should not be overlooked that there may be other forces affecting 3D printing technology in outer space and that there may be many unexpected variables when a 3D printer manufactured in a place of gravity is used in outer space. For example, solar wind, gravitational field waves, and changes and distortions of quantum ends of matter which can affect the exposure of 3D printers and materials are variables that should always be considered unless 3D printers are

Figure 4-66 Small 3D printer exhibited at CES

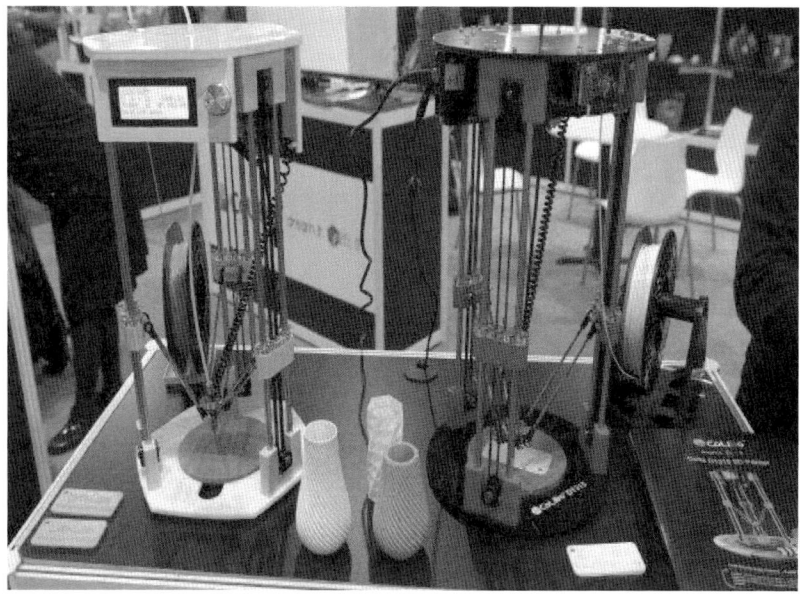

manufactured in space.

As described earlier, in October 2013, the European Space Agency produced metal parts used in spacecraft with a 3D printer, and at the 2019 Las Vegas CES (Consumer Electronics Show) International Consumer Electronics Show, a car made of a 3D printer that can be actually driven has been released. In other words, the rate of transition from plastic to metal is progressing faster than expected. Perhaps within a few years, a world may come in which even spaceships and robots can be created with 3D printers. Also, there may come a world where individuals own one or more 3D printers and use them to make and use things they need at any time.

Also, the construction market that uses 3D printers to make and use building materials is already active overseas, and the concrete curve forming operation, which is very difficult in the existing human process, is very simple with 3D printers, so it is used a lot.

In addition, 3D printer technology has the advantage of reducing weight and saving concrete materials because it is possible to form a skeleton to produce a similar strength without filling the entire interior of concrete, a common building material. Above all, it can significantly reduce the number of working people and significantly reduce the construction time.

In the field of architecture, there are reports that 10 houses were already completed in one day, and there were articles that the cost was only $5,000. Therefore, 3D printing technology is expected to bring tremendous innovation to the construction industry.

3D printers are also widely used in the military field. The lower frame of the AR-15, a firearm that can be printed by individuals, has already appeared and has been released. Because metal 3D printers are very expensive, gun manufacturing is still mostly made of plastic parts, and the main parts such as barrels and chambers that are subjected to strong pressure are mostly made of commercially available metal, so it is rare that they are actually made as firearms. However, in the US, it is very meaningful to be able to print only the lower frame. According to U.S. law, the only parts that are recognized as "firearms" are those with the number of the gun stamped on them, so parts that go inside the barrel, upper frame, and lower frame can be easily purchased without any registration. And although the case is different in other countries, it is also legal under US law to make guns that individuals can legally purchase. In particular, the pistol grip or grip that fits each person's body type, the eyepiece of the sight, and the buffer rubber of the butt are the most easily manufactured and replaced parts.

In general, guns printed with a plastic 3D printer are used as a substitute for toys, so there is no real military advantage. However, the fact that you can directly manufacture and use supplies such as military caps and uniforms or firearms in the actual field brings great tactical merit. In fact, being able to directly produce and procure war materials in the right place at the right time has a definite advantage that can determine the victory or defeat of the war. For example, in the Three Kingdoms era, when Silla fought a war with Baekje, Kim Yu-sin went to the battlefield with food for the Tang soldiers, and the fact that tens of thousands of soldiers were moved to protect the supplies A printer can also be a very useful strategic asset.

Anyone who has seen the movie Mission Impossible will remember this. You must have seen the scene where Tom Cruise, who plays the role of an American spy, the main character, went into the enemy camp wearing a mask that looked exactly like another person's face with a 3D printer on the spot to infiltrate the enemy camp. In this way, 3D printing technology can be used as a tool to conduct war and espionage in a very useful and efficient way in terms of war and military.

In fact, 3D printer technology is being actively used in plastic models and figures, both professional and amateur. Of course, thanks to the unique limitations of 3D printers, it is not a mass production system for 3D printers from beginning to end, but the method of making a 3D model, printing it out with a 3D printer, processing it, and then making a mold and duplicating it conventionally is being used. A world will come in which, as long as data is input, high-quality products that can be used immediately are printed on the spot. That time is not far away.

Also, if 3D printers become popular, a drastic change will occur throughout the scientific community. An example is a universal constructor (material recombination device) using a Nano Machine.

It was proposed by von Neumann and is a concept that appeared in science fiction such as Star Trek.

It is said that the 3D printer is composed of a Nano machine, and it is said that it has reached a stage where it can create anything regardless of material and shape by recombining materials from molecular units. Just think of the scene in the movie Terminator, where a bad Terminator from the future fights the main character while freely transforming and changing body and face shapes. In other words, it is the concept of freely changing the material and shape of a substance as desired.

In theory, it is said to be a production plant with virtually no restrictions except for the time and energy required for production. However, theory and reality are still different. For this to be realized, I think it will take much more time than the time for 3D printers to be commercialized for personal use.

3D printers have already been commercialized in the fashion and sporting goods industries. You can make shoes and ornaments that fit your feet, and ski shoes made by measuring the feet of players, racquet handles that fit your hands, helmets that fit your head, and saddles that fit your body are optimized for the user's body shape and convenience, and If tou are a sportsman, it will maximize your performance.

3D printers are also actively used in the medical field, and in simple terms, from the case of making bones prior to surgery, to directly manufacturing artificial organs.

Transplantable organ cells are cultured, printed with a 3D printer, and transplanted. An artificial organ, which is produced by culturing the patient's own organ cells and printed with a 3D printer, has the same cellular properties as the patient's own organ, so it has the advantage of adapting and setting itself up after surgery. In addition, it is said that if the bone marrow is transplanted into the hollow part of the artificial bone, it will gradually fill itself up, and through exercise and rehabilitation, calcium can be reinforced to make it as hard as the original bone. In the field of cell transplantation using a 3D printer, Dr. Atala of Wake Forest University is said to be famous.

A lightweight, snug-fitting splint for fracture patients made by scanning body parts has already been commercialized.

It is also used in the field of orthodontics, especially transparent orthodontics, and it is said that the principle is used that the teeth move when the teeth are moved and printed, and then a frame to fit the teeth is made and worn.

Figure 4-67 A car made with a 3D printer exhibited at CES

It is said that the total production period of the car made with the 3D printer mentioned above was one month. It usually takes at least three months to make a car with more than 20,000 parts by hand, and it takes at least two months to produce one car even if it is mass-produced in a factory. However, using a 3D printer has many economic advantages as it takes a higher quality product and a shorter production period. The advantage of 3D printers is the advancement and stabilization of technology, and there is no doubt about the choice of the manufacturing method. In addition, the trend that 3D printers will occupy in this manufacturing industry seems to be only a matter of time. 3D printers owned and used by individuals are also just a matter of time.

If an individual has a 3D printer, it is expected to bring about a big change in production as well as consumption. For example, if you purchase an item from an Internet shopping mall, the sales company only sends you a configuration drawing of the product, and the customer can make it with a 3d printer at home and use at home. However, there are a number of things to consider. A company is operated by inputting the sales proceeds to the customer and production cost through it but sending only product drawings without such a process and making the product by the consumer directly results in the subject of production becoming ambiguous. Therefore, such a prospect is only a fun imagination, and it is unlikely that the market will be formed like that in reality. However, if an individual owns a 3D printer, it is clear that one-man manufacturing will be activated because it will be possible to easily create and use products tailored to individual characteristics, and various related businesses for such one-man manufacturing will develop. Another interesting assumption is that the products that can be made by such a one-man manufacturing industry can be literally simple consumables, but they can also be automobiles or airplanes. This is the real Fourth Industrial Revolution. This is how technology changes the very structure of the world.

Part 5 Future of The Fourth Industrial Revolution

5.1 50 Knowledges for The Fourth Industrial Revolution

In preparation for the Fourth Industrial Revolution, this chapter selects and presents 50 common senses related to information and communication technology that should be know the most in real life. The list of 50 common sense to prepare for the Fourth Industrial Revolution is defined through simple and clear explanations for each small topic and structured to be acquired with basic knowledge.

(1) Image resolution and monitor resolution
The resolution of an image depends on its size of the image. Using pixels as the unit, the pixel dimension measures the total number of pixels along the image width and height. The resolution of an image also represents the density of detail in a bitmap image and is measured in pixels per inch (PPI). The more pixels per inch, the higher the resolution. The resolution of a monitor is described in terms of pixel dimensions. For example, if the monitor resolution and the pixel dimensions of the photo are the same sizes, the photo will fill the screen when viewed at 100%. How large an image appears on the screen depends on the image's pixel dimensions, the monitor size, and the monitor resolution settings.

(2) Differences between image formats PNG, GIF, and JPEG
PNG is an acronym for Portable Network Graphics, which is useful for overlaying graphics on top of other backgrounds, thanks to their support for a variety of colors and transparent backgrounds. Since this format uses

lossless compression, there is no loss of image detail, resulting in higher image quality than the JPEG format but a larger file size compared to JPEG.

There are two types of PNG: PNG-8 and PNG-24. PNG-24 supports more colors and partially transparent pixels. This is advantageous if you want to add a drop shadow to an image with a transparent background, or if the image you want to post online is rich in gradients (where the color transitions smoothly, such as a wide sky). The PNG format, unlike JPEG, keeps text and logos sharp even when posted online, making it suitable for social media cover images. It's useful for high-definition graphics for slide decks, high-quality images for posting in online photo portfolios, and more. Also, it is known that the image quality loss of Facebook's compression algorithm is lower in PNG compared to JPEG.

GIF stands for Graphics Interchange Format. It creates a small file size for web graphics with a limited number of colors (e.g., webtoon drawings), transparent backgrounds, or animations. Although GIFs are less popular these days for static graphics thanks to the high-speed Internet (which has higher PNG quality), they are still widely used for animated graphics on the web or slide decks.

JPEG is an acronym for the Joint Photographic Experts Group that developed the format. It is the most commonly used format in cameras and scanners because it supports a wide color gamut (also good for black and white photos). However, since JPEG is a compressed format, it reduces the file size at the expense of some details. This saves storage space on the camera memory card and is advantageous when posting photos online or sharing via email.

(3) Concept of image processing and image processing techniques

Image processing broadly refers to all types of information processing in which input and output are images, and processing of photos or moving pictures is a representative example. Most image processing techniques use a method of viewing an image as a two-dimensional signal and applying a standard signal processing technique to it.

Until the mid-20th century, image processing was done in analog, mostly optics. Although such image processing is still used for holography and the like, these techniques have been largely replaced by digital image processing techniques due to the improvement in computer processing speed. In general, digital image processing has the advantage of being used in various ways and being accurate and is also easier to implement than analog. Computer technologies such as pipelines are sometimes used for faster processing.

One of the most widely used image processing techniques is

- Euclidean geometric transformations such as zoom in, zoom out, rotate, etc.
- Color correction such as brightness and contrast, color mapping, tonalization, quantization, and color conversion
- Digital synthesis or optical synthesis
- Restore raw image format using filters
- Image registration, transformation, recognition, and segmentation
- Create HDR (High dynamic range) video by combining multiple videos
- 2D object recognition using geometric hashing

The most used digital image processing these days is literally processing images on computer. In a broader sense, image processing refers to all fields related to image generation, processing, interpretation, and recognition of images using a computer. Using this technology, we can see blurred images more clearly, restore the original image when the image is damaged, or extract only necessary information from the image and use it in various ways.

(4) Distinguishing between achromatic and chromatic colors

Achromatic color refers to the absence of color, and its representative colors are black, white, and gray. Since gray is a color made by mixing white and black, it is broadly classified as achromatic.

Conversely, chromatic color means a color with hue and brightness, and if you look at the type, the primary colors are combined to create intermediate colors. Dark red, orange, tangerine, light green, yellow light green, turquoise, sea blue, navy blue, indigo blue, purple, purple, etc. are applicable.

The biggest difference between an achromatic color and a chromatic color is the presence or absence of saturation, hue, and lightness. Almost all chromatic colors can be created with RGB (Red, Green, Blue), which we often talk about.

(5) Size difference between PNG and GIF

Although PNG uses a newer compression algorithm than GIF, it creates larger files than GIF because GIF only supports 256 colors. When compressing a true color picture to PNG, all the original colors are saved, whereas when saving as a GIF, the number is reduced to 256 colors and then saved. If the original uses only 256 colors, this difference does not appear.

You can also use the open source such as OptiPNG or PngCrush to reduce the size of the PNG file.

(6) Light seen by frequency band

Light is the visible radiant energy to the human eye and makes vision possible. Visible light is generally defined as having a wavelength in the range from 700 to 400 nanometers (nm) to $400 \times [10]^{(-9)}$m. These numbers do not represent the absolute limits of human vision, but as a rough approximation, they mean that most people can see it in most situations. Visible light is defined as 380 to 800 nm in a wide range and 420 to 680 nm in a narrow range. Under ideal laboratory conditions, people can see infrared light down to at least 1050 nm. Children and young adults can see ultraviolet light down to about 310 to 313 nm. The basic properties of visible light are intensity, propagation direction, frequency or wavelength spectrum, and polarization.

Light has a speed of 299,792,458 meters per second in a vacuum, which is one of nature's fundamental constants. Visible light is any type of electromagnetic radiation (EMR), which experimentally can always be found at the speed of its movement in a vacuum. What all types of electromagnetic radiation (EMR) have in common is that visible light is absorbed in small packets called emitted photons and exhibits the properties of both waves and particles. This property is called wave-particle duality.

A frequency band corresponding to visible light that humans can see is defined as light, and another frequency band is defined as a wavelength.

(7) Aliasing and anti-aliasing in image format

Aliasing is the phenomenon of principles related to image and signal processing and refers to the effect of preventing different signals from being distinguished during sampling. In other words, it is a distortion in which the image or signal differs from the original continuous signal or image as a result of reconstruction in the sample. It is also called a stair-step phenomenon, and to solve this problem, a technique called anti-aliasing is used. Anti-Aliasing is a technique that softens the jagged edge line that appears in games or videos. The image you see on your monitor is made up of pixels, which are small square-shaped dots. If you enlarge the diagonal line that appears on the monitor, it becomes a continuous form of small square dots. Therefore, smooth lines or textures cannot be expressed and are perceived as unnatural. Anti-Aliasing is a technology that makes up for missing data from the lines expressed by connecting pixels and adds neutral-colored pixels around them to express images naturally without any difference when viewed with the naked eye. Fundamentally, it is not possible to make a smooth oblique line or curve, but it is a principle that represents the approximate value as much as possible.

(8) Three properties of color

The three properties of color mean hue, brightness, and saturation. Hue is the name of color necessary to distinguish colors regardless of brightness or saturation. The color ring means that the seven colors seen in the spectrum and the numerous colors in between are arranged in a circle.

Brightness indicates the lightness and darkness of a color. Closer to white indicates high brightness, closer to black indicates low brightness, and intermediate level indicates medium brightness. In addition, saturation indicates the vividness of a color, and the more achromatic colors are mixed with pure color, or more chromatic colors are mixed, the lower the saturation.

(9) Image and graphic editing software

Image or graphic editing software can be classified into an image editing tool, a drawing tool, a painting tool, and 3D graphics software.

The drawing tool is based on the vector method, and Adobe's Illustrator and Corel's Corel Draw are representative.

The painting tool has raster-type data based on a pixel unit and has a feature that the data size is larger than the data of the drawing tool. MacPaint, Kid Pix, SuperPaint, Painter, etc. are representative examples.

Editing Tool Software is software for performing various graphic processing on photos or images obtained through input devices such as scanners or digital cameras. It provides various functions such as filtering, resolution adjustment, layering, and image processing. Photoshop and Image Folio are representative examples.

3D graphics software is largely divided into modeling and rendering software, including 3D Studio Max, True Space, Soft Image XSI, MAYA, etc. These days, VR tools such as Unity for virtual reality image work are in the spotlight.

(10) Lossless compression technology and algorithm

Compression techniques can be classified into several categories. It can be divided into two types: lossy technique and lossless technique. In terms of properties used for compression, it can be divided into entropy technique and object-based technique.

The lossless technique means that when compressed data is restored, the restored data completely matches the data before compression. That is, the restored bit stream completely matches the pre-compression bit stream. When this technique is compressed, no changes or modifications are made to the data to be compressed. This technique can be used for the compression of data where accuracy is vital in the multimedia information. The lossless technique is also called the bit-preserving compression technique.

The lossy technique refers to a technique in which the restored data does not match the data before compression. This technique is generally suitable for compressing continuous media - sound, video, and moving pictures. The lossy technique does not mean a difference to the extent that users feel that the information after compression/restoration is different from the original information. In other words, when users see the data compressed/restored by the lossy method, it should be enough to feel that it is almost identical to the original data.

Here, the entropy technique refers to a compression technique that does not consider the characteristics of the target to be compressed. The entropy technique does not use the unique characteristics of the target information to be compressed, but simply considers all data as a bit stream or a byte stream. For example, if the values of 10 consecutive bytes all have 0, using a special character and the number 10 is an entropy technique. In this way, repeating 0 has no meaning ten times, and since it is restored to the original value during restoration, all entropy techniques correspond to lossless compression techniques.

Entropy encoding techniques include a method of replacing a repeated sequence and a statistical method. The target-based technique uses the characteristics of target information to be compressed. For example, in the case of voice, it is easy to distinguish between a non-speaking section and a speaking section, and only the speaking section is important, so there is no reason to enter information corresponding to the non-speaking section. In the case of a moving picture, since there are many similarities between two consecutive pictures, compression is attempted by dividing each picture into several areas and finding which areas are similar.

The target-based technique shows better compression than the entropy technique. This is because the unique characteristics of the media to be compressed are used. The compression rate will vary depending on the actual input data. It is on the same principle that describing a pure white screen is much easier than describing a complex market landscape. The target-based technique may be a lossless technique or a lossy technique.

(11) Difference between a word processor and a text editor

In the text editor, only letters can be entered, and the size and color of the letters cannot be expressed. It is mainly saved as an ASCII file, that is, a text file. Therefore, the file can be read by any kind of text editor and cannot be encrypted. Notepad, which is built into the Windows operating system by default, is a prime example.

A word-processor can freely express the size, color, diagram, figure, photo addition, and multi-stage editing of text (letter).

Documents are stored as binary files, and therefore cannot in principle be read by other types of word processors. If you have a conversion program, you can read it, but a conversion program is just a converter.

Word processors can encrypt. MS Word (Microsoft Word) is used the most in the world and Hangul word processor (HWP) is used a lot in Korea. Windows also has a built-in word processor called WordPad.

(12) Difference between Hangul word processor (HWP) and MS Word (Microsoft Word)

Hangul word processor (HWP) is very strong in Hangeul processing. It fully supports Korean archaic language and includes a dictionary, so it is easy to write a translation. Because it is fully integrated, it is widely used by businesses around the world.

(13) Advantages and Disadvantages of PDF

PDF is a file format used by printing a paper book after editing, and you can get the same file as the edited result on the screen.

The advantage of PDF is that it is easy to convert from one format to another, and since it is used as a standard for document archiving in ISO, it can be easily used in various operating systems.

The disadvantage of PDF is that only the screen size determined by the editor is supported equally, so it is not suitable for an e-book format having various sizes.

(14) Difference between HTML and XML

XML was extended by introducing the convenience of HTML. By introducing the link function using URL, which is a function of HTML, a multi-link function that can designate multiple link locations is performed. In this case, it is also compatible with HyTime (Hypermedia Timebase Structuring Language) or TEI (Text Encoding Initiative Guideline), which are international standards for multi-link functions targeting SGML documents. HyTime's multi-link function allows you to designate an application program as a link location at the same time as the homepage. For example, it is a function that can display images created in a special format with a dedicated viewer. This is similar to Netscape Navigator's plug-in software, where plug-ins are only available in specific browsers, whereas in XML, applications, and data can be connected regardless of browsers.

When a web document changes from HTML to XML, the search method of the homepage also changes. In HTML, full-text searches were performed mainly because strings have no meaning. In XML, meanings such as 'title', 'summary', 'author', and 'published date' are given to text, making it possible to search for each category.

XML has the potential to create new applications based on documents. One of them is Push's information distribution function. Push-type information distribution such as PCN of Pointcast in the US and Casternet of Marimba is becoming a hot topic, but both currently require dedicated client software. Here, Microsoft proposed V\CDF (Channel Definition Format) as a standard Push-type information format in March. This CDF is also a kind of DTD based on XML. Distribution of the CDF file is realized by defining the channel name required for Push-type information sharing, time designation for sending/receiving the latest information, and historical information on how the user uses channel information, etc. in the DTD. The browser interprets the meaning of the character string in the tag in the CDF file, determines whether it is the data to be displayed on the screen or the data to be managed as change history information, and sends it to the relevant application.

(15) The need to use XML in Internet-based applications

XML has Push's information distribution function. Push-type information distribution such as PCN by Pointcast of the United States and Casternet by Marimba is becoming a hot topic, but both currently require dedicated client software. Here, Microsoft proposed CDF (Channel Definition Format) as a standard Push-type information format in March. This CDF is also a kind of DTD based on XML. Distribution of CDF files is realized by defining the channel name required for Push-type information sharing, time designation for sending/receiving the latest information, and historical information on how the user uses channel information, etc. as DTD. The browser interprets the meaning of the character string in the tag in the CDF file, determines whether it is the data to be displayed on the screen or the data to be managed as change history information, and sends it to the relevant application. What has been executed by the dedicated client SW so far is executed in the browser. In the future, a new DTD corresponding to the CDF will likely appear. When XML becomes the standard, the standardization of DTD will become the stage of the competition against the existing HTML extension competition.

XML is not just about writing documents but it's about creating databases. Therefore, it is useful and easy to write applications in XML rather than HTML because Internet-based applications can create applications more easily by using XML in the future and also include databases.

(16) Definition of Internet-based HTML5

HTML5 is the fifth complete version of HTML and is the core Mark Up language of the World Wide Web. In July 2004, the Web Hypertext Application Technology Working Group (WHATWG) started a detailed specification work under the name of Web Application 1.0.

HTML5 is the next standard proposal for HTML 4.01, XHTML 1.0, and DOM Level 2 HTML. It aims to enable users to easily view various additional functions such as video and audio and the latest multimedia contents in a browser without ActiveX.

On October 28, 2014, W3C announced that it had finalized the HTML5 standard.

HTML5 has backward compatibility, is easy to use with a simple syntax, and provides the ability to use SVG and MathML inline. Therefore, it has the advantage of being able to play media including video and audio without plug-ins.

(17) Appearance and Change of Tank Book

It is a generic term for digital books in which the contents of a work that has been published or can be published as a book are recorded in an electronic recording medium or storage device using digital data, and then the contents can be read, viewed, and heard with a computer or mobile terminal through a wired or wireless information and communication network.

An e-book is a digital file that can be read with a computer or a dedicated terminal through a dedicated viewer. The fields composing e-books can be divided into three types, e-book contents field, e-book distribution field, and e-book terminal field. In the content sector, publishers are mainly responsible for producing and distributing content themselves, or providing content to distributors, and then receiving a portion of the profits. The distribution sector plays a role in converting content into e-book format and providing e-book content to individuals (B2C) or institutions (B2B). In the distribution field, there are distribution companies specializing in e-books in charge of distribution and solutions, while online and offline bookstores such as Amazon, Barnes & Noble are in charge of distribution. Distribution companies are providing dedicated viewers for e-book users to read e-books. The field of e-book terminals is divided into dedicated terminals and general-purpose terminals. Dedicated terminals are specialized terminals for reading e-books, such as Amazon's Kindle, Samsung Electronics' e-reader, and iRiver's e-book terminal. Most of them are characterized by the adoption of E-paper. A general-purpose terminal refers to a device that does not have much inconvenience in using e-books because it has e-book functions such as smartphones, PMPs, electronic dictionaries, and netbooks such as iPhones.

E-book is a new media that appeared in the process of media convergence and new media development along with the development of existing electronic publishing technology as a book-like device made by applying the Internet languages HTML and XML. However, there is still no unified name. E-book contents are called Electronic Book, software for viewing E-book contents is called a viewer, and hardware is called E-book Device.

However, content, software, and hardware are collectively referred to as an e-book. In other words, E-book refers to a digital publication area that can be downloaded through the Internet as well as viewed on a PC or terminal through a dedicated viewer. Since e-books can overcome the limitations and problems of paper books, there is no doubt that they will be activated in the future. E-books will free us from the time and space constraints of paper books, allowing more information to be shared by more people at a lower cost. In addition to economic benefits, e-books will play a role in realizing equal values in the reading environment and publishing culture. In the electronic community, two-way communication between authors and readers will become more active, and anyone will be able to publish and distribute without commercial restrictions so that more diverse ideas and ways of expression can be freely expressed.

(18) Changes in multimedia due to the advent of e-books

In the fall of 2007, Amazon, an Internet bookstore in the United States, introduced the e-book device Kindle. Amazon, which has a strong market dominance with a market share of over 90%, has provided nearly 700,000 e-book contents. Free content without copyright or low-priced content under $2 made up a significant proportion, and readers' reactions to Amazon's e-book price incentives were warm.

Amazon paid about $13 (wholesale price) to publishers for a new e-book and sold it to consumers for $9.99. The retail price is set by Amazon. Amazon didn't give exact figures, but Kindle is said to have sold over 8 million units in 2010. Thanks to the success of the Kindle, the e-book market is said to have nearly tripled in 2009 compared to the previous year.

Thanks to the growth of tablet PCs, interest in the e-book market is increasing. The situation changed when Apple introduced the iPad, a tablet PC, to the market and sold e-books through the iBook Store.

Although the Kindle still had a high share of total e-book downloads, a change occurred in the e-book distribution model.

The reason the US e-book market is growing rapidly is that two urgent issues in the e-book market have been resolved to some extent.

First, the distribution of hardware for viewing e-books was quickly established, and the copyright problem was also solved through the platform business.

However, Amazon provides e-books through individual negotiations with authors, and Google is solving this problem through collective negotiations with the Copyright Council.

Apple is also solving this problem by voluntarily creating iPhone applications by content companies. In other words, with the advent of e-books, desktops, smartphones, and tablet PCs have developed a function to deliver e-book contents to the reader more realistically and intuitively compared to existing paper books. We are moving in the direction of additionally developing suitable content.

(19) Character recognition method for multimedia devices

The character recognition device consists of a photoelectric conversion device, a recognition processing device, a memory device, and an output device. The photoelectric conversion device converts the text on the ground into a voltage waveform, and at this time, the shape of the text, which is a two-dimensional figure on the ground, is the same as that of the TV. It is converted into a one-dimensional signal that is a time series change of a voltage waveform by the phosphor scan method. The storage device stores an arithmetic control program for controlling the recognition processing unit, and data expressing the recognized shape in a specific form.

The recognition processing device inputs and processes unknown characters through the photoelectric conversion device under the control of the memory device program, and the type of character corresponding to the pattern with the highest degree of matching compared to the standard pattern in the same memory device is recognized as the character type of the unknown character. In recognition by OCR, the reliability of the read result is important, and therefore, there are some restrictions on input characters in order to secure recognition information. There are OCR-A and OCR-B in the standard characters for OCR printed characters. In the beginning, OCR-A was used, but OCR-B is currently being used due to the problem that it is not easy for humans to read.

Unlike printed characters, it is difficult to strictly define the shape of handwritten characters with mechanical dimensions, so there are several problems in recognizing them. A natural shape, etc., is mainly considered as general indicators. In addition, the size and shape of the character entry column are simultaneously restricted to stabilize the size and shape of handwritten characters.

(20) Development trend of semiconductor technology

In the early 1940s, the device responsible for computation and memory in computers was a vacuum tube. ENIAC, known as the world's first computer, was equipped with a whopping 17,468 vacuum tubes. The vacuum tube was prone to breakage even with the slightest mishandling, and it generated a lot of heat and consumed a lot of electricity. In addition, there was a limit to miniaturization because the volume could not be reduced. Scientists set out to find a new material to replace the vacuum tube. In the meantime, it has been discovered that current flows limitedly when there are impurities in semiconductors such as germanium (Ge) and silicon (Si, silicon). In December 1947, William Shockley, John Bardeen, and Walter Bratton of Bell Labs developed a 'transistor semiconductor device' to replace the vacuum tube. It enabled miniaturization and popularization of electronic products. Since then, semiconductors have been called the flower of the electronics industry and rice of the high-tech industry and have come to stand at the center of the information and communication technology revolution.

However, silicon semiconductors have disadvantages such as slow electron movement speed, inability to emit light, and difficulty in processing smaller than 10 nm. In addition, if a high frequency of 2 GHz or higher is applied, semiconductor properties are lost and cannot be used in mobile communication devices such as mobile phones. Semiconductor experts predict that the era of silicon semiconductors will come to an end after 2020.

In the past, semiconductor technology has focused on increasing device density while reducing device size. This includes the 30-nano 64-gigabyte NAND flash developed by Samsung Electronics in 2007. However, this type of technological development has reached its physical limit. So, research on new materials has begun. The goal was to find a material that is as cheap as silicon and has superior electrical properties to silicon.

That's how compound semiconductors came about. Unlike single element semiconductors such as silicon or germanium, compound semiconductors are semiconductors composed of two or more elemental compounds. Gallium arsenide (GaAs), indium phosphorus (InP), indium antimony (InSb), etc. belong to this. Compound semiconductors are more than 10 times faster than silicon semiconductors, and consume only one-tenth of the power, so they are widely used in mobile communications. In addition, since it can emit light of various wavelengths depending on the element, it is also used in optical devices such as laser diodes and light emitting diodes or lighting devices. However, there is a disadvantage that the price is more than five times higher than that of silicon semiconductors.

(21) Next-generation semiconductor technology

M-RAM is a semiconductor that utilizes the principle that the magnetism of an object changes and the resistance value changes when a magnetic field is applied along with an electric current. Compared to DRAM, power consumption is only about 1/1000 and processing speed is fast.

R-RAM is a semiconductor that uses the phenomenon in which weak current flows when a voltage over a certain level is applied even in an insulator that does not conduct electricity. The structure is very simple as it consists of a metal electrode and an insulating film. It is being developed as an alternative to flash memory for portable devices.

P-RAM is a semiconductor that uses the principle that the internal structure changes when an electric current is applied to a material. Due to its small size and low voltage operation, it has the lowest production cost among next-generation semiconductors.

Next-generation semiconductors such as M-RAM, R-RAM, and P-RAM are characterized by being able to minimize current interference in ultra-fine circuits. Information is stored according to a change in the resistance value of the semiconductor device itself. Therefore, even if the circuit line width is reduced, the information does not disappear, and the memory capacity can be increased by increasing the degree of integration even more than now. In addition, these semiconductors are superior to existing semiconductors in both power consumption and processing speed. However, the way information is stored is different. M-RAM uses magnetism, the magnetic property of the device. Generally, there is a fine magnet inside each object, and it is magnetic, and the degree of magnetism is appropriately changed to store information. On the other hand, R-RAM is manufactured by applying a voltage to an insulator that does not conduct electricity. PRAM uses the principle that the internal structure changes when an electric current is applied to a specific material having a crystal structure.

(22) Mobile cloud environment

Mobile cloud means not just extending the concept of traditional virtualization to mobile, but also transforming mobile services themselves into a cloud platform to provide free mobility not only to users but also for the data, content, and services that the user uses and creates.

In other words, it is the concept of using cloud technology not only on smartphones but also on various mobile devices that users have to utilize desired content and services without time and space restrictions.

From the user's point of view, the mobile cloud has the characteristics of a private cloud for personal and corporate work and a public cloud for the use of various external services related to personal life.

There are two main ways to apply cloud computing in a mobile environment. The first method is to use a cloud server instead of a traditional server, and the other method is to run applications using the cloud and support major functions rather than the terminal itself.

Both are referred to as mobile clouds, and their distinction is increasingly blurred. The biggest difference between the above two methods is the initial application purpose.

Currently, as users' demands for personalized mobile services increase, complex mobile applications have increased, and social networking functions have been integrated into mobile applications, raising issues for real-time data processing and synchronization.

Demands for accessibility, sharing convenience, and stability of user data have increased, but there were difficulties in development due to the limited hardware resources of mobile terminals and the mix of various platforms. Mobile cloud, which emerged to overcome these limitations, provides personalized virtual storage services and cloud computing for complex computations such as voice interpretation and image recognition.

In general, mobile cloud applications are applications that require a lot of computing power, such as image combination or voice interpretation, large-capacity storage to provide high-quality photos or music, and continuously transfer data to different terminals or the same application in real-time. It is mainly used for applications that access, process, and synchronize.

(23) Green Information Technology

Information technology can now be said to be the core and peripheral technology that already occupies a large part of our lives. When information technology appeared in earnest, information technology was recognized as a new industry, and many services, technologies, and products appeared, but now information technology is recognized as the most important essential infrastructure in our society. In other words, online shopping, company-wide management system, video conferencing, and Internet phone service are the results of playing a key role in information technology to overcome the limitations of time and distance and to dramatically improve resource utilization and work efficiency. Information technology, which has played a key infrastructure role in economic growth in the 20th century, is drawing attention as a key means of realizing a sustainable society, which is being discussed in earnest around the world as we enter the 21st century. Information technology is a tool that can effectively respond to energy and environmental problems in each field of society, such as energy saving and carbon emission reduction, by using the characteristics of improving the efficiency of information and resource use.

Green information technology, that is, Green IT, is being defined as a key means of responding to global climate change by governments and private organizations in each country.

The Korean government defines Green IT as IT that contributes to solving energy and environmental problems in each field of society, such as home and industry, through energy saving, carbon emission reduction, and resource use improvement, and emphasized IT as a means to realize a sustainable society. The OECD defined Green IT as IT with a low environmental burden and IT used as a facilitator to alleviate the environmental impact of society, including eco-friendly IT itself and solving environmental problems using IT. As a result, Green IT is a concept that includes the minimization of environmental burden in the IT field for the realization of a sustainable society and the achievement of eco-friendliness and energy efficiency using IT.

The category of Green IT includes areas that promote efficiency improvement and eco-friendliness in the existing IT field, and areas that utilize IT to contribute to eco-friendliness, energy efficiency enhancement, and carbon reduction in other industrial fields. Greening in the IT field focuses on optimizing IT device resource utilization thorough high efficiency and eco-friendly material development of IT devices such as PCs and servers, electronic printing media, low-power networks, data center efficiency improvement, printer integration, server virtualization, dynamic resource management, etc..

Greening using IT aims to improve energy efficiency and build an eco-friendly ecosystem in each field of society, such as industry, home, building, transportation, and logistics. It optimizes resource utilization and supports the transition to a low-carbon society through energy management of factories, buildings, and homes, SW-based power management, intelligent system, and infrastructure using advanced IT, and remote work environment establishment through virtualization and cloud computing support.

Additionally, Smart IT refers to information technology that is a cutting-edge new growth engine that transforms traditional industries into smart industries by convergence in all industrial fields such as broadcasting/communications, home appliances, automobiles, medical/welfare, logistics, and national defense to realize a ubiquitous society. In the era of the Fourth Industrial Revolution, Green IT and Smart IT along with existing technologies will be the means to realize it.

(24) Multimedia display technology

The display has evolved from the first-generation display CRT (Cathode Ray Tube), which was installed in thick TVs, to a flat-panel display (LCD), a self-luminous display (OLED), and a TFT-LCD with improved image quality using thin film transistors.

LCD is an imaging device using a panel containing liquid crystals between glass substrates and consists of three-stage component materials such as backlight, liquid crystal, and color filter. The backlight is a part that acts as a separate light source, which is necessary because the LCD cannot emit light by itself and is also called BLU (Back Light Unit:).

The core material of LCD is liquid crystal. Although liquid crystal is a liquid, the alignment direction of molecules is a material with a certain structural regularity, that is, crystallinity, and the alignment direction of molecules is changed by external conditions such as heat, electricity, or magnetism. Liquid crystal molecules are usually elongated or plate-shaped, so the refractive index varies depending on the direction.

LCD uses that the alignment direction of liquid crystal molecules varies according to voltage. When an electric signal is applied from the outside, the arrangement of liquid crystal molecules changes to show a certain pattern. Accordingly, the light transmitted from the backlight is refracted differently according to the pattern as it passes through the liquid crystal panel, and as it passes through the polarizing filter and color filter, it becomes a single pixel with different colors and brightness. It is the principle of LCD that these pixels gather to form the entire screen. In addition, LCD is divided into the passive matrix and the active matrix depending on the driving method. The passive LCD uses a method of driving the liquid crystal at the intersection point by applying a voltage to the horizontal and vertical axes of the liquid crystal panel, so the device configuration is simple. It has the advantage of low production cost due to its simple structure, but it is mainly used for small products such as electronic calculators and watches because of its poor image quality and slow response time.

Active LCD is represented by TFT-LCD (Thin Film Transistor-Liquid Crystal Display), and the biggest characteristic of TFT-LCD is that it controls each pixel by using a thin film transistor as a switch. That is, unlike a passive LCD that drives pixels in units of axes, there is an advantage in that each pixel can be driven independently. It has a structure in which a thin semiconductor film made of silicon is covered on a glass plate. Since the thin film transistor controls and transmits electrical signals, TFT-LCD can realize higher image quality and resolution than passive LCD. Active LCD is divided into the TN method, IPS method, and VA method according to the liquid crystal arrangement method.

OLED is a display using a fluorescent organic compound that emits light when an electric current flows. The biggest feature of OLED is that, unlike LCD, it does not require a backlight and can make a display that can be bent or folded. This is because the pixel itself emits light. From a structural point of view, a three-layer panel made of a specific organic compound is placed between the anode and the cathode, where the liquid crystal panel should be placed in the LCD, and these three layers are composed of a hole transport layer, a light emitting layer, and an electron transport layer.

Electrons (-) are emitted from the cathode and holes (+) are emitted from the anode. These holes are precisely electron-free spaces but can be thought of as particles having the same size as electrons and having a positive charge.

Electrons and holes pass through the transport layer, respectively, and are combined in the light emitting layer made of organic material. Neutral particles formed by the meeting of electrons and holes are called excitons, which represent an excited state. That is, the energy of the organic material of the light emitting layer rises to an excited state due to the energy generated from the combination of electrons and holes, and when the energy of the excited state falls to the ground state, energy corresponding to the difference and band gap is emitted This is expressed as light to express an image. A metal electrode such as aluminum is used for the cathode, and a transparent ITO (indium tin oxide) electrode is used as the anode because light must pass through the anode. The band gap is a unique property of a material, and it varies depending on the type of organic material and the color of the light it represents. In general, organic materials representing Red, Green, and Blue are arranged in RGB to compose the panel.

According to the driving method, OLED can be divided into PMOLED (Passive matrix OLED), which is a passive OLED, and AMOLED (Active matrix OLED), which is an active OLED. It is the same principle that divided LCDs into passive and active types. PMOLED controls pixels in a row by sequentially applying signals to the horizontal and vertical axes to emit light, whereas AMOLED uses thin film transistors as switches like TFT-LCD to control each pixel independently. AMOLED is more expensive to manufacture than PMOLED, but it has low power consumption, and high resolution, and is widely used in smartphones because it can be made into a thin film.

Currently, the display of smartphones can be divided into IPS LCD and AMOLED. Most of Samsung Electronics' Galaxy series uses AMOLED-based panels, and LG Electronics' IPS LCD-based panels are mainly installed.

TFT-LCD can be divided according to the liquid crystal arrangement method. In the TN (Twisted Nematic) method, the liquid crystal molecules stay in the horizontal direction when no voltage is applied, and then switch to the vertical direction when voltage is applied to display the screen. The structure is a method of arranging liquid crystals by turning them 90 degrees between two glass substrates, and it is the most widely used method because the production cost is low. However, TN LCD has a disadvantage in that the viewing angle is limited in the vertical direction, and the IPS method compensates for this disadvantage.

In the IPS method, the liquid crystal molecules rotate in one plane to represent the screen, and since they rotate in one plane, theoretically, they have a wide viewing angle of 180 degrees. That is, there is an advantage that the screen is not distorted when viewed from any angle. Because of this feature, it is also called a wide viewing angle panel. However, it has a relatively low contrast ratio.

Apple's Retina is a display introduced with the iPhone 4, and it was named because the number of pixels per inch is higher than the limit that humans can feel, and the technical name is AH-IPS.

AH-IPS has all the advantages of existing IPS and has been developed in stable touch operation, power consumption, and brightness.

Currently, the most used smartphone displays are AH-JPS and AMOLED.

As mentioned earlier, AMOLED is an OLED that uses a thin film transistor as a switch, and AMOLED does not require a backlight, so it can be made into a thin film type. In addition, the viewing angle is wide because the device itself emits light. Because LCD has a backlight, even if it displays black, it is not completely black, whereas AMOLED's black is completely black because pixels are turned off. Therefore, AMOLED has better contrast than LCD and consumes less power. However, when displaying white, it consumes more power than LCD, and the RGB method is not yet accurate, so color bleeding occurs.

The common feature of IPS LCD and AMOLED is a wide viewing angle, and unlike a TV or laptop, which can only be viewed from the front, a smartphone is viewed from various angles, so the importance of the viewing angle is greater. Comparing the current IPS LCD and AMOLED, the IPS display is superior to AMOLED in terms of technical completeness such as resolution, and it is a panel that implements the current best technology. However, experts predict that the share of AMOLED displays that can be made thinner and more eco-friendly will increase in the future.

A flexible display using OLED is already becoming a reality. Because it has to be thin to bend, OLEDs that do not require a backlight are applied, and plastic OLEDs that use thin plastic substrates that can be bent without breaking easily are mainly used instead of glass substrates.

The display is QLED (Quantum dot LED). QLED uses a semiconductor crystal (quantum dot) of several nm that emits various light depending on the size and voltage. Compared to the band gap described in the previous OLED, which is determined by organic materials, the band gap of quantum dots can vary depending on the size, so there is no need to use different materials for one panel. Therefore, it is expected to exhibit excellent monochromatic light and photostability at a lower manufacturing cost than OLED.

(25) Five things that will lead the future innovation in the information technology market

CNN introduced 5 innovative technologies that will captivate future consumers. Flexible displays, smart clouds, long-lasting batteries, faster networks, and ultra-fast quantum computers were selected as the top five technologies to lead future innovation.

First, flexible display is easily understood by imagining that a smartphone can be wrapped around an arm. A flexible display has already been released, but its commercialization is a bit slow due to its high price.

Second, Smart Cloud is a work in progress. Future smartphones will act as smart assistants based on user information stored in cloud servers. If a flight is canceled on the way to the airport, the smartphone will make a reservation for the next flight, order coffee at a nearby coffee shop, and send an e-mail saying that it will be late for the meeting due to flight problems. Even now, these functions have already been implemented and commercialized at the basic stage.

Third, a battery with a very long lifespan is also in the works. Currently, about 70% of smartphones use lithium-ion batteries, but lithium-ion batteries have a drawback in that they are large. Lithium imide batteries are considered an alternative, but battery performance is improved by only 10% compared to the existing ones.

Fourth, faster networks are gradually being implemented through the commercialization of 5G. In this field, Korea is achieving rapid commercialization worldwide. However, it is not yet possible to provide a network speed sufficient for users of 5G smartphones to experience. It seems that the new base station and the stability of the network operating system are still under development.

Fifth, a computer applying quantum mechanics, or a quantum computer, is applied is expected to appear in the future. With the advent of quantum-mechanical computers, calculations that are significantly faster than current computers are possible. Many computer manufacturers, including IBM, have been focusing on developing quantum computers for the past few decades, but the results are still unpredictable.

Some of you readers have a plan to research or develop these 5 future technologies, and I have no doubt that if it succeeds, it will be a great opportunity to acquire wealth and fame at the same time.

(26) Five trends in future technology

The first is artificial intelligence and machine learning. Artificial intelligence is no longer a foreign word to us. However, the reason why it is ranked first is understandable if you think of Google's Alphago and Korea's Go player Sedol Lee. It was thanks to Deep Learning that the software called Alphago, created by information technology engineers, was able to defeat Lee Sedol, a 9-dan professional Go player, and win 4 times. Deep Learning is the most representative example of machine learning that forms rules by itself, unlike an expert system that assumes that an expert directly puts a rule corresponding to the number of all cases. It is a method that analyzes data and infers results through an artificial neural network made of artificial neurons as if a person were thinking. Machine learning of artificial intelligence is more closely related to our daily life than we think.

When uploading a photo to Facebook, it automatically recognizes people's faces in the photo and easily tags by asking, 'Is it Hong Gil-dong?' It is based on Deep Learning.

Many information technology companies around the world, such as Google and Facebook, the world's leading IT companies, are showing a lot of interest in AI technology and are working hard to develop new algorithms. In Korea, a portal company called Naver has launched an artificial intelligence translator such as Papago.

The second is cybersecurity. Cybersecurity is also not a new keyword. It is a keyword that will continue to be talked about in the era of the Fourth Industrial Revolution. In 2010, Symantec, a security solution manufacturer, surveyed more than 2,000 government agencies and companies around the world, and 94% of respondents said they should invest more in cybersecurity. The reason cybersecurity is emerging as the keyword of 2017 is that the frequency and risk of threats have increased significantly. Already, social infrastructure such as finance, security, transportation, and medical care, as well as individual homes, are being built and controlled through the Internet thanks to the Internet of Things (IoT) technology. In addition, all the data of each company is stored in the cloud or server instead of in the office filing cabinet, and since hacking occurs in countless ways and extraordinary ways, the efforts of companies to stop this are expected to increase. An example is Samsung Electronics' Knox, which is a security platform that fundamentally blocks personal information leakage by porting a security tool that existed only as software to its hardware.

Cyber security companies such as appthority and Argus are emerging one after another around the world, and cyber security will always be included in the core technology field in the future society.

The third is cloud and digital transformation.

Companies are digitizing their offline analog infrastructure to adapt and respond flexibly and flexibly in a rapidly changing environment. This is the reason why the sales of enterprise servers are falling sharply and the penetration rate of cloud computing systems is increasing. As such, the migration of companies to third-party platforms such as cloud, mobile, big data analytics, and social media is called digital transformation.

Among them, cloud computing is expected to play the most decisive role in popularizing digital transformation.

After 2020, more than 67% of enterprises will build a cloud-based IT infrastructure, and as this change progresses, it is expected that almost all enterprises will provide their own cloud services.

The fourth is augmented reality and virtual reality.

AR (Augmented Reality) and VR (Virtual Reality) have taken the world by storm for years. That's because of the location-based game Poketmon Go. It is predicted that over 30% of companies worldwide will use AR or VR as their marketing strategy in the future. In addition, it is predicted that AR and VR will be popularized from 2020 onwards, and 1 billion people around the world will access applications, content, and information through AR and VR. The popularization of AR and VR will soon lead to the activation of personalization services. Their impact on society as a whole is expected to be enormous, with advertisements tailored to individual characteristics exposed and necessary information automatically presented at the right time.

The fifth is the Internet of Things. The Internet of Everything means that everything in this world becomes a component of a network. The Internet of Things (IoT), such as wearables and smart homes, is already deeply embedded in our lives. You can connect your phone, TV, etc. to the Internet, control gas valves and boilers remotely through your smartphone, and adjust color and brightness according to your mood in home appliances such as smart refrigerators, water purifiers, and air purifiers equipped with a display. Philips' Hue lighting is a technology that will be widely activated in the future as it is difficult to find a part where the Internet of Things is not applied.

(27) Wearable Devices - Smart Watch

Smartwatches are a popular product for Early Adapters. However, since it has the following disadvantages, it seems that many improvements should be made from the point of view of the consumer who wears it.

First, if a smartwatch is to be activated, whether it can include a fashionable function as a wristwatch will also have a significant impact.

Although smartwatches can perform many functions today, many advancements are needed to replace the wristwatch, which is an item of fashion.

So far, the problem with smartwatches is incomplete operation. Because it is not in a technically stable state yet, there are many conflicts between related applications and malfunctions occur. Since the size of the battery cannot be increased, the lifespan is inevitably short. In many cases, regular watches run for more than a year on coin batteries. However, the current smart watch has the disadvantage that it has to be charged every day if it is used for a lot of time like a smartphone. Also, in terms of functionality, there are many overlaps with existing smartphones. Therefore, it is necessary to develop content that can maximize the advantages of a smart watch.

(28) QR Code pros and cons

QR Code (Quick Response Code) is a two-dimensional lattice code that can contain much more information than conventional barcodes. Various information can be provided by scanning with a smartphone or a dedicated scanner. QR is an acronym for Quick Response as a two-dimensional matrix code that contains various information in a rectangular grid pattern. It was developed by Denso Wave of Japan in 1994 and has been widely used in various fields since Denso Wave declared that it would not exercise its patent right. Existing barcode-reading terminals could only be owned by product sellers, making it impossible for consumers to grasp information using barcodes. Therefore, the use of QR codes has increased as the spread of smartphones has become more active.

The biggest advantage of QR code is that it responds quickly, can store 100 times more large-capacity information compared to existing barcodes, and is possible to recover from errors.

A QR code can store various formats and large-capacity information. The amount of information that can be stored in a barcode is about 20 digits, and only English and numbers can be recorded. It can store any kind of language and format. Therefore, unlike existing barcodes, QR codes have the advantage of being able to grasp the information by themselves even without a database. The amount of information can contain up to 7,089 characters when only numbers are stored, and up to 1,817 characters in Chinese or Korean characters. In particular, it can contain more than 20% more information than other two-dimensional barcodes because it can efficiently express one Chinese character with 13-bit bits.

Photos, videos, and voices can be stored as binary data. The maximum amount of photos, videos, and voices that can be stored in one QR code is about 3KB. The downside is security. That is, the overflow of numerous information may cause security problems in various fields such as malicious code or hacking between systems and may also cause problems of compatibility between reader programs and compatibility of the generation period.

(29) Common knowledge about microprocesses

Usually, in the case of a laptop CPU, an alphabet such as M or U is attached to the end of the model number. M is an abbreviation for mobile, meaning that it is for a general laptop which is different from desktop applications.

Of course, the M-series performance is slightly lower than that of a desktop, but it has excellent performance as a laptop CPU. When performance, power consumption, and heat generation are combined, performance is achieved in the most balanced way.

Among the M series, there are products with an additional 'Q', such as the Core i7-4700MQ, which means that this CPU has a quad-core configuration with four core circuits.

Like the i5-4200U, there are cases where a U is added to the end of the CPU model name, which is an abbreviation for Ultra Low Voltage, which means that it is a low-power product that minimizes power consumption.

The performance is somewhat lower than that of the M series, but instead, the battery life is much better due to low power consumption. For example, the operating speed of the Core i5-4210M is 2.6 GHz, but the operating speed of the Core i5-4200U is 1.6 GHz.

For this reason, the U-series Core i5 can only deliver performance comparable to the M-series Core i3. However, in the case of thermal design power, which is a measure of power consumption, the Core i5-4210M is 37W, while the Core i5-4200U is only 15W.

There may be differences depending on the usage environment and detailed specifications, but if it is a Core i5-4210M-based laptop, the battery life will be 2-3 hours even when fully charged. However, for a laptop based on the Core i5-4200U, you can expect about 6 to 8 hours of battery life.

If portability is more important than performance, it is of course good to choose a laptop with a U-series CPU.

(30) Definition of interactivity in information technology

In a broad sense, interaction refers to all actions that humans perform with certain objects, people, or beings in a given environment, and the medium that provides the possibility of such actions is called interactive. Such interaction can be divided into categories such as human-human interaction through one-to-one face-to-face, human-media interaction through a mechanical medium such as media or computer, and human-computer interaction.

Interactivity has been actively discussed as an important concept, especially in computer-mediated communications. Rafaeli defines interactivity as the degree to which subsequent message delivery in a series of exchanges of communication relates to communication through a previously delivered message, and more specifically, considers this to be sufficient interactions to affect the content or form of the media, the periodic situations in which two-way communication and a subsequent message relate to the previous message. Rice argued that interactivity is communication that allows humans to have control over the speed, structure, or content of communication in real-time or non-simultaneously. Neuman described interactivity as the quality of electrically mediated communication characterized by increased control of both the audience and the recipient. Rogers interpreted interactivity as a three-dimensional structure consisting of the exchange of control roles and interactive dialogue. Control refers to control over the content, timing, sequencing of communication actions, search for alternatives, storage, or transformation of content, etc., and role exchange means exchanging roles between message communicator and receiver. The reciprocal dialogue is when A and B talk, A's response to B depends on B's response to A in the previous conversation. It means that it happens sequentially. In particular, emphasizing the aspect of role exchange, Pavlik defined interactivity as two-way communication between a message sender and a receiver, and more broadly, a multifaceted communication that occurs between a number of message bearers and receivers, whereas Heeter defined interactivity as a communication between a message sender and a receiver. He stipulated that the distinction between message carriers and recipients does not exists in all media. Rogers explained interactivity in terms of interpersonal dialogue as the degree to which participants in the communication process can exchange roles and exert control over the interpersonal dialogue. The interactivity of the medium is also evaluated according to how well the mediated communication reflects the communication elements between individuals.

Research on interactivity is being actively carried out, especially in the virtual reality situation. In addition to vitality, which refers to the technical ability to create sensory-rich mediating environments, interactivity is defined as the degree to which the user can influence the form and content of the mediated environment, as it is the main factor constituting it. Steuer cited the three factors that affect interactivity: speed, which refers to how quickly the mediating environment responds to user manipulation, the number of attributes, such as temporal sequence and spatial composition, that the user can change to the mediating environment, , and the mapping, which refers to how naturally the user's actions are connected and expressed as actions in the mediating environment. Therefore, regardless of the type of media, the interactivity of the media can be said to be relatively high or low depending on how quickly, freely, and naturally the user can control the content or form as desired in the mediated environment. Interactivity increases realism, especially in virtual environments, by allowing users to control the relationship of their sensory senses to the environment. Realism refers to a phenomenon in which an experience mediated by media is felt as if it is actually experienced without being mediated. For example, while watching TV in the living room, the user experiences a sense of reality when the user feels as if they are real in a scene in a movie mediated through the television and feels that objects in the movie exist as if they exist in real life. Realism occurs when users can understand and predict the consequences of their actions in the virtual environment.

The influence on realism was tested by dividing interactivity into two categories: the user's search for the sense of control over the virtual environment and the predictability of the outcome of his/her action, which has been proven to be a factor inducing a sense of reality in reality.

Strain viewed interactivity in multimedia situations as allowing users to actively select and decide what content to receive, when, and how, and there are various levels of interactivity depending on the user's needs and technological sophistication. That is, the first stage refers to the stage in which the media allows the user to access the content. For example, on a television, it refers to the level at which a user can turn on/off or simply select a channel. Level 2 refers to the level at which users can choose their own path within the program according to their needs and intuition. For example, when working with a computer, it is said that selection and access to content are possible, and the user manipulates the order of information processing, edits, or changes the form of existing data and saves it. Stage 3 is somewhat closer to the theoretical level and can be seen as the stage to realize the highest level of interactivity. In this stage, the user becomes an author and can freely change the content, and depending on who the user is, the experience of the content can be different.

From the educational engineering perspective, Bork viewed the input required from the learner while reacting with the computer, the learner's response analysis by the computer, and the computer's activity itself as interactivity, while Damarin listed a series of interactive options as activities such as finding, following, using, constructing, creating, etc. Jonassen understood interactivity as the relationship between the computer-based user's control and its analysis and response. He said that interaction is the action between the learner's response and the computer's feedback on it and that the interaction is meaningful when with the response matches the learner's information processing needs. Therefore, interactivity has the characteristics of immersing and personalizing the user more than simply touching a mouse and pressing a button.

From an artistic point of view, Cameron saw interactivity as the possibility that the audience can participate and control a certain work or expression, and this intervention of interactivity can help to understand the meaning of Narrative as a finality in which the story elements are organically constructed under the author's intention. He said that, in particular, in a narrative situation such as a movie, a character creates a story, and when interactivity becomes possible, the audience controls it, and this deprives the character of an important function. Laurel said that interactivity is an experience like acting on a stage. Interactivity is a series of physical actions to the mediated environment and objects and beings in it, and a series of human reactions embodied in the mediated space. It is also consistent with Heeter's view, which emphasizes the organic relationship between elements in a given environment. All of these perspectives mean that, due to the increase in interactivity, which means that the audience's control over the work is increased, the audience, who was sitting in the audience watching the play passively, goes into the stage and plays with the actors.

Combining the various viewpoints discussed above, it can be seen that the user's controllability of information or certain elements in the physical world is positioned as a key concept in interactivity. This concept of control also appears in defining interactivity in advertising. In other words, interactivity is fundamentally in the control of information, whereas in traditional advertisements, consumers were passively and unilaterally exposed to product information, in interactive advertisements, consumers can actively select the product information they want to see. In the end, it can be said that with the development of media that provides interactivity, control over the flow of information has begun to be transferred from the seller to the consumer.

Roehm analyzed interactivity by dividing it into two dimensions, message and control, and the message is divided into interactivity due to form and interactivity due to content, and control is divided into consumers and sellers. In other words, "in terms of content", consumers can select information according to their level of interest, adjust the length or sequence of information presentation, and choose whether to view the same content as a video clip, print, or audio version in terms of form. From the seller's point of view, in terms of content, it means to modify the amount or order of information provided based on the reaction of consumers or to personalize and provide information to suit the tastes of specific consumers. Content-level interactions include highlighting certain characteristics of a product without altering the actual information or providing a printed version as a video.

Ghose classified the types of interactive functions into five major categories. The first is a consumer support function that provides consumers with an opportunity to ask questions or feedback, the second is marketing research that collects consumer satisfaction and opinions through a survey on the web, and the third is a keyword search or virtual reality display of products. The fourth is an advertisement promotion function using electronic coupons, prize lottery, user groups, or multimedia functions, and the fifth is entertainment through electronic postcards or online games. Cutler defined a new interactive medium as one that offered immediate advertising and sales and the possibility of collecting payments. Taken together, interactivity is being used as a variety of incentives to attract consumers who have an autonomous choice to sellers in advertising. It is moving toward making it easier for consumers to directly purchase products from sellers, which shows that interactivity is emerging as an important factor in marketing activities due to the increase in consumers' control over information.

Combining various discussions on interactivity in this mediated communication situation, interaction occurs through an interface that connects the two between the medium user and the medium. Among them, it can be said that it is a series of exchange processes that include not only the user's control over the content or form of the mediated experience but also the reaction of the medium or message recipient.

Interactivity personalizes information more and has the characteristic of actively immersing the user in the experience in the mediating environment, and there may be various levels of interactivity depending on the characteristics of the medium or the characteristics of the user.

(31) Conditions for a good interface

First, you need to make an effort to be consistent. When designing similar or sequential situations, try to ensure consistency by using familiar icons, colors, menu structures, events for actions, and user flows. Standardizing the way information is delivered allows users to perceive and apply context continuously, rather than with a single click.

Consistency plays a very important role in helping users adapt to the digital environment and achieve their goals.

Second, in general, you should provide shortcuts for highly skilled users. There is a need for a faster way to perform tasks more easily. For example, both Windows and Mac provide shortcuts for copying and pasting, allowing users to become more experienced users.

Third, useful feedback must be continuously provided. Users must know where they are located and what is happening. All actions must be timely and human-readable feedback must be provided within a predictable time frame. A good example of this is when a user fills out multiple questionnaires, giving feedback on how many questionnaires they have filled out in the process. A bad example would be an error message popup that displays a non-human readable error code.

Fourth, it is good to have the design communicate the message you want to convey. It tells you what to do in a given situation and encourages you to do it. For example, when users see the word 'Thank You' while shopping online, they can recognize it as a receipt indicating that the purchase has been completed as soon as the shopping is completed.

Fifth, it is to have a simple and quick error response capability. Systems need to be designed to do their best not to be stupid, but if errors are unavoidable, it's a good idea to provide users with simple yet intuitive Step by Step instructions for quick and easy troubleshooting. An example would be an interaction where the user forgets to type and displays a red flag in a text field that has passed.

Sixth, it is good to make it easy to reverse an action. Users should be able to easily reverse their actions. It is important to make this overturn possible at various points of time, and it is good to do it regardless of whether it is a simple single action, a single data input, or multiple actions.

Seventh, empowerment provides an internal place of control. Let users be the starting point for action. You need to give users the feeling that they have direct control over what's happening digitally. You need to gain confidence in your design from users by designing a system that works as they expect it to.

Eighth, it is better to focus on perception rather than memory. Human attention is limited, and it is said that the brain's short-term memory storage unit can store only about five items in the case of ordinary intellectuals. Therefore, the interface should be as simple as possible, have an appropriate information system, and should be designed in terms of recognition and understanding rather than memory. Recognizing objects is an easier operation than remembering, as it involves recognizing some sort of hint that makes it easier to access and associate information. For example, we tend to experience multiple-choice problems more easily than subjective ones, because it forces us to perceive and compute, not to remember.

(32) Touch screen technology

The global touch screen market size increased from 155 million units in 2006 to 785 million units in 2010, reaching an average annual growth rate of 49.9%. The field that is leading the high growth of the touch screen market is the smartphone. Portable devices account for the highest proportion of touch screens and have the highest growth rate. Among portable devices, the adoption of touch screens for navigation and portable game consoles is already increasing, but in terms of market size, smartphones constitute the largest market.

In particular, after 3G mobile communication service, 5G service is commercialized, and as the Internet of Things and artificial intelligence technology spread, the utilization of the wireless Internet is increasing, and accordingly, the demand for touch smartphones suitable for wireless Internet is also increasing significantly.

There are three types of touch screens: pressure-sensitive touch screens, capacitive touch screens, and infrared touch screens.

Originally, the pressure-sensitive type and capacitive type were used because of their respective strengths and weaknesses, but since the 2010s, the capacitive type has become the mainstream and technological development has followed. In fact, there are some people who draw detailed drawings using the Galaxy Tab 7.0 or iPad drawing app, so it doesn't mean that capacitive precision is poor anymore, it's just making a dedicated touch pen to give a feeling of writing. In other words, the decompression type was eliminated, and the range of use of the current decompression type was reduced to the use of a control panel for a manufacturing system in a factory or an input system for military equipment.

(33) Dubeol-sik QWERTY keyboard and Cheonjiin keyboard

Cheonjiin was originally a keyboard frequently used in mobile phones. Besides Cheonjiin, there are several types of mobile phone keyboards, but Cheonjiin is known to be the most convenient to use. This is because all vowels can be expressed with dots and ｜ and ―.

To put it simply, QWERTY is in the form of a computer keyboard, and Cheonjiin is in the form of a mobile phone keyboard. The good thing about the QWERTY keyboard is that it is faster than the Cheonjiin keyboard.

For example, if you try to enter ㄹ in QWERTY and CheonJiIn, QWERTY hits the keyboard only once, so you can write ㄹ at a time.

On the other hand, because Cheonjiin inputs by double pressing (ㄴ, ㄹ), it has no choice but to input more slowly than QWERTY.

For example, let's say you type the text "안녕(Hello)". When entering this string, QWERTY moves to the second letter '녕' by pressing ㄴ immediately after writing '안', which is the first letter.

However, for Cheonji, you must press space or the > key separately. Otherwise, a difficult case arises in which "안녕(hello)" is input as "아령 (dumbbell)".

In addition, since vowels ｜, ―, and dots are used separately, to enter one vowel ㅕ, you only need to enter QWERTY once, but you have to enter it three times for Cheonjiin.

(34) Web version (1.0 , 2.0 , 3.0 , 4.0)

With the advent of the Internet in the Web 1.0 era, that is, in the 1990s, we used the Internet in a hypertext-oriented Web environment. Text and links were the main forms, and the use of multimedia such as music or video was extremely limited. On the website, there was no service that provided dynamic data and could not be accessed other than what the operator showed. Therefore, there was no data collection through the participation of visitors. The computer was slow, the storage space of the hard disk was insufficient, and the bandwidth of the network was small, so flashy websites such as videos and flash were considered a waste of resources.

The first characteristic of Web 2.0 is openness. In a website with the characteristics of Web 2.0, no one monopolizes data and provides a platform where everyone can use data in the Internet environment. Therefore, all users can freely use all data uploaded or serviced on the website according to their convenience.

The second characteristic of Web 2.0 is that it improves connectivity in all directions. On the web, users and information cannot survive unless they are connected with other elements. Therefore, the connectivity between information and information and the social connectivity between users and users are inevitably strengthened.

The third characteristic of Web 2.0 is participation-oriented and interactivity. A new type of information is created by user participation and interaction between users, and collective intelligence that creates new value through active participation and sharing of content created by users and user groups is a very important feature.

The term Web 3.0 has been at the center of controversy since it was first used by New York Times reporter John Markoff in 2006. Web 3.0 only refers to the flow of the web development direction and has not yet been clearly conceptualized. However, when looking at the characteristics of the technologies leading Web 3.0, opinions are converging on personalization, intelligence, and situational awareness, so the evolutionary direction of the Web can be predicted.

Web 3.0 is an intelligent web that uses semantic technology to provide customized content and services to users through situational awareness. In other words, in the Web 3.0 era, the intelligent web provides the information users want.

Web 4.0 is the era in which computers become people. Previously, computers could not understand human speech and only process commands by receiving input from the keyboard. However, Web 4.0 is an era in which computers that provide the Internet can understand human speech. In the era where computers understand human speech and move autonomously, that is the time when Web 4.0 is completed.

(35) Biometric authentication in information technology

Biometrics means that biometric information (fingerprint, face, iris, cornea, hand shape, vein on the back of the hand, voice, etc.) that is different for each person is extracted and made to be identified. Biometric information is used as a means of identification for each individual.

The biggest reason that biometrics has emerged is security and convenience. That is, in the case of existing keys and access cards, there is a lot of room for theft, loss, duplication, etc., so security is relatively low, and it has the disadvantages that it is necessary to carry it with you, and it requires effort such as memorizing passwords.

On the other hand, biometrics uses human biometric information, and although there is a difference in degree depending on the reliability of the system, it has the advantage of satisfying the excellent security that is not released unless it is yourself and the convenience of not having to carry or memorize a separate device.

Among the types of biometrics, Vein Recognition is a method of recognizing the shape of blood vessels on the back of the hand or wrist. In the case of this method, replication is almost impossible, so it has high security, but there are disadvantages in that the hardware configuration is complicated and the overall system cost is high so the range that can be utilized is limited. In addition, palm recognition uses the palm creases distributed on a person's palm, and it was conceived from the fact that each individual's palms have a unique pattern. In addition, voice recognition is a method based on the characteristics of people's intonations and pitches of voices different from each other. It analyzes the characteristics of the voice transmitted through a microphone, etc., and finds the closest one. You can use it to verify your identity, and it does not require additional training to use, and has the advantage that the system price is low. However, there is a disadvantage that the recognition may be erroneous when a person has a sore throat due to cold or other factors, intentionally imitates another person's voice, or when there is a lot of noise in the surrounding environment.

In addition, face recognition has a disadvantage in that it is greatly affected by the user's expression changes or ambient lighting by comparing the face shape input by the camera with the database without contacting the machine. However, in order to solve these recognition errors, facial technologies using artificial intelligence that improve accuracy by learning the recognition data accumulated with big data are currently being released.

Iris recognition is the most advanced security system compared to fingerprint or retina recognition in terms of data accuracy, stability, ease of use, and processing speed, using the iris pattern outside the pupil, which is unique to each person. The iris usually does not change throughout life after a unique pattern is formed within 1 to 2 years of life, and it is a non-contact method that recognizes the iris pattern from a certain distance. And fingerprint recognition, which we are well aware of, has been used universally for a long time because it has a characteristic that does not change for a lifetime unless the dermis is damaged. The principle of the fingerprint recognition system is to identify the characteristic points of the fingerprint image, such as ridges, valleys, and shortcomings of the fingerprint, and compare it with the stored original data.

(36) Trends of information technology consumers

With the development of industries and technologies, various products and services are produced and competition has intensified. It is no longer possible to satisfy consumers simply by meeting their needs. This is especially true in the electronics and IT industries, where new products and services are introduced every day. Electronics and IT companies are in a situation where they have to constantly create new values in order to be selected by consumers. In this context, user experience is rapidly emerging as an important value in the recent electronics and IT markets. The key to user experience is how easy, convenient, and enjoyable it is for consumers to use products and services. User experience is evolving according to the three trends found by consumers: self-centeredness, sharing, and luxury.

The first trend is egocentricity. As digital video devices that anyone can enjoy easily and conveniently have become popular, and SNS (Social Network Service) is combined with this, it has become an era in which individuals become the protagonists. Consumers are taking the lead from content production to consumption, such as taking and editing their own daily lives. It is no exaggeration to say that the advent of the one-man media era started with the convergence of self-centeredness and IT infrastructure. Sony's continued release and popularity of products specialized for self-photography as well as wireless communication functions can be attributed to keeping pace with these consumer changes.

The second trend is sharing. With the development of social network services (SNS), people want to share and communicate with many people the content they produce. Through such a process, the meaning and value of content are doubled. The public, who want to share content, are constantly consuming each other's content, forming a circulation structure in which they buy new content and ideas. Recent IT devices equipped with Wi-Fi as well as Near Field Communication (NFC) and Beacon technologies are representative examples of helping to form such a content circulation structure. In addition, cloud-based services that can store, share, and consume content freely between smartphones and PCs are pouring in, which is also an answer from companies responding to consumer demand for easier content sharing.

The third is content enhancement. Modern society is an era in which the standard of living has improved more than ever before. As living standards rise, people naturally consume entertainment content such as movies and music, and IT technology, which has evolved dazzlingly at this time, is converging with the content industry, satisfying people's desire for high-quality content.

As described above, the main trends of consumers in modern society are personalization, sharing, and luxury. It is said that it ill be successful only when a product is produced based on this trend.

(37) Gaze communication technology

Gaze communication technology can be said to be a new concept of communication technology that connects directly to the object visible on the smartphone screen even if you do not know the identifier of the object to be connected. In other words, communication is possible by simply touching the target as if taking a picture after running the application on the smartphone.

The line-of-sight communication technology generates an electron beam such as a laser beam with strong straightness and is implemented in a way that a specific target device responds to the beam. It is possible to identify the unique ID by distinguishing the objects that have entered the current range of about 8 degrees, and it is possible to search only the devices near the direction of the target, making it less susceptible to interference from other devices. In addition, it implements a high speed of finding a target within 3 seconds and a high communication target recognition rate of 94%.

Existing device-to-device methods such as Wi-Fi and Bluetooth are technologies that can communicate directly between devices in a short distance, mainly targeting mobile devices. It has the disadvantage of being unable to connect without knowing the communication serial and searching for devices other than the target. In addition, although the communication connection process is complicated and takes more than 30 seconds, line-of-sight communication technology overcomes all these shortcomings and limitations.

The biggest advantage of line-of-sight communication technology is that it provides a variety of mobile services to users through direct communication with nearby devices without using a separate base station or wired/wireless network.

For example, even if you do not know the phone number of the other party, you can make a call or send a message to the other party. All you have to do is send a variety of data. Of course, an instant sharing service is also possible, such as allowing multiple people to listen to or watch the music or video on your smartphone through nearby audio or TV.

(38) The concept of new media

In general, new media is defined as media in which innovative changes are given to one or more of the four media areas: information collection and creation, information processing and processing, information transmission, and information use.

In particular, it refers to a new communication system and a medium of electronic information equipment that transmits information through new technologies in the fields of telecommunications and electronics and can provide services suitable for upgrading and diversifying people's information demands in the process of receiving information.

A general concept of new media is, in addition to the existing media such as newspapers, magazines, and TV, the media that dominates the mass media as a new means of information exchange and communication due to the development of electronic technology, combined with other existing media or new technologies. It refers to media that appear in the boundary area between these individual media and have more convenient and advanced new functions and practicality. one of the important characteristics of the newly formed communication environment in the mid-1990s is the communication networking phenomenon. For a new media format including multimedia to be widely popularized, a transmission network capable of transmitting a large amount of digital information at high speed is essential.

The high-speed information network is interconnected with the existing telephone line, cable TV network, and corporate local area network (LAN), thereby connecting homes, businesses, and government agencies to one communication network. The Internet is a representative example of an integrated communication network. The popularization of the Internet plays a pivotal role in modern society's politics, economy, cultural life, and daily communication activities by connecting homes, businesses, and government agencies around the world through a single communication network.

Due to the unique characteristics of media, new media integrated human communication, which had been divided into face-to-face communication and mass communication, in the existing traditional communication environment, and can collect information with media that integrates what needed a separate transmission medium into one single media depending on the type of information such as video, sound, text, and data. On the wireless communication side, a newly emerged media is divided into the media that transmits signals using microwaves and terrestrial radio waves, and the types can be classified as follows.

Teletext, text radio broadcasting, vehicular mobile phone, and cellular radio-based new media such as television media (that is, subscriber TV, low-power TV, multi-channel microwave broadcasting) and digital radio broadcasting, combined with text information transmission functions in existing broadcasting media Personal wireless communication media such as telephone, outgoing-only mobile phone, and personal mobile communication are included.

Using satellites, it does not use terrestrial waves or microwave waves but uses artificial satellites such as communication satellites or broadcasting satellites to use very high-frequency bands, and there are direct satellite broadcasting and VSAT networks.

(39) Relationship between Old Media and New Media

The development of digital technology advances the birth and development of new media such as social media, and the existing media such as newspapers and broadcasting are called traditional media or old media.

Old media is a media belonging to the industrial group in which the importance of copyright is emerging with the characteristic of one-sided information delivery such as publication, radio, and television, which were in the spotlight before the media revolution that came with the development of the Internet.

New media mainly belongs to the industry group that forms a platform that emphasizes communication with readers, with IT-based operators such as Google and YouTube being the majority. In fact, the Washington Post, one of the leading global old media companies, was sold to Jeff Bezos, the founder of Amazonone of the representative companies of new media in 2013, and Bezos announced that it would introduce a new platform to the Washington Post and reorganize it completely.

With the development of printing technology in the late 15th century, newspapers were created after the birth of newspapers, and then magazines were created. With the development of radio technology in the 1890s, radio and TV in the 1920s appeared, forming four major media. In the early 2000s, social media appeared and the whole world was engulfed in a craze.

Social media such as Twitter, which led the Egyptian revolution, Facebook, which has surpassed 1 billion members, and YouTube, have quickly turned the world into a single fence, and their influence is growing more and more in the future.

Old media such as newspapers and broadcasting and new media such as the Internet and smartphones are complementary to each other rather than competitors. It is right to view it from the perspective that users select new media in addition to existing old media, rather than consuming new media instead of old media.

(40) Social networking media

Social Networking Service (SNS) media refers to a platform where users who subscribe to social networking services such as Twitter and Facebook can share information and opinions with each other and expand their interpersonal networks. It is so widespread that it is difficult to find anyone who has never used a social networking service in a country where this platform has spread to people and a network system has been developed. Even today, the number of people using it is increasing at a tremendous rate. SNSs such as Twitter, Instagram, and Facebook do not use only one, but when one is used, other SNSs are also used. The speed of information that just spreads is very fast, but it got even faster by uploading humor and things you want to brag about. As a result, users of the SNS system share information with each other and the sharing spreads quickly to others. As a result, once an event or important information is posted on SNS, the speed at which information spreads can be seen, the power of SNS is beyond imagination now

(41) Changes in social networking media
Social Networking Service (SNS) refers to an online platform that creates and strengthens social relationships through free communication, information sharing, and network expansion between users. The most important part of SNS is that it creates, maintains, strengthens, and expands social network through this service. When information is shared and distributed through such a network, it can become more meaningful.
Most of today's SNS are web-based services, and besides the web, they provide a means for users to communicate with each other through e-mail or

instant messenger.

Recently, along with the increase of smartphone users and the expansion of wireless Internet services, the number of users of SNS is also rapidly increasing. The number of Facebook and Twitter users developed in the United States already exceeded 10 million in 2011 in Korea alone, and the continuous increase is not expected to stop for the time being.

The value of using SNS for marketing is emerging day by day in that it can identify and manage service users who can be classified into a broad and specific group at the same time using a database. This is because, from the perspective of the company, it is possible to execute customized marketing that can effectively reach the target group at a low cost. SNS companies are also building a strong profit model through the sale of advertising space on the SNS page and sales of social games and items, so the SNS market is expected to continue to grow in the future.

Early social networking websites started as generalized online communities. Early communities such as The Well, Theglob.com, Geocities, and Tripod brought people together and allowed them to chat in chat rooms, and provided publishing tools that allowed you to publish personal information or personal writings on your personal homepage. In addition, there are communities that connect people simply by e-mail addresses.

With the increase in smartphone use and the emergence of various types of services, the number of SNS users is also increasing exponentially. According to Facebook's Q1 2014 results, the number of users worldwide exceeded 1.27 billion, and the number of daily users exceeded 800 million. Twitter also has over 200 million monthly active users. In Korea, as of March 2014, the number of monthly Facebook users reached 13 million, of which 92% were using mobile devices at least once a month. Kakao Story, linked with the mobile messenger KakaoTalk, is Korea's largest SNS, and as of April 2013, more than 40 million people are using it. The usage status and usage behavior by age and gender can be known through the results of the SNS usage survey conducted by various organizations. First, according to a 2013 survey on Internet use by Korea KISA, 55.1% of Internet users aged 6 years and over were using SNS.

SNS is developing from the role of passive media that connects offline relationships online and digitally stores documents to active media that spreads users' thoughts and feelings. This means that SNS provided users with an opportunity not only to form relationships on the Internet, but also to establish themselves as a key player in production, distribution, and consumption, the process of the information (content) economy. This changed the previous information economy structure, which was centralized and one-sided, into a user-centered horizontal structure, and SNS played a major role in this change. In particular, as users break away from the portal-centric paradigm and participate as the main agents of content production and distribution, users can spread information faster and more accurately through their relationship-based network. In the relationship with unspecified people, users strengthened their networks around the content they prefer, and the use of content-oriented SNS has also increased rapidly based on the environment in which large-capacity content is exchanged.

(42) Closed social networking service (SNS)

Open SNS has gained popularity in that it can communicate with acquaintances anytime, anywhere. Twitter, Facebook, and KakaoTalk are representative examples. But now the advantage of such connectivity has become a boomerang. He felt tired of the openness that an unspecified number of people could come in through an acquaintance's SNS or search for it if they wanted to. As a reaction against this, closed SNS, where only a small number of acquaintances that one can control can send and receive messages, are emerging.

The criterion for classifying SNS into open type and closed type depends on how many people can communicate. For example, the group-type SNS Path, which has been popular in the United States since 2011, is evaluated as the beginning of a closed SNS in that it limits the number of friends that can be added to 150. It was a number based on the theory that the maximum number of human beings a person can have close relationships with is 150. Compared to Facebook, which can add up to 5,000 people, that number is reduced to 1/33.

In Korea, an application called Naver's Band is gaining popularity. It was launched in August of last year and has recently surpassed 10 million users. Band does not limit the number of users like a pass, but the feature is that only people you invite can join and view the content.

An app called Between, which shares photos and texts only between the two of them who are lovers, is an extreme example of a closed SNS. The symbolism of space with only the two of them makes the couple feel closer. Another popular factor of Bitwin is that unlike KakaoTalk, which does not know who the message is from when a message notification rings, it is immediately clear that it is a message sent by a lover. It was launched at the end of 2011 and is currently used by more than 3 million people. In other words, it is expected that closed SNS will become popular for a while in the future as users' tendencies and preferences are shifting to narrow but deep relational network services rather than wide and shallow relations.

(43) Social Networking Service (SNS) Problems

It is said that Facebook members, the world's largest global social networking service, make and maintain Facebook friends online, even if they are not very close or even hateful to see in real life. What's the reason? According to a recent study by US money-saving site CouponCodesPro.com, the reason people keep Facebook friends with people they hate is that people have a desire to keep spying on their daily lives.

CouponCodesPro.com surveyed 2,570 US adults who love to use social media. The questions were: how many Facebook friends do you currently have and how many of your Facebook friends are your closest friends? do you want to keep a close relationship online with someone you don't want to see? would you leave your seat if you run into someone you were friends with online but didn't like?

According to the survey results, the average number of Facebook friends was 671, the average number of real close friends was 18, and about 68% of respondents said they would maintain a friendly relationship online even if they are not really close. Half of the respondents said that they would leave the seat if they encountered him/her in their daily life.

Then, why do they want to keep Facebook friends with people they don't want to see?

69% of the respondents said that they wanted to know what they usually do. In this regard, CouponCodesPro.com said that the survey results show that friendships online are different from friendships in real life. With the development of social media, many people share their daily lives online, but in fact, the spying substrate to peek into other people's lives is also being discovered at the same time. The important thing is to know that other people are also peeking at your daily life as much as you are peeking at other lives through SNS. said to have In other words, there are many Facebook friends who want to satisfy their spying rather than actually maintain close friends, so it seems to be necessary to refrain from using SNS for indiscriminate exposure of personal information or desire to show off.

(44) Infographic

An infographic is the visualization of information. The word infographic itself is a compound word of information and graphic that represent information. It also called news graphics.

It can be found in newspaper articles, magazines, and public relations media such as the government and posters. It is often used in promotions by companies, etc. The information must be delivered concretely, practically, and intuitively. The term itself is recent, but the concept is more of an extension of the old. In a nutshell, everything that tries to convey information in a visual form can be viewed as an infographic. Illustrations and photos are included in a broad sense, but infographics contain the meaning of information processing. Surprisingly, it is a technique that many students have also tried, and panel production means making a panel with infographics.

The more familiar with the Internet generation, the more vulnerable they are to long texts, so the importance of infographics is growing.

(45) Decicorn

It refers to a more successful company than a unicorn, which is a startup valued at more than $1 billion. New meanings are given to existing words in the sense that such high-value startups are as rare as unicorns. But now Silicon Valley is said to be overflowing with these unicorns. Recent findings show that there are 131 unicorns in the tech industry, and startups are now so overvalued that startups worth more than $10 billion are classified as a neologism "decicon". It isalso called Decacorn.

(46) Dronevertising

The advertising industry is always looking for new places to advertise its products. Unusual places attract public attention because interest means the money in advertising.

When the quadcopter, or drone, appeared, someone thought that it would be effective if a drone had a billboard attached to it and flew it. So, dronevertising was born.

You can think of it as a combination of Drone and Advertising.

A new advertising agency has appeared that is fully looking forward to the possibility of drone Verification. Philadelphia-based DroneCast and Russian company Hungry Boys are examples.

(47) Faircasting

The method of going to a travel agency and purchasing an airline ticket is a thing of the past, and now everyone buys it on a website. In line with this change, new sites for finding the cheapest airfare have appeared.

Travelers looking to save even a penny are well aware that flight fares fluctuate frequently as airlines implement dynamic pricing policies to maximize profits. The concept of dynamic pricing is to set the initial ticket price high, catch the naive, and then lower the price as the departure date approaches. Then, when the seats fill up and demand outstrips supply, the price rises sharply again.

Here, targeting the optimal point of purchase is called faircasting. It is a new word coined by startup company Farecast, combining the words "fare" and "forecasting."

(48) Inculator

In the high-tech startup world, there are startup incubators and startup accelerators.

The Startup Incubator provides business resources, including business support and office space, for start-ups. One of Silicon Valley's largest incubators is AngelPad.

Accelerators are intensively supported for a shorter period. The key concept is to build a business in months, even weeks, so that the company is good if it succeeds, and if it fails, it goes bankrupt quickly so you don't lose a lot of money. Accelerators advise on the development of ideas and business plans and invest cash and manpower to speed decisions whether the company functions or fails. A representative accelerator in Silicon Valley is the Y Combinator. The new word incubator is a compound word of incubator and accelerator. An incubator is an accelerator, but it develops ideas and builds business for a longer period. In the case of accelerators such as Nine Plus, we think that entrepreneurs need sufficient time, so they provide services with a margin of time.

(49) Quinquagintacorn and Unicorpse

Quinqua Gintacon is a startup valued at over $50 billion. So far, the only Quinqua Gintacon is Uber, which has a valuation of about $51 billion on a funding site. So in other words, these startups are also called Ubercorns. In Korea, Jae-woong Lee of Tada is running a ride-hailing service with the goal of Ubercon. However, growth in the Korean market is not expected to be easy due to opposition from the taxi industry. Unicorps is a dead unicorn, a startup that was valued at over $1 billion and then went bankrupt before going public. There are rumors circulating that Evernote will be the first Unicorp.

(50) Edutainment

It is a compound word of education and entertainment, and it is an educational form that enables learning while having fun as if playing a game. In general, edutainment refers to software that aims for learning effects through entertainment based on multimedia images. In general, educational games refer to games that are intentionally designed from the production stage so that users can experience various learning processes in the course of the game. It is often described as a game for educational purposes, but in fact, it would be more appropriate to call it a game in which educational effects occur through fun. Because even if the purpose of education is not to have fun, the purpose cannot be achieved. Reflecting this point, the edu game refers to a case in which educational and game characteristics are integrated and educational effects are achieved through game play.

As described above, since games provide a functional aspect that cannot be overlooked in terms of education, games have a great impact on education.

5.2 Nano Technology and The Time Machine

Still, there are opinions that nanotechnology is not viewed as an established discipline, but as a convergence research trend that encompasses various disciplines such as physics, chemistry, materials science, mechanical engineering, and medicine. In particular, since the nano unit is used a lot in the chemistry field, there are many cases in which the nano unit is attached to the name of the department in the chemistry department at universities.

Carbon nanotubes are also a product of nanotechnology, and there are many parts that are grafted with nanotechnology in electronic engineering, electrical engineering, and materials engineering.

Looking at the history of nanotechnology, Richard Feynman foresaw the era of manipulating individual atoms and storing information from around the world in microscopic devices through a lecture called 'There is plenty of room at the bottom' on December 29, 1959, by Richard Feynman. Therefore, nanotechnology was first proposed. Then, in 1987, Eric Drexler, who is called the father of nanotechnology, directly mentioned nano-manipulation technology and nano-robots for the first time and argued that nanotechnology would be used in actual manufacturing technology and products with various functions would appear. That claim was possible because, as early as 1981, the invention of the scanning tunneling microscope gave rise to nanotechnology to control atoms and manipulate artificial nanostructures.

At that time, nanotechnology was merely a prediction that such technology would appear in the future. However, after the US government first discussed the development of nanotechnology in 1996, the National Science and Technology Commission (NSTC) was finally established in 1998, which rapidly accelerated the development of nanotechnology. The Bill Clinton government of the United States announced the National Nanotechnology Development Plan (NNI) and presented specific goals for nanotechnology. Korea also established a comprehensive national nanotechnology development plan in 2001 to create various nanotechnology, preoccupy the nanotechnology market, and solve energy and environmental problems through nanotechnology.

In general, nanotechnology is integrated to such an extent that it is statistically insignificant because the number of molecules constituting a nano device or a nano-sized object is only tens to hundreds. Even such a small object has such a small mass that the gravitational force becomes negligible and is affected by the Van der Waals force too much. At this time, a problem arises, because of the Van der Waals force, a few nanoparticles keep agglomeration, making individual manipulation difficult, and the surface area is too wide to adsorb surrounding water molecules, so the pure state continues to be lost. These problems arose when Richard Errett Smalley developed Fullerene.

Here, in physical chemistry, Van der Waals force refers to an attractive or repulsive force between molecules or between parts within a molecule, not between covalent bonds or electrical interactions of ions. In other words, when an instantaneous dipole is formed by the movement of electrons in a nonpolar molecule, the molecule next to it is also temporarily polarized, creating an induced dipole. The attraction between the instantaneous dipole and the induced dipole is called the Van der Waals force. It is named after Johannes van der Waals.

Also, fullerene is a generic term for molecules in which carbon atoms are arranged in spheres, ellipsoids, and cylinders. It was first discovered in 1985 and is a completely new material found in the soot left behind when a laser was fired on a piece of graphite.

Buckminsterfullerene (C60) is mainly formed by bonding 60 carbon atoms in the shape of a soccer ball. It consists of 12 5-membered rings and 20 6-

membered rings, and 5 6-membered rings are adjacent to each 5-membered ring.

It forms the shape of a nano soccer ball with a diameter of about 1 nm, and the name Fullerene is derived from the name of American architect Buckminster Fuller, who designed a dome with the same shape as this structure.

In 1990, Kretschmer et al. discovered a method of forming fullerene, which later developed into an arc method, and research on it has been active. It is obtained by extraction of organic solvents (Benzene, Toluene, etc.) of tin produced by arc discharge using graphite as an electrode in helium gas at a pressure of about 50 to 600 Torr. At this time, C70 in the shape of a rugby ball or higher-order fullerenes such as C76, C78, C82, C90, C94, and C96, which are smaller but larger in size, are also produced.

Using fullerene (C60) as raw material, two bodies (C120) or fullerene polymers in the form of two connected are also synthesized, which return to the original C60 when heated. Recently, fullerene, a metal introduced with an alkali metal, is attracting attention as it exhibits superconductivity at a higher temperature than conventional organic superconductors.

In addition, since C60 has a space with a diameter of 0.4 nm (0.4×10^{-9} m) and higher-order fullerene has a larger space, metal-encapsulated fullerene can also be made. This is generated when an arc discharge is performed using graphite mixed with metal atoms as an electrode.

By adding fullerene to the resin by using its oil-soluble property, it is being tried to improve durability and heat resistance, remove static electricity, and apply it as a noise filter. Research is also underway to use this to make hard and sharp cutting tools or very hard plastics.

When fullerene is subjected to a pressure of 20 GPa and a temperature of 2200 K, agglomerated diamond nanorods can be made. The hardness of this material is 1.17-1.52 times that of a diamond.

Here, if we look at the electronic engineering characteristics of nanotechnology, the space in which free electrons of a nano conductor or semiconductor particle can move is limited, so the freedom is lost and an energy quantization phenomenon occurs in which only a specific energy value is obtained. At this time, the electrons that lose their freedom and are trapped in the energy wall have energy proportional to their size and interact with photons of the same energy. In other words, it can have only a specific level of energy, and when it transitions to another level, energy absorption or emission occurs, and energy is emitted as fluorescence by the contact point between them.

It is possible to use this quantum tunneling phenomenon to make ultra-fine processes such as low-power, high-integration semiconductors.

It is impossible to measure objects in the nanoscale with ordinary microscopes as we know them. This is because the wavelength of light entering the human eye through a microscope is several hundred nanometers, so it is impossible to identify an object on the nano scale, which is smaller than the wavelength that humans can recognize. Therefore, in order to measure a nano object, it is necessary to measure it with a light source having a nano-level wavelength. At this time, the wavelength of accelerated electrons is mainly used, and it is about 0.01 nm, so nano measurement is possible. Electron microscopy includes scanning electron microscopy and transmission electron microscopy. Nanotechnology uses lithography technology based on measurement technology. Optical lithography is a technique that uses an optical mask and light to make prints. By operating an ultra-high-resolution scanning tunneling microscope (STM) at cryogenic temperatures, it is possible to grasp the properties of atoms in detail, and it is also possible to control this single atom. However, commercialization failed because it is quite inefficient to move atoms one by one to produce them. However, after Dip-pen Nano Lithography appeared in the world, nano control technology reached a turning point again. Most of the nano-controlled processes succeed in achieving breakthroughs using this technique by engraving the probe of Atomic Force Microscopic with a solution composed of Alkane Thiol and writing as its name suggests.

Alkane is a cycloalkane that is in the form of a chain or a ring. It is mainly used in chemistry. If the number of carbons is small, it exists in gaseous form, and as the number of carbons increases, it becomes liquid or solid. When the number of carbons is 4 or more, isomers with the same number but different bond types are formed, and when the number of carbons is 3 or more, a cyclic form is formed.

In addition, Thiol is similar to alcohol (R-OH) structure, but has a larger size, polarization, and oxidation degree than alcohol, and has smaller hydrogen bonding strength, boiling point, and basicity. It reacts well with mercury and heavy metals to form precipitates. Cysteine is a representative thiol compound.

Over the mid-2000s, this dip-pen nanolithography technology developed further along with the growth of computer simulation, and in 2014, it is said that nano-scale printing was successful.

Generally speaking, nanotechnology aims to be implemented with nanomachines.

Nanomachines were first coined in 1959 by Richard Feynman, a physicist and one of the scientists involved in the Manhattan Project.

He said, "I want to build a billion tiny factories, models of each other, which are manufacturing simultaneously. The principles of physics as far as I can see do not speak against the possibility of maneuvering things atom by atom. It is not an attempt to violate any laws it is something in principle that can be done but in practice it has not been done because we are too big."

Figure 5-1 World of Nano Technology

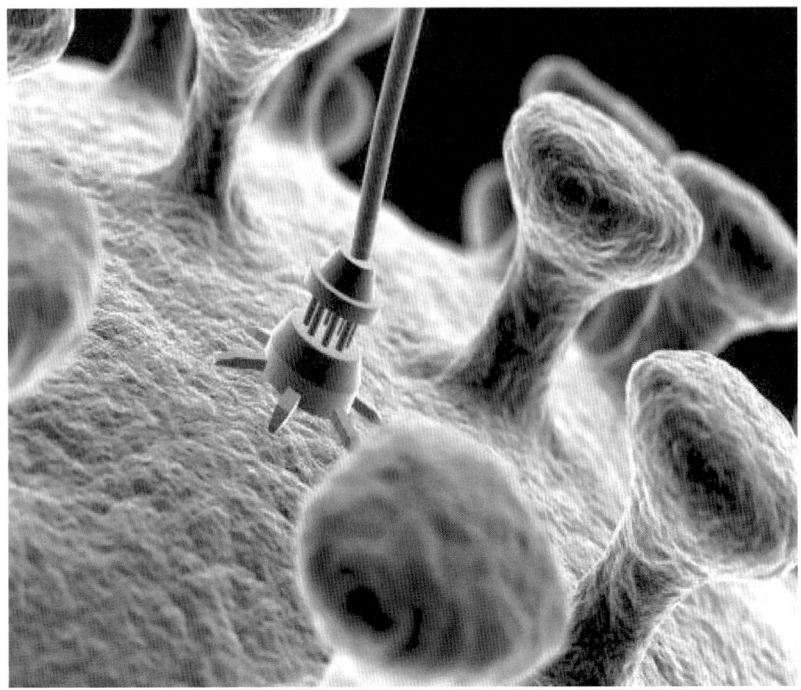

Have you seen the movie Ant-Man? The space inside the human body is described as space as big as the universe to the eyes of the main character, who has become so small that it becomes invisible and small enough to freely move in and out of the human body. As Richard Feynman said, the problem of size is always relative, and if the problem of relative size is solved, the basic physical properties can be applied consistently anywhere.

Nanomachines do not deal with the size that we know and see but are crystals of nanotechnology created through scientific phenomena that exist in nature beyond the relative size we think.

In general, when we talk about nanomachines, in order for nanomachines to work, in addition to physical or mechanical engineering principles, chemical principles will be greatly affected.

Figure 5-2 Nanotechnology - Catenane

If these nanomachines are put to practical use, it is expected to bring innovative changes to human civilization. That's why the movie Ant-Man includes nanomachine technology that maximizes human imagination.

In fact, there are cases where it gets smaller like Ant-Man, but like the movie Hulk, certain chemical substances are produced in nano-particle units that are smaller than molecular units, so if they enter a human body, they become superhuman, regenerate, and even change their appearance. All of these technologies are nanomachines.

Like the movie Hulk, the setting that the nanoscale molecule, the smallest unit of a person's body, changes by ingesting a certain chemical is a setting that does not exist now but can sufficiently appear sometime in the future. Similar progress is still being made today, and the most common examples are the actin-myosin system in muscles and intracellular molecular transport.

In fact, ATP Synthase, one of the enzymes used in cellular respiration, turns a motor when electrical stimulation is applied.

ATP Synthase is an enzyme that produces adenosine triphosphate, the energy source for all cellular activities. This enzyme is located in the inner membrane of mitochondria with a large surface area, and this protein phosphorylates adenosine diphosphate and produces adenosine triphosphate using the ph

Figure 5-3 Nanotechnology - Rotaxane

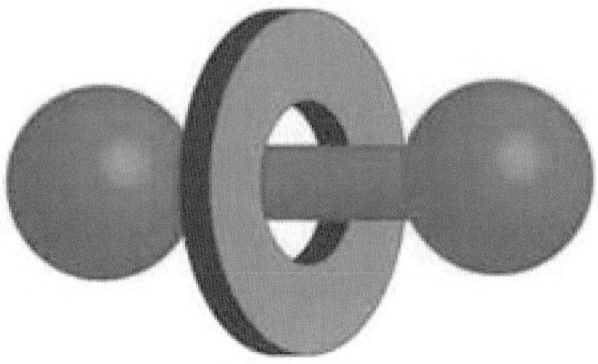

and voltage differences caused by the transfer of hydrogen ions, a subprocess of cellular respiration. Paul D. Boyer and John E. Walker, who explained this, were awarded the 1997 Nobel Prize in Chemistry.

And then, the 2016 Nobel Prize winners in Chemistry, Jean-Pierre Sauvage, Fraser Stoddart, and Bernard Feringa, pioneered the future of nanomachines by developing molecular machines.

In nanotechnology and nanomachines, the important concepts we must understand are the terms catenane and rotaxane.

Catenane refers to a molecular structure that has free-moving parts and does not break the bond by mechanically combining two molecules that are not chemically bound to form one molecule.

In other words, if this structure can be made as a chain of molecules, a structure with a movable molecular size can be made by linking the chains.

Rotaxane is the same as catenane in that it refers to a molecular structure that has free moving parts and does not break bonds by mechanically combining two molecules that are not chemically bound to form one molecule. It is characterized by the fact that it has a single ring and the end of the stick is closed so that the ring can move back and forth between the ends of the stick. Molecules with geometric structures can be used in various fields, for example, when a person controls a rotaxane molecule with a ring between sticks and commands one end to be ON and the other end to be OFF, it can be used as a switch.

In other words, nanotechnology is not a visible band that we can see with our eyes in reality, but technology at the molecular level that we cannot see. Until now, many developments have been made mainly in the chemical field, but in the future, it will be integrated with various fields such as electronic engineering, electrical engineering, architectural engineering, and material engineering.

This is an area where infinite development is expected.

This development of nanotechnology has had an impact on the field of physics, which was previously thought impossible, and made it possible to dream of actually making a time machine that exists only in people's imaginations. In the past concept of time, various interpretations of time travel could come out. In the case of simply viewing time as an absolute flow, time travel was impossible because the flow could not be reversed. Until Einstein's theory of relativity $E = mc^2$ came out, there was no case where time was clearly identified. However, after the advent of Einstein's special theory of relativity, the speed in time cannot go below zero, that is, time does not stand still. Because light has zero mass, we know that the sum of the velocities of matter in space-time is equal to the speed of light, and there are no negative velocities.

According to Einstein's special theory of relativity, the past, present, and future exist simultaneously according to the relativity of simultaneity. That is, the future of one inertial system may be the past in another because the present standard in a specific inertial system is different depending on the situation of that inertial system. In other words, if you go through another dimension, it means that you can travel through time either in the past or in the present. There is just no way to move. However, in nanotechnology, there are countless quantum mechanics that we have not yet discovered. If we go through this nanotechnology stage, it means that the physical volume and

Figure 5-4 Time and space exist in multiple dimensions

shape as we know it can change meaninglessly. As in the movie Terminator, the future Terminator can time travel and go back and forth between the past and the future.

A time machine is a dream of scientists and a regular subject in movies and novels. Stephen Hawking of England, who is known as a renowned scientist in physics, is also said to have done research on the time machine based on existing knowledge from time to time. But that was around the dawn of nanotechnology. However, in the future, nanotechnology at the time when the Fourth Industrial Revolution materializes is clearly expected to cause innovative changes in physics.

An American physicist named Ronald Mallett is said to have been continuously working on the time machine. According to the special theory of relativity, a time machine that goes to the future rather than the past is not theoretically impossible, so research is being conducted to send protons to the future. This also means being grafted into nanotechnology. This is because, when the movement unit of matter is reduced to an atomic unit, the dynamics of nanotechnology exist rather than the existing laws of physics.

The time machine can be said to be an Internet of Things to which a kind of physical nanotechnology is applied. For us to implement the Internet of Things environment and services, we inevitably need the microprocessor theory, which is the basic principle of electronic engineering, and the chip that implements it. Therefore, in the core technology of the Internet of Things environment, various technologies are fused together with such microprocessor technology, and this is where nanotechnology is applied.

The background for the Internet of Things environment is the development of wireless communication speed, improvement of computing speed, and miniaturization of parts. In other words, the miniaturization of microprocessor chips down to the Nano-scale unit has been established as a future technology in the Internet of Things environment.

IoT devices are being developed to operate indefinitely through the air, the sun, radio waves, etc. instead of the existing batteries with limited time and capacity.

The IoT service at present is used in various fields such as the medical field, home appliances, communication, and automobiles, and it is the most used to increase productivity by connecting the manufacturing process and applications of the product.

For example, Apple developed iBeacon, which utilizes Bluetooth low energy technology as an indoor positioning system and is providing the service with

IOS7. This is to automatically provide product-related information and discount coupons to a smartphone when a customer stands in front of a product in a store where a beacon is installed.

Through real-time product management, inventory levels are lowered to reduce costs, and it is also contributing to realizing a hyper-connected society that unites people, cities, houses, cars, and buildings.

There are various types of interfaces in the era of the Internet of Everything. When the voice controls various devices, the accuracy of voice recognition is an important measure, and such a voice recognition system can use a method of searching for and comparing sounds that are statistically similar to the input voice. Therefore, taking this voice control as an example, it can be seen that it is also connected to the big data discussed above. This is because there is big data for a lot of voice data, and accurate voice recognition will be possible. If a technology whose accuracy is determined according to the degree of holding such voice data is used, it can be used in various fields. That is artificial intelligence. For example, there may be fields such as games, education, automobiles, medical care, and logistics. In this field, artificial intelligence technology is converging a lot. In particular, automobiles are being developed in the form of autonomous vehicles by incorporating artificial intelligence.

Looking at how information and communication technology and infrastructure have developed to implement the Internet of Things, the infrastructure, or the platform, has been developed as follows.

The first generation is the period when computers are introduced for convenience in life.

The second generation is the period when Internet services are activated and a lot of information is collected.

The third generation is a time when various devices appear and technologies such as wireless, cloud, and big data are activated.

The Fourth generation refers to the present and is the time when various devices go through the convergence process and the Internet of Things environment is built.

The 5th generation can be regarded as the 5th generation when the technology of the Fourth Industrial Revolution is completed and applied.

When this platform classification standard is applied, it can be said that Korea is just entering the fourth generation along with the commercialization of 5G. It is not an exaggeration to say that the world is currently engaged in a platform war of information and communication technology. The evidence can be found in that the companies with the highest value in the world are also companies that provide information and communication technology platforms. As of 2019, companies that provide IT platforms such as Microsoft, Google, Apple, and Alibaba are the most influential in the world.

Apple made the world a single platform service through iPhone and iOS, and Google's Android platform, which started as a search engine, occupies almost half of the global smartphone market. Just as Microsoft, as almost everyone knows, dominated the world with its PC platform called Windows operating system, the smartphone platform is dominating the market around the world now. In recent years, mobile headset manufacturers such as Nokia have voluntarily made efforts to embed Location Base Service (LBS) into their devices, but originally LBS was developed in cooperation with mobile carriers and mobile content providers.

The most important advantage of location-based services is that wireless Internet users do not need to directly input addresses or regional identifiers while moving to multiple locations.

However, to realize this, satellite-based positioning technology such as GPS is not the only sub-element technology used. In a mobile communication network, a unique location management mechanism for managing the mobility of a terminal exists, and a number of non-GPS location-based services based on this exist. These days, PC-based wired Internet services are also converging with location-based service functions while continuing to expand beyond boundaries into the wireless Internet area.

For example, Apple's CarPlay is a Connected Car Platform that installs in-vehicle software on a smartphone and connects it to a car.

Sensing technology is the first element to implement a general IoT environment. Sensing technology is a technology that collects information generated from objects and information generated from the surrounding environment.

The second element is wired and wireless communication and network technology. It is a technology that supports various things existing in space to be connected to the Internet.

Finally, the third is a service interface technology, which processes and processes information suitable for various services, and serves to converge various technologies. This is the smartphone application we know easily.

In addition to this, security technology, the Achilles heel of information and communication technology, is absolutely necessary. In today's reality, where personal information and information are increasingly important, security technology has become the last important technology in all services using information and communication networks. If you make a Time-Machine and the time machine was hacked and you should go to 2020, but if you went to 2200, it would be a very difficult situation. In other words, technology to prevent hacking or information leakage for large amounts of data and technological elements of the Internet of Things is essential.

As described above, in order to implement the Internet of Things, the time machine, the development of nanotechnology, sensing technology, wired/wireless communication technology, service interface technology, and security technology are absolutely necessary and the fusion of these technologies may one day give us the opportunity to time travel.

5.3 Prediction of The Fourth Industrial Revolution

As stated in the introduction of this book, the core of the Fourth Industrial Revolution means technological innovation in six fields: big data, artificial intelligence, robotics, Internet of Things, unmanned transportation, 3D printer, and nanotechnology. The concept that encompasses all these technological innovations is the Internet of Everything.

Also, the field that will closely touch our human life in the future is the Internet of Everything.

Everything in this world exists and operates within a network.

In the future, in the era of the Fourth Industrial Revolution, the Internet of all things will ultimately change from device-centered to service or people-centered. Artificial intelligence, robotics, the Internet of Things, unmanned vehicles, 3D printers, and nanotechnology are all needed to cope with these changes.

The Internet of Everything is an extended concept of the era of Ubiquitous (a world in which the real world and the virtual world are combined so that computer resources can be conveniently used anytime, anywhere) in that things communicate with each other and exchange data by themselves without relying on people. It can be said that it is different from the existing general Internet of Things in that it interacts with all information in the real and virtual worlds as well as objects.

Gartner, a US market research firm, has published 10 strategic technology trends for 2020 with innovative potential classified into People-Centric and Smart Spaces.

According to Gartner, artificial intelligence is a key catalyst for enhancing human capabilities while improving automation processes.

And it is said that physical environments such as factories and offices will evolve into smart spaces where people and surrounding objects can interact through touch sensors and sensory channels.

Figure 5-5 Gartner's Top 10 Strategic Technology Keywords

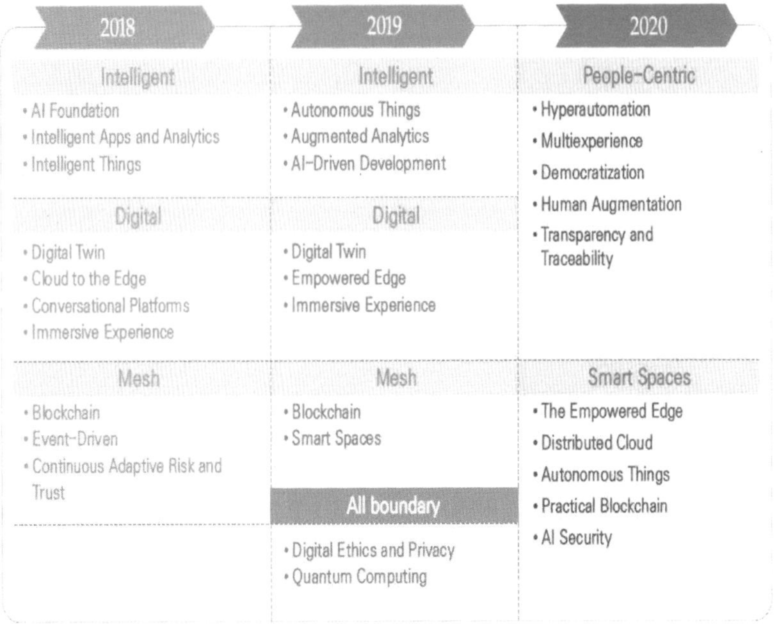

2018	2019	2020
Intelligent	**Intelligent**	**People-Centric**
• AI Foundation • Intelligent Apps and Analytics • Intelligent Things	• Autonomous Things • Augmented Analytics • AI-Driven Development	• Hyperautomation • Multiexperience • Democratization • Human Augmentation • Transparency and Traceability
Digital	**Digital**	
• Digital Twin • Cloud to the Edge • Conversational Platforms • Immersive Experience	• Digital Twin • Empowered Edge • Immersive Experience	
Mesh	**Mesh**	**Smart Spaces**
• Blockchain • Event-Driven • Continuous Adaptive Risk and Trust	• Blockchain • Smart Spaces	• The Empowered Edge • Distributed Cloud • Autonomous Things • Practical Blockchain • AI Security
	All boundary	
	• Digital Ethics and Privacy • Quantum Computing	

The 10 strategic technology trends identified by Gartner of the United States are as follows.

First, Hyperautomation - Performs tasks by combining machine learning, package software, and automation tools. Representative examples include RPA (Robotic Process Automation), iBPMS (intelligent Business Process Management), and Digital Twin.

Second, Multiexperience - Not only VR, AR, and MR, but also multi-channel human-machine interfaces (HMIs) are spreading, and the way we perceive and interact with the digital world changes significantly.

Third, democratization - It is possible to access specialized fields such as

Figure 5-6 Global artificial intelligence market Trend

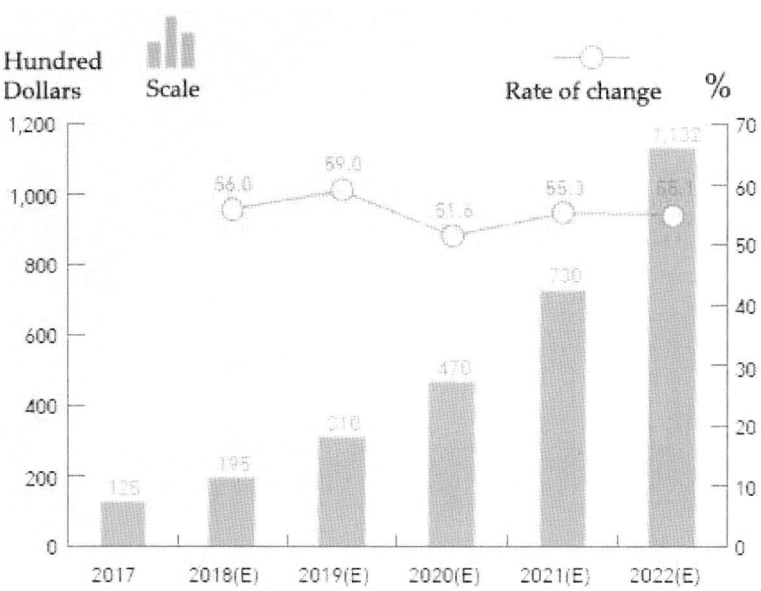

business process and economic analysis at low cost in a wide range without specialized education.

Fourth, Human Augmentation - It refers to improving human cognition and physical ability by using technology and science.

Fifth, Transparency and Traceability - It refers to various supports and actions that can provide an ethical approach to the use of advanced technologies, including AI, and secure trust.

Sixth, The Empowered Edge – As edge computing is enhanced with sophisticated and specialized computing resources and data storage, it will become an important factor in a wide range of industries.

Seventh. Distributed Cloud - A public cloud service is provided in another location (home, office, etc.) outside of the cloud provider's data center.

Eighth, Autonomous Things - AI performs the roles previously performed and performed by humans and expands the scope.

Figure 5-7 Global Human Enhancement Market Trend

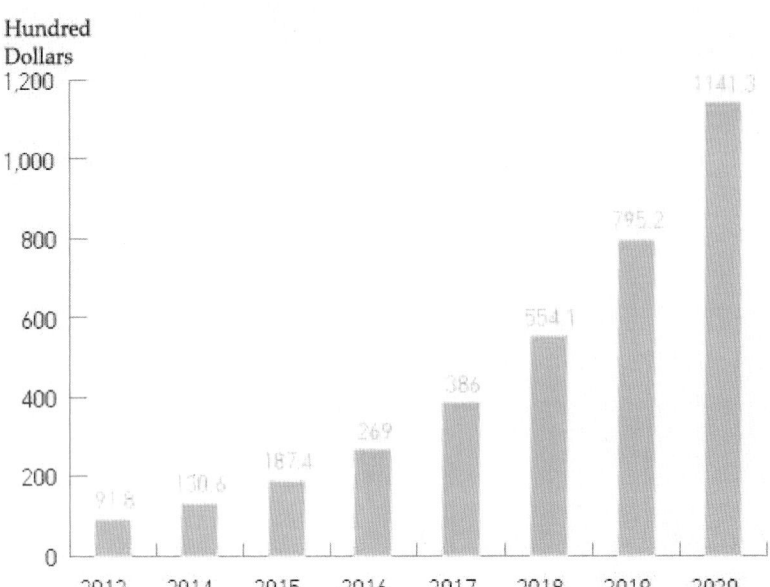

Ninth, Practical Blockchain - Blockchain, which is emerging mainly in various tests and small projects, is expected to expand in earnest by 2023.

Tenth, AI Security - As the exposure to cyberattacks increases in the hyper-connected smart space, the role of AI-based systems and processes that can protect them will increase.

As described above, Gartner revealed the top 10 strategic technology trends for 2020 and selected artificial intelligence as the most important part.

This is because artificial intelligence technology is the most important keyword among keywords in the Fourth Industrial Revolution era.

As we have seen before, the technologies of the Fourth Industrial Revolution do not all exist individually but are interconnected like an animal food chain. In other words, it can be called Vienna sausage one after another.

Figure 5-8 Artificial intelligence patent applications

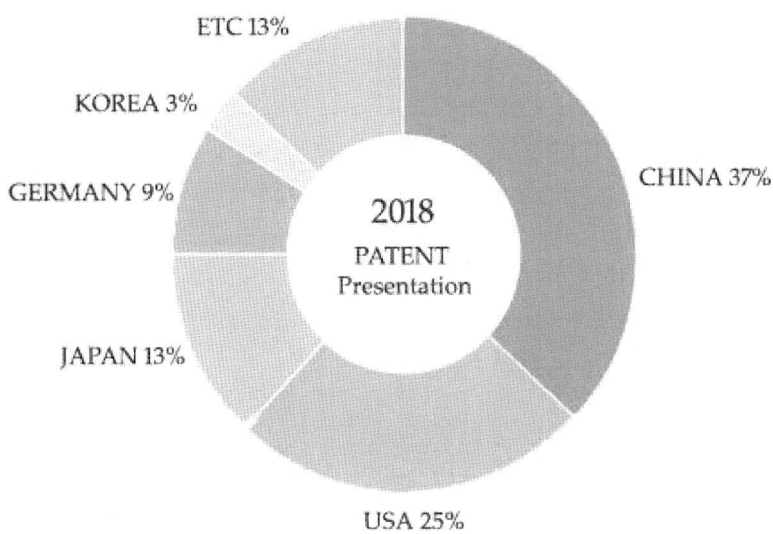

Internet of Things technology produces big data, big data is implemented with artificial intelligence, and artificial intelligence is only used in reality as robots and unmanned transportation means. Nanotechnology and 3D printer technology are integrated into the Internet of Things technology.

In other words, each technology does not exist separately from each other but is bound to each other like a chain through fusion and utilization.

As such, the Fourth Industrial Revolution can be explained as the Internet of Everything, where everything is tied to a network of technology and a network of points of view.

In other words, everything in this world, including big data, artificial intelligence, robots, unmanned transportation, 3D printers, and nanotechnology, is included in everything and included in the network.

The Internet of Everything can be recognized as a network from a macro point of view rather than a simple Internet network.

Figure 5-9 Artificial intelligence papers around the world

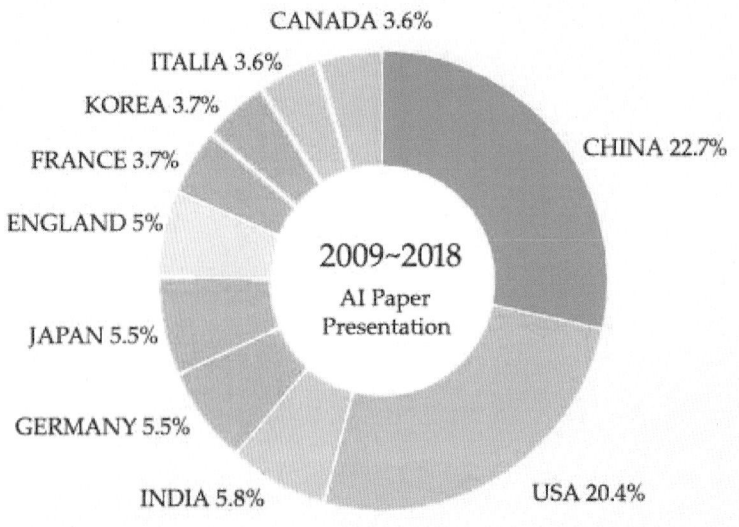

In the Fourth Industrial Revolution, the Internet of Everything means an era in which all things in the world, such as people, things, data, and processors, are connected and communicate through a network.

The current world is already the world of ubiquitous where information and communication technology dominates. Such information and communication technology is expected to undergo many innovative changes in the era of the Fourth Industrial Revolution. Expressing it in one word, it will be changed to a platform-oriented way so that it can be said, "All technologies in the world lead to a Platform" rather than "All roads in the world lead to Rome."

Even now, ownership of a platform is an important business area for a company to the extent that it determines the survival of an IT company, because its importance will increase in the future.

Taking Korea as an example in the Third Industrial Revolution, Samsung Electronics developed a mobile operating system called Tizen, and TMAX

Soft made an OS almost similar to Microsoft's Windows operating system. In other words, the platform war has already begun in the Third Industrial Revolution. However, even a well-made platform becomes useless if many people do not use it. Knowing this fact well, information and communication technology companies these days consider their own operating system-based platform as their core competitiveness and are pushing forward their efforts to become a platform used by many users as their top priority.

Therefore, the future era of the Fourth Industrial Revolution can be said to be the era of platform wars.

And the core of the platform war is in software.

The general information and communication technology industry structure is located in the order of hardware, operating system, middleware, and content. Everyone knows that the information and communication technology industry, which used to be hardware-centered, is rapidly changing to software-centered.

Bill Gates of Microsoft once said this.

"There will come a time when everything in the world will be implemented with software. That time isn't too far off." I totally agree with this statement because this software-centered society will be the era of the Fourth Industrial Revolution.

The future world of the Fourth Industrial Revolution will not be a material society, but a society with metaphysical characteristics that go beyond the limits of mind and matter, and the tool to implement it will be software. To make it easier to understand, think of the American movie "The Matrix."

In the era of the Internet of Everything, both people and things become a component of the network. This is because one component of such a network will be managed and controlled through software logic rather than being controlled through a hardware process.

Platform means software, and it is the software, not the person, that controls it.

As a prime example, users these days already place more importance on features and user experience than hardware performance. Of course, hardware enough to handle such software must be supported, but modern customer requirements are content, not containers.

Therefore, in the future, all companies are showing a tendency to place importance on the platform, or software, which can be said to support the future society, that is, the social structure in which the Fourth Industrial Revolution is completed.

If we look at the history of the information and communication technology industry in the past, the keyword for the second platform is convergence, while the keyword for the first platform was mobile.

Even in the era of the Fourth Industrial Revolution, the last topic in information and communication technology is security. No matter how good innovative technology and no matter how good innovative service, if security is weak, efficiency will inevitably lose vitality, and the value of content will be diluted. Therefore, even in the era of the Fourth Industrial Revolution, security is a part that should not be overlooked.

Even now, the impact of security on information and communication technology is very large.

These days, the security fields such as security using blockchain technology, which is a technology that uses the characteristics of an immutable node, and security using artificial intelligence are being newly developed in the concept of convergence and platform.

For example, in the case of insecure devices, well-known attacks cannot be avoided because they do not receive support such as firmware or patches, and the number of cases of damage caused by easy exposure to new hacking tools is increasing rapidly because they do not receive regular monitoring and new security patches.

The importance of such security is always a regular theme in movies.

For example, in the movie Terminator, the movie starts with the setting that Skynet, the Internet of all things covering the world, is infected with a virus due to hacking, and machines take control of humans. In the end, the earth will be destroyed because of the security vulnerabilities of information and communication technology.

As you all know, movies are made based on scenarios that reflect the possibilities of reality. In other words, the situation of the movie Terminator in the Internet of Everything environment called the Fourth Industrial Revolution tells us the possibility that it can happen in the future if security is not thoroughly implemented.

In the end, the Fourth Industrial Revolution is the Internet of Everything, Software, Platform, and Security that protects these three keywords for the Fourth Industrial Revolution described just before.

Copyright ⓒ LEE WONCHAN All rights reserved

Bibliography

[1] X. Chen et al, "Pipelined Back-Propagation for Context-Dependent Deep Neural Networks," Proc. InterSpeech, Sept. 2012.

[2] Q. Le et al, "A. Building High-Level Features Using Large Scale Unsupervised Learning," International Conference on Machine Learning, 2012.

[3] A. Coates et al, "Deep Learning with COTS HPC Systems," Proc. 30th International Conference on Machine Learning, 2013, pp. 1337-1345.

[4] R. Wu et al., "Deep Image: Scaling up Image Recognition," 2015.

[5] Spark Lightning-Fast Cluster Computing, http://spark. apache.org/

[6] H20 World Training, "Sparkling Water," 2014, https://h2o.gitbooks.io/h2o-training-day/content/hands-on_training/sparkling_water.html

[7] P. Moritz et al, "SparkNet: Training Deep Networks in Spark," ICLR, 2016.

[8] N. Irizarry Jr, "Mixing C and Java™ for High Performance Computing," MITRE Technical Report, Sept. 2013.

[9] B.-G. Chun, T. Condie, and C. Curino, "Reef: Retainable Evaluator Execution Framework," Proceedings of the VLDB Endowment, 2013, pp. 1370-1373.

[10] M. Weimer et al., "Reef: Retainable Evaluator Execution Framework," Proc. ACM SIGMOD International Conference on Management of Data, 2015, pp. 1343-1355.

[11] E.P. Xing and Q. Ho, "A New Look at the System, Algorithm and Theory Foundations of Large-Scale Distributed Machine Learning," Tutorials at KDD, 2015.

[12] H. Zhang et al., "Poseidon: A System Architecture for Efficient GPU-based Deep Learning on Multiple Machines," Dec. 2015, http://arxiv.org

[13] W. Wang et al., "SINGA: Putting Deep Learning in the Hands of Multimedia Users," Proc. 2Third ACM International Conference on Multimedia, 2015, pp. 25-34.

[14] Veles, https://velesnet.ml/jenkins/job/VELES_Python_Veles_Tests/ Veles Machine Learning Platform Documentation/

[15] Computational Network Toolkit(CNTK), https://cntk.codeplex.com/

[16] D. Yu et al., "An Introduction to Computational Networks and the Computational Network Toolkit," Tech. Rep. MSR, Microsoft Research, 2014, http://codebox/cntk

[17] T. Chen et al., "MXNet: A Flexible and Efficient Machine Learning Library for Heterogeneous Distributed Systems," arXiv Preprint arXiv:1512.01274, Dec. 2015.

[18] Encyclopaedia Britannica, https://www.britannica.com/technology/data-mining, 3d printer,5g, virtual machine, nano techonology, robot, drone, iot, industry revolution, distributed processing system, artificial intelligence Dec. 2019.

[19] Andreas M.Antonopoulos, Mastering Bitcoin, Second Editon, O'Reilly, 2017.

[20] L. Lamport, R. Shostak, M, Pease, The Byzantine Generals Problem, ACM Transactions onProgramming Language and Systems v.4 n.3, July 1982.

[21] Imran Bashir, Mastering Blockchain-Second Editon, Packt, March 2018.

[22] Gartner, Selecting Impactful Big Data Use Cases, 2015

[23] D. Wang, S. Lee, Y. Zhu and Y. Li,A Zero human-intervention provisioning for industrila Iot Devices, in Proc. of IEEE International Conference on Industrial Technology(ICIT), Mar. 2017

[24] R. Yang and M. W. Newman, Learning from a Learning Thermostat: Lessons for Intelligent Systems for the home, in Poc. of AMC UbiComp, Sep, 2013.

[25] MIT News, Brain-controlled robots, 2017. 3. 6.

[26] Google Research Blog, Federated Learning: Collaborative Machine Learning Without Centralized Training Data, Apr. 2017.

[27] McKinsey, The Internet of Things: Sizing up the opportunity, 2014.

[28] 5G Forum, 5G White Paper : 5G Vision, Requirements, and Enabling Technologies , 2015.

[29] M. R. Sama, K. Guillouard, L. Suciu, G. Simon, X. Lagrange, J-M Bonnin, "New Control Plane in 3GPP LTE/EPC Architecture for On-Demand Connectivity Service",CloudNet , 2013.

[30] European Telecommunications Standards Institute, Network Functions Virtualization, Retrieved July 31, 2015, from http://www.etsi.org

[31] Uwe Doetsch et. al., Mobile and Wireless Communications Enablers for the Twenty-Twenty Information Society (METIS) Final Report on Architecture , Retrieved Jan. 31, 2015.

[32] Open5GCore, Open5GCore – The Next Mobile Core Network Testbed Platform, Retrieved July 31, 2015, from http://www.open5gcore.net

[33] OPNFV, Open Platform for Network Functions Virtualization (OPNFV), Retrieved July 31, 2015, from https://www.opnfv.org/.

[34] International Telecommunications Union, Working Party 5D (WP 5D) – IMT Systems, Retrieved July 31, 2015, from http://www.itu.int/en/ITU-R/study-groups/rsg5/rwp5d/Pages/default.aspx.

[35] Gartner, Inc., Gartner Top 10 Strategic Technology Trends for 2020 https://www.gartner.com/smarterwithgartner/gartner-top-10-strategic-technology-trends-for-2020/

Closing Remarks

Before writing this book, I considered many considerations and various matters. I have been in the ICT industry for more than 20 years when I used ICT technology to work and carry out my business directly but I often overlooked the value of books as a medium of information and information delivery. However, It has changed as a medium for conveying information like e-books and internet books.

The book has been destined with human history, and I think that the meaning will continue without changing even if any multimedia information delivery media comes out in the future.

It seems to be a book that has the power to acquire information and create something through it. In that sense, I would like to define all multimedia today as a kind of book.

I have been working in the ICT industry for more than 20 years and have been working as a developer and as a CEO of the company. I have written this book in terms of providing a wider range of knowledge and ideas to people living in the generation of the fourth industrial revolution. The Third Industrial Revolution took place in the 20th century and people did not expect technology to change the world but only thought that everything would change conveniently.

However, now technology is changing the world, and technology is not leading the world, but technology is leading people. Therefore, I wrote this book to help people understand and adapt to the fourth industrial revolution.

Written by WONCHAN LEE

Copyright © LEE WONCHAN All Rights Reserved.